Where to Buy Property Abroad

David Cox and Ray Withers

crimson

This edition first published in Great Britain 2008 by
Crimson Publishing, a division of Crimson Business Ltd
Westminster House
Kew Road
Richmond
Surrey
TW9 2ND

First published 2006
Second edition 2007
Third edition 2008

A catalogue record for this book is available from the British library.

ISBN 978 1 85458 442 7

Printed and bound by Mega Printing, Turkey

Contents

PART II
INVESTMENT POTENTIAL OF INDIVIDUAL COUNTRIES

Foreword

Until now, there have been few comprehensive books catering for international property buyers whose primary motivation is investment. There are books on buying property in France or Spain, and many other countries, all of which may pay some attention to the investment aspect of buying property in those specific markets. But there is no book on the general subject of international property investment: discussing its principles, the required tools and techniques and providing analysis and comparisons of a broad range of markets across the globe. The purpose of this book is to fill that gap: to provide people with an accessible overview of many of the most exciting international property markets and how to purchase safely.

This book is also about guidance and access to information. Even when you have made a decision about where to buy, working out how the buying process works can be a complex and unrewarding task and there are a lot of unscrupulous agents that give the industry a bad name. In order to invest in property with confidence, you need access to the best possible information that is up to date and reliable. And it is here that people looking further than the UK and traditional markets tend to suffer. There just isn't enough written about markets beyond the historical holiday home hot-spots and a few books based purely on buy to let and property investment.

Surprisingly, although property is one of the largest of all the asset classes it is also one of the most misunderstood. Investment banks plough millions into the research of debt and equity markets and analyse them on a daily basis. This has not been the case within the international property market and there have been no unified and reliable sources for investors on international property markets.

That doesn't mean that the required information doesn't exist, simply that it doesn't exist in a format readily accessible to ordinary investors. Our advantage is that we are not professional writers but actual practitioners of property investment. In our professional capacity at Property Frontiers we analyse and assess international property investment opportunities on a daily basis. We are developers ourselves in a number of countries, and have learnt the hard way in a few. As such, we have a good understanding of both the methods of assessing opportunities and the sourcing of the data that our decisions rely upon.

The range of property investment opportunities around the globe makes it physically impossible to discuss them all in a book with a practical weight limit. But we have drawn on our own experience and the expertise of our colleagues to provide information on 44 of the most interesting and popular investment markets in the world today.

The first half of the book looks at *Where and what to buy* – not specifically but in terms of providing the tools and background understanding necessary to analyse property markets and investment opportunities. After introducing the international property market, its history and an overview of global trends, especially in the light of sub-prime crisis, we move on to look at market analysis, starting with a discussion of how markets work. In our discussion of market mechanics we look at the different forces that cause property price movements and look at some detailed case studies on the impact of factors, such as EU accession, hosting the Olympics and low-cost air travel.

In the second chapter of this book, *Where to buy abroad*, we introduce some tools for assessing the relative value of a property market and finally look at some specific considerations when buying in the city or countryside, in ski resorts or by the beach.

Chapter three, *What to buy*, provides a basis for developing an investment strategy and gives some simple tools for assessing the attractiveness of a specific property investment opportunity. This chapter also considers the pros and cons of old property, new build and off-plan. We also deal with the potential risks of buying abroad and ways in which those risks could be minimised through collective investment schemes such as funds and real estate investment trusts (REITs).

Chapter four, *Making a profit from property*, looks at the various ways you can profit from your investment, in particular buy-to-let purchases, and helps you calculate potential return before looking into the different aspects you should consider when purchasing a property to ensure you are able to exit and liquidate your property and release your profit.

Chapter five, *Good advice and information*, discusses the role of an agent and how to find one you can rely on. It also highlights some good sources of information and other resources that you will need.

Chapter six, *Financial considerations*, examines the financial considerations of buying abroad including mortgages, currency exchange, closing costs and taxation.

Finally, Part II looks at 44 of the most interesting markets. Each set of country details includes information on the best areas to buy, the type of property to look for, and the short and long-term prospects of an investment in this geographic location.

Above all we aim to equip people with the knowledge they need to identify good investment markets for themselves. Forgive the analogy, but this book is more fishing rod than fish. Tell someone where to invest and they may make money; teach someone how to identify good investments for themselves and it's 'hello Aston Martin'. Perhaps not quite, but knowledge and self-reliance are two of the most valuable assets around. Good luck.

David Cox and Ray Withers
September 2008

Acknowledgements

The authors would like to thank all of our colleagues at Property Frontiers who have made outstanding efforts to support the production of this book. All of the country experts have given extensive amounts of their time in supporting our research.

In particular a special thank you must go to Emma Holifield, Judi Williams, Elizabeth Birkett, Frayni Jones and Steph Williams for their many hours of editorial support. Without their efforts this book would be much poorer in detail and facts.

We would also like to thank the publishing and editorial team at Crimson Publishing for their expert guidance and support.

Acknowledgements

PART I

UNDERSTANDING WHERE AND WHAT TO BUY ABROAD

I Introduction

No matter which part of the English-speaking world you live in, you will undoubtedly be familiar with dinner-party conversations regarding either property investment or real estate investment. Whatever the terminology, property is a national obsession across the globe from Britain to Australia and numerous countries in between.

Over the last 30 years, more and more people have purchased a second home, some for their own personal enjoyment and some purely for investment. In the US this led to the evolution of prime second-home destinations such as the Gulf Coast of Florida and the snowy peaks of Aspen. For those of us who live in the less geographically diverse British Isles, we have tended to head to the sunnier climes of the Mediterranean. By dint of geography then, the international property industry is much more developed in the UK as people wanting a second home in the sun have had no choice but to buy abroad. However, motivations are changing. Recent decades have seen significant domestic property booms in the UK, USA, Australia and Ireland. A coincidence of circumstances (mainly related to easily accessible mortgage financing due to heavy competition in the banking sector) has democratised the ownership of real estate. Ordinary families have become landlords, re-financing their own homes to build a portfolio of properties that have generated a healthy return.

As a result of these recent booms, property investment has overtaken investing in equities in terms of popularity (particularly in the UK and Ireland), but it is no investment panacea. Real estate is most certainly part of a market place, subject to the same peaks and troughs as any other asset market. It is true that property markets tend to be more stable, partly due to the lack of liquidity (property isn't as easy to dispose of as other types of asset) and partly due to the fact that no matter how much prices drop, people still need a home. But the reality remains that prices may go down as well as up. The real estate markets in the USA, Spain, UK and Australia have all experienced a slowdown in recent years and at the time of going to press the impact of the sub-prime crisis had caused dramatic price falls across the western world. However, in today's age of international travel and the internet, people are very aware that there is a world beyond their doorstep and that world is full of places where property markets are just beginning to boom as others begin to fall.

The fact that we are writing this book for the third successive year is evidence enough that international property investment is a very popular topic. Brits have been buying property abroad for many years, but today around 40% of those doing so state investment (rather than a holiday home) as their main motivation and 38% are looking for somewhere to migrate to. Over 600,000 Brits own a second home and a staggering 360,000 of these are abroad. Second-home ownership has risen by a fifth over the past 14 years whilst house prices at home have tripled. Recent figures from The Office For National Statistics have claimed that some two million Brits will invest in overseas property by 2012 and at least 25% of first-time buyers will buy their first property abroad. In the US, the story is slightly different. US holiday home owners have mostly purchased in other parts of the country, meaning that the market for holiday homes abroad was small. However, as a result of the recent downturn in the US home market, a rapidly growing international real estate industry has sprung up in the US looking to service the requirements of investors looking for better returns overseas.

THE DIFFERENT MOTIVES OF BUYERS

Many international property buyers may be investors, but there are still many other buyers whose primary motivation is different; perhaps they are looking for a holiday home or even to relocate. Whatever the motivation though, the investment considerations discussed in this book play an important part in the decision-making process. Even people whose main motivation is to enjoy a holiday home in the sun must consider whether or not their purchase is a sound investment. Few people can afford to buy a holiday home that is a bad investment. The concepts discussed in this book are therefore as relevant to holiday homers and relocators as they are to hard-nosed investors.

When buying a property abroad, for any purpose, there are many questions to answer. Should you buy in somewhere like Spain or France where there is a long history of foreigners buying property, or an emerging market where prices may be much lower and potential returns much higher, but where the process is more complicated and the investment potentially riskier? Is an off-plan development better than an older house? Are rentals for ski chalets higher than for beach houses, and how do you find out about banking, taxes, fees or how to find the notary or estate agent who can give you the best service?

In the UK, overseas property programmes, exhibitions, articles and magazines seem inescapable, but despite the ubiquity of coverage there is a lack of clear information on countries other than the more traditional holiday home favourites of Spain, France and Italy. Understanding the property market and buying process in less well-trodden destinations can seem like one of the labours of Hercules. And that is what makes this book different: the breadth and depth of information given.

Recognising that people's motivations are different, and that they are buying more adventurously, this book aims to explain how to buy property in Malaysia as well as Canada, Brazil as well as Turkey, Slovakia as well as Mongolia.

Growing numbers of people have the incentive and budget to invest in property abroad, but are uncertain about where to spend their money. The information in this book is provided for all those people. If you are interested in buying property but unsure where and what to buy we will help you to understand the basic concepts of international property investment, to understand why prices rise in a certain area and where they should rise over the next two or three years.

The great global property boom

The rise in house prices

Why is property investment a topic of such broad appeal? Well there are several reasons but one of the most significant is that the Western world has just been through the biggest property boom in history. This means that there is a whole generation of people who have experienced what a good investment property can be. They also have a great deal more funds available to invest as the values of their own properties have risen so dramatically. In fact, over the past decade house prices have boomed in almost every developed market with the exception of Germany and Japan.

Although this growth has now slowed, the rising value of property over the last 10 years has made a whole generation of people feel financially secure and encouraged consumer spending which benefits the wider economy. Generally over the last decade, even during periods of economic instability, household spending has proved surprisingly resilient – and the reason for this resilience has been linked to rising property values and lower costs of mortgage borrowing. With mortgages rising and property prices dropping, this resilience may now be floundering in some areas but not all markets are dropping. The table overleaf shows remarkably healthy growth although this may reflect the use of annual rather than monthly figures and by the beginning of 2009 it is a fairly safe bet that the picture will not look quite as rosy.

Whilst this boom has created a generation of potential property investors, it has also left them feeling that they have missed the boat. Some developed property markets or areas within developed markets still present a good opportunity (despite recent levels of growth) whilst others do not. What is certain though is that there are many property markets across the globe that have not yet reached these levels of growth and it is these emerging markets that are rightly catching investors' attention.

Fig 1. Real House Price Change (1997–2008)
(*The Economist*'s house-price indicators)

Country	Percentage change
South Africa	401
Ireland	220
Britain	202
Spain	195
Australia	174
France	151
Sweden	150
Belgium	147
New Zealand	125
Denmark	124
Italy	102
Netherlands	99
US	92
Canada	80
Switzerland	19
Hong Kong	−23
Japan	−33

How property has outperformed shares

The debate between investing in stock and property is one which has been ongoing for a substantial amount of time. Property investment greatly increased in popularity between 2000 and 2003, corresponding with a 40% fall in the value of stocks. This fall in the stock market dented investor confidence and raised concerns over the reliability of pension funds. In a world of fiscal uncertainty, the tangibility of property becomes extremely attractive.

Property is perceived as a reliable investment, and will often be used by serious investors as a low-risk venture suitable for balancing the distribution of risk in a portfolio of investments. Whereas stocks and shares are vulnerable to the whims of the investor, the world financial system and to the slightest dip in confidence, property values are much harder to shake. Even now it is easier to borrow money to finance a property purchase than it is to borrow to play the stock market. And for most people, following the daily or even hourly fluctuations of the stock market is a practical impossibility, too complex, too hard, and too reliant on having prior information. In contrast, as well as being an investment, property is something that most people encounter as part of their daily lives. For most people, property is familiar and easier to understand than other, less tangible, investments. The fact that a property investment is an investment in something real also gives added security. Generally, a house stays where you have left it. In the worst case the value of a house may decline, but leaving aside the possibility of earthquake or fire, it is unlikely to vanish overnight like fairy-gold or an investment in Enron.

'Whereas stock and shares are vulnerable to the whims of the investor and the slightest dip in confidence, property values are much harder to shake'

International support for the right to buy overseas property

As we saw above, the level of property prices in developed markets has led investors to examine international markets at an earlier stage in their growth cycle. However, there has also been another driver behind the growth of international property investment and that is the increasing level of international support for investors to be able to safely buy in different countries. Today, countries recognise the value of outside investment. Over the last decade, barriers have been lowered and the right to buy extended to foreign nationals by many countries.

With the WTO (World Trade Organisation) upholding investment rights there is more security for money being sent abroad. The WTO also plays an important role in ensuring international commitment to enforcing property ownership, and systems of law and government which uphold reciprocal rights.

Governments benefit from the international property industry and have an incentive to provide as much protection to buyers as possible. Taxes and fees provide money for governments to spend on infrastructure and development but the property market also brings work: employment for solicitors and translators and of course construction workers. Foreign buyers can also help to preserve older housing stock. In Morocco crumbling riads have been lovingly restored by foreigners with the time and inclination to bring these lovely courtyard houses back to life and in the Far East, many of the few remaining colonial villas have been restored by foreign buyers.

The opening up of the former Eastern Bloc countries and certain areas of the Far East has presented a whole new range of opportunities. The economies of these countries are only just beginning to experience the full benefits of the open market and many are set to experience very high levels of economic growth. Property prices in such countries have historically been held at artificially low levels and are likely to rise dramatically as the wealth of the local population increases. Many of these countries are very receptive to foreign investment as a means of providing the funds required for rapid development.

All of these advantages ensure that governments have an incentive to treat international buyers and developers well, working together to ensure that cross-border investment is both safe and straightforward.

Example – the Valencia land grab

A good example of the international commitment to reciprocal property rights has been provided by the co-ordinated response of governments and international organisations to recent property seizures in Valencia, Spain.

Badly drafted legislation in the Valencia region enabled developers to take land away from homeowners, under the cover of development. The 1994 *Ley Reguladora de la Actividad Urbanistica (LRAU)* states that all land can be converted for property development unless it is protected on historical, cultural or ecological grounds. Under the LRAU, developers can request that land should be reclassified from rural to urban land without asking for the owner's permission. They can then compulsorily purchase the land, paying compensation which can be far below market value and even forcing the property owner to pay for infrastructure improvements such as water installation or road building.

The Valencia land grab laws have been one of the most embarrassing problems in international property over the last two decades, but the case has also shown the amount of support available for property owners. After over 15,000 complaints to the European Parliament the government of the Valencia region announced in June 2008 that it intended to overhaul the urban planning laws, including the infamous 'land grab' laws. This was the second time in only a few years that the Valencian government had been forced into changing their urban planning laws. The original 'land grab law' was replaced in 2006 by the *Ley Urbanistica Valenciana (LUV)* which, although a slight improvement on the original, did not stop unscrupulous developers and politicians carrying on as before. Sadly, similar practices have already been adopted in Andalucia and Murcia and parts of the Canary Islands. The Valencia case has shown that governments are prepared to campaign internationally for the rights of buyers. The quality of information now available internationally was another key element helping to create co-ordinated opposition. The higher standard of information, not least the way that journalists now regularly cover stories about issues affecting buyers overseas, is one of the changes that have made people feel safer.

> **'Ten years ago, buying outside of France or Spain without detailed personal knowledge of the country meant leaping in to the dark. This is no longer the case'**

Ten years ago, buying outside of France or Spain without detailed personal knowledge of the country meant leaping into the dark. This is no longer the case. There are still countries where buying can be a challenge – property title in the Turkish Republic of Northern Cyprus is, for example, distinctly dubious, and although there have been some heavily publicised cases and many debates, at the time of writing there is still no definitive answer as to whether buying property in certain areas of Northern Cyprus is 100% secure.

The problems in Valencia and Northern Cyprus have been all the more unusual because modern economists and governments recognise the value of encouraging foreigners to buy houses. Foreign investment is good for a country, bringing in money and rejuvenating economies. This money disappears the moment people begin to feel that their investment may not be safe.

As word spread about the unjust laws in Valencia, property sales noticeably declined and prices plummeted for land considered to be at risk. According to CB Richard Ellis there is a severe oversupply of property in the Valencia region, with some one million Spanish properties on the market at the time of writing: 5–10% of these were in the Valencia region. It is estimated that it will take between two and three years to soak up this oversupply. In addition, the National Statistics Institute has released data stating that new home-build permits in Spain dropped 50.2% and home sales fell 27% between January 2007 and January 2008. According to the Spanish National Institute of Statistics (INE), the total number of businesses and individuals in the country declaring bankruptcy during the first quarter of 2008 soared 78.6% year on year, and 45.7% of these were from the construction and property industry.

International property investment: coming of age

As property prices have rocketed across the Western world, investors have begun to look elsewhere for potential gains. This has led to a coming of age for international property investment. Buying property abroad is not new, as we see below, but never before has buying property in another country been so accessible or driven by people whose primary motivation is pure investment.

This new breed of international property buyer is both the child of the 'great international property boom' and of a tradition which stretches back much further into the past.

Buying property abroad: early beginnings

The appeal of a second home in the sun is by no means a notion restricted to modern tastes: even the Romans had their villas at Baie! The origins of the international property market as we know it lie in the expansion of tourism in the 19th century. English travellers who had developed a taste for the southern sun began to buy property in Europe, either wintering abroad or swapping Brighton for Cap Ferrat on a permanent basis.

The moneyed beneficiaries of the Industrial Revolution quickly developed a preference for the promenades of Europe over the dark, dank mills of home. This influence is still reflected in place and hotel names across Europe. The hotel names Carlton, Majestic and Bristol reflect the importance of British customers to their proprietors. To top this off, the Brits invented winter sports tourism by flocking to the Swiss resort of Zermatt. By 1901 half a million travellers crossed the English Channel every year.

The next key development was the extension of affordable air travel. In the 1960s air travel was combined with the affordable package tour and a world of tourism was born. With the development of affordable international travel people could divide their time between a working life at home and relaxation abroad. The second-home market in France and Spain opened up in the 1960s, a decade that also saw the launch of the first international property magazines in the UK. From the beginning of the 1970s pioneers began to explore Italy and then, in the late 1980s and 1990s, Portugal, Greece and Florida joined the market, and buying overseas property became a desirable end in itself. The markets in Spain, Italy and France exploded and a secondary interest in winter sports destinations developed. The World Travel and Tourism Council estimated that between 2006 and 2015 tourism and related industries would contribute 10.9% of world GDP.

The opening up of Eastern Europe

In the 1990s the fall of communism opened up vast new markets in the east of Europe and contrary to the picture held by many people of grey crumbling walls and Soviet era tower blocks, the majestic beauty of the mountains and lakes of Eastern Europe has proven very popular.

An important part of this success has been prices which, to Western eyes, looked ridiculously low. Houses in Bulgaria or Romania used to sell for a few thousand euros. The prices available in Eastern Europe have helped to democratise the international property market; buying a home overseas is no longer the preserve of the wealthy.

'The prices available in Eastern Europe have helped to democratise the international property market; buying a home overseas is no longer the preserve of the wealthy'

The lower costs in Eastern Europe have been a pleasant surprise for many buyers, who still raise finance off the back of their homes. The average amount of money that people expect to spend on a second home is close to £180,000 – an amount which would buy a newly built four-bedroom house with two bathrooms, a private swimming pool and a sea view in even the most popular corner of Turkey.

Finally, with buyers realising the sheer range of possibilities and prices available, the number of viable markets has exploded. Britons spent £24bn on overseas property in 2007 (according to the Association of International Property Professionals) and countries which are now fair game for investors include Malaysia, Brazil, Morocco, Grenada, Argentina, Poland, India, Mongolia and many others.

Emerging markets

Over the last few years, interest in emerging markets has blossomed. People are travelling further and becoming familiar with new parts of the world. The primacy of France, Spain and Italy is being rapidly overtaken by new destinations. Italian machismo took a knock as far back as 2005 when China ousted the country from fourth place in the list of most popular destinations, and Turkey entered the top ten destinations by more than doubling the number of visitors per year. The World Tourism Organisation forecasts that by 2020 Europe will still be the world's first choice for tourism, but that the region's share of the market will have dropped dramatically. Rather than catching the ferry to France or taking a flight to the Florida Keys, tourists will be more likely to hop on a long-haul flight to Hainan or Brazil. Long-haul holidays are one of the fastest growing segments of the tourist industry, with 17.2 million Britons travelling abroad in 2007.

This roaming spirit contributes to the emergence of property markets further overseas. As people see more of the world and destinations once seen as exotic become familiar and therefore feel safe, the traditional markets can look rather tame. You do not have to travel halfway round the world to find exciting new property investment destinations. For example, the coasts of Morocco and Spain are so close that a 39km tunnel is being planned to link the two countries, yet a two bedroom apartment which would cost £120,000 on the south coast of Spain costs from £25,000 in Morocco.

The threshold to get into emerging markets is becoming much lower, extending appeal beyond the typical 40-something investor or holiday home buyer to younger people and even first-time buyers hoping to get onto the property ladder but priced out of the market in their home country.

A good example of a market where investors have recently become active and successful is **Mongolia**. Mongolia is a commodity-rich country with the world's largest copper mine and rapidly developing oil and gold industries. With the incessant growth of China, the demand for copper, coal and oil has fuelled a rapid growth in entrepreneurial business in Mongolia. With global mining giants such as BHP, Ivanhoe, Centerra Gold and Rio Tinto all opening up operations in the capital, demand for high-quality accommodation from both high-profile executives and ambassadors in Ulaan Baatar is extremely high. With strict planning regulations and most of the population living in traditional Ger settlements there is simply not enough good housing to go around, so rents are constantly being driven higher and yields of 10% are achievable. Recent analysis has suggested that an additional 4,000 new homes are needed to be built each year in this tiny capital city. With no mortgages available in Mongolia prices here reflect the true value of the property which continues to grow at around 20% per year.

With property in Eastern Europe, Latin America and beyond available for the price of a new car in the West, it can be easy to get carried away. Ultimately, rather than a ramshackle farmhouse which costs €5,000 but is 200 miles from the nearest town, research suggests that the properties which do best are attractive developments in areas with strong fundamentals of demand, i.e. city centres or emerging tourist resorts where people are likely to travel. With a little thought, it is possible to find a property which will provide a solid rental return while appreciating in value by up to 20% per year. And this is what investors should look for. Low prices alone do not indicate that prices are on the way up.

Overview of the world property markets

The areas where people buy are changing. This is partly due to the emerging pre-eminence of the profit motive amongst buyers and partly because even holiday homers are trying to get more for their money. This can be seen as both a positive and a negative development. From one perspective there is more choice and therefore more opportunity. From another, greater choice creates greater confusion.

Whatever viewpoint you hold, the reality remains that developed western markets are not necessarily the best place to invest in property. For example, property in much of Western Europe is very expensive and offers low rates of return, especially once rental yields are swallowed up in management costs and taxation. Overbuilding in favourite areas helps supply to outweigh demand, creating competition for rental business and putting deflationary pressure on property prices. The dangers of over-building are particularly apparent in Spain, which holds the crown for using more concrete than any other country in the EU – laying down more than 50 million tonnes every year. In the past decade Spain has built over five million new houses, most of these situated along the coast to accommodate the endless number of foreign investors.

Overdevelopment on this scale has a big impact on the market. Over 70% of European property investment comes from Britons alone. In 2003, 55% of these buyers headed straight for Spain, attracted by the near-perfect climate of the Mediterranean coast, but this percentage has dropped dramatically with many now looking instead at Eastern Europe and Asia.

Eastern Europe

The main factor pulling buyers towards Eastern Europe is initial cost. Low prices make investment in property more widely accessible. But it isn't all about low prices. Many parts of Eastern Europe have delivered excellent returns for the investors who arrived on the scene early. Some parts of Bulgaria apparently saw price rises of almost 50% in one year whilst capital cities across the region have also proven to be good choices. The opportunities in Eastern Europe are tied to two key factors, the first of which is domestic economic growth. Burgeoning local economies are increasing the wealth of local residents, thus creating greater demand for housing. Additionally this economic growth has the benefit of attracting foreign companies and their workers which contributes positively to the local economy and creates further demand for property. This factor will be most obviously felt in major commercial centres and capital cities.

The second factor is increasing tourism. The natural heritage of many Eastern European nations is set to make them extremely popular with tourists. Investing in areas where tourism is likely to grow can be a good choice as more tourists mean more tenants and more development means increasing property values. A word of caution though: timing is even more important when buying in tourist resorts. Rampant speculation and over-development can lead to the creation of a property market bubble. It is important therefore that you consider the sustainability of the resort which is primarily dependent upon the existence of underlying factors that make it an attractive destination to holiday. To put this into a practical example, we wouldn't personally invest in **Bulgaria**. The Bulgarian coast simply doesn't have an attractive enough climate to compete with resorts in the Mediterranean.

This doesn't mean that investors haven't made profits in **Sunny Beach**; they have, but that statement is in the past tense.

Despite this, Eastern Europe does present interesting opportunities within tourism locations. The states of Eastern Europe have some extremely important historical and cultural attractions as well as good skiing, all of which attract tourists. Our tip is therefore to buy in cities that will attract short-break visitors such as **Budapest** and **Krakow** or in ski resorts with reliable snowfall such as the **High Tatras** mountains.

Asia and the Pacific

Beyond Eastern Europe lie other areas which have shown impressive growth in recent years. Investment buyers have been attracted to the high profits in expanding economic centres such as **China** and **India** (half of the BRIC (Brazil, Russia, India and China) nations who are predicted to eclipse the current richest nations by 2041). There has also been considerable growth in investment purchasers in key tourist and second-home destinations such as **Malaysia**. Many of these countries are actively pursuing foreign property buyers as they realise the obvious economic benefits of converting tourists into buyers.

Investing in paradise is not always as cheap as people expect. Prices in Thailand, for example, reflect just how desirable a location this has become. Even the most modest of one-bedroom apartments in **Phuket** will cost £65,000 ($128,482).

Whilst we all recognise Asia's exotic appeal, it is its economic performance which should be of most interest to investors. **Vietnam** is one of Asia's most exciting economies and its rapid level of development and internationalisation since 1986 has resulted in a GDP growth rate of 8% in recent years. With a thriving export industry in textiles, footwear and seafood and a rapidly improving infrastructure there has been a dramatic increase in standards of living. As a direct result rental yields in **Ho Chi Minh City** are around 10–14%.

Outside of Vietnam, the Asian economic growth story extends to many nations in the region and brings with it excellent investment opportunities. Two examples of markets to watch are the Malaysian capital of **Kuala Lumpur** and the capital of the **Philippines, Manilla**. Both these cities demonstrate strong underlying growth drivers which should see property prices rising significantly in the near future.

A more unusual Asian market which is currently creating a buzz in the property investment world is **Mongolia**. The country is attracting a great deal of mining interest (Mongolia has the largest copper deposits in Asia), and large numbers of expatriate workers are moving into the capital, Ulaan Baatar. Accommodation in the region is generally poor with a large percentage of the population still living in traditional Gers. As a result there is a severe shortage of executive standard accommodation and the few high-quality developments which are under construction sell out extremely quickly. Investors who enter the market early should see substantial profit.

Australia and **New Zealand** are still two of the most popular with younger buyers yearning to emigrate, but both markets are in a vulnerable position as a result of the international credit crunch. Average house prices in Australia doubled between 1996 and 2004 but then took a turn for the worse and began to fall. According to 'Global Property Guide', Australia experienced a property boom in 2007 with property prices rising an average of 12.3% in many major cities, due to lack of supply, but then this again began to falter. After years of fast growth the housing market in New Zealand has significantly slowed recently. By 2007 house prices were 82% higher then they were in the last quarter of 1999 having risen a staggering 70% relative to household income – one of the biggest increases in the world.

Africa

In Africa, overseas buyers have tended to concentrate on only a few specific markets. **South Africa** is one of the strongest second home markets in the world. At the other end of the continent **Cape Verde** and **Morocco** are creating a new challenge.

South Africa has seen some of the fastest increasing property prices in the world. According to the global house price indices tracked by *The Economist*, house prices in South Africa grew by 401% between 1997 and 2008, by far the highest growth rate in the Western world – almost double that of Ireland which lies in second place. South Africa is also predicted to benefit from strong tourism growth during the coming years. In 2007 tourism levels in South Africa rose by 9% worth around £24.8bn but with their hosting of the 2010 football World Cup, it is estimated that this figure will reach $60bn in 2017.

'The choice of where to buy depends on the degree of risk that you are willing to accept and your rationale for buying'

Northern Africa, Morocco and the Cape Verde Islands are becoming popular with buyers keen to find an emerging tourist hotspot within reasonable travelling distance of Northern Europe. The historic cities of Morocco began to capture the attention of trendsetters after World War II and the designer Yves St Laurent credited Morocco with introducing him to colour. Winston Churchill was a famous fan describing himself as 'captivated by Marrakech'. To this day our love affair with Morocco has not diminished and many choose here instead of Spain as a holiday home destination.

The Cape Verde Islands are a newer market; this group of nine islands lies off Africa's west coast, following the curve of the continent beyond the Canary Islands. A host of articles and travel programmes in early 2005 testified that Cape Verde was gaining a reputation as one of the hot new markets. The islands were first colonised by Portugal in the fifteenth century and now have one of the most stable governments in Africa. The Cape Verde islands have become a haven for ex-patriots, to the point that foreigners may now outnumber native Cape Verdeans. The strange, wild beauty of the islands combined with property prices from €50,000 for apartments to around €145,000 for luxury villas mean that the Cape Verde Islands are becoming an increasingly popular investment opportunity with a 25% annual increase in tourists visiting each year.

A more unusual destination worth considering from a purely investment perspective is **Angola**, where the burgeoning oil industry, gas resources, hydro-electric production and diamond mines have turned the country into the second fastest growing economy in Africa and one of the fastest in the world. However, after years of poverty and war, Angola is still one of the poorest countries in the world with all the inherent problems thus associated so this is not an investment for the faint-hearted.

Central and South America

Central and South America are home to some of the best examples of 'true emerging markets' in the economic sense of the term. Many of the countries carry the characteristics of newly emerging economies and this means that problems with stability remain across the continent. However, this doesn't mean that opportunities do not exist. There are places in South America though where only the hardest nosed investor would consider buying. One example that springs to mind is **Colombia**. The property market in Colombia has grown rapidly over recent years, but as the country is commonly referred to as one of the most dangerous places on earth it may be a place where profit comes at too high a price.

More stable options exist in **Brazil** and **Argentina** as well as in Central American states such as **Belize** and **Panama**. In areas such as the north coast of Brazil, developers are taking advantage of the verdant rainforest, stunning beaches and sense of space to work on luxury developments. In the first quarter of 2007 alone, tourism to Brazil increased by 9.6% and with a cost of living considerable cheaper than that of the UK or the USA and a booming economy, Brazil's two principal cities – Rio de Janeiro and São Paolo – offer excellent investment opportunities. In Central America Belize offers a wealth of natural delights and arguably the most attractive incentive programme for foreign retirees anywhere in the world, plus, it is the only country in South America which has English as its principal language.

There is also much excitement about parts of **the Caribbean** where prices have been rising by as much as 20% per annum. Although renowned for their laid -back lifestyle, excellent diving and crystal clear seas, a number of the Caribbean islands also offer excellent tax advantages – **Tobago, St Kitts, The Cayman Islands** and **Bahamas** to name but a few. However, one of the best investment opportunities lies in **Grenada**, which is yet to experience the levels of development seen on other Caribbean islands and therefore has lower prices and greater potential for growth.

Conclusion

The inescapable conclusion is that investors are looking further afield for their profits. And whilst the markets above are some of the more popular options, there are very few limits on investing anywhere overseas. Overseas property agents now receive daily enquiries about buying in the **Ukraine**.

The choice of where to buy depends on the degree of risk that you are willing to accept and your rationale for buying. If you are interested in a specific country, maybe one of those mentioned above, the country information in the second part of this book should help to get you started. Alternatively, for buyers more concerned with the amount of profit to be made than the country in which they make it, the chapters below should help you to work out which opportunities to consider.

2 Where to buy abroad – analysing markets

How property markets work

Before we can understand which property markets offer the best opportunities, we must have an understanding of how property markets work. Don't worry, we are not about to launch into an extended monologue on economic theory. We don't need to. The reality is that understanding property markets is less about technical knowledge than about understanding the behaviour of people; you certainly don't need a PhD in economics.

THE VALUE OF PROPERTY: SUPPLY AND DEMAND

Just like the price of any asset or commodity, the value of property is based upon the concept of scarcity. Simply put, the supply of any resource is finite (there will be a limited amount of land and therefore properties within a city). Thus the more market demand there is for it, the more its price will rise. This is the principle of supply and demand, the two concepts that make market economies work. Supply and demand determine the availability of every commodity or asset (including properties) and the price at which it is sold. This principle is fundamental to the analysis of property markets; if you want to know how any event will affect the property market you must consider the implications of that event on the supply of property and the demand for property.

Essentially, when supply and demand are balanced, prices are stable. When supply exceeds demand prices fall. And when demand exceeds supply, prices rise.

Without becoming too concerned with the theory, the levels of supply and demand are dependent upon the behaviour of market participants – people; how will a particular event make people feel and act? It is judging the behaviour of people and their response to certain events and actions that stops economics from being a pure science. The genius of people such as Warren Buffet and George Soros is not their in-depth understanding of finance and economics, but more their ability to predict how people will react to certain events. After all, it is people who make up markets and the actions of people that determine whether prices rise or fall.

The market reaction to some events is easy to predict. For example, when interest rates rise so does the cost of mortgage repayments and therefore the cost of property ownership. In a real-estate market where many of the participants rely on mortgage financing to purchase a property, this will reduce demand for property and therefore have a deflationary impact on prices. It is important to remember though that the effect will be relative. In this example, higher interest rates may reduce demand, but demand may still exceed supply (albeit by less than it did before). In this scenario prices will continue to rise but at a lesser rate.

Other events may have a less obvious effect on a market because the reaction of people is harder to predict. For example, a change of government could either increase or decrease demand for property. The reaction to the event depends on people's *opinions* of whether the new government will make property ownership more or less desirable as a result of their policies, on tax for example. A further complexity is that some market participants will base their decision not on whether they think the change in government will have a positive or negative effect on the market, but on their opinion of what other market participants will feel about the change. Some people may personally believe that the new government will be positive for the housing market but may not buy because they believe the other market participants will have a contrary belief. In situations where the consequences of an event are not clear, you often see a slowdown in market activity as people wait to see the response of other market participants.

What then allows us to assess property markets and make predictions is our understanding of the factors at work within the market, otherwise known as **market forces**. Whilst supply and demand are market forces in themselves it is the market forces that affect supply and demand that need to be understood if you are to successfully assess a property market. The problem is that no market is 'perfect.' Perfect markets are essentially fictional economic models used to explain the principles of how markets work. No market in the real world is perfectly predictable as people will make irrational as well as rational decisions.

'Irrational behaviour' is what makes markets difficult to predict. In addition, property markets have their own peculiarities that need to be borne in mind. Firstly, people don't buy property purely on financial motivations. Whether or not a property market is falling or rising, people need somewhere to live. Shelter is a basic human requirement. Additionally, people often choose a house because they like it rather than because it has good investment potential. A key influence on people's buying decisions is taste and as the saying goes, there is no accounting for it. Personal perceptions of where is a desirable place to live mean that markets can be so subjective that prices which are acceptable in one town are regarded as outrageous in the next. That doesn't make property markets unpredictable; it simply means that we need to be aware of the factors that make one location a more desirable place to live than another. The question then is: what do people find attractive when choosing somewhere to live?

Secondly, property is not a liquid asset. Property doesn't lend itself to the easy tradability of assets such as stocks and shares. Properties take longer to sell and have high transaction costs (costs of buying and selling). This means that people hold on to real estate even when prices are falling. It also means that property markets react slowly to market forces and events. From an investor's point of view, this is one of the most attractive characteristics of property investment; markets are relatively slow moving and stable. A property price crash is a very different beast to a stock market crash. Global stock markets have been known to lose 15% or more of their value in a single day. A property market crash that wipes 15% off property values is likely to take a matter of years to bottom out.

'No market in the real world is perfectly predictable as people will make irrational as well as rational decisions'

From an economist's perspective the biggest problem with property markets is that they are so localised. Property markets are more influenced by local factors affecting supply and demand than they are by broad economic trends. According to The Economist, 'Fluctuations in property prices can arise not only owing to cyclical movements in economic fundamentals, interest rates and the risk premium, but also as a result of the intrinsic characteristics of the property market itself.' This is perhaps the real key to understanding property markets: they move to their own rhythm. For all the importance of economic factors, the really significant factors are things like local supply. Research carried out for the International Monetary Fund suggests that 'almost three fifths of the overall variation in housing prices can be explained by innovations in the housing market itself. The combined effect of other explanations, such as GDP, interest rates, bank credit and equity prices, accounts for the rest.'

The largely independent nature of individual property markets therefore makes generalisations and broad projections dangerous. However, it also means that uniform increases and falls in value are unlikely. A statement such as 'over the last three years property prices in Russia have risen dramatically' is invariably misleading. It is much more likely that certain cities or neighbourhoods in Russia have seen dramatic increases in prices, whilst others have been stagnant or even dropped. The truth in the statement is that the average value of property across Russia has risen dramatically, but this doesn't mean that any Russian property would have been a good investment.

The fact that property markets are localised and relatively independent of one another doesn't mean that local property markets have not been subject to the impacts of globalisation. The fact that you are reading this book proves that they have.

For example, the real estate market in the Costa Del Sol will be closely related to the economic health of the UK and Ireland whose residents make up a major proportion of property owners (market participants) in the area. If there were an event in the UK which reduced the ability or desire of UK-based buyers to buy in the Costa Del Sol (as has been the case over the last year), this would reduce demand and have a deflationary impact on prices. This means that one of the most important steps in analysing a property market is to identify who the market participants are. Only once you have done this are you able to consider the market forces which may impact upon their behaviour.

The important point to take away is that to understand what is happening in a property market and, more importantly, to predict what will happen, requires an analysis of all of the factors affecting supply and demand at a local, national and international level. In other words, you need to consider both the microeconomic and macroeconomic influences on supply and demand.

Below we consider some of the most common microeconomic and macroeconomic influences on supply and demand in a property market. The factors discussed here are not intended to be exhaustive, but merely illustrative. The intention is that these examples will help you to understand what other events may impact on supply and demand in a property market that you are assessing.

Some potential events causing price movement in property markets

	Will Influence Supply	Will Influence Demand
Macro	Law Changes (e.g. increasing the amount of land that can be built on) Taxation incentives for developers National or regional level infrastructure	Income growth (GDP) Cost of ownership – tax Finance availability Change in law Membership of trade organisations
Micro	Building restrictions Local business activity (perhaps factory closures may open brownfield sites) Price of land	Local population growth and immigration Local infrastructure developments Tourism Local level of employment

The above diagram lists just a few of the factors that could stimulate movement in a property market. When evaluating the result, or potential result, of any one or more of these events on a market we must proceed with caution. The impact of one event on another is never direct or simple in the real world. We cannot say that EU membership directly causes property prices to rise. This would, at the very least, oversimplify the situation. In the real world, events happen in chains of events linked to one another by causality. Also, there may be other, omitted variables that have an effect. Relationships between real-life events are neither isolated nor linear, unidirectional nor normative.

We couldn't possibly hope to map and understand every variable at work within a property market, but we can use past experience and common sense to work through potential scenarios highlighting the most logical chain of events. Sticking with the EU example, why is it that people believe that membership leads to property boom? Much of this belief comes from past experience of other members joining the Union such as Ireland (see below), but there are many potential chains of events which logically link this cause and event, for example:

EU entry
↓
More trade with other members
↓
Increase in levels of employment and rates of pay
↓
Increase in wealth of the local population
↓
Increased demand for privately owned housing
↓
Increases in house prices

This example remains oversimplified and is just one of a vast range of possibilities. We could create an equally logical argument to suggest that EU membership will cause property prices to fall;

EU entry
↓
Ability for local workers to migrate to other parts of the EU in search of higher paid jobs
↓
Decreases in local population
↓
Less demand for housing
↓
Decreases in house prices

In reality both of these series of events may occur at once. Certainly Poland is an example where the local population is falling due to emigration whilst at the same time Gross Domestic Product (the wealth of the country) is rising. What, therefore, will be the net impact on the property market?

This is neither a simple nor easy question to answer. The above example shows why the international property industry employs experts to analyse these situations. Whilst it might not be possible for ordinary investors to work through all these scenarios or stay abreast of all the events that may impact on property markets across the globe, it is important that you are aware how complicated markets can be and are able to be more questioning when someone suggests that a particular event will have a direct and certain impact on property prices.

Despite the conflicting possibilities above, we do believe that it is possible to make an educated assessment of what is happening in most markets. Whilst it might not be possible to evaluate every cause, effect or scenario we can rely on past experience and common sense to come to an opinion on what is likely to happen in the future.

Financial advisors always tell us that past performance is no indicator of future performance, but it is a good place to start. You will see in a later case study what EU membership did to property prices in Ireland and why, therefore, many people expect the same results in current and future entrants. EU entry provided Ireland with investment in infrastructure and increased its levels of trade. Both these effects will also be felt by more recent entrants. However, whilst the Irish experience suggests that Eastern Europe will experience significant growth, we cannot simply map the Irish experience onto other countries.

The following are case studies which give some practical consideration to how some topical events may impact on property values in different markets.

Case studies of topical market forces

Picking up one of the international property magazines it is easy to identify a number of factors used almost as a synonym for capital appreciation. First among these is European Union entry, followed by the hosting of international sporting or commercial events. For example, Beijing has been one of the most popular investment buys of the past couple of years and much of its popularity has been related to its selection as host of the 2008 Olympic Games.

The excitement about the ways in which single events can impact on property prices is sometimes justified. Ukraine's prospects before and after the Orange Revolution of 2004, for example, could not be more different. Yet it often pays to be slightly cynical about the impact of any single factor on the market. As a general rule, big name events like the Olympics justify a rise in property prices only if backed by other factors such as investment in infrastructure development.

Case study: the benefits of European Union accession

Anyone considering buying property in Eastern Europe will be well used to predictions that property values will grow at a rate of 5–10% every year until accession, followed by an immediate doubling of values on the day that integration is formalised. Working on the principle that any prediction taken so seriously and allotted such attention is always worth questioning, the section below examines the true benefits that lie behind EU accession, helping you to work out just how much of a difference it will make to property prices.

Accessions are planned a long time in advance – Turkey began preliminary membership negotiations in October 2005 but isn't expected to join the Union before 2015. Beyond this, Croatia, Bosnia and Herzegovina, Serbia, Montenegro, the former Yugoslav Republic of Macedonia, Albania and potentially even the Ukraine and Georgia may also join the EU. Beyond the geographical limits of Europe, Cape Verde is also interested in joining.

If some of the claims made by agents are correct then all of these countries should see prices rising, but the 'magic effect' of joining the EU may not appear. The idea that countries joining the European Union will see an automatic and impressive climb in prices owes a great deal to the Irish experience.

THE IRISH EXPERIENCE

When Ireland joined the EEC in 1973 GDP per head was 63% of the EU average. By 2001 this had climbed to 126%. This economic success has been matched by increasing real estate prices. Over the last 12 years alone the value of property has climbed by 270%.

Unfortunately, Ireland may be the exception rather than the rule. More recent accession states have seen a slower pace of growth. Greece joined the EU in 1981, but in the years of Ireland's greatest triumph, had an economy which remained almost stagnant at around 69% of the Union average.

It looks very much as though the rules of enlargement are changing. Ireland succeeded so dramatically because it is a small country and, as one of the first and best value entrants, enlargement caused foreign investment to flood in.

Limits to the impact of EU accession

EU accession isn't quite the magic solution that some agents believe. The key to price rises in Eastern Europe is more often economic development than EU entry, though often the two go hand in hand. Some highly developed countries have opted to stay out of the Union – for example, Norway – but few property agents would argue that EU accession would have any impact on property prices there. Given the fact that they remain out of the EU, Norwegian property has continued to increase annually with a rise from 12.4% in 2006 to 14.2% in 2007.

In the Baltics, wages have risen by 10% in a single year. Outside investors have been able to make profits by betting on this rise. The average price of property in Latvia rose 39.2% between July and September in 2006 and Bulgaria was not far behind with growth of 19%.

The most recent wave of accessions has been in the Mediterranean and Eastern Europe, in areas where prices were naturally going to rise anyway. Cyprus and Malta have benefited from the rising numbers of people retiring to the sun. The price rises in Bulgaria and Romania have arguably more to do with artificially low property prices after the end of communism than with the effects of accession.

'The key to price rises in Eastern Europe is more often economic development than EU entry, though often the two go hand in hand'

What EU membership does do is make buyers feel more secure. In order to be invited into the Union, countries need to have stable economies, removing the risk of a currency crash or profit-eroding inflation. The European Union also provides 'fundamental freedoms,' including free movement of people and money. Citizens have the right to live and work anywhere in the EU and no limits will be placed on investment.

In some ways the benefits of EU accession are more symbolic. This is especially important where countries were part of the communist sphere but have now embraced market economies and are keen to turn towards Western Europe. European Union entry carries real prestige – shown by the long list of often slightly surprising countries who see accession as an eventual aim.

ACCESSIONS IN EASTERN EUROPE

If nothing else, the increasing numbers of entrants (10 in 2004) means that the 'magic effect' of joining the EU may not appear. Believing that 10 countries can all see a simultaneous increase at the levels predicted by some commentators slightly stretches credibility.

Enlargement has now turned towards the larger populations and vast geographical area of Eastern Europe. With such a variety of new markets and so many areas in which to invest, there may not be enough of the old EU accession magic to go around.

The 2004 accessions increased the surface area of the EU by a quarter and the total population by a fifth. The accession of Bulgaria and Romania on 1 January 2007 further increased the total number of people living within the EU to 490 million, and another generation including Croatia and Turkey waits in the wings.

Economic benefits of membership

With the Union growing at such a rate, the pace of economic growth linked only to accession will be limited. This doesn't mean that EU accession states don't have a bright future, only that expecting EU entry to act as a universal panacea is unduly optimistic.

Having set out the reservations and the provisos, the limits and the reasons for a degree of pessimism, it is only fair to balance the picture by noting that EU entry is very good for any fledgling economic power. Far from being conferred from the outside by EU entry, this is the result of hard work within the country.

The complex economic criteria required for accession are designed to establish a 'stable market economy'. This sounds straightforward enough, but in reality means bringing fledgling economies up to the standard where they can compete on equal terms with the original EU 15. Finally there is the long process of adopting the whole body of EU law, known as the *acquis communautaire*. Candidate countries are required to step into line with the EU, and this can mean anything from eliminating corruption in Romania to altering water standards across vast swathes of Eastern Europe.

In return for this considerable effort, large amounts of money are transferred to the candidate countries. Since 2000 Romania, for example, has received substantial financial assistance from the EU, with pre-accession funds exceeding €1bn and allocated post-accession funds amounting to €19,688bn between 2007 and 2013. The money can be used for infrastructure improvements or for projects such as developing education, improving employment opportunities and promoting tourism. These factors all have an indirect impact on property prices.

The advantages of entry also include higher rates of foreign investment. Outside investors feel more confident about the security of their funds and the standard of treatment that they will receive at the hands of local government. More importantly, accession states get to join the free market, greatly improving potential for economic performance. The conditions for investment are also improved. As economies fall into line and financial markets are opened, interest rates fall sharply. Low interest rates encourage people into the housing market and are one of the best preconditions for rising prices.

THE IMPORTANCE OF TIMING

If you do want to buy hoping to take advantage of price rises around accession, timing is important. Property prices go up when buyers feel at their most confident. This is not necessarily at the actual moment of accession, but is generally months or even years before. Buyers who wait until the date is set may miss the boost effect.

The Czech Republic joined the European Union in 2004. In 2003 prices rose by 20%–25% in expectation of joining. Just prior to entry prices faltered, with people feeling that they had been over optimistic. Then, after entry, prices began a slower but more sustained rise based on greater internal wealth.

As a local businessman interviewed in the *Prague Post* said, 'There is no immediate impact on the real estate market, because all participants have already projected it in their expectations a long time ago'.

Impact of future accessions on property prices

The next country to join will probably be Croatia. At the time of writing, Croatia's candidacy has been resumed after the EU accepted that the Croatian government was making genuine efforts to co-operate with the UN War Crimes Tribunal at The Hague. The country looks set to be granted membership in 2009 or 2010, providing that the criteria for membership are met and that the treaty of accession is ratified by the parliaments of the other member states.

From October 2005 membership talks have also been opened with Turkey, an official candidate from 1987 – seven years before applications were received from Poland and Hungary. Turkey has been making progress on human rights and other requirements, but membership is unlikely to mature before 2015 at the earliest.

Turkey's candidacy has caused concern in some of the EU countries because of the size of the population as well as a number of other factors (some of which have been seen more as xenophobia than legitimate objection). Opening talks in 2005 signalled that these concerns have been overcome and that Turkey will eventually be welcomed into the Union. However, the conditions set on Turkey's candidacy are extremely stringent. For the first time, there is a criterion that the EU must have the capacity to absorb a new country. Turkey's membership, which has been seen by some as a step too far, is by no means assured yet.

Opinion polls taken at the time of the establishment of the European constitution showed a noticeable cooling regarding further accession. Turkey's official candidacy has been delayed too long for the EU to fob Turkey off, but we may now see a couple of years of consolidation before the EU begins to consider the next wave of accessions.

Having said this, there are definite signs that Montenegro is on the way to joining the Union since independence was gained from Serbia in 2006, although the country is currently experiencing ecological, judicial and crime-related problems that may hinder its bid. Other countries recognised as 'potential candidate countries' (the EU specialises in this kind of coy language) are Albania, the Federal Republic of Macedonia, Serbia and Bosnia and Herzegovina.

Of the recent and future member countries, Turkey's popularity as a second-home destination means that accession is unlikely to make much of a difference to property values in the second-home resorts along the Mediterranean coast. Of all the potential new member states the best opportunity of all is in Montenegro, a small coastal state next to Croatia on the Adriatic.

Before the war in the former Yugoslavia disrupted tourism in the region, Montenegro was a popular destination with the yachting crowd – a position it is rapidly regaining.

Timeline of European Accession

Year	Country
1952	Founding members included Belgium, France, West Germany, Italy, Luxembourg and the Netherlands
1973	Denmark, Ireland and the United Kingdom
1981	Greece
1986	Portugal, Spain
1990	East Germany reunites with West Germany and becomes part of the EU
1995	Austria, Finland and Sweden
2004	Cyprus, Czech Republic, Estonia, Hungary, Latvia, Lithuania, Malta, Poland, Slovakia, Slovenia
2007	Bulgaria, Romania
c.2009–10	(Potentially) Croatia, Montenegro
c.2012–15	(Potentially) Turkey, FYR Macedonia, Albania, Bosnia & Herzegovina, Serbia

The impact of low-cost airlines

There is a close relationship between cheap flights and second-home ownership, so much so that the growth of the second-homes market can hardly be imagined without the no-frills airlines. Research suggests that most owners of second homes visit their property six times a year.

As long as you are fairly relaxed about the area where you hope to buy, identifying a region set to attract cheap flights is a sure-fire way to find a property on the way up. The link between flights and homes is so close that airlines now often advertise property in their in-flight magazines.

'The growth of the second-homes market can hardly be imagined without the no-frills airlines'

A landmark survey by Savills Research and Holiday-Rentals.co.uk in 2006 found that the average price of a property located within 10 miles of an airport served by a low-cost airline is 39% higher than for properties within the same distance from an airport without a low-cost carrier. Rents were also found to be up to 30% higher for properties within 10–20 miles of airports.

How to find out about new routes

By importing such vast numbers of visitors, cheap flights can have a radical impact on house prices and rental potential. This makes new destinations one of the factors most closely monitored by house buyers. Working out where flight routes are going to open up is easy. Airlines announce future routes in the news sections of their websites and announcements are also often placed in the national press.

Risks of buying to be close to destinations served by budget airlines

Buying solely because of the introduction of another cheap flight destination is, however, a risky strategy. The value airlines can be ruthless about cancelling routes that are not proving sufficiently popular or if airport costs rise. This creates a danger that the airlines may pull out and anticipated appreciation vanish like the morning mist. Some analysts have also registered concern about flight costs rising if an area is over dependent on a single carrier.

The question also arises – Will low-cost airlines continue, given the international outcry about their impact on global warming and the massive increases in fuel charges they are being forced to pass on to their customers?

Impact of hosting the Olympics and other international events

Part of the arguments put forward for hosting the Olympics are the benefits that accrue to the host cities. These include employment and tourism growth as well as the vast amounts of money visitors spend whilst the Games are on. The area will also benefit from what economists call the 'Multiplier effect', with the money then being spent and re-spent in the city.

A survey by Halifax Building Society, which coincided with the announce-ment of London's successful Olympic bid, suggests that there is a correlation between hosting the Games and house prices rising. The survey found that in the five years prior to the 1992 Games, Barcelona saw a 131% increase in prices compared with an average across Spain of 83%. Athens, the host in 2004, saw a 66% increase in prices over the four years and nine months before the Games, compared with a 47% price increase across Greece. Halifax's research suggests the average increase among host cities has been 66%.

Other benefits of the Olympics are harder to measure. Research by Price Waterhouse Coopers suggests that the 'extensive media exposure during the Games may enhance the reputation of the city as an attractive business centre, further attracting new investment and trade from global companies'. This investment may also be supported by the fact that local people may be encouraged to learn valuable new business skills, for example being given training in languages and customer service.

Hosting the Games can also galvanise governments into proceeding with long-meditated infrastructure improvements. This is expected to be the primary benefit of the 2012 Games for London. Already an internationally famous tourism destination, the chief advantage of the Games will be in the improved transport links and lasting developments to be constructed in east London.

The building projects and infrastructure developments linked to international events are the real reason that prices rise. Barcelona, Athens and Sydney all saw significant work on the urban environment. In Barcelona 78km of new roads were created; the city also saw a 78% increase in green zones and beaches and a 268% increase in the number of ponds and fountains. In Beijing, a dozen Olympic sports centres, a new cross-city underground railway, a host of office towers, a massive airport terminal and a colossal French-designed theatre were completed before the 2008 Olympics. The Olympics have boosted Beijing's property market dramatically – in 2001 alone Beijing saw a 40% rise in real estate when the capital was rewarded the right to hold the 29th Olympic Games.

Olympic opportunities

All of the analysis on the Olympics suggests that countries benefit most if they don't have a high profile before holding the Games. The evidence suggests that cities which already have an international reputation may benefit less from the Olympics than the less well known. With the winter games in Vancouver 2010 and the summer games in London in 2012, the Olympic Committees seem to have chosen the next two cities where the opportunities for property investors will be limited.

The difference between the impact on Olympic cities and across the host country suggests that it is also important to be specific. To take advantage of the Olympic factor you need to buy as close to the events as possible, right down to looking for something next to the Olympic villages. Prices in Beijing rose fastest between the third and fourth Ring Roads – where the Olympic stadium was built.

Other sporting events

Buying ahead of the Olympics works because the sheer size and prestige of the Games guarantees heavy investment. But they may be more the exception than the rule. Sporting events generally have a short shelf life. And there may just be too many sporting events around. The number of World Cups, championships, games and contests means that an event will have to be fairly special to justify the build-up.

However, smaller-scale events can have some benefit in the right circumstances. For example, prior to the 1995 Rugby World Cup, Johannesburg International Airport was severely underfunded; after the event it was world class. The Rugby World Cup may only have lasted for a couple of months but it made a lasting contribution to the city.

Perception or reality? Knowing when growth is sustainable

Within any property market, there are three general types of buyer: end users (people who want to live in their property all or some of the time), investors (people who want to let their property out for profit) and speculators (people who buy in the anticipation that prices will rise). Thinking about market participants in this way allows us to make better judgements as to whether the market we are analysing is experiencing growth based on economic fundamentals or whether it is a bubble.

The underlying concept is that sometimes price growth is based on fundamentals (supply is exceeded by genuine and sustainable demand) and sometimes growth is self-perpetuating, i.e. price growth attracts buyers, which makes prices rise further. In such a scenario speculators believe prices will grow and therefore buy property. If enough speculators buy property, demand increases and prices go up. Such a market is based entirely on fragile human confidence and when the speculators lose their confidence and stop buying or start selling prices plummet as there are no genuine end-users in the market.

'Problems arise when rampant speculation takes over a market. Price rises become more dependent on speculative investment than they do on demand'

Speculation is essentially second guessing how other market participants will respond to certain stimuli and then gambling on it. Speculation is a valid investment strategy used by many different types of investors and is not harmful to a marke *per se*. The problems arise when rampant speculation takes over a market and price rises become more dependent on speculative investment than they do on fundamentally driven demand. An excellent example of speculation leading to a bubble followed by a crash is the Asian Economic Crisis of 1997. This particular economic phenomenon was only partly related to real estate investment but it did play a part. Once speculators lost faith in the markets of South East Asia they pulled their money out. As a result stock markets in the region crashed, currencies plummeted in value and the real estate markets went into free fall.

What does this mean for international property investors? It means that when deciding whether or not to invest in a market, you must decipher whether any price rise or fall is the result of underlying fundamentals or whether it is down to the second guessing of speculators.

Deciding whether a market is overvalued or undervalued

It goes without saying that the best property investment is in a property which is currently undervalued and set to increase in price. The difficult part is knowing whether a market is undervalued, overvalued or valued correctly. Knowing whether a market is valued correctly is a good starting point when considering where to invest. Undervalued markets will not always increase in value but usually will. Overvalued markets may not necessarily fall. Just because a formula says that a market is overvalued doesn't mean that people will stop buying. However, an overvalued market does not make a good investment.

There are formulas which help us to identify anomalies, compare markets and to make a decision on whether a market is ripe for investment or may be about to crash. Two key tools discussed below are the price to earnings ratio and the affordability ratio. It is also important to look at vacancy rates and the ownership ratio. We have focused on these because they are measures which allow us to connect a property's price with its underlying value as an asset and its underlying affordability as a home.

The price to earnings ratio

The price to earnings ratio (the P/E) is a measure used by investors when considering many forms of investment. A quick flick through the stock market indices will show a column giving the P/E for each stock. The P/E can also be used as a tool to evaluate and compare house prices.

In the case of a property, its net earnings are the amount of revenue received through letting minus costs (maintenance, property management, mortgage financing etc). The P/E is the purchase price of the property divided by the net earnings.

$$\text{House P/E} = \frac{\textbf{Property price}}{\textbf{Earnings after costs}}$$

The house P/E provides a direct comparison to P/E ratios used to analyse other uses of the money tied up in a property investment. This means that you can use this measure to compare two property investment opportunities or compare a property investment opportunity against an alternative use of the money.

The P/E is effectively the inverse of yield. Therefore what it is assessing is the value of the property based upon its income. In a property market where average net yields are 10%, the P/E would be 10; or in other words, the value of the asset (the property) is 10 times its net annual profit (rent). When comparing markets, therefore, we want to see a low P/E ratio which means that rental yields are high. When the P/E ratio is high, say 25, yields would be unattractive for investors and we could say that the asset is overvalued compared to returns.

Rents, just like corporate and personal incomes, are generally tied very closely to supply and demand fundamentals; one rarely sees an unsustainable 'rent bubble' (or 'income bubble' for that matter). Therefore a rapid increase of house prices combined with a flat renting market can signal the onset of a bubble. This would be highlighted by an increase in the P/E ratio.

Occupancy rate

The *occupancy rate* (opposite of *vacancy rate*) is the number of occupied units divided by the total number of units in a given region (in commercial real estate, it is usually expressed in terms of area such as square metres for different grades of buildings). A low occupancy rate means that the market is in a state of oversupply brought about by speculative construction and purchase. In this context, supply-and-demand numbers can be misleading: sales demand exceeds supply, but rent demand does not. This scenario would lead to falling yields compared to property prices (an increase in the P/E ratio) and may signify the beginnings of a bubble.

OWNERSHIP RATIO

The ownership ratio is the proportion of households who own their homes as opposed to renting. The ownership ratio gives a good indication of the relative levels of demand for renting and home ownership. Markets with low ownership ratios can offer low price property with high yields. The ownership ratio can partly depend on culture, but it also tends to rise steadily with incomes. Governments can sometimes play a role by enacting measures such as tax cuts or subsidised financing to encourage and facilitate home ownership. If a rise in ownership is not supported by a rise in incomes, it can mean either that buyers are taking advantage of low interest rates (which must eventually rise again as the economy heats up) or that home loans are awarded more liberally, to borrowers with poor credit – as was seen recently in the USA.

The interesting point regarding ownership ratios is that they tell us where purchase demand may be set to rise. A country with a growing economy combined with a low ownership ratio would be a very good bet for price growth.

The affordability ratio

The affordability ratio is the ratio between property prices and household earnings. As an example, analysts believe that a healthy ratio is 1:4; in this case an average household income of £25,000 should mean that the average cost of a home should be £100,000. The cost of a house in the UK and US is now out of kilter with this equation – one of the reasons for the downturn in both markets.

If house prices become too out of line with household incomes then prices will probably stagnate if not fall. Market growth where there is already a ratio of 1:6 or 1:7 is unlikely to be sustainable. Although the recent falls in property values across much of the Western world cannot be put down entirely to affordability, it has been a major contributing factor.

This tool is more useful when evaluating a market where the primary market players are local residents as the relationship between earnings and prices in a holiday home market will be very different.

Market cycles: Does boom lead to bust? – The credit crunch

As with any asset class, over-heated property markets do sometimes fall.

Most recently the 'credit crunch' that hit the UK market as a direct result of the American sub-prime mortgage crisis is a classic case in point. But before we go on to consider how to deal with a fall in the market it would be useful to explain the basic underlying problems.

Today there are more financial innovations in the world's money markets than ever before. Banks debt, including your very own mortgages have been converted, chopped up and put together again under a dizzy array of combinations, then sold and resold to other banks, hedge funds and all other manner of investors all around the world. The debt that your local bank took on when it gave you your mortgage may now be owned by a private investor in Japan. This new securitisation of debt has created an incredibly huge global market, and has helped alter the world of finance.

This new way of repackaging and off-loading debt was closely tied into the housing market and in particular the American sub-prime mortgage market. In the 10 years leading up to 2006 American house prices rose on average 124%; in the same period the UK saw increases of 194%, Spain 180% and Ireland a staggering 253%. Markets were buoyant and consumers and lenders' confidence was sky high resulting in mortgages of up to 95% (LTV) being offered to people who under normal circumstances would not have been able to secure a loan. As long as house prices increased everybody was a winner. However, house prices didn't continue to rise as they had before and the market started to cool; once the introductory rates on home loans increased, sub-prime defaults started to rise. One study had the number of homes bought in California in 2007 with very lax credit checks at around 70%.

'This is an exciting time to be investing in emerging markets',

Large banks in America who had massive exposure to these sub-prime securities found that they had suffered huge losses. Bear Stearns was the first major bank to announce the write-off of billions of dollars worth of debt, but unfortunately this was just the tip of the iceberg. Confidence vanished from the market overnight and globally banks stopped lending to each other, tightening regulations and placing conditions on their hedge funds. Liquidity drained from the US securitisation market and the UK saw its first run on a high street bank in over 100 years. It showed that the markets across the world were now so intertwined with each other that problems in one could spread across the globe at breakneck speed.

This isn't the first time stock markets have fallen so dramatically. On 19 October 1987, so called 'Black Monday', stock markets plummeted and the US economy was plunged into financial crisis. With correct handling by the central bank (US FED), normal service soon resumed and investors continued to use the markets. Many looked for parallels during the sub-prime crisis hoping that the central banks would do their job again and pull the economy through. The only problem, however, is that the stock market crash 20 years ago was based on equity markets and not debt. Sub-prime hadn't even entered the public's vocabulary in 1987, and new financial theories and technological developments have transformed the markets further than ever before. However, the saving grace in all this mess is the surfacing of the world's 'emerging markets' and in particular the emerging BRIC (Brazil, Russia, India and China) superpowers. We should also take heart in the fact that as the credit crunch has put the brakes on global economic growth, the first 5 or 6 years of the 21st century have seen healthy international growth. According to the economist.com 'between 2003 and 2006 global GDP at market exchange rates grew by 3.5% a year'.

We are now likely to see a shift in the balance of power, from the developed economies to the emerging ones. Goldman Sachs published a report in 2003 in which the term BRIC was first coined. In this they concluded that China would overtake the US as the world's largest economy by 2050. Subsequently in a report released three years later, Goldman Sachs conceded they may have been wrong.

The sheer pace in which China has already grown has led analysts to believe it could take over as the world's largest economy by 2041. Analysts have now coined a second term 'NII' which is shorthand for the next 11 countries snapping at the heels of BRIC. These are Bangladesh, Egypt, Indonesia, Iran, South Korea, Mexico, Nigeria, Pakistan, the Philippines, Turkey and Vietnam. It is hoped that these emerging countries will be able to take over the reins on the global economy as the West starts to falter.

The question for the investor is how to take advantage of this swing in economic fortune. It is an exciting time to be investing in emerging markets and as long as the correct diligence has been done and the market is well researched, these countries offer a multitude of opportunities for the savvy investor.

The lessons to be learnt from the sub-prime crisis are valuable, and in a way help the global economy in the long term. Tighter regulations and a better rating system for securities and junk bonds, means that we shouldn't see a repeat of this crisis again.

RAMPANT SPECULATION

It has to be seen therefore that the biggest predicator to a bust is rampant speculation. When property prices become so out of line with underlying fundamentals, like affordability, or their price bears no resemblance to their earnings potential, trouble may be imminent. Outside of the real estate world, we can look at the internet bubble of the late nineties and early noughties. In this case investors saw the internet as an entirely new business model that changed the parameters of the game. As a result, over-excitement among investors caused them to invest in internet companies whose shares were very highly priced yet were earning no profits. The P/E ratio should have told people that the price of the shares was out of kilter with their underlying value. The internet did not change the rules of the game; even in the new e-world, businesses still have to make money.

Ultimately the bubble burst and share prices dropped to more realistic levels. A lot of people lost money and got burned but this doesn't mean that they have learned their lesson. It is a strange fact of human nature that people will buy into an investment once they have seen other people doing well. This is what happened with the internet boom. Every day people watched the bull market rising and rising until they could resist it no more. They invested their nest egg just before the bubble burst and then watched the value of their investment plummet.

When a market's success is compounded by other people jumping on the bandwagon due to that very same success, there should be warning bells. Regardless of whether you are investing in equities or properties, you should tread very carefully in a market where prices cannot be justified by underlying returns.

The answer to the question 'does boom lead to bust?' is a resounding 'not necessarily'. The fact is that property markets are generally very stable, but when there is rampant speculation a bust may well follow. Markets don't need speculation to boom. Ordinary homebuyers may enter into fierce competition for properties, but when the number of speculators outstrips the number of investors and home owners, there are fewer people to hold on for better days. Speculators have no ties to the market and are liable to cut their losses and move on elsewhere.

If you do get caught in a falling market and decide to hang on for happier times, research suggests that the waiting period will be limited to an average of just over four years before prices recover. If you do decide to sell, remember that falling markets often create a vicious cycle. People are reluctant to buy in case prices fall further, sellers have to drop prices again in order to tempt buyers in, but then buyers become even more reluctant . . . This means that if the market starts to fall and you are in a position to sell out, prompt action is essential. However, if you can afford to hold on through the hard times (which should be possible if the investment generates a positive cash flow), then this might be the most financially rewarding scenario in the long run.

Specific considerations for different types of markets

Considering a property investment is a very different process from deciding on where to buy a holiday home. Investment is a financial decision and must be made with the head, not the heart. Just because you love that beautiful old farmhouse in the heart of the French countryside, it doesn't mean that you will make any money out of it. The question of whether you want sun-drenched beaches or an equally sun-drenched terrace overlooking a medieval old town, ceases to be relevant. The real question is: is it better to invest in a city, the countryside or a tourist resort?

City or country

Research suggests that over the long term, the rental and resale potential of properties in cities outperforms that of properties in the countryside. Prices in cities are, however, often more volatile than in the countryside, partly because the supply of land is more limited and partly because of higher rates of population mobility.

What attracts investors to countryside properties, particularly in emerging markets, is price. However, low prices don't necessarily suggest that prices are going to rise. You may be able to buy a run-down village house in Romania for a few thousand pounds, but part of the reason that these properties cost so little is that nobody wants to live there. Even if your country house investment is close enough to new infrastructure, entertainment or commercial developments to increase demand, prices have got to go a long way before you make any significant profits in absolute terms. Our tip: stick to cities and major towns.

Buying in resorts: the impact of tourism

Many property companies focus on selling properties in resort areas. This is partly due to the fact that many people buying abroad are buying a holiday home, but it is also partly a result of increasing investor interest in resort properties.

Increasing levels of tourism bring increased wealth and demand for short-term holiday accommodation. In theory, with more people comes more demand. However, it is the intentions of those people that are important to decipher. Genuine resort investment opportunities exist in places where there will be considerable tourist demand for holiday accommodation and where buyers are landlords or holiday-home purchasers rather than speculators.

Determining the longevity of an investment in a resort area is based on simple common sense. There must be genuine, fundamental reasons why people would choose to holiday in the resort and even buy a holiday home there. For example; will the Black Sea coast of Bulgaria with its short summer season actually be as popular a holiday and second home destination as Spain? The answer is probably not.

'Investment is a financial decision and must be made with the head, not the heart'

Climate and local attractions are important. People will always want to holiday and live in the Mediterranean area because of the climate. Equally, people will also always want to holiday or live near Disneyworld. Florida and Spain might be very mature markets, but there is a reason that prices have reached the levels that they have: there is genuine demand. When looking for emerging resort markets we have to look out for the same demand motivators.

There is also a potential, non-financial benefit to having a property that you can use yourself in a resort. In a holiday resort, your property is likely to be used for short-term visitors rather than long-term tenants and it is therefore likely that it will be available for you to use at least some of the time. On many purpose-built resorts, developers offer packages where they let your property for you for most of the year but keep it open for your personal use at set times. This can be a good investment in your lifestyle as well as your financial future.

When considering a resort investment, we need to consider the main driver of rental and purchase demand: the number of tourists. As a starting point, the

10 countries forecast by the World Travel and Tourism Council to show some of the highest levels of real growth up to 2015 are as follows:

Country	Expected GDP Growth in Travel & Tourism in 2008 (%)	Average Growth per annum until 2018 (%)
Montenegro	17.0	5.6
China	11.3	8.8
India	7.9	7.6
Reunion	13.7	5.1
Croatia	6.4	7.1
Sudan	8.0	5.2
Vietnam	6.0	7.5
Laos	5.0	4.3
Czech Republic	3.1	6.0
Slovenia	3.7	4.8

These countries offer real opportunities.

Montenegro, in the top place for tourism growth, has often been named as the single best destination when trying to find a holiday home. Like neighbouring Croatia, Montenegro has a stunning coastline dotted with islands and a wooded interior studded with lakes which are largely UNESCO protected (reducing the likelihood of mass overdevelopment). Both countries gained a reputation as high-class holiday resorts in the 1960s and 70s. In Montenegro's upmarket Sveti Stefan resort, Elizabeth Taylor and Richard Burton are said to have disturbed other guests with their arguing, whilst Sofia Loren gave the chef lessons in how to cook pasta.

The tourist market in the region fell off during the 1990 war in the Balkans, unfairly in the case of Montenegro which had little involvement. There are no restrictions on foreigners buying property in Montenegro and prices have been relatively low, but are increasing rapidly. The average price for a new, off-plan one-bedroom flat is £82,400 going up to £300,000 for a three-bedroom house. This is one of the reasons that Montenegro may be a better bet than Croatia, a favourite with German and Italian buyers for many years. Prices in Croatia start from a higher base with two-bedroom apartments in an off-plan development with sea views costing over £125,000. In luxury new developments this sum might just stretch to a one-bedroom apartment.

The Czech Republic is already one of the great success stories of the last 10 years. The market for city-centre property in Eastern Europe was practically invented in Prague and it is a model copied in many European capitals. There is arguably too much existing competition for the market to prove particularly profitable. Opportunities do, however, exist outside the capital. The Czech government is making greater efforts to attract visitors to spa towns and destinations outside Prague, and is seeking millions of euros in extra development funds from the European Union. The money will be put towards tourism growth and improvement of infrastructure throughout the country. Spa towns such as Karlovy-Vary are attractive areas for second homes; property here is good value for money and prices are now likely to increase faster than in Prague.

India is an interesting nomination: high levels of interest have been sparked after a loosening of restrictions on foreign investment. Like China, India should be seen as a long-term investment with the chance of significant long-term capital appreciation.

Turning to other areas of South East Asia, Vietnam is one of the countries generating a real buzz at the moment. Construction has started on several prestigious second home developments on the coast. Designed to appeal to those who have fallen for this exotically beautiful country when travelling, these developments could also prove popular with the second-home market drawn from China and Japan.

Ski property

Second homes might generally be associated with escaping to the warmth and the beach, but rental yields in ski resorts can be higher. The supply of ski resorts is still far below that of beach holiday destinations, meaning that demand for accommodation can be high.

Skiing holidays are becoming increasingly popular. The Ski Club of Great Britain's analysis now estimates UK visits to ski resorts at over 1,313,000 – a 12.5% growth since the 2000/2001 season. However, with an average cost of over £600 for a week in the Alps, the cost of such holidays may be prohibitive. This gives the new resorts in Central and Eastern Europe an opportunity to break into the market.

The rental season for ski property may also be longer. Resorts are often in areas which can appeal to people throughout the year. For example, the Alps now have a thriving summer market with people enjoying walking holidays and adventure sports.

Ski Destinations: Four key markets still dominate world skiing, accounting for two-thirds of the world market: Austria (56 million visits), France (57.6 million), the US (52.2 million) and Japan (52 million), but the market share of these countries is shrinking fast. The number of visits to Japan declined by 40% between 1996 and 2006.

Eastern Europe: There is a strong perception that the Eastern European markets offer the best value for money. A week in a Romanian or Bulgarian resort, including costs such as a week's lift pass, can cost a third of the price in France or Switzerland. The facilities in Eastern Europe are not bad either – Bulgaria put in a bid to host the 2014 Winter Olympics, and although the country was not shortlisted, the improvements made to the resorts of Borovets, Bansko and Pamporovo to support the bid make it a world-class skiing destination.

The Tatras, the range of mountains bordering Poland and Slovakia, also merits a look. The High Tatras in Slovakia is a particularly notable region, providing the only real competition for Alpine skiing in Eastern Europe. Skiing here is Olympic standard, with reliable snow and good facilities. The best known resort is Strbske Pleso, which is also a centre for adventure sports including paragliding and bungee jumping.

The High Tatras are a good bet because the high standard of skiing is backed up by a very solid housing market. With 19% flat income tax, a burgeoning economy and a tourist industry that the World Travel and Tourism Council expects to grow by 4.9% annually over the next 10 years, Slovakia presents a very interesting opportunity.

Emerging Markets: Eastern Europe appeals to skiers from the west of Europe because of the comparatively low prices and reasonable flight times. There is, however, evidence that dedicated skiers are prepared to travel further and further for good snow.

Skiing in exotic locations is easier to arrange than people realise. Buyers looking for something further abroad could try looking at Chile, Japan or even China.

Skiing is one of the biggest trends to hit China in years. A decade ago, less than 200 people in China were believed to have tried skiing; now it's one million. The market is expected to grow to 12 million. The best resorts are in the northerly province of Heilongjiang. Yabuli, the site of the third Asian Winter Games, has excellent facilities and one of the longest toboggan runs in the world. Buying here could be the equivalent of investing in Whistler 20 years ago.

Renting Ski Property: As with beachfront property, it is possible to agree rental contracts with holiday companies. You may want to look for a development with a leasing agreement or guaranteed rental scheme already in place. More than 60% of ski holidays are sold as inclusive packages. The six key companies to look for are Airtours, Crystal, Inghams, Thomson, First Choice and Neilson. Renting directly should also be possible. Figures from the Ski Club of Great Britain show that people arranging independent trips has grown 9.7% year on year since 2000, whereas the tour-operated market has only grown 1.7% annually.

Beach destinations

The sheer number of beach resorts, everywhere from the Americas to the Black Sea, means that the relationship between supply and demand is not nearly as favourable as with ski property. Nonetheless, 18.7% of buyers still say that they are looking for a property close to the coast. The majority of these buyers are looking for personal use rather than investment property. Prices are often higher on the coast and in most countries the number of second homes at the coast will ensure intense competition for holiday lets.

For those people determined to buy on the coast, the most favourable conditions are often in emerging markets where there is little competition. Prices may be low on the Black Sea coast, but with the number of people buying in Bulgaria and Turkey, rental yields are going to be low. In Brazil or Goa, the numbers of apartments built to the standard expected by Western tourists is lower, meaning that rental yields on high-quality property are likely to be more satisfactory.

'Research suggests that over the long term, the rental and re-sale potential of properties in cities outperforms that of properties in the countryside'

Another policy is to buy near a beach, but in an area which also has other strengths. The Costa del Sol in Spain has benefited from proximity to Barcelona; Dubai attracts tourists to the beach, but also for the shopping and leisure and sporting facilities. Prices have risen much more quickly in these markets than in straightforward beach towns.

Some of these 'beach extra' markets are still in their infancy and provide a good opportunity for buyers. Gdansk, for example, is a beautiful Hanseatic town in Poland which attracts high numbers of tourists. Attractive beaches lie just outside the city limits, but with the relatively short summer season it is the city's other attractions which provide a basis for demand. The south of Italy and Sicily also combine historical attractions and beautiful cities with glorious beaches.

The newer markets in the Middle East can also be good places to look. The Middle East is becoming more and more fashionable with vast numbers of British and Russian tourists visiting Egypt every year. As Marrakesh and Dubai join the mainstream, cities such as Doha and Muscat may be the next Middle Eastern hot spots.

Whilst the Caribbean islands have long been associated with luxury beaches there are other areas in Central America also worth considering. Panama and Belize both offer beach living with many tax advantages for the retiree. Investing in Belize is also considerably cheaper than neighbouring Nicaragua or Honduras, plus it has the advantage of being the only English-speaking country in South and Central America.

3   What to buy – assessing opportunities

If you are buying a home, or even a holiday home, deciding what to buy is reasonably straightforward. If you need three bedrooms, you buy a three-bedroom house and if you are a beach lover, you will buy a home in the sun and near the sea. Knowing what to buy for investment is decidedly trickier.

What makes a good investment is dependent on so many different things which relate not only to the property itself, but also to events in the local, national and international market place. In chapter two we looked at the issues of where to invest. In this chapter we narrow our analysis down to examining what type of property to invest in. There is no one answer to this and the range of good property investment opportunities out there is equalled only by the range of bad opportunities.

Best to invest: old or new build?

Research suggests that more than three-quarters of potential international buyers want to buy either an off-plan or new-build property. Whether to look for new-build or older property is a question that depends on your reasons for buying. Putting aside the question of personal preference, this is about working out which type of property will be the best investment in any given area.

Older property

In France, for example, the market is calibrated to older property and buyers tend to look for something with charm rather than novelty. This is also partly a case of buyers adapting to availability. With an ample supply of older housing and strict planning laws, something older may be easier to find and provide better value for money.

Italy is another country where the market is adapted to older properties. It is not insignificant that these countries are among the most sophisticated and developed of second-home markets. A link can often be made between the youth of the market and the youth of desirable housing. People prefer new developments in Eastern Europe because the quality of existing housing is not good.

The key to the appeal of new builds is the confidence that they instil in the buyer. The thought of older houses, with the potential for dry rot and rising damp, can put off even the most determined buyer. And whilst coping with a leaking roof and fragmenting walls is possible if you are living in a house, coping with the manifold disasters that may beset your paying tenants several thousand miles away can be spectacularly daunting.

Newer property can sometimes also seem better calibrated to social and cultural developments. This is not a case of 'all mod cons', but of the growing demand for smaller properties across the world. The trends for later marriage, higher divorce rates and more single households ensure that prices for apartments often climb faster than for houses.

New builds

New properties may also be easier to maintain than older buildings – an important consideration if you are stuck a thousand miles from a building with a flooding washing machine. If you buy on a new development the developer may even have made arrangements for management before completing the project.

For people looking for a second home, there is often some comfort in numbers. Master planned communities can include facilities which older housing can't match. This doesn't just mean swimming pools integrated into the design of the house but can extend to golf courses, shopping centres and water parks.

A sense of community can add value to a rental property, especially if you are aiming for holiday lets. If a development is well placed, close to the sea or a ski resort, and attractively planned, you will hold a competitive advantage over other properties in the area which lack these benefits. With new builds the reputation and prior experience of the developer is often a useful guide. Large developers have to run their businesses on very professional lines and this gives the buyer a chance to demand good service. Asking to look at references, to look at completed developments or even to talk to people who have bought before are all valid requests. You won't get this level of service from someone selling their family home, but then, you can explore a completed house at leisure, whereas a new build may not be completed for two years after purchase.

There is also a less positive side to newer builds. Just as the presence of developers can be an advantage, showing you that an area is very much on the way up, in areas where a great deal of new building is under way, there is a danger of over-supply.

The joy of off-plan

A number of structures have been developed to cater for the investment market. By far the most popular is off-plan property. Buying off-plan means purchasing a property before the building is complete; instead of touring a property the buyer works from images, plans and computer simulations. At best, this arrangement benefits both developer and purchaser. Off-plan property is sold at a discount in order to compensate buyers for the inconvenience of waiting for completion. On some projects prices rise in three or four stages. As the development nears completion the developer's risk exposure lessens and they raise prices.

Off-plan property does cost less, and often carries other advantages; for example, people buying a property before completion may be able to influence the design. However, there is also some risk attached and it is a good idea to make sure that the developer is able to deliver the property that is promised.

Selecting a development

The primary reason for selecting a development is that you believe it is a good investment. Perhaps there is a five-star hotel on site to help attract paying tenants, or perhaps you feel that the off-plan prices are undervalued compared to comparable properties. Whatever the investment rationale, you also need to ensure that the off-plan promise is going to translate into reality when the development is finished.

There are simple measures that you can take to ensure that you are making the right choice of development. Ask the developer for some information on their track record; see what developments they have done before. This will provide a good indication that the developer is credible and should give some confidence in their build quality. In emerging markets, however, you may find that you come across many first-time developers. This doesn't automatically mean that they won't be good. In this scenario, check that the promoting agent has completed sufficient due diligence, that the contract paperwork is in order and that the developer has sufficient finances to deliver the project.

'Developer insurance, taken out by the company and guaranteeing at least your money back if the project falls through, will help keep your investment safe'

You also need to look at floor plans with a critical eye. Look at the shared areas as well as the design of your individual property. Is the swimming pool generous enough to cope with fifty families? Does the design look crowded and where are restaurants and recreation facilities in relation to your apartment?

SAFEGUARDING YOUR INVESTMENT

Think also about what lies beyond the edge of the development plans. Is more building planned in the area and do you have guarantees that high-rise buildings won't spring up around the charming low-density development on the plans? This is something that a lawyer can help with (another reason to have a good professional enlisted before beginning your hunt for property). Ask your lawyer to conduct a search as soon as possible, looking at plans and regulations on surrounding sites. This is particularly important for properties with a sea view – you'll pay a premium for this and the property value will fall if developers squeeze another property in between you and the coast.

The staged payments common with off-plan property are themselves a form of guarantee. The points at which instalments will be needed differ under various jurisdictions; a typical schedule in Europe would be a reservation deposit – which will be legally binding in most jurisdictions, and then four instalments on completion of foundations, the shell of the building, roof and finish.

In some markets, developers should have a sheaf of independent guarantees and should be falling over themselves with eagerness to present these to customers. Developer insurance, taken out by the company and guaranteeing at least return of your money should the project fall through, will help to keep your investment safe. Developers sometimes also offer bank guarantees which offer similar protection. However, many emerging markets do not have these systems of guarantees in place and so you need to be even more certain that the developer can and will deliver on their promises.

It is also important to ask about completion dates – something that a surprising number of buyers seem to be relaxed about. Off-plan property is most likely to be sold in areas where demand outstrips the existing housing stock. But if demand is high, developers will be tempted to take on as many projects as possible, cranes may be booked up, there may be a shortage of qualified construction staff…even with the best intentions in the world, they can fall behind schedule.

A good contract will include penalty clauses for every day beyond the scheduled completion date that handover is delayed. For example, developments have been found which offer refunds of a small percentage of the purchase price for every single day of delay, and if delivery is held back for more than 90 days the buyer is offered their money back. With this kind of penalty in place, delay can be quite profitable. If nothing else, you will be saved the frustration of seeing your money tied up in a project that seems to be going nowhere.

Finally, check the contract for clauses limiting your right to resell before completion. This is called *flipping* and is extremely common in markets like Dubai. When markets grow at an unsustainable rate, local governments may encourage or require developers to take action by inserting contractual clauses making flipping illegal. This can be good for the market, encouraging stability and preventing markets from spiralling out of control, but if there is any chance that you will need to resell prior to completion of the property, you need to be sure that this right is specified before buying.

Off-plan: too good to be true?

The excitement of flipping leads us to the second problem with buying off-plan: the dangers of the 'too good to be true' stories of instant capital appreciation and instant profit. Search 'off-plan property' on the internet and you will find a hundred 'true stories' starring ordinary folk who put down a deposit on an off-plan development and then re-sold it before completion for enormous profit. It's an appealing story and, where people have made a clever choice of development, sometimes true. According to the Global Property Guide property prices on The Palm in Dubai increased considerably between 2003 and 2007, from 3,563AED (£490,00) per square metre to 8,224AED (£1,131.00) per square metre; this averages out at an incredible 226% increase. This, however, is not always the case and buying property purely in the expectation of such swift capital appreciation and resale is a dangerous policy.

In some areas, buyers have been so confident that the real estate markets are rising, that they have taken loans in order to buy several properties, even if they depend on resale in order to meet the final instalments. Others have leveraged in order to buy more than one apartment or house, hoping to make profit on as many properties as possible.

When buying off-plan you have to be sure that there are underlying reasons why someone will want to rent or buy your property from you when it is completed. In some cases where markets are dominated by off-plan property, you may find that new market entrants only want to buy direct from the developer as well. This is a very typical scenario in a market dominated by speculators. If the growth drivers in the market are genuine, people will be desperate to buy your completed property from you in order to live in it or rent it out. If you don't believe that there is a queue of people waiting to buy completed property, then you should avoid any off-plan developments and probably avoid the market altogether.

Reducing risk

Firms dealing with the emerging markets will often encounter clients worried about the security of their rights to purchased property. Spain and China are two of the most common countries of concern. The opportunities for capital growth in China are enormous but potential buyers worry about the constitutional protection of property. Chinese law says that the government can confiscate land for other uses, provided that they pay fair compensation.

What many buyers don't realise is that similar laws are in place in many other countries where property rights are considered perfectly safe. The US government has similar powers to confiscate private property; these rights which are known as *eminent domain*, have been debated over for several years now with no clear conclusion.

'Most risk lies in ignorance'

The truth of the matter is that most risk lies in ignorance. Investing in almost any part of the world can be safe provided that you know what you are doing and that you take due care and consideration. At a property level, the risks are rather limited, beyond the obvious dangers of buying something which is falling down or that you don't actually own. Most risks exist at a market level; some are predictable and therefore avoidable; some aren't. Some risks just have to be accepted; who knows if there will be a natural disaster which could ruin a particular property market for years?

At a property level you can manage your risks by using a lawyer, commissioning a survey and by taking time to make a logical and considered decision about what to buy. This, however, will not protect you from market level events which could strike at any time. To manage risks at this level there are two main options: diversifying by buying in more than one area or country, or, if you don't have the resources for this approach, investing through collective investment schemes.

Diversifying and building a portfolio

Diversifying is simply a matter of hedging your bets. You may find a development that seems guaranteed to double in price, but to buy up as much as possible of a single development or area is risky. Any unexpected change in the market will endanger the whole, rather than a small proportion, of your investment.

The ideal approach is to split your investment and buy as large a range of property as possible. At some stage this may mean commercial and industrial property as well as residential. These markets are more complicated however, and price entry thresholds are higher. Most new property investors will prefer a first venture into commercial property to be in their home country.

For those people taking their first step into property investment, look instead for different kinds of residential property and in different countries, or different continents even. Because property markets are often localised (usually at a national level), buying in a range of countries helps to reduce your risk. Buying on different continents will reduce your risk exposure even more, by limiting the impact of regional events on your portfolio. In the late 1990s property prices plummeted across the whole of South East Asia. Property investors who had all of their investments in the region suffered significant losses. For those who owned South East Asian properties as part of a broader portfolio, the events of 1997 were less of a concern.

'Buying on different continents will reduce your risk exposure even more, by limiting the impact of regional events on your portfolio'

Even if you are absolutely devoted to a single market and determined to pick up as much as possible in the country of your choice, there are ways to diversify risk by buying different kinds of property. Dubai has been one of the favourite investment destinations of the last few years. In Dubai apartments have traditionally been more desirable than villas. This has caused many investors to concentrate exclusively on building a portfolio of apartments, whilst those who diversified and invested in villas as well benefited from their sharper rises in value.

If your first property is in a sunny holiday resort, try to balance this with something in a city. If you have been busy buying up houses with five or six bedrooms, then balance your portfolio with a couple of one-bedroom apartments or studio flats. After all, the size of the family is shrinking and more people are living alone than ever before. Part of this diversification is trying to put together a portfolio where the properties carry different levels of risk and will react differently as an investment in different circumstances. Put simply, it is the old adage of not putting all of your eggs in one basket.

Whilst diversifying your investment helps to reduce your risk, overstretching yourself can be equally damaging. If you only have enough money to buy one property, the best option is to buy something generating significant yields and then save that income towards your next property in a different market. Over time you will end up building a healthy, sustainable, low-risk and diversified portfolio.

Collective investment schemes: property funds and REITs

For those with limited budgets, there are ways of investing in a portfolio of high-quality properties without mortgaging everything you own. There are a range of collective investment schemes available which offer the opportunity to participate in large-scale property investments for a relatively small amount of cash. Collective investment schemes operate like funds in which investors' money is put together to purchase a range of properties.

Collective investment funds have numerous benefits, not least of which is that someone with only £20,000 ($35,000) to invest could gain access to the sort of returns only usually available with larger-scale investments. Another benefit of collective investments is that they let people duck out of the process of researching markets, assessing when to buy and when to sell and all of the difficulties of finding and keeping tenants. They also allow people to invest in commercial and industrial property, the thresholds of which are set too high for most investors.

Different investment funds will have different objectives. Some might have the purpose of developing a resort or tower block allowing investors to make the same kinds of returns as developers; others may buy a range of off-plan properties from across the globe and flip them before completion. Whatever the purpose of the fund, its objectives will be laid out in a prospectus for investors to examine prior to committing their funds. The actions of the fund managers will be governed by the parameters set out in the prospectus, so you can be certain how your money will be invested.

BENEFITS OF COLLECTIVE INVESTMENT SCHEMES

- Opportunity to benefit from property without the hassle of organising buying, letting or arranging sales
- Your investment will be managed by experts
- Opportunity to expose even small investments to a broad portfolio of properties and countries
- Funds can use their buying power to arrange bulk discounts
- Some funds have tax benefits. In the UK, investors can invest in many types of funds with money held in ISAs and even SIPPs (self-invested personal pensions)
- No sleepless nights over letting, tenants, vacancy rates and so on

Types of funds

The types of funds on offer vary dramatically in their structure and their investment objectives. In the US and Australia, readers will be familiar with Real Estate Investment Trusts (REITs) which are regulated funds managed by major financial institutions and operate in a similar way to unit trusts. The UK launched REITs in January 2007, and they took South East Asia by storm in 2005 and 2006. In the United States, REITs recently celebrated their 40th birthday.

Other forms of investment trust do, however, already exist. From the informal syndicate of friends to collective property funds, people are buying property through a variety of different instruments.

The rules and regulations surrounding investment funds make describing their various forms difficult here, but in outline there are several different forms which are usually made available to different types of investor.

Onshore or offshore

Often funds will be referred to as offshore or onshore funds. This typically refers to the country they are domiciled in and therefore the jurisdiction which regulates their activity. In the UK for example, an onshore fund would refer to one that is regulated by the UK's Financial Services Authority (FSA). Onshore funds need to meet certain criteria and the greater level of regulation usually allows them to be offered to a broader range of investors.

Onshore funds will often be structured differently from offshore funds due to regulatory requirements. Often onshore funds will have greater liquidity making it easier for investors to sell their interest in the fund when they want to. (See open-ended investment vehicles vs. close-ended investment vehicles below.)

Maintaining the UK example, an offshore fund would not be regulated by the FSA. The fund would, however, be regulated by the financial regulator in the country in which it is domiciled. The domicile of an offshore fund will usually be in a jurisdiction with low taxation and a reliable financial system which investors have confidence in. Typical locations for offshore funds include Jersey, Guernsey, The Isle of Man and the British Virgin Islands.

Whilst offshore funds are not regulated directly by the onshore regulator, the sale of shares in those funds is a regulated activity. In the UK, FSA regulations state that offshore funds can only be offered as an investment to 'sophisticated' or 'high net worth' investors. Investors need to self-declare themselves as being in one of these categories before a qualified financial advisor can hand over details of the fund.

Open-ended investment vehicles vs. close-ended investment vehicles

Open-ended investment vehicles are funds which allow investors to sell their units or shares almost without restriction. This makes these funds very similar to unit trusts which hold a range of equities. In order to facilitate the movement of cash in and out of the fund as new investors buy units and other investors sell units, the fund needs to maintain a certain level of liquidity.

In other words a fund which allows investors to take their money out of the fund as and when they wish, needs to have the cash available to pay them what they are owed. This would be difficult if the fund only owned property as property is not a liquid asset. Instead therefore, these funds have to hold more liquid assets like shares in other companies (usually property companies of some sort to maintain the theme) and even cash.

Most onshore, regulated funds will, by order of the financial regulator, be open ended. As a result these funds are open to all investors, including those who are viewed as neither 'sophisticated' nor of 'high net worth'.

Close-ended investment vehicles do not allow investors to sell their shares in the fund when they want. Instead, investors commit their money to the fund for a fixed time period in which the fund managers invest in properties to generate a return and then dispose of them to liquidate the assets and release cash back to the investors.

The 'lock-in' time on these funds will vary, but will always be set within a band as laid out in the investment prospectus offered to investors before they commit. Because these funds do not have the liquidity requirements of open-ended vehicles, the fund manager is able to invest all of the investors' money in property. The lack of liquidity in this type of fund is one of the primary reasons that the FSA only allow them to be offered to self-declared sophisticated and high net worth investors.

Real estate investment trusts (REITs)

Buying into a REIT is just like buying shares in any other kind of fund. Whilst they have the advantage of being based on property investment, they enjoy the liquidity of equity-based funds. Another appealing factor is the tax advantages that most governments package up as part of the deal. In the US and UK REITs escape corporation tax by distributing up to 90% of the income derived from rents or capital appreciation on real estate sales as dividends. The money is then taxed as income against individuals.

There are different forms of REITs, some of which look more like a financial than a property investment. Equity REITs invest in and own properties taking income primarily from rents. Mortgage REITs deal in investment and ownership of property mortgages, lending money for mortgages to owners of real estate. Income is earned primarily through interest charged on mortgage loans; this type of REIT accounts for less than 10% of the total.

Choosing a REIT: There are a couple of considerations to bear in mind when choosing a REIT. First is diversification. This is one of the great strengths of a REIT and if you are placing money into property through this kind of investment structure why not go the whole hog and pick a fund which enables you to invest in the full range of property including commercial buildings?

Secondly, because REITS are different from the common run of equities, assessing the relative success of any trust can be a complex task. Experts recommend judging a REIT according to 'funds from operations', a figure on the balance sheet which doesn't include depreciation. Property rarely depreciates – quite the reverse! And calculating success by funds from operations may therefore give a more accurate picture of performance.

Costs: Investing in a REIT can seem comparatively expensive. Initial charges can account for up to 5% of the value of the investment and a yearly management fee will be charged. But compared to the annual growth targeted by property funds, often between 15% and 20%, this looks reasonable. A good fund should return up to 15% annual growth and 6% yield; given the amount of research and administration necessary to identify and invest in growth areas, the fees begin to look comparatively reasonable.

In most jurisdictions, REITs have replaced ordinary property companies as the favoured way of holding property. However, there are some bonuses to staying outside this system in the UK. Here, REITs are restricted in how much they can borrow and how much development they can do, and overseas property owned through foreign subsidiaries is not eligible for tax-free status. As a result, most will be UK-focused and act more as landlords than developers, although they may still build new schemes. Many investors may therefore prefer the higher risks and potential gains of direct investment in foreign property or development.

4 Making a profit from property

What makes a good investment?

The Oxford English Dictionary defines an investment as 'a thing worth buying because it may be profitable... in the future'. This is often the interpretation taken by most people, but a better financial definition is 'the purchase of an asset which produces a financial return in the form of income'.

In countries like the UK and the US, people often think of their homes as their biggest investment. This point of view is based upon the assumption that your home is an asset because it may increase in value. This is not only wrong, it is the exact opposite of what is actually the case; your home is a liability.

To understand this statement, we need to be clear about the difference between assets and liabilities. Assets are things that we own which produce cash. Liabilities are things that we own which drain cash. In the case of your home, you will need to pay the mortgage, the utility bills, taxes and maintenance costs. It costs you money to live in your house. The capital value of your house may rise but this 'profit' is a myth. You cannot realise that profit. You still need somewhere to live and if your house has risen in value, so will the cost of other houses you may choose to live in.

If we look at an example of a buy-to-let property, we can see that it is an asset. A buy-to-let property should generate positive cash flow and potentially increase in value. The capital appreciation on an investment property can be realised and reinvested or spent elsewhere as you do not need it to live in. There will (or at least should) be a positive difference between the costs of owning the property and the rental income. This net income is passively generated by the asset and is available to you to be reinvested or spent as you wish.

It is clear that owning assets is a good thing. However, building up your assets is a means to an end for an investor. The actual goal of investment is to generate enough income from your assets to support your lifestyle. Once you have done this you are freed from the toils of work. Income is therefore the ultimate investment goal. If you only had assets and you had to keep selling them to generate enough cash to live, you would eventually run out of assets and therefore cash. However, if your assets consistently generate income, that income can be sustained forever.

Therefore, in answering the question of what to invest in, we can clearly say, invest in assets. In the context of property this means investing in property which generates a net cash inflow which can be reinvested into more assets that also generate cash. This is the virtuous investment cycle. If you keep reinvesting income from your assets into more assets, you will eventually be generating enough cash to live on.

For a more detailed explanation of the concepts we have discussed here, you should refer to the *Rich Dad Poor Dad* series of books by Robert Kiyosaki. These provide an excellent grounding for developing an investment philosophy and are a useful resource for investors in any field. More details can be found on the website www.richdad.com.

Investment versus speculation

For most people starting out in international property investment, or investment of any kind for that matter, it is important to focus on buying assets and generating income. This is the basis from which to build a portfolio. This isn't to say that investing purely for capital growth is not a viable approach. In fact when selecting an investment property, the ideal scenario is to find one that generates cash and increases in value, but the rental yield will always be the bottom line and the possibility of capital appreciation a bonus.

The danger for investors with a small portfolio comes when you invest in property purely for capital growth. If you are investing in a property which only breaks even in terms of income, or even worse costs you money every month, but you expect it to increase in value over time, you are not actually investing: you are speculating. These capital growth oriented investments have a place in an investment portfolio, but the cash generated by other assets in your portfolio should comfortably generate sufficient income to fund your outgoings on any speculative investment.

'If most players in the market are speculating on future capital appreciation and are not generating yield on their investment, then it is likely to be a bubble'

Understanding the difference between speculation and investment is also important from the point of view of analysing markets. If most players in the market are speculating on future capital appreciation and are not generating yield on their investment, then it is likely to be a bubble. On the other hand, a market where all the property owners are investors generating attractive amounts of rental income on their properties will be sustainable.

One of the most important aspects in ensuring you will make a secure and profitable investment is to research the market. Many agents and developers offer additional incentives such as 'discounted property' or 'guaranteed rental yields' but many are inflating the initial price to offer headline grabbing discounts. Simple internet research will enable you to tell whether the prices are in line with the local market.

When deciding what type of property to buy, you need to consider how you intend to profit from the investment. Below, we look at the three main ways in which property can generate a return on investment: rental yield (buy to let), capital appreciation and profit.

Buy to let

Rental yield

Buying for rental income is probably the best long-term investment strategy available. Not only can the cash generated from the investment be used to re-invest into additional assets, it can also be more profitable than buying and selling property. There is an old Farsi saying which goes 'hold the property and it will hold you'. This simply means that when you buy property it is better to keep it. This is true for several reasons. Firstly, historically speaking, property prices always go up over time. There may be peaks and troughs at different points but the price trend is always upward. Secondly, when a property you own increases in price, you make money. If your property increases in value from £100,000 to £200,000, you have made £100,000. In most countries this profit is entirely tax free until you sell it. In theory therefore you could make a million pounds a year or more and not pay a penny in tax. Additionally, when you realise your profit by selling you will incur a variety of transaction costs.

If you keep a property, over time it will increase in value as will the amount of income you make from it. The value of your assets will grow and you will incur no tax or costs for the privilege.

Letting a property

Letting a property abroad can be a hard slog. Setting up websites, finding tenants, arranging advertising, taking enquiries, finding someone to take day-to-day care of the property, the list is endless. The anxiety of trying to control events from a distance can be difficult. However, this doesn't have to be the case. If you take the time to select the right property and instruct the right professionals to maintain and let your property, you should be able to sit back, and enjoy the income. On new developments built specifically for the holiday or second-home markets, the management company may be as much part of the development as the swimming pool. Communal and management fees are specified in the initial contract and cover services such as ground maintenance, local rates and sometimes also electricity and water costs. It is, however, potentially more difficult for people buying an older property with no built-in letting and management system.

'Buying for rental income is probably the best long-term investment strategy available'

Another recent and popular scheme that many developers and hotel operators are now offering is the ability to purchase a room or suite within a fully managed hotel. This can be a secure way of ensuring you maintain a steady and sufficient income from your investment with the additional benefit that many schemes offer one to four weeks free usage per year. Many operators are starting to offer either a guaranteed rental scheme or a split of the revenue generated. With the right location, using a management company with a good track-record, the purchase price may be higher than a standard apartment, but you are likely to benefit from long-term and secure rental potential. This is especially true when you buy though a large or respected hotel chain.

Fees

Management fees will usually be charged whether you rent out a property on a development or not. However, you should be particularly aware of these when renting as they will impact upon your returns. Management fees are often expressed as a charge per square metre or square foot. The charges can vary significantly though and you will need to read the contract carefully to ensure that fees are realistic.

When letting your property, the management company will also charge a percentage of rental income for the services that make rentals feasible, such as finding tenants and maintenance. The level of management fee will often depend on whether you are renting to long-term or short-term (holiday) tenants. Management fees for holiday lets are usually higher because there will be more cleaning involved for changing over tenants on a weekly basis. In most places you should expect to pay between 5% and 20% of the rental income.

Calculating rental potential

Rental potential is a simple equation based upon the daily, weekly or monthly rental price (depending on the time periods you are letting the property for) multiplied by the occupancy rate. For example, an apartment with a monthly rent of £500 would deliver an annual rental income of £6,000. However, you may only be able to find tenants for 6 months of the year. The actual rental income would therefore be £6,000 × 50% = £3,000.

After the gross rental income, you will then need to deduct costs which will usually include management fees, rental management fees, maintenance costs and taxation.

Working out occupancy rates

One of the most important determinants of your rental income is occupancy. The agent and developer should both be able to give a realistic idea of occupancy rates but you should also check this from an unbiased source. In relation to holiday lettings, you need to consider the length of the letting season; information on this can usually be found on the internet or from the local tourist board.

When assessing likely occupancy try not to be unduly cynical, or to automatically disbelieve people who tell you that the letting season is comparatively long. Cities are a cert for year-round letting and there are areas of the countryside which also attract people in summer and winter. The Alps attract high numbers of summer visitors for walking holidays and the mountain resorts of Eastern Europe look like developing in the same way.

Whether to rent to locals or try for the international short-let market

Part of working out the expected occupancy is deciding whether you will market to locals or to holiday lets. The two markets are very different. Renting a house to the local market will provide a more reliable income, with tenants often booking an apartment for a year or more. (This is typically the case in city-centre locations.) It is also sometimes possible to rent to businesses or international organisations. In Brussels, for example, apartments are sold with a rental agreement with the European Union already in place. The EU uses your apartment to house politicians or diplomats and you receive a regular and generous income. In Mongolia, yields are high due to the number of companies that have partnered with developers to offer long-term rented accommodation for their international workers. Similarly in Fort McMurray, Canada, apartments are being built 'California style' (designed for two to share) specifically for the numerous oil industry workers.

LONG-TERM VERSUS SHORT-TERM RENTALS

Long-term lets

Renting long-term is the simplest and often one of the most profitable ways of renting, especially when the property is let to tenants all year round. Long-term lets are often easier to find in city centres rather than holiday resorts. There is no need to arrange for tenants to be met at the airport, no need to clean between lets or to arrange for the garden to be maintained. Your tenants will also expect less; you won't have to put in a swimming pool or worry about access to an airport if you are renting to local business people. Of course, what your tenants expect will be determined by local norms so you need to make sure your property is competitive. On the other hand, your rental on a daily basis will be much lower than for holiday lets and you won't be able to holiday in the property yourself.

The advantages of long-term lets include:

- Reliable long-term income
- The possibility of agreeing long-term contracts with businesses or international organisations
- Hassle free
- Lower management costs

Short-term lets

Short-term lets can offer a greater financial reward, but there is less security. If you invest in a holiday resort, you are more likely to let your property to people staying in your property for only one week, who will expect to pay a relatively high price for that week compared to someone renting an apartment for a year. An apartment that generates £400 a month if let yearly could generate £50 a night from tourists. However, with short-term lets, you will always have void periods. How long the void periods are depends upon the length of the letting season (often dictated by the climate) and local competition in the letting market. It should be emphasised that short-term letting is not just restricted to holiday destinations. Many European cities such as Barcelona, Prague, Krakow and Gdansk have opened up to cheap, direct flights and are proving popular long-weekend destinations, meaning higher yields are now attainable.

The advantages of short-term lets include:

- Higher rental value
- Opportunity to book the property for your own use and to occupy it during the low season

Disadvantages:

- Possible void periods making income less reliable
- High rental management costs

As we keep reiterating, it is important to conduct research on the local market. Certain countries and regions have a culture of renting (e.g. Germany) whereas others are focused on home ownership (e.g. the UK).

In some countries, rents have not always kept up with the increase in property prices, giving compressed yields. This has certainly been the case in many Eastern European cities where there has been an oversupply of property put onto the markets by investors.

If you have already purchased overseas without any management contracts in place, there are a number of ways to find tenants for your property:

1. Local agents
2. Advertising in the local press
3. Large or international companies in the area who may be looking for accommodation for their staff
4. British embassies who may be looking to relocate new arrivals to a country
5. The internet – there are many local and international portals (www. holiday-rentals.com) who list property for rent

Guaranteed rental schemes

An increasing number of developments offer the potential of guaranteed rental returns. Guaranteed rental is exactly what it suggests. When you buy the property, you sign a contract with either the developer or a management company to lease the property from you for a fixed annual amount for a set number of years. The management company will then use your property to let to tenants and take the risks and rewards from doing so. Whatever happens, you receive your pre-agreed rental. Yields tend to be 6% to 7% or more of your initial purchase price and the term can last from one to 20 years. These schemes can take much of the stress and effort out of investing abroad. It is, however, important to remember that the guaranteed income you hold is only as good as the company guaranteeing it. These schemes may seem very attractive but we have seen and heard of developers increasing the purchase price to compensate or cover the yield. A simple way of checking this is to look at the price of comparable developments in the area.

'Remember that the guaranteed income you hold is only as good as the company guaranteeing it'

It is also prudent not to be blinded by the initial guaranteed rental period. Many of you will be buying for investment so it is essential that you consider what will happen once the guaranteed rental period has elapsed. Is it likely that you (or the person you sell your apartment to) will be able to rent it out and generate a good yield? Often, in areas where there is a lot of development (such as the Black Sea coast in Bulgaria or parts of Cyprus) many developers offer schemes to differentiate themselves. You have to remember that your apartment will be competing with other apartments in the vicinity once the guaranteed rental period is over, so you will need to be confident that there is sufficient demand.

Personal use

A common advantage of guaranteed rental schemes is that they often allow owners to use the property for free for a set number of days each year (typically from one week to one month per annum). Many of these schemes are associated with hotel complexes, which means that owners also get use of the hotel facilities when staying in their property.

Capital appreciation

Research suggests that most people evaluate potential investments primarily on the capital appreciation that they offer. In fact many people specify that they are more interested in capital appreciation than rental income. On the basis of the points made earlier, this means that the majority of 'investors' are in fact 'speculators'.

For small or new investors, the pursuit of pure capital appreciation is a dangerous strategy. This is primarily because property ownership incurs expenses and if the property isn't generating cash then you have to fund the expenses from elsewhere. It sounds obvious, but it is always worth remembering that you can only pay for things in cash. It doesn't matter if your property has increased in value by £30,000; if you do not have the cash to pay the mortgage you will lose the property. Therefore, a good property investment should generate sufficient cash to cover expenses, and cash can only be generated through rental income. For those who want to build a portfolio, every investment should generate enough cash to cover expenses and leave a profit which you can use towards further investments in your portfolio.

Having said all this, capital appreciation is important and is often the single biggest contributor to your overall profit from the property. The ideal investment is therefore one which pays for itself through rental yield whilst appreciating at a healthy rate. The two objectives of yield and growth are not mutually exclusive: both objectives can be met in one investment.

Many investors' demands for capital appreciation are unrealistic and it is worth noting that a property which appreciates in value by only 7% per year will almost double in value over 10 years. This is growth which, compared to other asset classes, is both generous and sustainable.

Exit strategy

In order to realise the capital appreciation from your property investment you need to sell and liquidate it. Whether you are a speculator buying for short-term gain or an investor buying for the long term you should always consider how easy it will be to liquidate your asset.

Often people are (and we have both been ourselves) blinded by the attractiveness of a new-build resort that is offered for sale and do not think about how attractive the property will be in a few years' time. This is especially important in areas of fast touristic and economic growth. You must consider what competition there is (or is likely to be) in the area and how likely it is that you will be able to sell to either another investor or an end-user of the property.

Resale

When the time comes to sell your property, there will be several options. A private sale through a newspaper or internet site is the first, although this will be a time-consuming and difficult process.

'Whether you are a speculator or an investor buying for the long term you should always consider how easy it will be to liquidate your asset'

A better idea is to talk to the agent who sold you the property in the first place. Most agents will be prepared to help people who bought through them, even if the company does not specialise in re-sales. They will also already be familiar with the area and development, and should have marketing materials to hand. Finally, if you are selling on a particular development, your agent should already be linked in buyers' minds with the property. They may even keep a list of people waiting to buy re-sales in the property. And even if the agent can't sell the property themselves, they should have enough of a relationship with the developer and other agents to be able to find someone who specialises in re-sales locally. Approaching the developer will pay similar dividends with the additional bonus that developers often keep sales offices on the site of the development. The sales office may receive enquiries about buying into the development and they can pass these potential clients on to you. For a list of some key agents please refer to part II of the book.

Profit

The third means of making money from property is profit. Whilst in general terms profit can refer to any money made, it does have a specific meaning which is money made as a result of discount purchasing or renovations. Profit in this sense is the money made by buying and selling a property, not including capital appreciation. This shows that you can make money from property even if prices in the market are not rising. As an example, if you were able to buy a property for 10% under market value and then sell the property at market value, you will have made a profit, even if the market value has not risen.

There are two basic strategies for generating profit from property. The first is discount buying and the second is adding value. It is possible to buy property below market value when buying off-plan as developers often give genuine discounts to get early sales before construction starts. Bulk buyers can also buy below market value as they are likely to negotiate a discount for buying a number of properties in one development. However, these bulk discounts can also be available to people even when they only buy a single property. This is usually achieved through bulk buying as an organised group. This could be as informal as getting together with some friends to buy a number of properties, or could involve joining a property club or syndicate where the club arranges bulk buy discounts on behalf of its members. Buying through clubs like this can prove very profitable, as long as the discounts being offered are genuine. Before buying through a club, check that the savings stack up as you will usually pay some form of fee for the privilege of receiving the discount.

Profiting by adding value to a property usually involves renovation and modernisation. This is a good strategy in your home market, but very difficult to organise when the property is abroad. Unless you are doing it on a large scale and therefore able to employ a turnkey project management company, it is best to steer clear of this approach to international property investment.

5 The most valuable tools – good advice and information

Buying property is complicated. Even in well-established markets like the UK or US, the process of purchasing a property isn't a straightforward transaction like buying a car. No matter how experienced an investor you are, you will always need professional advice; unless of course, you are a qualified lawyer, surveyor, financial advisor and real estate broker. Without this unlikely cocktail of qualifications and experience you will need help and advice when buying a property, and especially when buying a property overseas.

When considering investing in overseas property, the first place you will start is research. It is recommended that you undertake thorough independent research before you approach an agent to at least get a feel for the area you want to invest in. Agents can play many roles in assisting your purchase; one of these is providing information and expert opinion. In most markets there will be many agents selling property and it is worth speaking to several of them, even if you have already chosen an agent to work with.

The first section below provides guidance on where and how to gather information on international property markets. This chapter then goes on to describe the role that agents and other professionals play and how to get the best out of them.

Sources of information

Rather than wondering where to find information about international property, the question exercising many people's minds may be how to escape it. Property television shows, newspaper articles and even radio shows have proliferated almost to the point of ubiquity. A number of magazines are now targeted at international property buyers; most tabloid and broadsheet newspapers carry at least weekly sections on overseas property and most libraries will have a shelf-full of books telling you how to buy. The available information is, however, rather lopsided, with most books and articles dealing with the traditional markets in Spain, France, Italy and Florida etc. – although a number of more useful books have been published recently, focused mainly on buy-to-let markets.

In addition, much of the information available has a very 'lifestyle' angle to it and tends to skate over the surface, looking at individual properties or attractive local vistas and leaving you none the wiser about how the market works. However, most of the information available does have some value to investors as many articles will contain information on some aspect or other of the buying process. It becomes somewhat of a jigsaw, but collecting articles can help you achieve a good level of knowledge.

Despite the usefulness of this form of 'light' coverage, there is a gulf between information absorbed passively from light reading and the research that will really help you understand where and how to buy. The fact is that it will take a lot of short articles to be able to deliver the specific, often very local information that will help you to make the optimum investment. You need to source information on the numbers; how prices, taxes and demand are operating; and what market forces are at work.

Buying a house touches on a lot of subjects, with some of them, for example taxation, having the potential to be very dry. Professional property investors will make a decision based almost entirely on the financial detail of an opportunity and the surrounding market forces. Consider the value of understanding where domestic interest rates are in their cycle: are they going to rise or fall?

This means that you need to look beyond the core property media to develop a deeper understanding of the market. In fact, the UK is very well served with reliable sources of information and thanks to the wonders of the World Wide Web, so is everyone else.

Newspapers and magazines

A good place to start is with broadsheet newspapers like *The Financial Times* or *The Wall Street Journal*. Not only do these publications often carry property specific news, but they will undoubtedly refer to social, political and economic developments around the globe which will affect local property markets. If interest rates are set to rise or property law is about to change, newspapers like this will report it in reasonable detail. Almost all good broadsheets also have excellent websites.

Additionally, most countries will have an online edition of the local English language newspaper. From the Baltics to Singapore, a local English language newspaper is now published almost everywhere and there is no more absorbing topic than the local property market for local newspapers. Searching within the property section of a local newspaper's website will also often dredge up translations of government statistics which would otherwise lie buried in thousands of results returned by Google.

News magazines can also be useful. One of the best sources is *The Economist*, which regularly publishes comment on the state of the global property industry as well as more localised information. *The Economist* in particular is useful as it actually collates data on global property markets and many of its articles carry in-depth leadership pieces on what is happening to property markets internationally. Other magazines which may be useful include weekly business journals and investment magazines.

There is also a plethora (in the UK at least) of specialist magazines on the topic of overseas property. These magazines often have a more holiday-home appeal but can be useful because they publish articles on a whole range of countries and also carry adverts. Scanning through these will give you an idea of local prices and provide contacts for agents covering the area you are interested in.

NEWSPAPERS AND MAGAZINES

- *The Financial Times* – www.ft.com
- *The Times* – www.timesonline.co.uk
- *The Wall Street Journal* – www.wsj.com
- *The International Herald Tribune* – www.iht.com
- *The Real Estate Journal* – www.realestatejournal.com
- *The Economist* – www.economist.com
- *Homes Overseas* – www.homesoverseas.co.uk
- *A Place in the Sun* – www.aplaceinthesunmag.co.uk
- *Property Investor News* – property-investor-news.com
- *International Homes* – www.international-homes.com

Organisations with online resources

There is, unfortunately, no single worldwide authority distributing information on property markets. However, many multinational institutions publish property related information, albeit at a very macroeconomic level. Nevertheless, useful information can be gathered from the World Bank (www.worldbank.org), the International Monetary Fund (www.imf.org) and the Organisation for Economic Cooperation and Development (www.oecd.org).

Other useful resources include the CIA (https://www.cia.gov/library/publications/the-world-factbook/index.html) whose fact book is always a reliable source of information on prevailing economic and social conditions and trends in a country. The US Heritage Foundation (http://www.heritage.org/research/features/index/) publishes an index of economic freedom which includes a useful country by country assessment of property rights and investment conditions. Finally, the Mercer cost of living index (www.mercer.com) gives an idea of comparative costs in different counties.

Europe is better served in terms of research than many parts of the world. The Royal Institute of Chartered Surveyors (RCIS) produces the annual *European Housing Review* which covers countries including Western Europe, Austria, Hungary and more. The RICS report draws an unimpeachably accurate picture of the property markets in each country and is available online at www.rics.org.

Government statistical websites can also be a useful source of information on the property market within a country. The National Statistical Institute of Bulgaria, for example, leads the way in Eastern Europe by analysing and translating price statistics which are then published at their website, www.nsi.bg. This degree of information is, however, slightly unusual and other countries may leave statistics untranslated or even uncollected.

Other excellent resources can be found by using a little lateral thinking. There are many organisations involved in various professions within the property industry and their websites can often prove useful. These include industry bodies, investment banks and financial services companies. Just because a magazine or website is aimed at people working in the real estate industry, doesn't mean that it isn't relevant to potential investors.

Websites to check include the National Association of Realtors (www.realtor.org), and the Overseas Property Professional (www.opp.org.uk). Investment banks invest billions in global property markets and therefore conduct excellent in-depth research. Try the websites of companies such as Merrill Lynch, JP Morgan or UBS Warburg.

Last but not least, international real estate companies also publish extensive market research and analysis. This information is usually targeted and comprehensive, making it an excellent starting point for your research.

PROPERTY INVESTMENT SHOWS AND PRESENTATIONS

The UK has a number of international property shows. Each brand hosts a number of events every year and aims to cover the different areas of the UK. Details of up-coming events are available on the internet and you can also often apply for free tickets. The top events are:

The Homebuyer Show	www.homebuyer.co.uk
The Property Investors Show	www.propertyinvestor.co.uk
A Place in the Sun Live	www.aplaceinthesunlive.com

If you do decide to attend a show, try to make time for a seminar or two. The teaching sessions are run by property professionals and as well as providing useful information, there will often be time for asking questions.

Other parts of the world are less well served with international property shows but this is changing fast and there are now excellent property shows from Moscow to Dubai, from Oslo to Hong Kong. It is also worth looking out for road shows and training seminars held by international property firms. Many real estate agents and property clubs also hold useful seminars which invariably have the dual objective of educating attendees as well as presenting the company's latest investment opportunities.

Next steps

Carry out research in sufficient depth and no matter which country you are interested in, there shouldn't be anything in the transaction that takes you too much by surprise. But research will only take you so far. Ultimately you will need the support of a professional, or more likely, professionals. Whilst there is no logical end to research and there is no such thing as too much knowledge when you are considering spending thousands of pounds, there is a limit to the amount of information that you will be able to access as a non-professional and, in most cases, without fluency in the local language. There is also something known as 'analysis paralysis', the condition of having so much data and information that it is impossible to know what to do. At this point, seeking out, and listening to, good independent advice is essential.

Working with property agents

Why buy through an agent?

The authors of this book work for one of the leading international real estate companies and it is therefore unsurprising that buying through an agent is highly recommended here. However, the truth of the matter is that dealing directly with a developer or vendor carries far greater risks and has no real benefits. In the majority of cases, the services of an agent are free to purchasers. Agency fees are usually paid by the developer or seller and are not usually an addition to the price of the property. Typically, the price of a property is fixed by the vendor and if they use an agent, the cost comes out of the vendor's profit. Even in markets where buyers do contribute towards agency fees, a good agent is more than worth the cost.

THE ROLE OF ESTATE AGENTS

The role of an agent is to bring buyers and sellers together. They therefore put a great deal of effort into attracting buyers and this includes offering a wide range of services from research to after-sales care; all of which are of significant value to investors. Technically speaking, when the seller of a property pays the agent's fees, the seller is actually the customer. However, it is impossible for an agent to make money and survive without buyers, which means that they should be very keen to turn you into a loyal customer.

The concept of customer loyalty in the real estate industry is, in many ways, tied in with the investment market. With the primary residence and even holiday-home markets, people complete transactions very occasionally and are more interested in the specific property than the agent they buy through. In this market, customer loyalty isn't such an issue, although every agent realises the value of reputation.

In the investment market, especially with agents that cover many countries and multiple investment options, customer loyalty is a much bigger issue. Investors will undertake many transactions throughout their lifetime and if they are confident that a particular agent is capable of providing top-notch advice and finding them the best investment opportunities, they will come back time and time again. The role of an international property agent in the investment market is somewhat akin to that of a stockbroker: helping clients make the best investments on an ongoing basis.

If nothing else, agents provide access to properties that would otherwise be difficult or impossible to find. You may be able to find a project promoted directly by the developer, but you should ask why there is no agent representing them. Agents are commercial operators. The more properties they sell, the more money they make. It is a foolish agent that makes enormous effort to sell a bad property. Investors are savvy and even if an agent succeeded in selling second-rate properties for a while, their reputation would soon catch up with them.

The key to a successful international agency is the ability to identify and source the best properties. Good properties sell themselves and it is far more financially rewarding for an agent to invest his effort into analysing markets and sourcing good properties than employing a hard-core sales team. This may seem like a sidetrack but it is a critical point. The research teams of good agents will have put in more resources, time, money, effort and expertise into locating the best investment properties than any lone investor could ever do.

This approach has nothing to do with altruism, simply good business sense. An agency dealing in international investment properties wants to source excellent investments and sell them to their loyal customer base of property investors. Honest agents will take a long-term view and will do most of the leg work to find the best property for you while making a profit for themselves.

The last few paragraphs have sung the praises of international real estate agents, and in most cases this is well deserved. However, it is a sad and unavoidable fact that some companies out there are not up to the challenge, have a short-term 'sell anything quick' attitude or are just plain dishonest. Thankfully though, they represent a minority. Property Frontiers (www.propertyfrontiers.com) is not the only international agent to operate in a way that benefits investors. There are many organisations in the marketplace whose services are also of great value. They vary from the likes of large multinationals such as Savills (www.savills.com) or websites like that run by E-quity (www.e-quity.com), to smaller, boutique agencies like Some Place Else (www.someplaceelse.co.uk).

We have made our argument for using a good agent, but what should an investor expect from an agent and how should you choose which agency to buy through?

What to expect from an agent

As discussed above, the most important thing that an agent should do is source the best investment properties. This involves conducting research into which countries, regions, cities and even streets present the best opportunity. It also involves undertaking comprehensive due diligence on the developer and answering questions such as: does the developer own the land? Do they have the right licences? Do they have sufficient financial backing? What is their track record or experience? You would be surprised by the number of agents who would be unable to answer these fundamental questions.

'You can't reasonably expect an agent to know the answer to everything, but if they are a quality company, they will admit what they don't know'

As a result of the agent's research and background checks on a developer they will be able to provide you with detailed information on the market, the location, the property and the buying process. A good agent will provide you with this information. If they don't, ask for it. This is absolutely within the rules; any salesman worth his salt should never make you feel that you are being demanding or asking for too much information. In the UK we can be overly diffident about asking for information. American buyers have no such qualms, reasonably regarding information as a right instead of a privilege and expecting information on how comparative property is priced, local growth rates, standard of build and all of the things that are required to make you feel confident about a decision.

WHAT TO LOOK FOR IN AN AGENT

You should also expect a good agent to give you options. They should listen to your requirements and then offer a range of suitable properties or countries, depending on your enquiry. An agent promoting a single project has a motive and indeed a need to convince you that it is the best property for you. This may well be the case, but it is difficult to judge without comparison.

Similarly, an agent focusing on just one country is more likely to skip over any negatives surrounding the market. Every market has its pros and cons and an agent who covers multiple countries will be more likely to discuss them with you openly. This doesn't mean that single country focused agents are unreliable; it simply means that they believe in the market they are selling and are going to push the benefits. An agent covering multiple countries is more able to offer a balanced review of each market. It's the difference between having markets to fit the customer and making the customer fit the market. It is a fact that different markets offer a different balance between reward and risk.

Your agent should also be capable of providing a packaged service. This includes being able to support and guide you through the purchase process as well as recommending or even organising currency exchange services and mortgage financing. As an example, Property Frontiers has a large 'after-sales' department whose sole role is to help investors through the paper work involved with buying property and a separate division specialising in overseas mortgages. A packaged service means that you will not be abandoned as soon as you have signed on the dotted line. It is also a strong sign that your agent has the necessary connections, experience and expertise that you would expect.

If you are looking at investing in a number of properties over a period of time, the logical step up from a packaged service is a relationship. An agent is going to want to build a relationship with you and present you with the best opportunities that come onto their books. A good agency will be able to offer you someone to effectively act as your account manager, a dedicated point of contact who will answer ongoing questions as well as present you with new opportunities.

Some agents will also offer portfolio services, effectively a formalisation of the account manager service but paid for. An agent with whom you have a good relationship will offer you the best opportunities first, but if you want them to provide advice and guidance even when you are buying a property through another agent, you will normally need to pay. Whichever level of relationship suits you, a good agent will be able to offer a service to meet your needs.

Selecting an agent

In some cases, the agent you use is dictated by which agent is selling the property you want. However, the reliability of the agent should play as much of a role in your decision as the attractiveness of the investment opportunity as it will have an equal impact on the success of the venture.

Checking That Your Agent is Reliable: Do your research and you will be able to test whether an agent really knows their market or whether slick internet marketing is making a company seem more competent than is really the case. Can your agent answer specific questions about the country and area where you are looking? Do they know about taxes, fees and can they advise on whether you will be able to resell a property easily?

You can't reasonably expect an agent to know the answer to everything, but if they are a quality company, they will admit what they don't know, commit to finding the right answer and do so quickly.

A good idea is to look for an agent selling a range of properties, or working in more than one country. An agent could be linked to only a few developments, and will be responsible for marketing those developments in the UK or US. If the company is focused on too limited an offering they will be forced to push you toward what they have available. It is much better to use a company offering a range of options so they can find the one that suits you.

In many countries, estate agents are regulated and it is worth looking at letterheads and other paperwork for membership of a professional body. You can also ask for details of a firm's liability insurance. A good idea in the UK is to look for an agent registered with the Association of International Property Professionals (AIPP) or the Federation of Overseas Property Developers, Agents and Consultants, an organisation which rejoices in the acronym FOPDAC.

Whether to work with a local or international agent

Contacting estate agents and developers in the country where you hope to buy has some advantages. They are likely to have in-depth knowledge of the country and what is happening with the local market. Being locally based, they will also be available to show you around the area if you choose to visit the country.

On the other hand, using an agent operating from the UK, US, Ireland or your home country may have advantages. Firstly and most importantly, buyers have the potential for legal redress if an agent breaks the law or can be proved negligent. A firm based in the UK or your home country is easier to deal with – simple things such as telephone calls and receiving papers will take less time and energy.

Working from a distance can also give an agent a useful sense of perspective. An international company will be able to look at a local market with a critical eye, and if the market begins to drop, will be able to turn to an alternative area or country. In contrast, an estate agent with close links to a particular region will naturally tend to be biased. The really international companies, those that operate in several countries at a time, can also advise buyers on the countries and conditions that will best suit their needs.

Inspection trips

Advantages and disadvantages

At their best, viewing trips offer you the chance to look at the property in context, to measure for yourself how far it is to shops and airports and to work out whether the property really does have the rental potential that the estate agent has rhapsodised about. At worst, you can feel under immense pressure to buy and may spend an acutely miserable weekend fending off a salesman trying to flog a property which is unappealing and not appropriate for your needs.

In either case, inspection trips are arranged to encourage people to buy. Companies will arrange flights and accommodation at rock bottom or subsidised prices and arrange for you to be met by a salesman or local representative based in the country you are interested in; you will then be taken on a tour of properties that fit your criteria.

INSPECTION TRIPS ARE NO HOLIDAY

While in the country you will spend almost every moment in the company of a salesman who will earn a commission if you buy. It is emphatically not worth considering an inspection trip because you feel like a cut-price holiday. Quite apart from having no time for the beach, you may be lucky to have the evening meal unaccompanied. The busier the market, the worse this will be. Real estate agents in Florida have a reputation for lurking in hotel foyers hoping to lure away clients from rival companies!

Avoiding pressure to buy

It stands to reason that companies would not arrange viewing trips if they didn't stand to benefit. To avoid the pressure to buy, it may be better to arrange your own flights and accommodation and make up your mind in a more relaxed setting. By all means meet vendors, but arranging the trip on your own should be straightforward and may just make for a more comfortable experience as well.

If you have enough confidence in a country to buy there, you should presumably also have the confidence to explore on your own. Doing so allows you to see the less attractive areas of a country, building a three-dimensional picture. Hiring a car at the airport and finding a ski resort in the middle of the Carpathian Mountains is a daunting thought – but then, if you can't find the house or apartment, it will also be difficult for tenants.

Weaken during a buying trip, however temporarily, and you will have a contract placed in front of you. It's almost a certainty that you will get some form of hard sell. You will be told that properties are running out, that time is running out, that you have to make a decision now! Nine times out of 10, this will be an exaggeration.

When you want to sign a contract on the spot

If you have been convinced by a property whilst at home and seeing the site adds that final grain of conviction, or if there really is a queue of people clamouring to buy, you may wish to sign a contract while you are in the country. In this case you will usually be offered one of the following kinds of contract:

- A reservation contract: under this you reserve the right to buy the property for a certain period in return for payment of a relatively small deposit. If you do not sign a full contract within the specified period – usually three weeks – you will lose your deposit. This is similar to the option contracts used in the UK.

- Preliminary purchase contract. This commits you to the purchase come what may – unless, for some reason, the seller is unable to proceed. Even in that situation, whilst you will be legally entitled to recover the deposit paid, it might in practice be difficult or not cost effective to do so.

This is where having a lawyer waiting makes sense. Even in the most rushed buying conditions you can fax or email a copy of the contract to your lawyer and have them examine it for evidence that the transaction is not quite what it seems. Firms specialising in international property transactions will commit to this service whenever you need them. Of course, it's better not to allow yourself to feel hurried into a transaction in the first place, but in those rare circumstances where there really is a queue of people keen to buy – as has been seen recently in both Sao Paulo in Brazil and Ho Chi Min City in Vietnam – it's good to be prepared.

Professional advice

Lawyers

Before choosing a property and getting caught up in the buying process, you should try to have some arrangements in place. Better to have mortgage funding in place than to find a property with fabulous investment potential and then watch it being snapped up as you stand by waiting for your bank manager to make a decision. Making preliminary contact with a lawyer will also save time and preserve you from hours spent deep in the European countryside trying to find a lawyer through the local language version of the yellow pages.

The process of seeking advice should begin before you find a property. And of all the advisors that you will need, an English-speaking solicitor familiar with local conditions should be top of the shopping list. A good solicitor will ensure that the property title is sound, that you will not be liable for unpaid taxes or charges on the house and that the purchase runs smoothly.

A good lawyer should be seen as an investment, not an unnecessary indulgence. In particular, you should never sign anything until an official translation has been checked by your lawyer. Although the majority of agents are honest, if you sign a contract while unsure of the contents you may be committed to arrangements that you don't understand, which may impose unfair terms and will not be designed for your benefit.

To paraphrase Mae West, a good solicitor is hard to find. If you are looking for a lawyer in the country where you hope to buy, at the very least you should try to find someone on personal recommendation. Use an untrustworthy or negligent lawyer abroad and you may find yourself stuck with large financial liabilities, no house, and a lack of legal redress. The laws governing solicitors varies widely. In some jurisdictions lawyers may not even be obligated to keep money entrusted to them separately from their own!

International law firms

As a more expensive but secure alternative, a number of solicitors in the UK specialise in international property transactions; companies such as Bennett & Co (www.bennett-and-co.com) or The International Law Partnership LLP (www. lawoverseas.com) employ bilingual lawyers but are based in the UK and governed by UK law. This gives you redress under UK law should anything go wrong; firms will carry heavy indemnity insurance to protect buyers in case of any negligence. The Law Society maintains a database of English-qualified solicitors working abroad and foreign lawyers working in the UK. This can be found at www.lawsociety.org.uk; follow the link to 'choosing and using a solicitor'.

Whether you opt for a home or locally based law firm is very much a matter of preference. As is often the case, the decision boils down to the relationship between cost and risk. A local lawyer will probably be cheaper – but local law may allow you no redress in case of incompetence or negligence. How much risk you are prepared to accept is entirely up to you.

Deciding where to look for your lawyer should also be influenced by the level of risk in the market where you are looking and the amount that you are preparing to spend. As a general principle, any purchase above £50,000 may warrant using a lawyer at home, or at least using a local lawyer recommended by a credible agent. It is sometimes said that lawyers in any EU country should be reliable. Unfortunately, the distinction isn't this easy. For some reason, problems are most often reported in Spain, although this may reflect the number of transactions rather than the relative competence of Spanish lawyers.

Aside from the greater feeling of security, international firms may offer a service better tailored to the needs of people buying across borders. Lawyers will either be bilingual or qualified translators will be kept on hand. Either way, no room will be left for ambiguity about the meaning of legal terms and responsibilities. International firms are also better placed to understand which aspects of a legal system are apt to confuse or mislead overseas buyers, and will be used to explaining the process from beginning to end.

'A good lawyer should be seen as an investment, not an unnecessary indulgence'

Against this, an international firm will lack the close personal knowledge of an area that a local solicitor will provide. However, close personal knowledge can be too close and too personal: you should avoid using a lawyer recommended by or associated with a developer. One of the developments in international property has been the increased number of developers offering legal services as part of a comprehensive package. Nine times out of 10, this service is honestly meant and carried out, but no one wants to be the 10th person. Whether you look for a lawyer abroad or at home, you want to find someone who has your best interests, rather than those of the developer, at heart.

Surveyors

Taking independent advice should also extend wherever possible to having a full survey of your property. Your agent should be able to find you a surveyor working in the area. Alternatively, the Royal Institute of Chartered Surveyors publishes a database of surveyors working around the globe at www.rics-firms.co.uk. Using the RICS database will find a qualified surveyor anywhere from Croatia to Mexico.

Surveys on new-build properties are rare as few buyers choose to have them. This is often because new-build properties come with a range of guarantees from the developer. In most cases these guarantees should be sufficient, but if you have any doubts a surveyor will be able to assess the materials and build standards on your behalf.

In new markets a surveyor can also be an invaluable way to learn about the market. If you are considering an off-plan purchase for example, you may feel overdependent on the estimated completion price given by the developer. And developers looking for sales may be unduly optimistic. A qualified surveyor should be able to give you a more accurate idea of the resale value of the property. If this sum is half the price that you have been told to expect, you may want to think again.

TRANSLATORS

Most international property agents will arrange notarised translations as part of the service they provide. Should you need to have contracts translated, the translated version should be notarised as an accurate copy. In most legal domains the original version will be legally binding.

Financial advice

A surveyor can stop you buying a 20-bedroom French chateau which is actually close to becoming a 20-bedroom French heap. A translator can prevent you from signing a document which says 'I, the buyer, give all my money to the owner of this heap and expect absolutely nothing in return'. Yet there is one more advisor who may prove equally invaluable – a financial advisor.

Financial planning is an integral part of buying property and can be a complex topic. Few people will be able to pay for a property with a single lump sum, leaving the majority of buyers at the mercy of stage payments, international mortgages, currency fluctuations, varying tax regimes and more.

Financial and taxation regimes vary widely and taking advice based on your individual circumstances is critical. This is something to think about before beginning to look seriously: deciding how to share the tax burden and under whose name to register the property have significant financial implications. Most financial advisors will be able to help you plan for your domestic financing options and liabilities, but there are also firms specialising in the international market of which Blevins Franks (www.blevinsfranks.com) is the best known.

6 Financial considerations

Part of the appeal of investing in overseas property is that it is interesting, exciting, even 'sexy'. However, when it comes down to it, it is the relatively dull aspects of finance which determine the success of the venture. Considerations of financing, exchange rates and taxation can make the difference between profit and serious financial headaches.

The reality is, however, that with a little forethought the financial aspects of investing abroad can be taken care of quickly and simply. The three areas that need consideration are: being aware of the additional costs involved (both in terms of upfront costs and taxation); making adequate provisions for currency risks; and selecting the best financing option.

Calculating the final rather than the asking price

Most experts advise adding 10% to your budget in order to cover taxes, fees and unexpected expenses. However, making general assumptions of the cost is dangerous. Underestimating the costs could mean that you have to find extra money for the purchase once you have committed. This could be difficult, especially if the amounts involved are in the thousands. Equally, overestimating the costs could mean that you pass up an excellent opportunity because you assumed the purchase costs were higher than they were in reality.

Broad percentage estimates are simply not good enough and aren't actually necessary. Any agent will be able to give you an accurate breakdown of the costs involved and you should request this if it is not volunteered. Some of these costs, such as stamp duty, will often be derived from a fixed percentage of the property value. Others however will be fixed fees, regardless of the property price.

The best approach is to have a list of all potential, additional costs and write down the actual figures for the property in question. If you have access to Microsoft Excel or another spreadsheet programme use this as it will enable you to easily calculate the absolute values of percentage costs and to add all of the costs together. Holding the information in a spreadsheet makes it easier to compare the total costs of several investment opportunities at once.

As a guideline, the list below shows many of the potential additional purchase costs that you may encounter:

- Stamp duty/purchase tax
- Agent's fees
- Lawyer's fees
- Translation fees
- Survey fees
- Mortgage arrangement fees
- Notarisation fees
- Travel costs
- Bank set-up fees
- Currency transaction fees.

Financing your purchase

When it comes down to it, you only have two options for financing your overseas property investment: use your own money or someone else's, such as the bank or even the developer themselves. As we saw earlier in the book, gearing your investment by using the bank's money to finance your investment is the ideal situation as it reduces your cash requirements and actually improves your return on investment from a capital gains perspective. If you decide not to use your own money to finance your purchase then there are three options available:

1. To raise a mortgage on the property you want to buy.
2. To re-mortgage against another property that you own already.
3. To find a property where the developer is offering delayed stage payments.

International mortgages: raising a local mortgage against your investment

In many ways, raising a local mortgage for your property is ideal. One of the main benefits of financing your purchase this way is that your borrowing and repayments will be in the same currency as your rental income meaning that currency fluctuations will have no impact on your ability to make repayments.

Having the mortgage abroad will also make you feel more secure as your other assets will be left out of the equation. This creates a balance between assets (the property) and liabilities (mortgage debt) which is important. If you fall behind on payments the investment property is the only asset placed at risk.

However, in many countries the mortgage market simply won't be developed enough for you to be able to get a mortgage there. Mortgages might not be available to foreigners (or even at all). If mortgages are available they may have restrictive lending criteria or prohibitive interest rates.

Outside the Eurozone, were interest rates were around 5% at the time of going to press, most places have higher rates than the UK or US. In places such as South Africa and Ghana rates are often much higher – 12% in Ghana and 15.5% in South Africa at the time of writing. Rates like this will heavily erode any rental income. Lending conditions are also tighter. The amount that will be lent will often be less than in more established markets. Typically, banks will lend no more than 80% of the property value, although this is changing as the overseas mortgage market becomes more established. Repayment terms will also be shorter than the 25 to 30 years that many investors are used to. Often, repayment terms will be between 10 and 15 years – again, though, this is changing as overseas property investment becomes more common. This significantly increases the cost of monthly repayments. There are often restrictive age limits on lending, making it difficult for anyone over the age of 60 to borrow.

As a general rule, the more 'emerging' a market, the less likely it is to have a developed mortgage system. Buyers can easily borrow in order to buy in Western Europe, the US, Australia and parts of the Caribbean, but in countries outside of these areas it can often be a different story. A first step to finding out whether mortgages are available in the country you want to purchase in is to ask an agent dealing with that area. Agents realise the value of mortgage financing to investors and will be very keen to let you know when it is available.

Alternatively, there are some financial services companies which specialise in arranging mortgage finance overseas. It is worth speaking to them as they sometimes manage to arrange special deals on mortgage financing in countries where it is not usually available to foreigners. Property Frontier's 'Frontiers Financial Services' can organise financing in countries around the globe including Malaysia, Poland, Canada, the Caribbean and Slovakia. You can find out more by visiting their website at www.frontiersfs.com.

COUNTRIES WHERE IT IS POSSIBLE TO BORROW LOCALLY INCLUDE:

Albania, Andorra, Australia, Austria, Belgium, Bosnia, Bulgaria, Canada, Caribbean, China, Croatia, Cyprus, Czech Republic, Estonia, Finland, France, Germany, Ghana, Greece, Holland, Hong Kong, Hungary, India, Ireland, Israel, Italy, Latvia, Malaysia, Malta, Montenegro, Morocco, New Zealand, Panama, Philippines, Poland, Portugal, Romania, Slovakia, Slovenia, South Africa, Spain, Sweden, Switzerland, Turkey, UAE, USA. There are more being added all the time.

Advantages of a developing mortgage market

A developing mortgage market is one of the most reliable indicators that a country is on the way up. Without a developed mortgage market there is a limit to how far prices can climb. Where there is no mortgage market, the majority of transactions are in cash, purchasing power remains low, and prices stay artificially low.

Turkey is a good example of a mortgage market which has just taken off. Previously, interest rates have been as high as 22.5% and repayment terms were 60 months for loans in lira and 180 months for loans in foreign currency. Mortgages are now readily available from a number of banks with interest rates from 6.4% over a term of 20 years.

Re-mortgaging to finance an overseas investment

Another option is to re-mortgage your home or other properties that you own in your country of residence. This has become relatively common practice in countries like the UK and Ireland where house prices have risen dramatically, giving people access to large amounts of equity.

The advantages to this approach are that you will be able to arrange finance before you find a property abroad, meaning that you will be ready to proceed when necessary. You are also likely to have an established credit rating and be familiar with the borrowing, process making it far less complicated than raising finance abroad. There is also the issue of interest rates which in the UK and US have been relatively low in the past. Because you will be borrowing against the value of an existing property, you may also be able to finance 100% of the purchase cost of the overseas property, giving you 100% gearing.

The downside of borrowing at home is that you may be exposing your main residence to risk if you fail to meet your repayments. There is also the currency risk. If you are letting out the overseas property, you will most likely be receiving rental income in the local currency. However, your repayments will be in your domestic currency. As the values fluctuate between the two, your rental income may drop relative to your mortgage repayments, making it harder to meet the repayments.

Whether you raise finance domestically or internationally is a personal decision which should be made in light of careful consideration of all of the benefits and risks. If you are unsure which option suits your needs best, speak to a professional financial advisor who can help ensure that you make the right decision.

Developer financing

A potential alternative to mortgage financing to watch out for is developer financing. In areas where finding a mortgage can be difficult, some larger developers may offer financing or deferred payment schemes. Confident developers may agree to take money in regular instalments, bringing apartments and villas within the reach of more people. To all intents and purposes developer financing works like a mortgage although developers don't always charge interest.

Deferred payment schemes are different from stage payments. Stage payments are a limited form of financing where you pay for the property in stages until it is completed and you take ownership. Deferred payment schemes include stage payments but the stages continue well beyond the completion of the building. A typical deferred payment scheme would allow you to pay chunks of the property price at regular intervals over a seven-year period even though the property is completed and you are given ownership within two years.

'To all intents and purposes developer financing works like a mortgage although developers don't always charge interest'

Developer financing is of course a marketing strategy that helps the developer sell more properties. In instances where the developer doesn't openly charge interest on the deferred payments, you may find that they have added a premium to the purchase price. Check this by comparing similar properties without developer financing. Adding a premium for this form of payment plan is perfectly reasonable and should be expected; just make sure that the premium isn't excessive and you are not paying over the odds.

TIPS FOR FINANCING A PROPERTY

1. If you are arranging finance on the property, ensure that this is stated in any contract and you have an 'opt-out clause' if the loan is not agreed (which will ensure any deposit paid is refunded).
2. Have mortgage financing arranged before agreeing to purchase, or before signing contracts and paying a deposit. This will help you to avoid delays and difficulties should your application be rejected.
3. Open a bank account in your chosen country and ensure you get a Certificate of Importation for the money you bring in from your home country. This will make repatriation of funds much easier.
4. Set up standing orders in a local bank account to meet bills and taxes. Failure to pay your taxes in some countries, such as France, Portugal and Spain, could lead to court action and possible seizure of your property.
5. Consider using a specialist overseas mortgage broker – this will be invaluable when dealing with the red tape associated with foreign banks and as previously mentioned they will be able to negotiate better rates and terms.

Currency and foreign exchange

People often underestimate the impact of currency fluctuations, but it is worth remembering that movements in exchange rates can turn profit into loss very quickly. However, it is also worth remembering that it can equally turn a loss into a profit.

Currency markets are an investment opportunity in themselves and you should always consider the impact of currency movements when evaluating a property investment. As an example, between July 2007 and June 2008, the pound rose from €1.48450 to €1.49680, then fell to €1.23460 before ending at €1.27540. This meant that a property costing the euro equivalent of £200,000 in July 2007 fluctuated in value by over £52,000 in less than a year, purely as a result of currency movements.

An extreme example of a currency where investors have made substantial profits is the Chinese currency, the RMB. For some years the RMB was pegged to the US dollar at a rate which kept the value of the currency artificially low. This made Chinese goods significantly cheaper in global markets than would otherwise be the case. In July 2005 the Chinese government removed the peg, associating the RMB instead with a basket of currencies composed of euros, yuan, other Asian currencies and the dollar and allowing the value of the currency to float based on market supply and demand. In April 2008, the RMB hit a milestone as for the first time in over a decade the dollar bought less than 7 yuan, trading at 6.9920 yuan to the dollar, a 16% increase since the removal of the peg. The yuan is still rising in strength against the dollar, although the growth rate is slowing due to a combination of domestic inflation and slow growth in the United States, China's biggest export partner. It is still frequently suggested that the currency is undervalued, and analysts initially predicted rises of up to 40% relative to other currencies in 10 years. This would present an excellent opportunity to international property investors who invest in property in China, with a possibility of seeing the value of their property rise in value by up to 40% in pound or dollar terms even if the price in RMB doesn't change at all.

Knowing where currencies are going to move would be an extraordinary gift, but international money markets are complicated and it would be very difficult for ordinary investors to predict currency movements. These sorts of considerations are best left to the experts, but the good news is that there is an entire industry whose job it is to monitor currency movements and their services are readily available to international property investors.

When you purchase abroad you will need to transfer currency from your home country to the country you are buying in. You could use your bank to do this but you are unlikely to get a good rate of exchange. The sensible option is to use a currency broker such No 1 Currency (www.no1currency.com), HIFX (www.hifx.co.uk), Currencies Direct (www.currenciesdirect.com) or Moneycorp (www.moneycorp.com). Not only will these companies be able to save you thousands of pounds by offering a better exchange rate at the time of transfer, they will also be able to offer a range of associated services from advice on future currency movements to hedging currency risk.

> ## 'Always remember that movements in exchange rates can turn profit into loss very quickly'

Currency brokers publish research on potential currency movements and will be able to help you understand what is likely to happen to the currency of the country in which you want to buy a property. They will also help you plan the best means of transferring money between your home country and the country in which you are investing. Depending on which way the currency you want to buy is moving, they will recommend when to buy the currency that you need. They will also provide the option of a forward contract where you book the currency now at an agreed exchange rate using a deposit of around 10% of the amount of currency you want to buy. This can be a very good option when you have stage payments to pay. For example, imagine that you are buying a home in Thailand and that the value of the Baht is rising against the pound – meaning that the price of your property will cost more in sterling. The purchase price has to be handed over in three months' time. Under a forward contract you could agree to buy the Baht at today's exchange rate, or tomorrow's, or whenever your broker thinks the optimum exchange rate is available. After paying the deposit, whether the Baht continues to rise is a matter of supreme disinterest as in three months', time the money will be delivered at the rates agreed. You can fix exchange rates in this way up to two years in advance.

If you are transferring money between countries regularly, for example for mortgage payments, transfer fees can be an unpleasant surprise. Bank fees can be as high as £50 for a single transfer and with little regard for the size of the transaction. In this case it may be worth looking at a regular transfer plan. Currency brokers offer regular transfer plans which reduce the transaction costs and can be used for mortgage payments or even for transferring your state pension payments overseas if you live abroad.

Taxation of overseas property

Taxes vary widely from country to country and unless you are planning to make a permanent move overseas, owning property abroad may have implications for your taxation liabilities at home. Tax filing dates, procedures and requirements may vary widely and penalties for making a mistake can be severe. This makes the need to seek specialist advice doubly important. Wherever you buy, you will need to take advice on local taxation and the implications for your tax status at home. The information below highlights some potential issues, but professional advice from a qualified tax expert should always be sought.

Taxation can make the difference between a rewarding investment and a pocket-emptying plunge. This means that the level of taxation is one of the invisible driving forces behind the dispersal of buyers across different property markets. For example, higher rate income tax in Germany is 45% whilst Slovakia has a flat tax of 19%. Investment conditions in Germany would have to be very strong to compensate for the tax burden.

MAIN TAX CONSIDERATIONS

- How will any gain on the property be taxed in the country you wish to invest in?
- How will rental income be taxed? Is there a minimum tax on rental income? Is there a withholding tax?
- What is the level of inheritance tax?
- Are there any other local taxes to consider? These could include purchase taxes, annual rates (for example, the UK council tax) and annual wealth tax (countries with this include France, Switzerland and Greece – although many countries are now in the process of abandoning the wealth tax. Spain has just abolished wealth tax, coming into effect in 2009)
- Will any profits be taxable in your home country?

Forms of taxation

There are several forms of taxation with the potential to make life seem very rosy or very blue for property investors. Some taxes are easy to calculate and your estate agent should be able to give you a good idea of the fees attached to buying in any particular country. Stamp duty, for example, is calculated as a percentage of the purchase price and is correspondingly easy to work out.

Other taxes are harder to calculate. Capital gains and income tax on renting can swallow up money like a starved boa constrictor but these taxes will depend on the amount of money made during the period of ownership. Reporting taxes in a foreign jurisdiction and working out which allowances apply is a matter for a specialised accountant. This is something else that will have to be factored into your costs.

Taxes can also impact on people in a way that they don't expect. Some countries operate a withholding tax, where a tenant is obliged to keep back tax on the payment of rent when the landlord is overseas. This can be levied at rates of over 20%, creating problems for landlords dependent on rental income for interest payments or mortgages. Other jurisdictions, France for example, levy a wealth tax. This is collected annually on a sliding scale between 0.55% and 1.8% depending on the value of your property.

Capital gains

Capital gains are a charge on profit made whenever a company or individual sells an asset to someone else and makes a profit. Capital gains are levied on all sorts of goods, from paintings to stocks, although many countries operate a dispensation on homes used as a primary residence.

However, if the property you own abroad is an investment, the dispensation given on primary residences will not be available to you. This means that when you sell the property you may be liable for some form of capital gains tax.

'Taxation can make the difference between a rewarding investment and a pocket-emptying plunge'

The rate of capital gains tax and how it is calculated can vary significantly from country to country. Some countries offer taper relief which reduces the amount of capital gains owed for each year that you own the property. These sorts of schemes are often in place where governments are trying to stop rampant speculation in the property market.

Capital gains tax is usually charged against profit, but what is defined as profit will vary. Some countries may define the capital gain as the difference between the purchase price and selling price, whilst others may make allowances for other costs incurred such as purchase costs, selling costs and even property maintenance.

Care should be taken when it comes to capital gains as some countries have been found to be far from transparent in their dealings. At the time of writing it would seem thousands who sold property in Spain between March 2004 and December 2006 could be owed a 20% tax rebate from the Spanish government. British non-residents who sold their Spanish properties during this period were charged 35% capital gains tax whilst a rate of just 15% was paid by Spanish nationals – this contravenes European Community Treaty rules. Sadly those who sold pre January 2004 have also been affected but cannot issue a claim as the four-year claims period has now elapsed.

Income tax

Income tax will be charged against rental income. The rate of tax will vary from country to country and may also vary according to the amount of income you make. In many countries, foreigners will be entitled to the same income tax allowances as locals. This means that you pay no income tax on some of your rental income, but then pay increasingly higher levels of tax on amounts of income above and beyond pre-defined thresholds.

You will also need to understand any allowances on offer to offset against your income. Some tax departments will tax you on your gross rental income, whilst others will allow you to deduct some costs such as mortgage interest, maintenance and even travel before taxing you on the net remaining income.

Inheritance tax

Inheritance or death taxes can be particularly problematic for overseas property holders. Some countries have very high death taxes and it is also worth considering inheritance laws as in many countries, property doesn't automatically pass to your next of kin. You will almost certainly find that your existing will is insufficient and that you will need to make a local will for all the assets you own abroad.

For countries where inheritance rules for property are against your interest, the usual response is to buy through a wholly-owned company. Even if this overcomes local inheritance and taxation issues, you should also be aware of the taxation of your estate in your home country. For everyone domiciled and resident in the UK, inheritance tax may be payable on your total worldwide assets.

Double taxation

Many people select a country in which to invest based upon its attractive tax environment. However, this approach often overlooks the fact that whilst there may be no taxation in the country in which you are buying, it doesn't mean that you don't owe tax at home. A classic example of this is Dubai, where there are no capital gains or income taxes of any kind. People buy in Dubai for this very reason, perhaps choosing it as a preferential place to invest over a country such as Bulgaria where capital gains tax is 15%.

The problem that many people don't realise is that their total tax liability is likely to be the same in both circumstances. If you are domiciled in the UK or US, the Revenue is likely to want to take a slice of any capital gains you make in Dubai or Bulgaria at your usual rate. If your usual rate of capital gains tax is 18% then you will pay 18% capital gains tax on the gain you make in

Dubai or Bulgaria. The only difference is that, as long as a double taxation treaty between your country of domicile and Bulgaria exists, you would pay 15% capital gains tax in Bulgaria for which you would be given a tax credit in your own country to reduce your liability there to 3%. Either way you end up paying the full 18%.

DOMESTIC TAX LIABILITY

Many international investors are entirely unaware of their domestic tax liabilities resulting from overseas property. This is very dangerous as a failure to accurately declare your interests could be seen as evasion. It is essential that you take appropriate advice and report all of your activities as necessary, both at home and abroad.

For all that has been said above, it is important to be aware of the existence of double taxation treaties. These treaties are formulated between governments to ensure that you are not taxed twice on the same slice of income. If you invest in a country where there is no double taxation treaty you may find yourself paying both local tax and domestic tax. If there is a double taxation treaty in place you will be given a tax credit for paying the tax locally and therefore only need to pay the difference in your home country.

The UK has more than 100 bilateral double-tax treaties, the largest network in the world and agreed with countries from Uzbekistan to Myanmar. World-wide, there are more than 1,300 double-taxation treaties. The treaties work to the advantage of countries as well as individuals. Companies are more confident about trading overseas if they know that they won't be taxed twice.

If the UK doesn't have a double-taxation agreement with the country where you own property, UK tax payers may be entitled to special relief called 'unilateral relief' or to something called a foreign tax deduction. Your local tax office should be able to give you more advice about whether you are eligible for this relief.

PART II

INVESTMENT POTENTIAL OF INDIVIDUAL COUNTRIES

- ANGOLA 254
- ARGENTINA 295
- AUSTRALIA 350
- BELIZE 302
- BRAZIL 307
- BULGARIA 100
- CAMBODIA 198
- CANADA 314
- CAPE VERDE 258
- THE CARIBBEAN 322
- CHINA 204
- CROATIA 105
- CYPRUS 111
- DENMARK 117
- EGYPT 264
- ESTONIA 95
- FRANCE 122
- GREECE 129
- GUAM 211
- INDIA 216
- ITALY 136
- KAZAKHSTAN 223
- LATVIA 95
- LITHUANIA 95
- MALAYSIA 229
- MONGOLIA 236
- MONTENEGRO 143
- MOROCCO 270
- NEW ZEALAND 356
- PANAMA 331
- PHILLIPINES 241
- POLAND 149
- PORTUGAL 156
- ROMANIA 163
- SLOVAKIA 170
- SLOVENIA 175
- SOUTH AFRICA 279
- SPAIN 180
- THE BALTICS 95
- TURKEY 187
- UNITED ARAB EMIRATES 287
- UKRAINE 193
- URUGUAY 338
- UNITED STATES OF AMERICA 342
- VIETNAM 248

Introduction

Readers should now have a range of ideas and frameworks for analysing both markets and investment opportunities. In Part II we examine 44 different property markets to make assessments of their attractiveness as property investment destinations.

Each country profile looks at the range of specific factors which make that country a good investment option or, in some cases, a bad investment option. Whilst we comment on the opportunity in each country, telling people where or where not to invest is not the objective. These 44 examples are practical applications of the theory discussed in Part I. The idea is to show by example what to look for in a market so that similar characteristics can be identified when analysing any market of your choice. It is also worth emphasising that we are not tipping every country we discuss. Featuring in this section is not necessarily an endorsement.

We have not hidden our opinions on each of the markets we discuss. If we believe there are good investment opportunities we say so. If we believe the market has had its day, we say that too. The commentary on each country therefore reflects our own opinions. Some may disagree. After all, in most cases our opinions are based on economic analysis and it is well known that finding two economists with the same opinion on anything is a difficult challenge. We are confident in our opinions nevertheless. There are of course no certainties and we do not carry crystal balls, but the following comments have been written from the point of view of where we would invest our own money. We can do nothing more than that.

Omissions

Many readers may look at the 44 countries chosen to feature here and wonder why some countries are missing. We are aware that there are some 'obvious' omissions. However, this book like any other has practical limitations and cannot cover everything. The final list was chosen not because the countries are the most popular with investors, but because they give a good range of examples. As was stated at the beginning of the book, its aim is to be more fishing rod than fish: to provide a basis of understanding that allows you to make your own analysis of your country of interest whether it is featured here or not.

Future editions and more information

The information contained herein will date quickly. Laws change, events happen and markets move. Therefore, there is a practical lifetime to the accuracy of the information in each of the country profiles. To overcome this, updates to the book will be published by way of future, updated editions and also through the book's website **www.aninvestorsguide.com** and on The Property Frontiers Website **www.propertyfrontiers.com**. Both the websites and future editions will expand the range of countries covered as well as the depth of information on each of those countries.

If the country or area of a country you are interested in is not covered in this edition, you may be able to purchase a profile online or request its inclusion in the next edition of *Where to Buy Property Abroad – An Investor's Guide*, by emailing info@propertyfrontiers.com.

Guide to the risk and opportunity ratings

At the end of each country profile, we have given a risk rating and an opportunity rating. These ratings are a summary of our analysis indicating the levels of risk when investing in a market and the level of opportunity to profit from it.

The ratings themselves are simple. Both work on a scale of one to five. The opportunity rating is indicated by the $ symbol. A single $ equals a low opportunity whilst 5 of them ($ $ $ $ $) equals the highest opportunity ranking.

For risk we have used the ⚠ symbol. A ranking of ⚠ equals a low risk rating whilst ⚠ ⚠ ⚠ ⚠ ⚠ equals the highest risk rating.

Guide to the mortgage charts

LTV – Loan to Value – the percentage of finance given in relation to the value of the property

TERM – The number of years the mortgage is loaned for

CURRENCIES – The currency the mortgage is provided in

RATES – The interest rates levied on the original amount of money lent

STATUS – Means of segregating those eligible for a mortgage – applicants usually have to be either employed or self-employed

SPECIAL CONDITIONS – Any special conditions which affect mortgage acqusition.

Please note that the tables were compiled with the help of www.frontiersfs. com, www.connectoverseas.co.uk and www.mortgagesoverseas.com

Contacts

For contact telephone numbers and websites of financial advisors, lawyers, currency services, media resources and for general information on individual countries see the Contacts List in the Appendix.

The Baltics

LATVIA: Currency: Lat
Exchange rates:
100 Lats = £112.4   £1 = 1 Lat
100 Lats = US $222   US $1 = 0.45 Lats

LITHUANIA: Currency: Litas
Exchange rates:
100 Litas = £23   £1 = 4 Litas
100 Litas = US $45.2 US $1 = 2.2 Litas

ESTONIA: Currency: Kroon
Exchange rates:
100 Kroon = £5.1   £1 = 20 Kroon
100 Kroon = US $10   US $1 = 10 Kroon

Introduction

Although independence was declared at the close of the First World War, the Baltic states of Latvia, Lithuania and Estonia were under Soviet and Nazi German rule until the early 1990s when their independence was finally recognised by the Soviet Union. The freedom of the last two decades has enabled the countries to develop, trying to match the status of their fellow European counterparts. All three countries have been members of the EU and NATO since 2004 and look to join the euro by 2012.

The historic centres of the three Baltic capitals – respectively, Riga, Vilnius and Tallinn – are listed as UNESCO World Heritage Sites and are on the short-breaks circuit, with Vilnius expected to be the European City of Culture in 2009. Vilnius has Gothic, Renaissance and Baroque buildings whilst Riga stands out for *art nouveau* architecture, and Tallinn has an astonishingly attractive medieval Old Town. Ryanair and EasyJet both fly to the Baltics from the UK and visitor numbers are rising steadily. The Baltic States are described by The World Travel and Tourism Council as each being a 'fast growing travel and tourism economy'. Tourism rates are expected to grow by an average of 7.7% across the region during 2008 and by an average of 4.6% per annum in real terms between 2008 and 2018.

The Baltic states have enjoyed considerable growth over the last few years as international interest in the area has developed. The population is steadily becoming richer, with mortgages available on attractive terms and low fees and taxes. The quality of build is also extremely high. All of this engendered a healthy property market that offered investors good rental returns over the medium to long term. However, recent economic developments have altered the state of the market, making investment into the area a much more risky prospect.

Is this a good place to buy?

This time last year, the Baltic states were one of the most sought-after investment markets of the moment as house prices rose at extraordinary rates. However, predictions that these rates could be unsustainable have proved correct. Having taken the top three positions in the Knight Frank Global House Price Index in the third quarter of 2006, all three countries have now fallen considerably in the rankings as their property markets have stumbled.

According to Knight Frank's figures, Latvia had been in pole position with a growth rate of 56.9%, a rate that in 12 months has fallen to just 10.2%. Whilst the current growth rate itself is still healthy enough, a closer examination of the current market state reveals prices dropping in many sectors of the property industry, with the apartment sector bearing the brunt. Inflation is also at a worryingly 12-year high of 17.5%. Estonia tells a similarly negative story with a growth rate of 5.2%, down from 16%, whilst Lithuania's growth rate fell from 20.3% to 5.6% by the close of 2007.

These sudden changes are a product of overheating economies that could not sustain the massive growth rates, leaving the governments no choice but to resort to methods to contain the knock-on effects as the markets topped out. The property boom in the Baltics was fuelled by demand from both local and international buyers. As the countries recovered from Communist control, wages increased enabling the nationals to move out of Soviet-era accommodation and purchase new properties. International purchasers moved in to take advantage of low prices. All too quickly housing prices spiralled up, pricing locals out of the market and leaving foreign investors with no exit strategy. Rising interest rates to combat the unsustainable growth have helped slow the market as international interest dwindles.

These recent developments, although disheartening, are not entirely catastrophic. Whilst the Baltics are not the investment potential they were 12 months ago, given time they can still be a viable option. The rising interest rates, implemented to try to control the high growth, will realign the economy of the region and tightening credit conditions strive to do the same. They are also working to bring the Baltic economies in line with the euro, something all three states hope to join by 2012. The slowdown could actually make joining the euro more achievable and create a more stable platform for further growth.

Whilst housing prices are dropping dramatically in some areas, others seem less severely affected. Tallinn Old Town in Estonia, and its surrounding area, has remained stable in terms of growth. Rental values have been increasing as demand for property in the tourist areas remains strong, and many nationals priced out of the buying market are turning to the rental market instead.

> *'The greatest demand remains for renovated apartments in higher quality city-centre buildings. Good quality townhouses are also likely to do well'*

The Baltic Times predicts that prices are likely to continue to fall throughout 2008 as consumers adjust to new government-implemented property acquiring policies. There is no doubt that the market will take time to recover as consumer confidence has fallen and potential investors are waiting to see what happens next. Estonia has slashed its growth forecast for 2008 from 5.2% to 3.7%; however, the country remains positive for recovery prospects, having raised the 2009 growth forecast from 6.1% to 6.4%.

Investors already engaged in the Baltic property market are having to weather the storm. Despite prices falling by up to 20% in Riga and 10% in Tallinn in the latter half of 2007, investors are confident that the enormous growth of the past few years will still yield a considerable profit on their property. However, net yields in Tallinn have fallen as low as 4% as prices outpace rents, and mortgage rates are slowly escalating, meaning times are currently hard.

Which type of property should you go for?

Different areas of the property markets in the three states reflect varying effects of the economic changes, and due care should be paid to ensure the stability of a sector. In Riga, for example, the apartment market has suffered the greatest decline in prices, whilst prices remain stable in the detached house market in the city centre. The Old Town in Tallinn still retains a strong demand for property, although new-build properties are proving hard to sell, having witnessed the greatest decline in asking prices.

INSIDER TIP — It is important to note that new property in the Baltics is often sold as a unit without tiles, flooring, lighting, bathroom or kitchen, so it is important to know how you expect the finished apartment to look and allow an extra €200 per square metre to complete the refurbishment. In order to encourage sales, some developers are not reducing prices but instead offering additional fittings included in the price.

The greatest demand remains for renovated apartments in higher quality city-centre buildings. Good quality townhouses are also likely to do well. The majority of new developments are one or two-bedroom apartments and the average size of a new apartment has increased from 65 square metres to 77 square metres in Latvia and Estonia. The reverse is true in Lithuania where the average area of a newly constructed apartment is around 62 square metres. Buying smaller properties here is seen by locals as a way onto the housing market which has been escalating in price wholly out of line with incomes. Some Soviet era property is of poor quality but new builds are generally well put together and their prices will reflect this.

Until the economy and housing markets stabilise further, it is hard to project any real investment prospects. This is not to say that they do not exist, but firm guarantees are unavailable, and with the current situation as it is, any investor would surely have to be involved solely for the long-term.

Hotspots

The search for potential property should be limited to the capital cities and surrounding areas as anywhere further out is unlikely to have the necessary interest to warrant a viable exit strategy.

Tallinn

Estonia's capital, Tallinn, is a fascinating blend of the cultures of its various rulers: an extravagant Tsarist palace and ornate buildings lie juxtaposed against symbolically powerful Soviet architecture, with a background of winding, medieval streets and properties. One bed-room apartments generally start at around £50,000 ($98,220), whilst high end, more luxurious apartments start from around £90,000 ($176,840). In an article published by *The Financial Times* in February 2008, a spokesperson from developers Ober-Haus describes how of the 3,500 units built in Tallinn in 2007, 1,000 are still unsold.

Riga

Situated in Latvia, Riga is the largest city of the Baltic states, a fascinating blend of the medieval and the modern, with the largest collection of art nouveau buildings in Europe. Property-wise, both renovations and off-plan developments are available, with off-plan tending to offer better quality, although this can vary on an individual basis. Prices for one-bedroom apartments, off-plan, can be found starting from £70,000 ($137,650).

Vilnius

The marks of the motley heritage of Vilnius, Lithuania, are all too evident around the city, with beautiful architecture dating back various centuries and a variety of religious buildings accounting for the different phases of its rulers. The planned European City of Culture in 2009, Vilnius is stepping up its efforts to promote its local culture within the EU. Property prices in Vilnius are slightly lower than the other Baltic capitals, with off-plan one-bedroom apartments starting from around £40,000 ($78,660).

Buyer's guide

Although foreign investors are free to purchase apartments in Estonia, Latvia and Lithuania they are subject to some constraints when buying land. Those looking to buy coastal, forest or agricultural land must have lived in the country for at least three years and have contributed to agriculture in some way. (Source: http://www.housebuying.eu/en/lithuania/property-buying-guide.html)

Mortgages

Finance is not yet available in the Baltic states.

Key risks

With reliable forecasts for the foreseeable future unavailable, investment in the Baltic states is a risky venture. The sudden crash from the booming economies seen in 2007 has left the area in a state of flux and although unlikely to face a recession, the region has suffered from a drop in confidence which is an offshoot from the current negativity in the international arena.

The Baltic property market is currently one defined by high risk, with investors being advised to sit tight and see how the market develops over the next 12 to 24 months. The climate in the Baltics means that none of these countries is going to become a tourist hotspot beyond the city-break market, but they are still popular, and in time this could again generate demand for property.

Rating: ⚠ ⚠ ⚠ ⚠

Key opportunities

The current slowdown in property construction means that once the economy has recovered, there will be a shortfall in terms of supply and this will be the time to invest and benefit from a recovering economy (although this scenario is currently out of sight). There is no doubt that there is not the demand for property that there once was, and although one could take advantage of the decreasing property prices, exit strategies are few and far between making any investment a large gamble. The rental market offers slightly stronger opportunities as locals are priced out of the buying market and forced to rent. However, with high mortgage and interest rates the rental market currently does not offer much of a return either.

Rating: $$

Europe

THE BALTICS

Bulgaria

Currency: Lev
Exchange rates:
100 Lev = £40.36
£1 = 2.48 Lev

100 Lev = US $80
US $1 = 1.25 Lev

SOFIA

Introduction

Inhabited since prehistoric times, Bulgaria is home to a host of traditions, cultures and peoples. Possessing remnants of the oldest processed gold in the world, the most ancient copper mines in Europe dating back to the 5th millennium BC and examples of treasured Thracian architecture from the late Bronze Age, the country is underscored by a wealth of historic archives.

Currently one of the least populated European states, Bulgaria is approximately the size of England, but with a population of only 8 million people. Not only enjoying 354km of Black Sea coastline with 10 blue flag beaches, the country also boasts 37,000km of mountainous hiking paths, a series of Roman, Greek and Thracian historical attractions, including nine UNESCO world heritage sites and a blossoming ski culture.

On the back of strong economic and tourism growth, Bulgaria's property market has become renowned. With 98,000 mentions in the international press in 2007 (according to Ernst and Young), few can have missed the huge media hype accompanying this country. Stories detailing the phenomenal gains of up to 47.5% early investors have made, namely along the Black Sea coast and in Sunny Beach have had a knock-on effect for investors. Spurred by tales of such returns, foreign investors in their masses sought to buy here, prompting a period of rapid construction and development. In 2008, Bulgaria has become one of the most popular property investment destinations for British buyers, who between them invest in thousands of Bulgarian properties each year. Despite regular price rises, entry costs are still low by European standards although the merits of the country's investment future have recently come into question as problems with overdevelopment come to the fore.

Figures from the Bulgarian National Bank (BNB) show that foreign buyers purchased real estate totalling €729.3m over the first 6 months of 2007 and that between January and March of the same year, investment increased by 63% compared to the same period for 2006 (www.thepropertybank.com). Overall, Britain remained the biggest investor in the Bulgarian economy for the second consecutive year with FDI totalling €901.5m in 2007 – a 23% increase (www. propertywisebulgaria.com).

> *'In 2008, Bulgaria has become one of the most popular property investment destinations for British buyers, who between them invest in thousands of Bulgarian properties each year'*

In a bid to preserve the beauty of its landscape and protect itself from over-development, restrictions are now in place in a bid to stave off a slump in demand. However, whether these measures have been introduced too late remains to be seen. Planning permission is now only granted to the highest calibre projects and restrictions such as limiting the number of storeys in new build developments are in place.

Aside from Bulgaria's property industry, the country's tourist market is also reaching new heights welcoming 7.7 million foreign tourists in 2007 and named as the top emerging destination for the same year by Opodo. According to the World Tourism Organisation the country is now one of the world's most attractive new destinations and visitor numbers are expected to be in excess of 20 million by 2010. With Easyjet now flying from Gatwick to Sofia, affordable accessibility is readily available.

Since accession to the EU in January 2007 Bulgaria has benefited from billions of euros in EU funding directed towards transportation infrastructure. Sofia airport has recently opened new facilities, Varna Airport has doubled its capacity by adding a new terminal and Burgas has a new terminal scheduled. In line with this, increasing numbers of budget airlines are introducing new routes to the area opening up accessibility and furthering tourist capacity. Road, rail and metro facilities are also being improved.

Is this a good place to buy?

Bulgaria's economic past has been somewhat turbulent with dramatic declines throughout the 1990s such as the collapse of its COMECON system and the subsequent loss of the Soviet market. Recovery became evident in 1994 when GDP growth recorded its first positive increase and the implementation of an

Europe

BULGARIA

economic reform package coupled with a currency board regime backed by the IMF and World Bank in 1997 afforded Bulgaria the stability it sought. A three-year loan secured by the country in 1998 was used to develop financial markets, social safety net programmes, the tax system, to reform agricultural and energy sectors and to simplify trade and has had a lasting effect on the success of the economy. Accession to the EU confirmed the confidence economic statistics were starting to show and it is hoped that the euro will replace the Lev in 2010.

The National Statistics Institute states that GDP growth reached 6.2% in 2007 and the International Monetary Fund expects that growth will continue to be a positive 5.5% in 2008. Meanwhile, FDI is expected to reach €6bn in 2008, up from 2007's €5.3bn. So significant has Bulgaria's recent growth been, that Ernst and Young awarded the country 3rd place in its Southeast Europe Attractiveness Survey 2008 in terms of general attractiveness whilst the IMB World Competitiveness Yearbook 2008 place Bulgaria's economy as 39th in the world.

Although the Bulgarian economy has come a long way, it must be reminded that the country's per-capita PPP GDP is still only a third of the EU25 average whilst its nominal GDP per capita is only 13% of the EU average.

Still among the lowest in the EU, monthly incomes are rising and averaged €180 during 2007. This very gradual proliferation of new wealth is creating a slow-growing middle class now able to consider entering the local property market, and with the rate of new development, they have plenty of choice.

The recent strength of Bulgaria's economic indicators means that the international community now sees the country in a more positive light. The World Bank's director for Romania and Bulgaria has identified Bulgaria as 'a good place for investment' noting that in three years, Bulgaria rose from being the Bank's lowest-rated country in the region to the highest.

As far as the property market is concerned, Bulgaria's communist background coupled with a slow entrance onto the economic scene in the 1990s meant that property prices were, and still are, low by Western European standards. It is partly these low entry prices that have allowed such growth in capital. Inline with a steadying economy and confident tourist market, property prices have risen, rewarding those early investors with big returns.

ERA Real Estate believes, that 15% capital appreciation can be achieved in 2008 and shows that the number of property transactions in Bulgaria grew between 4% and 5% in 2007 to reach a total of ~325,000 (www.themovechannel.com). Further findings from the Bulgarian National Statistical Institute reveal that residential property prices increased by almost 7% in the first quarter of 2008 which means, according to these statistics, the country looks to be on track to achieve the 28.9% growth in residential property prices that were recorded in 2007 (National Statistics Institute, www.opp.com).

INSIDER TIP

Some investment opportunities may still exist in Bulgaria's capital, Sofia, but because of the nature of speculation in Bulgaria over recent years, these are probably best left to large scale, institutional investors.

Although phenomenal growth was achieved by early investors, those looking to invest now will most likely be disappointed. The phenomenal growth rates which were achieved several years ago and which some sources claim can still be achieved are paper returns only and are very unlikely to be achieved in practice. The coastal areas and the mountain hotspots are all vastly over-developed meaning that the rental and re-sell markets are almost non-existent. Buyers hoping to turn a quick profit in hotspots such as Sunny Beach or Bansko are finding that it has become increasingly difficult to sell their property due to a proliferation of new builds catering for the speculative investor. A malign supply and demand imbalance has developed, meaning a viable exit strategy is now very hard, if not impossible to find.

Those determined to invest on the coast or in the mountains need to be aware that it is very unlikely to prove a profitable venture and more than likely will lead to substantial losses as the speculative bubble in Bulgaria unwinds.

Which type of property should you go for?

There is an old phrase which says 'if you can see the boat you've missed it' and Bulgaria is most definitely a missed boat. Many buyers piled into the market because prices were low and the potential for capital appreciation was strong. Indeed the early investors have seen this capital appreciation, but mainly because their investments prompted even more people to buy for the same reasons. The fundamentals in Bulgaria simply don't add up and, for this reason, we would suggest that any property investment in the country be avoided.

Hotspots

We do not believe that any hotspots remain in this market.

Buyer's guide

Foreigners may obtain title and real rights for properties in Bulgaria but are not allowed to own land. If, however, foreigners set up or join a company, under Bulgarian legislation full ownership land rights, including those on agricultural land, can be acquired. Setting up a local company then is a common solution for alien investors.

Mortgages

LTV %	TERM	CURRENCIES	RATES %	STATUS	SPECIAL CONDITIONS
75	25 years	EUR	7	Employed or self-employed	

Key risks

Bulgaria has almost become a victim of its own success and may well be the best current example of a speculative bubble in the world today. Prices have risen dramatically in recent years as more and more speculators have poured into the market. As a result prices asked for new developments have soared, leaving market fundamentals way behind. This means that today's prices are precarious to say the least. We fully expect a huge price correction in the market to bring prices back in line with local incomes and realistic holiday let incomes. The risk therefore in this market is huge. Our best piece of advice to anyone considering investing in Bulgaria today: don't.

Rating: ⚠ ⚠ ⚠ ⚠ ⚠

Key opportunities

Due to the overinflated prices being asked for current off-plan developments, we believe that no real opportunities currently exist.

Rating : $

Croatia

Currency: Kuna HRK

Exchange rates:
1,000 Kuna = £109
£1 = 9.2 Kuna

1,000 Kuna = US $216.5
US $1 = 5 Kuna

ZAGREB

Introduction

Steeped in centuries of colourful history, home to one of the world's most well-preserved fortified cities and blessed with an idyllic Adriatic coastline, Croatia's appeal is extensive. Its borders brush the slopes of the Alps, plunge deep into the Pannonian Valley and overlook the Danube and Drava rivers. Its interior comprises verdant forests, deep gorges, a collection of magnificent lakes and rich vineyards as well as smatterings of quaint villages, romantic castles and stately manors. Named 'the Pearl of the Adriatic' by George Bernard Shaw, and enjoying a blend of Mediterranean, Southern European and Balkan cultures, Croatia is one of Europe's best kept and most beautiful secrets. With 1,185 islands lying just off its coastline, Croatia offers a host of secluded beaches and tranquil island living.

'Enjoying a blend of Mediterranean, Southern European and Balkan cultures, Croatia is one of Europe's best kept and most beautiful secrets'

Travel and tourism now accounts for around 25% of the country's GDP, 28.7% of its total employment and is expected to grow 6.4% in 2008 in line with the government's plans to attract 11 million tourists by 2010. With further increases of 7.1% per annum in real terms expected over the next decade, it's no surprise that Croatia sits in 9th position in the World Trade and Tourism Council's ranking of the growth rates of 176 countries.

Before the dissolution of Yugoslavia, the Croatian Republic was one of its most prosperous and industrialised areas, with a per capita output around one third above the Yugoslav average. After a mild recession in 2000, the economy stabilised, and growth has averaged 4–6% for the last few years. This should be accelerated by the country's expected accession to the EU, scheduled for 2010.

INSIDER TIP **Where foreign investment is concerned, the government has introduced several measures to make the climate more attractive, including the establishment of the Agency for Trade and Investment Promotion which has a mandate to assist potential investors in Croatia. Foreign investors have the same rights and status as domestic investors (providing a condition of reciprocity is satisfied with their country of residence) and may invest in nearly every sector of the economy, although it is necessary to seek permission from the Ministry of Foreign Affairs before making any property purchases.**

Croatia is currently a non-permanent member of the United Nations Security Council for the period 2008–2009, and in October 2007 it received an invitation to join NATO. Along with the much heralded accession to the European Union, forecast for 2010, these recent developments conspire to prove Croatia's status as a main European player.

Is this a good place to buy?

The country has a number of natural advantages as a tourist destination, including an average of 260 days of sun a year, brilliant sandy beaches, a large number of Venetian-style towns and Dubrovnik, one of the world's best-preserved fortified cities. In addition there are plenty of direct flights from the UK with a number of low-cost carriers flying to all five coastal airports as well as the capital. The travelling time is only two and a half hours from the UK, and flights to Zadar can be found from as little as £60 return. Croatia is well situated in central Europe and is easily accessible by road, rail and sea, meaning European tourists can visit the country with minimal effort.

Although the recent Balkan wars may give cause for concern with regards to the political stability of the country, Croatia has actually recovered well and reports show that the infrastructure is well established and meets the European standards as prescribed by EU accession prerequisites. Living costs are generally low if compared with the UK but are expected to rise. Consistent interest from foreign investors has allowed Croatia to develop a healthy economy which has in turn enabled many Croatians to become first-time buyers. With locals now able to apply for mortgages, the property market has been bolstered with prices increasing by an average of 11.3%. Demand for property is high but it is not being met by suitable supply. In 2006 around 30,000 new apartments were required to satisfy Zagreb's accommodation needs, but a mere 5,000 were built.

Renting or ownership of a property here is enough to obtain a residence permit and there are restrictions on development which mean that the country should never become as overdeveloped as the Costa del Sol, in Spain – houses must not be more than three storeys high or built within 300m of the sea, and there are targeted financial incentives to avoid creating concrete jungles. These factors therefore increase Croatia's appeal as a second home or retirement market. However, the main reason cited for purchasing property in Croatia is pure investment, both for rental and for capital growth, with some agents forecasting returns of 15%–20% on city properties. If Croatia is accepted into the EU its economy can be expected to mirror those of the more successful entrants in years to come. As this happens, property price rises of 10%–15% have been predicted.

'In 2006 around 30,000 new apartments were required to satisfy Zagreb's accommodation needs, but a mere 5,000 were built . . . the beauty of Croatia lies in its underdevelopment'

Whilst Croatia is undoubtedly attractive and a popular European destination for tourists and investors alike, it is not quite the spotless choice that it is sometimes touted as being. The country is still plagued by corruption, an issue that was highlighted as a major challenge for the country by the EU in their progress report of November 2007. This is a problem that is still rife in many sectors of the economy and can be encountered when trying to purchase property. Although Croatia is battling against it, this remains for the moment a deep-rooted problem, which potential investors should most definitely take into consideration. What is more, the inflation growth rate is set to soon overtake GDP growth, with inflation currently sitting at around 5.7% and GDP growth rate expected to decline in 2008 to 4.4%, down from 5.3%. In a recent survey on choice of investment property location, *A Place in the Sun* discovered that Croatia now ranks 17th in popularity, having been placed at 11th last year, a result perhaps of neighbouring countries' increasing appeal.

The beauty of Croatia lies in its underdevelopment. It is no longer the bargain corner of Europe as too many investors have latched onto the secret; some are even beginning to call it expensive. The restricted supply has ensured the country remains uncrowded, and to have such stunning scenery within easy reach, coupled with good financial prospects, one can see how Croatia is still considered a bit of a catch. With the prospective accession to the EU just around the corner, there isn't much time left to get on board to reap the financial benefits before prices face a dramatic rise; predictions from various financial and real estate institutions for increases in real estate value range from 50% to 300%. As such, the market could become erratic and unstable.

Which type of property should you go for?

Property in Croatia varies from beachside and city apartments to spacious, detached villas in acres of rambling countryside. The real estate market here is still in its infancy, and land and house prices are just favourable, especially on the islands where there are beautiful stone houses built in the traditional style. The Croatian government is committed to protecting the country's coastline and natural beauty, and the restrictions on building which this commitment entails means that seafront properties will be at a premium, although there is still no shortage of opportunities. Dubrovnik, in the popular southern region, is the most expensive area in terms of property, with a one-bedroom apartment costing just under £100,000. In mid-Croatia, prices become more reasonable; a one-bedroom apartment being around £45,000, whilst apartment complexes being built in coastal regions offer prices starting from around £65,000 for a one-bedroom apartment.

Hotspots
Istria
The north-western area of Istria is highly popular due to its easy, inexpensive access and its proximity to Italy. The stunning scenery, the beautiful, historic coastal towns of **Porec**, **Rovinj** and **Pula**, and the warm summers all conspire to give validity to the nickname, 'Tuscany of Croatia'. Due to high demand, property here is expensive.

North and South Dalmatia
The south-western coastal regions of North and South Dalmatia contain some of the most beautiful cities of the country. **Dubrovnik**, a UNESCO World Heritage Site, and **Split** are medieval cities with cobbled, narrow streets and

old city walls looking out over the South Adriatic's most crystal clear waters. The relaxed atmosphere, aided by the regional warm summers and mild winters, entices foreigners and nationals alike to make the region one of the most popular, with property prices to match. Split's five marinas prove favourable with avid sailors.

Zagreb

Travel further inland finds the capital, Zagreb, the political and administrative hub of the country. For years a focal point of culture and science, Zagreb is a bustling, beautiful city that has retained its Baroque charm, offering busy markets, open green parks and abundant shopping opportunities. It was promoted as *the* place to buy to let in 2008 and unsurprisingly, prices here are high. Northern Croatia offers cheaper property in the smaller towns, although a much quieter lifestyle is to be expected.

Buyer's guide

Foreign investors can purchase and own property in Croatia providing that a reciprocity agreement has been signed with the foreigner's country of residence and special approval issued by the Ministry of Justice. Proof of reciprocity agreement is obtained from the Croatian Ministry of Foreign Affairs and can take up to 12 months. Once this is received, the buyer can resister the property in his name.

This process becomes obsolete if foreign investors establish a company in the country and buy through this avenue. A Croatian company set up by a foreign person is considered to be a Croatian legal entity and can therefore purchase property without seeking prior permission or being subject to any restrictions. Typically a Croatian company takes around a month to set up.

Those looking to use their property for letting purposes will have to buy in the name of a Croatian company.

(Source: The International Law Partnership, www.lawoverseas.com)

Mortgages

LTV %	TERM	CURRENCIES	RATES %	STATUS	SPECIAL CONDITIONS
70	20	EUR	7	Employed or self-employed	Completed properties only

Key risks

It is important when investing in any emerging market to seek local legal advice. In the past, Croatian property was sold by a simple contract between local people and never recorded in the Land Register. This means people who are deceased or not involved in the sale can still be registered as owning the land concerned. To secure a clean title, your solicitor may have to trace anyone directly involved with the property since the last record to obtain each of their signatures.

Another problem incurred with many older properties is the possibility that records are out of date and inconsistent. Permission to buy can be refused, incurring legal fees and expenses if there are problems with the title. The same goes for changes which have been made to the property previously – always check for records of planning permission. A good local solicitor who is familiar with the intricacies of the legal system is vital, and is likely to charge 1–2% in fees.

It is also important to shop around when buying in Croatia, both for properties and estate agents. It may be that the same property is listed on different web sites for different prices, as a vendor will have a base price to which estate agents may add their commission. Also, very few properties are advertised, and there is little consistency in prices.

To find a reputable estate agent, look for a company registered as *nekretnine* ('realty' in Croatian), under a name ending with the letters 'd.o.o.'. Make sure that all fees are outlined before proceeding, as different agents will charge for different things.

Rating: ⚠ ⚠

Key opportunities

Croatia, despite the above, undoubtedly offers some good investment potential. Although not the financial bargain it once was, the country remains hugely popular with British and European tourists meaning demand is sustained and the property market remains healthy. The beauty of the country makes it an attractive place both for immigrants and tourists so occupancy should always remain consistent and high. The accession of Croatia to the EU will only ease the property buying process for foreigners, but the assumed price rises that this may bring with it is something that buyers should be aware of. Property investment **pre-accession** then, is recommended for those set on buying in the country.

Rating: $$

Cyprus

Currency (SOUTH): Euro €

Exchange rates:
10 € = £8
£1 = 1.23 €

10 € = US $16
US $1 = 0.64 €

NICOSIA

Introduction

Standing at a crossroads between the mighty empires of East and West, Cyprus embodies a rich and varied cultural heritage that draws inherited influences from the Ancient Greeks, the Persians, the Egyptians and the Ottomans. As a result, Cyprus is a multiplicity of traditions, mythologies and cultures, with evidence from each scattered across the island. A land of beaches, mountains, castles and villages, Cyprus has a charm that is like no other, and with a climate that offers 340 days of sunshine a year, a low crime rate and an economy that makes the island an effective tax haven, especially for the British, it is not hard to understand Cyprus' popularity.

Although some may have Cyprus down as a contemporary clubbing haven for the young and reckless, travel inland reveals medieval stone villages that have barely altered over the decades. Inhabited by aged Cypriots, these tranquil, hilltop hideaways afford fantastic sea vistas and absolute tranquility. The southern Troödos Mountain range offers a decent ski season, with a variety of abilities catered for, and although the limited size of the resort may not constitute enough to make it a top ski destination in itself, the fact that within an hour one can go from sunbathing by the pool to shooting down the snowy slopes should count for a lot. Such diversity appeals to a range of visitors and means that 2.8 million holidaymakers visit Cyprus each year.

Following the Turkish invasion of Cyprus in 1974 the country became divided in two. Turkish Cypriots inhabited the northern third of the island, forming the Turkish Republic of Northern Cyprus (TRNC), and Greek Cypriots took the lower part of the island, becoming the Republic of Cyprus. Whilst the Republic of Cyprus is internationally recognised, the TRNC is acknowledged only by Turkey. As a result the TRNC is overdependent on Turkey, with a stagnant economy and an international embargo that prevents Northern Cyprus from engaging in any political, economic, social or cultural activities. As a result they remain completely isolated from the rest of the world. In comparison with the Republic of Cyprus' prosperous and booming economy, good infrastructure and international involvement the TRNC seems like the ugly sister, doomed to being ignored. However, with the election in February 2008 of a pro-unification president Dimitris Christofias, the conflict looks closer to being resolved than it has done for many years. Meetings between the two prime ministers of the island took place throughout the early months of 2008 to discuss the possibility of this reunification and the ensuing ramifications it may induce. Further, on 3 April 2008, Ledra Street, the symbolic partition of the two sides dividing the capital city, was reopened amid support from both Greek and Turkish Cypriots. The prospects for a unified Cyprus then, are looking up.

The majority of this chapter focuses on the Republic of Cyprus, and so unless stated that the TRNC is concerned it should be assumed that facts, figures and discussion are relevant to the Republic of Cyprus.

Is this a good place to buy?

The most recent major development in the progress of Cyprus is the island's adoption of the euro as of 1 January 2008, following its accession to the EU in 2004. With these two developments in place Cyprus is in a much better trade situation, as the euro brings price transparency to the EU market, encouraging competition and lower prices, and facilitating more freedom of movement to and from the island. It has also been suggested that the euro may succeed where other methods have failed and actually assist in bringing the two sides of Cyprus together by increasing trade across the dividing line and to the rest of the world.

The Republic of Cyprus has enjoyed a stable economy over the years although its heavy reliance on tourism means that it has been subject to periods of erratic growth and loss further to political instability and European economic conditions. The service sector accounts for 78% of the country's GDP, with tourism bringing in just under £2.8bn in 2007. The importance of tourism to the economy cannot be overemphasised, which is why the government is taking firm steps to increase the number of tourists visiting Cyprus each year. A new terminal for the airport at Larnaca is under construction with a view to opening in June 2009, increasing passenger capacity to 7.5 million. Further expansion plans to increase capacity to 9 million by 2013 are also under way, whilst the international airport at Paphos is undergoing similar expansion. Recent offshore discoveries of oil could further stabilise the economy if strong export links with

Egypt and Lebanon are established. If handled sensitively, this oil could put Cyprus in a much stronger global position.

The country has now seen the arrival of its first retirement village, a purpose-built development focused entirely on the increasing number of mature homeowners, with the facilities to cater for their specific needs. Golf and marina developments complete with restaurants, shopping and leisure facilities are multiplying rapidly, generating property hotspots. In line with increased tourist appeal, and to complement the airport expansions, talks are in progress with budget airline companies about increasing flights to the island. Kept buoyant through the adoption of the euro and fuelled by a rush to buy before a 15% land VAT was implemented at the beginning of 2008, Cyprus' property market was one of only two European countries in 2007 where the market actually improved on its 2006 growth at an annual rate of 9%. Cyprus also managed to retain its position at the top of *Jet-to-Let* magazine investment survey as the number one country their investors would choose to buy.

Cyprus has a good infrastructure, with a legal system that is not dissimilar to that of England. Its tax sector is very attractive as there are no inheritance, wealth or gift taxes and the country has double-taxation treaties with many countries, therefore ensuring that people are not taxed twice on the same income. Cyprus is also a haven for retirees as their hard-earned money can go further due to the small 5% tax on UK pensions. Retirees are also entitled to a duty-free car and free state medical care.

> **INSIDER TIP**
>
> **The Cypriot government is careful to nurture its property market, ensuring that overdevelopment of certain areas does not occur by implementing restrictions on the size and number of properties – especially in coastal areas. For those wishing to restore older properties, restoration grants of up to 40% of the restoration costs with a limit of £46,400 ($91,700) are available.**

Whilst most attention regarding tourism and property development focuses on the Republic of Cyprus, it is worth mentioning the North of Cyprus with a view to investing. New legislation that will enable foreigners to purchase property in the TRNC on a long-term lease is currently under review. If passed, non-residents will be able to resell property and also apply for mortgages, creating a far more viable property market than previously encountered. The fact that large banks have started doing business in the region is also encouraging to the prospective investor, although at this time Northern Cypriot mortgages are unavailable so the full amount would have to be paid straight away in cash, something that is out of reach for most investors.

The division of Cyprus though has created severe land ownership issues as displaced Cypriots are returning to reclaim old properties. This can wreak havoc for those investors who have bought in the north as they may find their property repossessed within a very short space of time. With the land registry somewhat out of date, confirming accurate title deeds is a near impossibility, meaning any investment here should be undertaken with the utmost caution. Ownership issues aside, the property market is strong and with annual rental returns of 4%–6% the buy-to-let market is looking healthy too.

In the Republic of Cyprus, the market potential for capital growth is strongest over the medium term rather than the immediate short term. This means that for those looking for a quick sell, Cyprus is not the best place to invest. Although house prices are expected to rise at encouraging levels of 7%–8%, investors who bought into the Cyprus market a couple of years ago are finding it more difficult than expected to sell. With no clear exit strategy in place, capital gains are at present inaccessible. It is also worth noting that non EU property owners cannot rent out their property, meaning their buy-to-let potential is immediately extinguished.

Which type of property should you go for?

Non-Cypriots are entitled to buy an apartment, house or land, although any land, with or without property, must not exceed 1,388 square metres. On the whole, the market is currently geared towards off-plan and new-build purchases, for which prices are rising rapidly but there is very little demand for re-sales (even off-plan). Some potential property owners may prefer to renovate older properties or else purchase fully renovated homes. Both of which are viable options within the country.

Hotspots
Paphos
The ancient city of Paphos, with calm seas and stunning sunsets has proved popular with tourists and developers alike and a plethora of resorts and off-plan developments have sprung up around the area. Its popularity has pushed up house prices, making it the most expensive area of Cyprus. A new luxury development by developers, Pafilia, will be selling apartments from £223,000 ($440,600). Other developers offer a studio apartment from £119,000 ($235,100) going up to £224,000 ($442,600) for a two-bedroom apartment.

Limassol
Cyprus' second biggest city is also highly popular, with beaches, a huge variety of nightlife and a dash of ancient culture provided by a castle and mosque amongst crumbling, old-fashioned artisan streets. It is relatively commercialised and has a year-round tourist season which is good for the rental market.

Available property is mostly off-plan, with luxury apartments starting from £205,000 ($404,800), more reasonable villas available at around £123,530 ($240,000) and central urban apartments costing from £79,590 ($157,000).

Larnaca

This quieter and less-developed town offers a more relaxed lifestyle and property up to 20% cheaper than in the most expensive regions. It is said to be the only area in Cyprus to have seen steady increases of property prices by 8%–10% a year. The nearby airport makes for reduced travelling time and ease of access. Apartments on developments can start from £105,000 ($207,340).

Nicosia

The capital sits further inland on the dividing line across the island. With a year-round tourist industry, Nicosia boasts high returns and increasing prices as land becomes scarce. Again, most property is off-plan and much is sold within the early stages of development. One and two-bedroom apartments in the outer regions of the city can be bought with prices starting from £75,000 ($148,000), whilst a two-bedroom apartment in the centre can be bought for £115,600 ($228,270).

Buyer's guide

EU nationals whose primary residence is outside of Cyprus and who are looking to invest in either a second or holiday home need to respect various formalities and restrictions detailing the number of properties to be acquired and what they will be used for. Permission from the Council of Ministers also needs to be sought. Such requirements, however, are expected to expire imminently as they do not honour the freedom of establishment fostered by the European Union.

(Source: Law Chambers Nicos Papacleovoulou, *The International Comparative Legal Guide to Real Estate 2008: Cyprus*, available at www.iclg.co.uk)

Transfer taxes will be levied on the purchaser when proof of ownership is confirmed by the Land Registry Office. Further, investors will be subject to immovable property tax of between 2.5% and 4% per thousand, according to the Price Waterhouse Coopers Going Global 2007 Report.

Mortgages

LTV %	TERM	CURRENCIES	RATES %	STATUS	SPECIAL CONDITIONS
60	25	EUR	4.35	Employed or self-employed	

Key risks

Cyprus is essentially a second home or retirement market; not the most appropriate market for those looking for investment and capital growth, despite what many specialists say. The whole market here is based on new-build properties, and new developments are constantly being built. Consequently, once a property has been purchased, it could be possible to find that the price of an identical property in an off-plan development will have risen by perhaps 40% in two years; however the apartment bought new-build two years earlier will not even have a resale value equal to that at which it was purchased. The vendor will be competing against brand new properties sold by developers, and will therefore have real problems selling.

Whilst the risks associated with buying in the north have been briefly mentioned, it is worth reiterating that the repercussions can be severe. There have been some extreme cases of foreigners who have bought in the TRNC and ended up being fined, forced to knock down property, or even being sent to jail. The purchase of immovable property belonging to Greek Cypriots situated in the area of Cyprus under Turkish occupation constitutes an illegal act which will expose the purchaser to grave legal and financial consequences. That said, property owned by Turkish Cypriots or foreigners prior to 1974 avoids these issues and would constitute a safe investment, although prices for such properties are much higher and they are difficult to come by.

Rating – South: ⚠ ⚠ ⚠
Rating – North: ⚠ ⚠ ⚠ ⚠ ⚠

Key opportunities

These factors notwithstanding, for a second home, holiday home or a retirement scheme, the Republic of Cyprus has a lot to offer. The climate, traditions and lifestyle will suit many buyers, whilst the low cost of living will mean that a pension stretches much further than at home. In addition, the infrastructure and health services are excellent. As the GBP has weakened against the euro in recent months, property prices have increased for British buyers. However, these issues are somewhat alleviated by the lower rates on interest loans and so the property market is still favourable to the British. There are a couple of points to bear in mind. Although EEA nationals won't require a visa before moving to Cyprus they will need to apply for a Temporary Residence Employment Permit Category F. In addition, those Looking to retire to Cyprus must have a secure income of a minimum of just over £8,000 per person (around $16,000) and will not be allowed to work once their application has been approved. It is also wise to draw up a Cypriot will, as inheritance laws otherwise default all property to the spouse or children of the deceased as beneficiaries.

Rating – South: $
Rating – North: $$$

Denmark

Currency: Kroner
Exchange Rates:
100 Kroner = £11
£1 = 9.46 DKK

100 Kroner = US$21
US$1 = 5 DKK

Introduction

Boasting one of the highest standards of living in the world, with one of the best social welfare systems, and the highest gross national product per capita, Denmark is often seen as a model state. Though the majority of land is used for agricultural purposes, Denmark's main areas of employment are based in services, manufacturing and industry. The country is a long-standing EU member and has strong trade and business links within Europe, in particular with Germany.

Like all Scandinavian countries, Denmark has a highly educated and skilled population that is generally fluent in English and is business orientated. It also has a flexible and efficient workforce and the Danish telecommunications system is one of the most advanced in the world whilst the level of computer literacy is excellent. Unemployment sat at a healthy low of 1.9% at the beginning of 2008.

Taxation is extensive in all areas, leading to a higher cost of living compared to other European nations; however, Denmark provides enviable public services, healthcare, education and infrastructure.

Is this a good place to buy?

Denmark is once of the world's thriving business hubs and was ranked top of the 2008 Economist Intelligence Unit's six-month Global Business Environment rankings as the world's best place to do business in the next five years. Denmark has also topped surveys ranking countries in terms of citizen happiness, the peaceful nature of the country, and in quality of life. Geographically it is also well placed to conduct business with both established and emerging European markets and many of the world's biggest companies have their Nordic headquarters in the Copenhagen region. The Danish infrastructure and transport links are also of the highest standard with four airports offering good international connections with the UK, northern and Eastern Europe, and the Baltic states.

'Quality projects in restored historic or iconic buildings that appeal to the cities professional classes should continue to be a good investment'

With free trade and movement between all Scandinavian countries there is a great deal of mobility amongst the populations in this corner of Europe which leads to a healthy demand for high-quality properties to let. Given the high property prices in and around Copenhagen (which attracts the lion's share of migration) this is a potentially prosperous buy-to-let market.

Denmark may find that the strength of its investment future is mapped out by its economic performance throughout 2008. Following years of strong economic growth that resulted in increasing housing prices, the economy slowed considerably in 2007. Following a peak in 2006, certain areas of the residential market witnessed a slump in prices, with some owner-occupied flats dropping in price by 14%. Since the fourth quarter in 2007 some banks have even been reluctant to finance certain investment ventures, creating difficulties for some potential investors. Whether the country manages to recover economically is likely to have a direct effect on its property market.

Another issue to keep an eye on is unemployment. Whilst the unemployment rate is at a commendable low, it is actually creating a labour shortage, expected to increase over 2008, which will in turn create strong wage pressure and increase the risk of the economy becoming overheated.

Which type of property should you go for?

The booming market in Copenhagen has seen a lot of very standard new-build apartment buildings and, as the market slows, it is these projects that are reportedly suffering slower sales. Quality projects in restored historic or iconic buildings that appeal to the city's professional classes should continue to be a good investment, particularly those within the centre or easily accessible suburbs.

However, in Copenhagen and other cities with a large student population and a young workforce, more standard, lower-priced properties intended as buy-to-let investments should always be considered as having strong potential.

Denmark often has good summer weather and a large proportion of the local population traditionally enjoys taking holidays or weekends along the country's North Sea coast. The area is also becoming increasingly attractive to overseas tourists who are looking for alternatives to Mediterranean destinations. Therefore, cottages in coastal locations can offer both an attractive second-home option and viable buy-to-let purchases.

Hotspots

Copenhagen

Because it is such a small country, investment tends to be centred around the capital city. Copenhagen has seen increasing investment over the past few years by the government as well as from commercial sectors. This includes an airport that is considered one of the best in the world, a new metro system, and the Øresund Bridge, which opened in 2000 to link Copenhagen to the prosperous city of Malmo in Sweden in just 20 minutes. Increased immigration to the city from employees of multinational companies, as well as Danes, coupled with a limited amount of building land has significantly improved property prices and continues to generate a healthy demand for accommodation.

Despite the slowing of the economy and housing market Copenhagen sustains high demand due to its desirability. Most property in the city comes in the form of apartments and these can be some of the most expensive in the world, with an average apartment costing £3,661 ($7,165) per square metre, according to Global Property Guide. Expected rental yields vary between 4% and 6%. A new, glamorous, city-centre building is being developed by trendy company, YOO, with 60 apartments and six penthouses planned, and at around £7,000 ($13,693) per square metre the cheapest apartment works out at a cool £476,000 (£931,507).

Aarhus

Aarhus is Denmark's second largest city and is the main employment hub outside the capital. The town has around 300,000 inhabitants, a large number of resident companies and good regional transport connections. Aarhus is also a university city, creating a well-educated workforce. There has been much harbour-front regeneration in recent years and, as a result, property is as sought-after as in Copenhagen. Latest figures from the European Council of Real

Estate Professions give the minimum cost of a house in the city as £1,632 ($3914) per square metre, whilst the maximum is £4,710 ($9217) per square metre.

Other towns

Of the more provincial towns, key locations are **Skejby**, which is rapidly attracting a large number of biotech and IT firms, and **Viby**, also popular with smaller companies. **Aarlborg**, once the bastion of heavy industry and manufacturing, is attracting new industries, such as communications, IT and financial services. It has a ready workforce, thanks to the expansion of the university. **Odense**, is also a university city undergoing renovation of its old harbour. A large number of service-sector industries, including banking, accountancy and insurance have settled here and it is in a good location for connections to other areas of northern Europe.

INSIDER TIP Holiday cottages are popular with the local market as places to spend the long summers or for weekending and can also be rented to overseas tourists. Popular locations include the long coast of Jutland, including Skagen, and the islands of Falster and Lolland. Restrictions on foreigners buying property are especially prevalent in popular coastal areas so it may prove slightly harder to buy here than in other places. Prices have risen quite dramatically in the past five years and you should expect to pay from around €500,000. Rental returns can be between €400 and €1,500 per week depending on property and season.

Buyer's guide

Restrictions apply to non-resident foreigners wanting to buy property in Denmark. Permission must be sought from the Danish Ministry of Justice which, in the past, has been somewhat reluctant to grant it. If, however a foreign company acquires real estate through a company registered in Denmark, all restrictions are lifted and permission need not be sought.

(Source: Accura Advokataktieselskab, *The International Comparative Legal Guide to Real Estate 2008: Denmark*, available at www.iclg.co.uk)

Mortgages

Finance is not yet available in Denmark.

Key risks

Denmark is not the obvious choice for a potential investor wanting to make considerable gains on his or her capital. The property purchase process is not as simple as in other countries, with various permissions and certificates needed, and it is not an ideal place to have a personal holiday home as guaranteed occupancy is by no means assured. Rental yields are not particularly high, whilst taxes are, and there is not the level of property available for large-scale investment ventures.

Rating: ⚠ ⚠ ⚠

Key opportunities

As a country though, Denmark is a thriving, business orientated nation with probably the best welfare state system in the world and a high standard of living. All indications suggest that Denmark, particularly its capital Copenhagen, will continue to thrive as property prices remain high due to constant demand.

As such, good property investment opportunities can be found. With the reputation Denmark holds for quality of life and the level of care it receives from its government, it is not surprising that so many people visit the country each year, creating dependable short-term rental opportunities. This is no longer a market where high profits via fast capital appreciation should be expected, though steady, sustainable growth can be anticipated

Rating: $$$

Europe

DENMARK

France

Currency: Euro
Exchange rates:
100 € = £79
£1 = 1.3 €

100 € = US $157
US $1 = 0.64 €

Introduction

France is famed for its delectable cuisine and elite wines, its sunflowers and its lavender. Home to some of the world's most sought-after vineyards, famous artists and pungent perfumeries, it is a country brimming with culture and time-less appeal. Thanks to its extensive and varied interior France caters for a range of tastes and interests. To the east stand the Alps, offering some of the highest peaks and the best skiing in Europe, whilst to the south-west are the Pyrenees, equal in stature and appeal. Some of the world's finest cities and regions are also found within French borders. Paris, the city of love, is also the centre of French tourism, art, music and architecture and is eternally popular with tour-ists the world over. Similarly, the medieval Alsace, 18th-century Bordeaux, the sun-drenched vineyards of Provence, as well as the stunning beaches and busy seaside resorts along the Mediterranean coast, all exert an unyielding appeal that accounts for the 75 million visitors drawn to France each year. It is reputed to be the most visited country in the world and, according to a survey run by *A Place in the Sun*, is the second most desirable overseas destination for UK property buyers, a statement supported by the fact that almost two-thirds of French property sold to foreigners is to British people. Property prices here, whilst high, are on average 30% cheaper than in the UK.

Economically, France is maturing into an economy reliant on market mecha-nisms rather than government intervention, with increasing privatisation in certain sectors and reduced governmental influence. Accounting for 50% of the country's GDP, French tax is high, compared to the British tax contribution of 42%. Yet Sarkozy is trying to redress the situation. He has introduced tax relief on mortgages, cut wealth and income taxes, has reduced the inheritance tax laws quite dramatically and has plans to alter the traditionally French 35-hour working week so that hours over the 35 are paid tax free. Sarkozy's sweeping tax reforms will have a major effect on, amongst many other elements of French life, the French property market as citizens suddenly have more capital available to invest into property than before.

Is this a good place to buy?

Lifestyle and investment purchases are two very separate concepts which take into account differing criteria. Whilst good investment potential is judged on rental returns or long-term capital gains, a lifestyle purchaser is more likely to make their buying decision based on more aesthetic, emotional factors. As far as France is concerned then, those looking for low costs and fast, high returns may find that this country is not as suited to investment as it is to second-home and lifestyle purchases.

Having said that, opportunities for investment can be found. Figures from Investment Property Databank show that French capital growth stood at 11.8% in 2007, down from 15.4% in 2006. Although this figure is lower than in many of the riskier new emerging markets, French property does offer stable growth and a safe, tried and tested marketplace in which to invest.

As with most countries at this time, official statistics show that the French housing market is witnessing decreases in the price growth rate following the highs of last year. Overall, prices rose 3.1% in the 12 months, ending March 2008, but much of this growth can mainly be attributed to certain prosperous areas that support the national growth rate with their constant popularity. Other areas over the same period saw a considerable drop in prices. It is important to note here that, as ever, statistics can be manipulated to create a certain impression and some are arguing that this is the case with some organisations within France. It seems to be universally agreed that the market *is* slowing but the extent of the decreases cannot be agreed upon.

'As far as France is concerned then, those looking for low costs and fast, high returns may find that this country is not as suited to investment as it is to second-home and lifestyle purchases'

For anyone considering purchasing property in France it is necessary to examine their chosen area in detail to determine the strength of the property market. Figures can vary greatly from *département* to *départment,* as well as in the type of property in question. It is also necessary to take into account the weakening pound-euro relationship. As of April 2008, figures showed that the value of the pound against the euro had fallen by 16% in the last year, close to a record all time low. There are fears that these discrepancies are becoming more pronounced, creating a financial gulf between price conversions that the British are less able to cross. The French property market is likely to suffer as a result as the British hold back on their spending deterred by the higher prices. However, the IMF predictions that the UK's economy will eventually regain its former prowess means that the GBP will at some point become a more powerful currency. For the moment then, potential investors are advised to sit tight and wait for these improvements to materialise.

As a result of price drops and a slowing market it is almost unanimously agreed that at least the first half of 2008 was a buyer's market; however, this also means that now is a very difficult time to sell as demand for property abates and investors tighten their purse strings.

Which type of property should you go for?

The type of property to purchase obviously depends on the requirements of the buyer. The French housing market offers plenty of choice in location, style and price. You can buy beach homes, city apartments, suburban family homes, farmhouses, chalets and even vineyards or a *château*. A popular choice is to buy a farmhouse or another large property in an area popular with tourists and convert it into a gîte or guesthouse, thereby gaining an income as well as being able to make the most of the country lifestyle. However, the popularity of this trend means that in many areas the number of gîtes has outstripped demand, meaning they are harder to rent out.

For those planning retirement or wanting to buy a second home, new builds and off-plan properties are often the preferred choice. These types of property offer the ultimate in terms of comfort and guarantees, and also constitute a hassle-free, low-maintenance package that appeals to many. It is also useful to note that if you are planning to relocate to France the health and education systems in the country are classed among the best in the world.

INSIDER TIP Current inheritance tax laws state that children take precedence as heirs, so it is a common situation for young French people to rent for many years before inheriting either a property or the capital with which to buy a property. A substantial market for long-term rentals is therefore created. However, with Sarkozy's plans to all but abolish inheritance tax for most French citizens the situation may change in the future, although this will take time to come into effect.

The government is also trying to encourage property ownership; currently only 57% of French people own their own home, compared to 70% in the UK and 84% in Spain. Tax incentives and eased planning laws are expected to encourage first-time buyers, creating a demand for property that could be capitalised on by prospective investors.

'France is not a place for speculative investment – the market is tightly regulated and fees and taxes are high, although many have found that it is a destination worth putting their money and time into for gains other than the financial'

The French government is also trying to improve the quality and quantity of holiday property in the country, and has therefore introduced a leaseback scheme. Through this, buyers accept limitations on the amount of weeks per year they are allowed to spend in their property in exchange for a number of benefits, including a guaranteed annual return of around 4.5% for a fixed period (usually 9 to 11 years – and the rental is usually index-linked, so as prices rise, so do returns), all maintenance costs paid, and VAT repayment on the property, which on new developments is 19.6%. If the property is sold within 20 years then the VAT discount has to be repaid to the government.

Hotspots

France is composed of many regions, fiercely proud of their individual characteristics, creating such a range of choice that it is hard to decide on the one most suited to the prospective buyer's needs. Almost all of France could be considered for second-home property or investment potential, either due to continuing trends of reliable popularity or by the fact that a region is less developed and less popular, thus offering more of a bargain and possible greater investment potential. Key hotspots especially popular with the British will offer reliable demand, although prices will be higher, whilst less tourist-saturated areas are likely to offer lower prices and a greater proportion of French neighbours.

Normandy and coastal areas

With a convenient proximity to England, Normandy has long proved popular with the Brits thanks to its improved climate and surroundings that are not too dissimilar to that of England. Coastal properties tend to reflect prices 30% higher than those inland, fuelled by demand for sea views and easy access to cross-Channel travel. A studio apartment in the more desirable **Cherbourg** can be found from £65,000 ($127,500), whilst a two-bedroom house in the cheaper area of **Manche** can be bought for £100,000 (£196,000).

The Loire Valley

This area has also proved popular over the generations, with its myriad post-card-perfect chateaux, verdant riverbanks and resplendent towns. Property in the area ranges from cheap shells in need of renovation to modern comfortable homes more suited to British standards. The average house price is around £209,600 ($411,000).

Provence and the French Riviera

Provence and the **Côte d'Azur** prove highly desirable year on year, with the French Riviera especially popular with jet-setting millionaires. According to the 2008 Knight Frank Annual Wealth report, **St-Jean-Cap-Ferrat** saw capital appreciation of 39% in 2007, with property costing an average £34,320 ($67,300) per square metre, making it one of the most expensive residential areas. Sea-side residences can be found for considerably less further west along the south coast, with a three-bedroom off-plan apartment in the reasonably-priced **Camargue** region costing from just £115,000 ($225,500). Further inland into Provence larger properties can be bought for under £250,000; a large farm-house for £240,000 ($470,700); or a two-bedroom villa with a pool half an hour from **Cannes** for £128,000 ($251,000).

INSIDER TIP

For those who are keen to take on more than the average, habitable property, bargain opportunities are cropping up in some of the traditional vineyard regions due to a struggling wine industry that has forced some winemakers to sell up. Period properties, with and without a variety of land and vineyard attachments and in varying states, are available. £203,000 ($398,144) to £271,000 ($531,500) should buy you a habitable two or three-bedroom property in the Bordeaux **region, whilst prices can head into the millions as hectares of land and outbuildings are added. In the less developed but still easily accessible winegrowing region of** Beaujolais **(north of Lyon) prices range from £237,000 ($464,750) for a two-bedroom property to £305,000 ($598,000) for a three or four-bedroom house, to £312,000 ($611,825) and over for large family houses.**

Languedoc-Roussillon and southern areas

As a popular French holiday spot and busy British retiree destination, the property market in Languedoc-Roussillon is buoyant thanks to competition from French and British buyers. A decent seaside apartment can be purchased for £100,000 ($196,000) to £170,000 ($333,300); a village villa and pool can cost from £240,000 ($470,560) to £300,000 ($588,180); whilst a top-end farmhouse and land would set you back £400,000 ($784,240) to £550,000 ($1,078,200).

Increased access, predominantly provided by expanding TGV routes, has opened up the more tucked-away corners of the country to tourists and potential purchasers, raising house prices as more people discover places such as **Strasbourg** to the east, **Brittany**, to the south-west and the south of France.

Ski areas and beach resorts

To complement the strong summer tourist industry France also has a huge winter industry, located in the two main ski areas of the **Rhone-Alpes** and the **Midi-Pyrénées**. The most expensive of these is the Alpes, offering better skiing, where the average property price is £383,168 ($751,150), whilst the average cost of property in the Haute Pyrénées is £293,838 ($576,030).

Beach and golf resorts are a good bet for rentals. New golf resorts are springing up all over France, and a new-build property on one of these can cost as little as £50,000 ($98,015). For those wanting shorter-term and seasonal returns, **the Alps, the south of France** and **Paris** probably represent the best opportunities in terms of yield.

Paris

Having held the top investment rating for a number of years, Price Waterhouse Coopers' 2008 report on emerging trends in European real estate now shows Paris slipping from the top spot to fifth in terms of investment prospects, and sixth for development prospects. However, the city still provides some of the best property opportunities in France in terms of real investment as its market is characterised by consistent demand and a severe shortage of rented accommodation. According to Knight Frank's Paris office, the resale market is very active because there is little new residential development due to lack of space and tight planning restrictions. Rental yields of 4%–6% are generally to be expected in Paris, whilst the many leaseback options available offer a guaranteed rental return of 4.5%–5%, and a VAT rebate of 19.6%. Due to lack of space for new building, the new leaseback developments are found within a 20 kilometre radius. In the 15th arrondissement luxury apartments start from £190,000 ($372,460) for 30 square metres and £553,600 ($1,085,223) to £633,000 ($1,240,870) for 70 square metres.

Buyer's guide

Non-resident foreigners will not be subject to any restrictions when purchasing property or land. Freehold, usufruct, bare and leasehold rights are all granted within France.

(Source: Ashurst LLP, *The International Comparative Legal Guide to Real Estate 2008: France,* available at www.iclg.co.uk)

Mortgages

LTV %	TERM	CURRENCIES	RATES %	STATUS	SPECIAL CONDITIONS
85	30	EUR	4.75	Employed or self-employed	

Key risks

In France, as in Spain and Italy, the property market is considered to be mature, and therefore entry prices are high. In remote and hidden corners of the country it is still possible to find properties for comparatively low prices but they tend to be priced as such for a reason and require an inordinate amount of renovation work. If you intend to buy a property to renovate, be aware of the intricacies of planning permission laws which may prevent you from modernising as you would wish. If buying to let, consider your chosen area carefully, assessing whether it has a year-round market or whether occupancy is likely to drop off out of season. Investors will often find that it is worth spending more to get a desirable property in a good area so that occupancy and demand can be relied upon. This is not a country to invest in if you have a low budget especially as taxes are also high.

Rating: ⚠ ⚠

Key opportunities

The main opportunities in France are therefore suited to those looking for a place to settle down or to own a holiday home. The leaseback scheme offers substantial savings and could be a practical and viable option, but it is definitely a long-term strategy which may put some people off. Higher returns and easier exit routes may be achieved by buying independently and hiring a letting agent yourself, although going down this route brings with it a much greater level of risk and absolutely no guarantees.

France then, is not a place for speculative investment – the market is tightly regulated and fees and taxes are high, although many have found that it is a destination worth putting their money and time into for gains other than the financial.

Rating: $$$

Greece

Currency: Euro
Exchange rates:
100 € = £79
£1 = 1.3 €

100 Euro = US $157
US $1 = 0.64€

ATHENS

Introduction

Greece is one of the world's great roots of Western cultural civilisation. Its iconic sites are recognisable the world over and attract tourists from far and wide with a blend of mythical fascination and the sense of an inherent cultural heritage. The 15,000 kilometres of mainland coastline bordered by the Aegean and Ionian sections of the Mediterranean offer lengthy sand and pebble beaches with quiet bays ideal for swimming. Meanwhile the plethora of rocky coves and natural harbours are ideal for sailors and sunbathers alike. Scattered across these seas are 2,000 islands of which only 160 are inhabited. Inland areas vary from dry hillsides covered with herbs to pine-covered mountains. The land is fertile and lends itself to a wide range of agricultural uses from salad crops to olives, while the sea has created communities dependent on fishing.

With its rich cultural history and dramatic coastline, Greece has been a popular tourist destination since the mid 1950s and the explosion in package tours in the 1960s and 70s only served to increase popularity. Today tourism accounts for approximately 17.2% of the Greek GDP, a figure that is expected to increase by 3.7% in 2008, according to the World Travel and Tourism Council. Greece is currently welcoming record numbers of visitors to its islands, with total figures standing at around 15 million tourists per annum.

Several of the world's best-known business names hail from Greece, including legendary shipping magnate Aristotle Onassis and EasyJet founder Stelios Haji-Ioannou. However, apart from agriculture, shipping and construction, tourism is the main lifeblood of the Greek economy, which has grown at a steady rate since the country joined the Euro-zone in the mid 1990s. Despite strong economic growth, public debt, unemployment and inflation are all above the Euro-zone average, and the Greek government is working to reduce these, an effort that some say will be a long-term challenge.

This economic growth was consolidated when Greece hosted the 2004 Olympics Games, which led to a cleaning up of Athens, the creation of a better infrastructure and an increase in tourist numbers. Nevertheless, investment from overseas businesses has been somewhat hampered by the government's extraordinary levels of bureaucracy and red tape. Following pressure from the business community, there is currently a move to reform the procedures by which companies can invest in the country. This, it is hoped, will encourage investment and boost tourism further.

Is this a good place to buy?

Though winters in many parts of Greece can be cool and wet, the holiday season is considered quite long, and generally lasts from early June to the end of September, with temperatures ranging from the low 20s into the mid 30s in high season.

One difficulty facing property owners wishing to access their second home is the lack of transport options to many locations during the winter months. Direct flights to all but the largest islands reduce or cease operation from October to early May and transport is then by ferry or connecting flights via Athens. However, the recent increase in low-cost flights during peak season should have a positive affect on both the tourist industry and property sales. Following Easyjet's purchase and takeover of GB airlines, access to the country has improved. Departing from London Luton, London Gatwick and Manchester, frequent flights are available in high season to Athens, Corfu, Crete, Mykonos, Rhodes and Thessaloniki.

In terms of home ownership, there are a range of options, with each island or mainland area having distinctive characteristics. There has been little of the rampant overdevelopment seen in comparable holiday destinations and building laws limit both where and how much one can build in sensitive locations. Official permission from the local authority must be sought before building outside a designated urban zone. There are no restrictions for EU nationals wanting to purchase property in Greece; for non-EU nationals there is a little more paperwork involved, with certain documentation and certificates required.

Europe

GREECE

Greek property is still considered highly affordable in comparison to other holiday destinations such as Spain or southern France and interest has increased from overseas buyers, which, in turn, has contributed to a fast rise in prices.

One major concern that various property advisors have highlighted is the cost of buying in Greece. Historically it has been wise to put aside up to 20% of the cost of the property to cover the buying costs – a considerable amount when we remember that the cost of buying is usually around 5% in the UK. If buying for financial investment with the intention of renting out a property it is worth doing calculations to ensure that profit is still attainable, including these extra costs.

Which type of property should you go for?

Those seeking rural or coastal locations have the option of buying land for building, traditional stone houses (many in need of restoration), or newly built villas or apartments. In many locations a car will be essential as public transport is limited. In addition, Greece's package tourism industry has created a large number of busy and well-developed resorts with clubs, bars and retail outlets appealing to mass tourism where demand for short-term accommodation will be high.

The property market is considered to be underdeveloped in comparison to other southern European countries, especially considering Greece's many natural assets and attributes. However, as interest has increased the market has started to move on from being very locally based, with sales centring around individual land plots or homes for restoration, to larger-scale, new-build developments in popular locations such as Crete, Rhodes and Corfu.

Buying a village property is still possible in many locations and may be an option that suits those who are willing to integrate with the local population, particularly those willing to attempt to learn the local language and show respect for customs. Such residents are generally welcomed into the local community. The winter months in many rural locations, especially inland and in the mountains, may be cold and wet or even see heavy snow, thus buyers will need to carefully consider when they expect to use their property. Restoring rural property often entails certain restrictions – such as only using local materials and techniques, and limiting the height of the property – to ensure the building is in keeping with local character.

'Buying property in Greece does not present a real risk if approached in a correct and diligent manner; the market is by no means saturated and could provide good returns on investment if considered carefully'

Property in busy resorts is likely to have high occupancy at the peak of the season but many towns that are heavily dependent on mass tourism close for the winter season and may not be suitable for those wanting a year-round life-style or rental option.

Hotspots

Most buyers are attracted to the main islands of Greece, such as Crete, Corfu and Rhodes. The mainland is less well known to property buyers, save for the capital, Athens, but areas such as the Peloponnese offer both coastal and village property and prices can be lower here and winter access easier. Prices from www.worldofproperty.co.uk and www.sunshineestates.net have been included merely to give a basic idea of what to expect in each area; these are not to be taken as rigid guidelines.

Athens

Vibrant, lively and now considered very desirable, Athens is too busy and pol-luted for some but since the 2004 Olympics the capital has cleaned up its act. The infrastructure is far better than previously and there are lots of upmarket shops, hotels and restaurants. Standard apartments, even in central locations, can be remarkably cheap, while prestigious suburbs such as Ekali or the nearby island of Aegina can command very high prices. Prices for apartments to three-bedroom townhouses vary from around £65,000 ($125,990) to £390,000 ($755,940), with larger townhouses carrying price tags of £600,000 ($1,162,985) and more.

Peloponnese

A large land mass joined to the Greek southern coast, the area is a mix of devel-oped coastal resorts, a wealth of historic sites, peaceful mountain villages and rural areas which are attractive to Athenians keen to escape the city. Like the islands, property ranges from standard apartments and new-build develop-ments in popular tourist locations to small cottages in undisturbed villages or coastal towns. A three-bedroom villa would set you back around £130,000 ($251,989).

Crete

Crete is the largest of the Greek islands and very popular with both Dutch and UK buyers. Two airports mean both halves of Crete have their fair share of tourists. To the western side of the island are the busy towns of **Chania** and **Rethymnon**, while the east has the major towns of **Heraklion** and **Malia**, a sprawling resort. There are many small pretty villages both inland, among the mountains, and along the coast that offer a mix of traditional stone houses, renovated property and ruins ripe for restoration. There has been an increase in new-build villas and apartments and several developers have now moved into key coastal locations. As a result of the increased interest prices have risen significantly in the past few years. An old stone country house with two bedrooms costs as little as £33,500 ($64,935) but is unlikely to be up to British standards so would require a little extra work. A variety of off-plan two and three-bedroom villas on developments around the island start from £130,000 ($252,000), with optional extras available. Top luxury three-bedroom villas, an hour outside Heraklion start from £600,000 ($1,162,985).

Corfu

Corfu is a very green island, with pine forests and a mix of long sand beaches and small shingle coves. Property tends to be divided into high-end villas, often in small fishing villages on the north-east coast, cheap apartments in large-scale resorts and village properties. Much of the island is very well developed due to the long history of tourism and this offers scope for a longer season. A development in Corfu Town offers apartments from £118,250 ($229,160) and villas from £172,300 ($333,915) and £253,350 ($490,988). A four-bedroom townhouse in a development in the north-east of Corfu Town costs from £250,000 ($484,496).

Rhodes

In the Dodecanese islands, Rhodes is one of the largest and sunniest islands in Greece. It has a mature tourist market and offers a combination of cultural and historic sites, good beaches and lively resorts. There are restrictions on development to protect the coast and rural areas and there is a large expat population of all nationalities. The northern part of the island is less developed by tourism and is popular with property buyers. Popular towns such as **Lindo** and **Tsambika** are particularly expensive. A development in the town of **Lahania** has apartments and semi-detached maisonettes available from £128,326 ($248,695) and £195,886 ($379,626) respectively. A resort near **Kalathos** offers a development of three-bedroom villas costing from £199,243 ($386,132).

'Buying a village property is still possible in many locations and may be an option that suits those who are willing to integrate with the local population'

Europe

GREECE

Other islands

There are many islands in Greece to choose from depending on the lifestyle and type of property you prefer. Smaller, less developed places such as **Thassos** and **Skopelos** will appeal to those wanting more secluded and peaceful islands but travel services and the kind of property on offer may be more limited whilst prices will not necessarily be any cheaper. Larger, more developed islands such as **Kefalonia** and **Zakynthos** often offer the best of all worlds: a good tourist season, good infrastructure and local services and a mix of properties in all categories and prices.

Buyer's guide

Foreigners can acquire property in Greece without restriction. Acquisition of real estate in the country's border zones, however, will be protracted. For non-EU nationals there is a little more paperwork involved, with certain documentation and certificates required before purchases are allowed.

Mortgages

LTV %	TERM	CURRENCIES	RATES %	STATUS	SPECIAL CONDITIONS
80	20	EUR	5	Employed or self-employed	

Key risks

Although as a tourist destination Greece is very mature, as an international housing market it is considerably less established. According to the World Travel and Tourism Council Greece is underperforming compared to some of its EU neighbours, especially given its natural assets and attributes. Whilst the market is not exhausted it seems to be overlooked in favour of other countries, and the potential investor should take this into account. Of course this means that the advantage can be played and gains made where others fail to take advantage but as stated, this is not considered an investment market as such. The government is still struggling to keep the economy in line with the obligations of the EU Growth and Stability pact, and inflation, unemployment and public debt are still on the high side. Falling international interest in the form of committed investment are in part due to a rigid, inflexible labour market. With regards to the property market, high transaction costs could also be off-putting. It is also important to be aware of the small details involved in plot purchasing regarding boundaries, multi-ownership of land and ownership rights to olive trees on a plot.

Rating: ⚠ ⚠

Key opportunities

The allure of Greece's ancient Mediterranean relics set in bewitching landscapes and warmed by the brilliant sun are proving hard for tourists to resist so the country's tourism market is a very healthy one.

As an EU democracy with a stable economy Greece witnesses modest growth, and whilst there are economic issues to be aware of, the government is committed to correcting these deficiencies. The large amounts of investment poured into the country for the 2004 Olympic Games, especially into improving the infrastructure, have paid dividends and Greece is now a much more efficient country to travel through. The strong and thriving tourism market looks set to rise along with increased travel to the islands, so as cheap airlines improve their flight supply the country can expect to see more visitors. There are no restrictions to EU nationals buying property on the islands, and with the rising tourist figures, demand for holiday property should, at least in the short term, remain high.

In short, buying property in Greece does not present a real risk if approached in a correct and diligent manner; the market is by no means saturated and could provide good returns on investment if considered carefully.

Rating: $$$

Italy

Currency: Euro
Exchange rates:
100 Euro = £79
£1 = 1.3 Euro

100 Euro = US $157€
US $1 = 0.64€

ROME

Introduction

The birthplace of opera, Dante and Da Vinci, Italy epitomises artistic elegance and cultural prowess. Home to magnificent beaches, unspoilt countryside, ancient cities, an enviable climate and a vibrant history, Italy is one of the world's favourite holiday destinations. Over 45 million tourists visited Italy in 2007, helping the country retain its position in the top five most visited countries in the world, a ranking it has enjoyed for over 50 years. The cost of living is comparatively low, the health service and transport infrastructure are excellent, and the pace of life is refreshingly easy-going. Also, due to more stringent planning regulations than in Spain and other countries, Italy has kept its charm and remained largely unspoilt. It is also home to the greatest number of UNESCO World Heritage Sites in the world. For lovers of the outdoors, there is climbing, skiing and snowboarding in the mountains, while the more gentle hilly areas of Tuscany and Umbria are ideal for hiking and mountain biking. Numerous beach resorts dotted along Italy's coastline also provide excellent opportunities for watersports including sailing, windsurfing and scuba diving.

'Continued high levels of demand have pushed prices up, and Italy's property market now stands among the highest priced in Europe'

Economically, Italy is moving fairly slowly although it still produces one of the world's highest GDPs. Over the last decade the government has pursued a tight fiscal policy in order to meet the requirements of the Economic and Monetary Unions, and has benefited from lower interest and inflation rates. Numerous short-term reforms have been implemented, aimed at improving competitiveness and long-term growth, but other improvements, such as lightening the high tax burden and overhauling the rigid labour market, have not yet been put into practice. This is partly due to the economic constraints placed on the leadership by the budget deficit, which has breached the EU ceiling. Having said that, the economy performed well in 2007, with a 1.9% GDP growth rate, higher than the 2001–2006 average of 0.7%. The rate of unemployment has also declined steadily from 7.8% in 2005 to 6.9% in 2006 to 6.7% in 2007, whilst inflation at 1.7% remains below the average euro rate of 2%.

The property market in Italy is well established and attracts large numbers of investors keen to enjoy a slice of the beauty and passion that the country has become so famous for. Continued high levels of demand have pushed prices up, and Italy's property market now stands among the highest-priced in Europe. A marked economic imbalance, however, divides the country into two distinct areas. The north has traditionally been the main area of interest for foreign investors, and the market here is well and truly emerged. The south of the country on the other hand is somewhat less developed and offers a range of more affordable properties. It is these parts of southern Italy then that have the greatest potential for capital growth.

Is this a good place to buy?

Italy guarantees a great quality of life, a secure investment and a fascinating cultural experience. It also has the advantage of no inheritance tax and, unlike France or Spain, there is no capital gains tax if you sell after five years. As mentioned earlier there is still the potential for significant growth in the less developed southern regions of the country. If you are buying to rent, you will be committed to a four-year contract with your tenant in compliance with the 1998 Rental Law and as such will be restricted to fixed rental rates. As the law is strongly pro-tenant, it can make renting unattractive for the landlord; however, it does mean that you will have guaranteed rental for four years. Whilst house prices throughout Italy have been growing at an average rate of 8.1% between 1999 and 2006, rents grew by an average of only 2.7% in the same period, therefore indicating the fragility of the rental market.

The market now appears to be experiencing a slight cool down with the 2007 national price growth rate of 6.1% being the lowest for five years (according to www.globalpropertyguide.com), although it still regularly tops the charts as the most searched-for country by British investors on various property search portals. It must be said though that different regions experience vastly different growth rates. The main cities that are constantly popular with tourists experience a reliable and consistent demand for accommodation, whilst new, up-and-coming regions in the south of Italy are experiencing high growth rates as they begin to register on the tourist radar.

Which type of property should you go for?

Whether you're looking for a *trullo*, an apartment or a large luxurious villa, Italy has a property to suit every budget. At the lower end of the property scale, renovation is often needed. However, the charm of traditional stone-built homes occupying amazing plots with tremendous views does make this process worthwhile.

As in any market, the type of property to go for depends on the buyer's aims. For those focused on securing high rental returns it is probably advisable to purchase an apartment in one of the more important Italian cities such as Rome, Milan or Florence where demand will be consistent and high. It must be remembered though, that Italian law is strongly pro-tenant and as a result the rental market has dwindled in recent years. Wealthier purchasers looking for a second home will obviously buy where they feel is best for their needs, though popular areas are those in the countryside, Riviera or Lake District.

INSIDER TIP

When discussing investment potential in Italy there are three areas that never fail to be mentioned: Calabria in the 'toe' of Italy's boot, Abruzzo on the east coast across from Rome, and Le Marche, to the north of Abruzzo, all up-and-coming areas that look to offer the most capital appreciation in the coming years. Puglia is also a newcomer that looks set to become more popular due to its low prices, good flight connections, unspoilt, beautiful countryside and proximity to the sea.

Hotspots

The Italian Lakes

At the top end of the market are areas such as the Italian Lakes, or the larger cities. The Alpine region around the lakes is a playground for many wealthy Italian second-home owners thanks to its proximity to Milan. This part of Italy boasts the romantic lakes of **Como, Maggiore, Garda** and **Lugano**, but also has a huge range of property available, from period villas to brand new apartments. The area attracts people of all ages, and there are a variety of activities, from watersports and fishing to skiing in the winter, creating a year-round market for tourists. Lakeside properties regularly sell for well over £700,000 ($1.4m), and a more modest family home away from the water will cost upwards of £250,000 ($500,000). If investors are prepared to commit to renovation projects however, properties can still be found from around £50,000 ($100,000). Prices vary in accordance with proximity to the lakes.

Cities

Investors seeking rental potential should look to the larger cities, such as **Rome, Florence, Venice** or **Milan**. These areas symbolise Italy both in their historic and spectacular architecture and in their fashionable shopping districts, which are considered to be some of the best in the world. As a result the cities are never short of visitors and therefore a constant demand for accommodation is assured. The story is pretty much the same in each of these cities regarding cost of property, with many luxury apartments costing well into the millions of pounds, whilst more conservative apartments have prices that tend to start around £200,000 ($392,000) and quickly escalate. In Venice you are unlikely to find anything under around £400,000 ($783,500) that does not need renovating. Rental yields vary, but all tend to remain under 10%.

'Italy guarantees a great quality of life, a secure investment and a fascinating cultural experience. It also has the advantage of no inheritance tax and, unlike France or Spain, there is no capital gains tax if you sell after five years'

Tuscany

Italy's best-known region is probably Tuscany, with the areas around **Pisa, Siena** and **Florence** being the first place many UK residents think of when looking for second homes. Consequently, the area is now considered to be saturated in terms of investment potential, and whilst the tourist market in the area remains strong, there is little opportunity to buy a cheap property and expect it to generate a high return. It is estimated that Tuscan property prices have risen by over 40% since 2000. A ruin can be purchased for just over £100,000 ($196,000) in need of severe renovation, whilst a four-bedroom house can be purchased for just over £300,000 ($587,600). New apartments being built cost on average just under £2,000 ($3,900) per square metre. The north of the region, however, is considerably more affordable as it is often overlooked due to its mountainous setting.

INSIDER TIP

Umbria, a sleepy, verdant region dotted with medieval towns and castles, has until recently, been relatively overlooked by prospective investors. This in itself is one of the reasons for its popularity, as purchasers prefer the uncrowded region to that of Tuscany and other popular areas. Whilst prices remain cheaper than the most popular regions, they are on the rise as more and more cheap flights become available and people latch onto Umbria's potential. Property tends to be most expensive in the two main tourist towns, Orvieto and Assisi, and also in the south of the region, but prices are more reasonable around Lake Trasimeno and further north around Citta Di Castello and Umbertide. It is possible to buy a small village property requiring work for around £55,000 ($108,000); a two-bedroom apartment in good condition for around £110,500 ($216,500) and a completed farmhouse for £277,000 ($542,500). Renovation in Umbria costs about £690 ($1,350) per square metre. Both Tuscany and Umbria are extremely popular with second home and investment purchasers, and the holiday rental market here is good, generating competitive rental returns, although these vary significantly with location and size of property.

Le Marche, Abruzzo and Calabria

The popular regions of Italy mentioned above are all beautiful and worth considering for a second home, but they offer little in way of real investment potential as the markets are well established and mature in their growth cycle, thus, whilst demand may be reliant and strong for at least the holiday market, there is no potential for good capital gain. This is not the case though in the regions of Le Marche, Abruzzo and Calabria whose main attraction is their lack of development. All three regions have easy access to skiing and beaches allowing for a year-round tourism industry that maximises rental capacity. And with Ryanair now flying to four airports in the south of the country, the tourist and real estate sectors look set to take off. Be aware that the lack of development also means that these areas do not offer quite the same high standards of living as in more popular areas.

Prices are considerably cheaper than the rest of Italy, with Le Marche offering prices up to 40% and 30% less than the prices in Tuscany and Umbria respectively. A typical budget in Le Marche is around £136,000 ($266,400), with £160,000 ($313,500) able to purchase some fantastic properties. In Abruzzo

£35,000 ($68,500) buys an apartment near beach and ski resorts, £76,000 ($149,000) buys an off-plan studio apartment on a development and a two-bedroom farmhouse has a price tag starting from £80,000 ($156,700). Calabria has property prices to rival those in Eastern Europe, with off-plan apartments starting from just £30,000 ($58,700). Renovation property inland is also cheap at £20,000 ($39,000) to £30,000 ($58,700). Fortunately for investors, Calabria looks as if it won't be making the same mistakes as other emerging coastal markets, such as in Spain, as the local government has ruled that new development is not allowed within 300m of the beach, and with the mountains restricting building to the rear, overdevelopment looks unlikely. Those who do pick up some of the best beach front property could see returns of 10%–15%.

Buyer's guide

Foreign buyers are not subject to any restrictions when buying property in Italy providing a reciprocity agreement has been signed with the purchaser's home country. Property rights and contracts although secure are subject to lengthy judicial procedures.

Mortgages

LTV %	TERM	CURRENCIES	RATES %	STATUS	SPECIAL CONDITIONS
80	25	EUR	5.95	Employed or self-employed	

Europe

ITALY

Key risks

Italy is a mature, well-established nation with a strong, healthy economy and a political security typical of a founding member state of the EU. These are not risks in themselves but from the perspective of a potential investor they are not good signs as they demonstrate that Italy is categorically not an emerging nation and thus extremely unlikely to offer the favourable conditions necessary to create the best returns on investment. Italy has long been one of the most popular tourist destinations in the world and has the mature property market to show for it. The market in much of the country is more or less saturated in terms of investment potential and entry prices are high, making a good return harder to achieve. It is not a market for short-term ownership as capital gains tax will be charged if a property is sold within five years of purchase, and those looking to buy a cheap property in order to renovate should be aware that the bureaucratic process can be long and complicated, especially with regards to planning permission. The south of Italy still has traces of corruption too that purchasers should also be aware of.

Rating: ⚠

Key opportunities

The points raised above, although included under the title *Risks*, are not the same as risks associated with an emerging market. The risks of Italy are in reference to making an investment where high returns are expected. The fact that Italy is a secure market can be a positive thing as it is categorically a non-risky market. It has a long economic history full of trends that give transparency to the market with no hidden pitfalls. The well established tourist market makes for dependable demand, with many areas providing year-round tourist attractions, and the main cities especially have a high turnover rental market. The Italian government is learning from the mistakes of other countries that have become saturated by property developers and has implemented building restrictions to curb over-development. This also allays investors' fears that their chosen location may be swamped by myriad developers.

Italy is generally regarded as being a market for the private buyer and the non-professional investor. Whilst investment potential *is* achievable, Italy is more a country of second homes and private rentals than lucrative property investments.

Rating: $

Montenegro

Currency: Euro
Exchange rates:
100 Euro = £79
£1 = 1.3 Euro

100 Euro = US $157
US $1 = 0.64 Euro

PODGORICA

Introduction

Recently propelled into the public eye via the medium of film, Montenegro triggers images of stunning lakes, captivating coastlines and a 'Bondesque' gracefulness and style. It may be one of the smallest countries in Europe, but it contains some of the most bewitchingly stunning scenery: vertiginous mountains skirting around plunging, dark lakes; elegant, pale-walled cities that are national heritage sites and mile upon mile of golden beach arching alongside glossy, vibrant seas.

In the 1960s and 70s, Montenegro's upmarket Sveti Stefan resort exerted a magnetic attraction over the rich and famous. Elizabeth Taylor and Richard Burton are said to have disturbed other guests with their arguing, Sofia Loren gave the chef lessons in how to cook pasta and Montenegro's status as a popular tourist destination grew and grew. However, the war in the former Yugoslavia had a detrimental affect on this industry and although Montenegro itself never saw fighting, visitor numbers plummeted and the tourism industry suffered. Only in the last few years has tourism in Montenegro returned to anything like its pre-war supremacy, with 2007 being particularly successful generating revenues of over $1bn. Since its split from Serbia and ensuing independence in 2006, the country has once again begun to attract the well-heeled visitors that frequented its shores during the 1960s and 1970s, and is now being dubbed as 'the next Monaco'.

'Hailed as the one of the top three 'fastest growing travel and tourism economies in the world' for the fourth consecutive year by the World Travel and Tourism Council, Montenegro is powering towards a very promising future'

The nature of the market also seems to be changing. Traditionally a favourite with Italians, Germans and Russians, the British and Americans are now falling for Montenegro's charm and arriving in droves. English is widely spoken, and the beach resorts are being redesigned to attract wealthy higher-end tourism comparable to that in Croatia and Italy.

The World Travel and Tourism Council rates Montenegro as one of the top countries concerning tourism growth for the future. In 2007 the country recorded a 19% increase in tourist visits from the previous year, welcoming 1.13 million tourists who generated over $1bn. Expectations are that visitor numbers will continue to grow over the coming years. With a limited choice of industries to develop, Mongolia's main economic emphasis is its tourism sector. Consequently, the government is making a concerted effort to improve the country's facilities in a bid to foster consistent foreign visits and encourage potential investors. As a result, Montenegro is fast becoming a regular fixture as a holiday destination, and is widely tipped by many industry professionals as offering some of the best investment opportunities around.

Is this a good place to buy?

Hailed as the one of the top three 'fastest growing travel and tourism economies in the world' for the fourth consecutive year by the World Travel and Tourism Council, Montenegro is powering towards a very promising future. Many infrastructure improvements are now in progress to cater for the predicted rise in visitor numbers, with numerous private and public investors pouring millions into updating local amenities. In total, more than €500 million has been channelled into new developments and rebuilds. This level of investment will stand the country in excellent stead for the future, helping it to mature into a high-quality tourist spot and lucrative investment destination.

Alongside infrastructure improvements, several building projects are beginning to crop up throughout the country. Reconstruction of Montenegro's tired Soviet-era hotels are under way whilst the now decrepit island resort of Sveti Stefan has been bought out by luxury hotel group Aman Resorts and is due to open in 2008 or 2009. Despite this redevelopment, careful planning is in place to help Montenegro avoid becoming buried in the depths of a concrete jungle like many of the other Black Sea states.

In June 2008, Montenegro Airlines launched direct flights between Gatwick and Tivat, meaning visitors no longer have to suffer the impracticalities of transferring from Croatia or flying indirectly. It is expected that these flights will have an inordinate effect on Montenegrin property and tourism sectors, opening the markets up to a wider range of buyers.

An overspill of investors from Croatia is now starting to filter into neighbouring Montenegro, giving the property market here a large boost. Prices are therefore rising fastest in the north of the principality and with only 290 kilometres of coastline, the balance of supply and demand should favour early buyers and keep prices high.

Based on the results of the 2006 referendum, Montenegro declared independence on 3 June 2006. It became the 192nd member state of the United Nations, and in May 2007, the 47th member state of the Council of Europe, as well as being a member of the WTO and the IMF. Independent from industrial Serbia, the principality is concentrating on establishing itself as a tourism hotspot and is officially recognised as a potential candidate for the EU, with a projected accession date in 2015 boosting the country's profile.

Montenegro is also steadily getting richer. EU funding is being used for new roads and infrastructure and, since 2006, the value of real estate has soared. As far as return on FDI is concerned, the country leads the way receiving more FDI per capita than any other European nation – in 2007, FDI exceeded €785m (Source: www.tourismroi.com).

Which type of property should you go for?

Montenegro has all the qualities required to make it a top holiday and second-home destination and for those with renovation or project management skills this might be the place for you. However, early-bird investors who got their teeth into this market a couple of years ago have snapped up a lot of the renovation bargains meaning they are now much harder to come across, at least in their virgin states.

For most buyers then, it probably makes most sense to invest in one of the new apartment or villa developments being built along the coast which offer increasing opportunities for buy-to-let investment. Montenegro is aiming to become an upmarket destination and new-build trends are starting to reflect this, making off-plan investment both viable and attractive. A lack of rental accommodation throughout the country means there is excellent potential for those interested in buy-to-let investments, especially in the more popular tourism zones. With foreign and domestic investors given parity of treatment, a stock of attractive good-sized buildings available and a growing tourist industry, Montenegro also has scope for people hoping to set up bars, cafes and seasonal lets.

Hotspots

A new wave of buyers has explored Montenegro after crossing the border from Croatia, meaning the majority of interest is focused predominantly towards the north of the country and particularly towards Kotor Bay.

> *'For most buyers then, it probably makes most sense to invest in one of the new apartment or villa developments being built along the coast which offer increasing opportunities for buy-to-let investment'*

Kotor

Kotor is a UNESCO World Heritage Site and a medieval fortress city, which makes it more than just the usual beachfront resort. The area has already seen substantial investment and prices in this area are generally well above the national average, and are comparable to the most expensive areas in Croatia. It is limited in terms of space so overdevelopment is unlikely to occur. A one-bedroom apartment here can sell for over £100,000 ($198,160), while a four-bedroom house can go for £310,000 ($614,300). Although the market remains popular, it has more appeal amongst those looking for holiday homes than amongst dedicated property investors.

Coastal areas

In coastal areas south of Kotor, property prices are considerably lower and **Herceg-Novi, Budva** and **Bar** are emerging as popular resorts and investment hubs. Budva is a walled town placed just outside Sveti Stefan surrounded by 24 miles of beach and, with pale stone town walls, it is frequently compared to Dubrovnik. It contains all the criteria for a thriving tourist resort and welcomes over a quarter of a million visitors every year. It offers great opportunities for investors looking for 'jet-to-let' options. This area around Budva and Sveti Stefan is one of the most intense areas of development throughout Montenegro with prices for one-bedroom apartments starting from over £160,000 ($317,000).

Tivat

Tivat is also tipped as a hotspot and property prices are set to rise significantly over the coming years. Its airport makes it very accessible and it is also the site of a huge marina and resort projected by the tycoon Peter Munk.

In general, opportunities for capital appreciation are now better in the south or inland at mountain and lake resorts, although any properties near beaches like Buljarica or Becici are also likely to see a healthy price rise. Another good bet is Ulcinj, which has eight miles of beach and prices which remain at a reasonable level.

Podgorica

There are increasing numbers of projects available in other regions of Montenegro, including the capital Podgorica, and the area around **Skadar Lake**. The capital offers a more traditional buy-to-let investment opportunity where strong demand is currently outstripping existing supply. Most importantly, given the minimal investment to date, the mountain regions are now hotspots for investment and government, donor agencies and non-governmental organisations are now promoting these heavily.

Buyer's guide

Foreign investors performing economic activities in Montenegro can acquire property for the purpose of business activities providing reciprocity is granted in the foreign buyer's country of origin. Otherwise, foreign nationals can acquire ownership title to apartments and residential buildings, again on condition of reciprocity. Unless foreigners can gain rights to use the land, foreign persons cannot acquire ownership title to land.

(Source: Schoenherr in cooperation with Moravcevic Vojnovic Zdravkovic oad, *The International Comparative Legal Guide to Real Estate 2008: Montenegro* available at www.iclg.co.uk)

Mortgages

LTV %	TERM	CURRENCIES	RATES %	STATUS	SPECIAL CONDITIONS
70	15	EUR	9.33	Employed or self-employed	Completed properties only

Key risks

In its brief history of independence Montenegro has proven itself to be a highly attractive market. However, given its age there are elements of the market and the country as a whole that deserve consideration. Firstly, it is important to realise that Montenegro is not the bargain investment venture it was just after its split from Serbia; prices have risen fast meaning entry costs are no longer low.

Whilst Montenegro is showing progress in its political stability, it still retains some of the scars of its troubled past. Land is not always registered officially and often has been owned by the same family for many generations, meaning claims over land can become tangled. It is essential to use an independent lawyer who can thoroughly check all paperwork.

Montenegro's rapid rise to stardom has been astronomical, especially compared with some of its longer established Balkan neighbours; however, the country's poor infrastructure has not caught up with the levels of visitors the country now receives. Previous potential investors have found the lack of infrastructure somewhat disabling. Trying to reach the less popular and developed areas can be practically impossible meaning their investment potential is erased before it has even had chance to establish itself. Those buying in these areas then, may well have to wait many years before they start to see any kind of positive return.

Rating: ⚠ ⚠ ⚠

Key opportunities

Montenegro seems to be the golden child of the Balkans. It has been hugely popular, not least with property investors, and for good reason. Economically Montenegro has a lot to show for its few years of independence. High GDP growth rates and an impressive amount of foreign direct investment demonstrate international confidence in the country as well as enormous potential for the future as FDI begins to bring improvements. Its thriving tourism industry is going from strength to strength creating a growing demand for accommodation that can be exploited by potential investors. Confidence in the tourism market is demonstrated by developers such as Aman Resorts who have bought a number of sites to develop, including the iconic Sveti Stefan resort, and Peter Munk who has plans for a multi-million marina development in Tivat.

Planning complications have meant that property supply has still not met the increased demand. The introduction of direct flights from the UK will only increase tourism and demand for property further. Potential EU accession should further augment the attractiveness of the country.

Whilst Montenegro is not the investment opportunity it was 18 months ago, profit can still be made. There are enough positive signs to suggest the Montenegrin market is a good, long-term bet for investment but it is not so established that the market has become stultified. It is a beautiful country and a great location for either a second home or apartment to rent out. As always, careful consideration of location and appropriate legal caution is vital.

Rating: $$$$

Poland

Currency: Zloty

Exchange rates:
100 Zloty = £24
£1 = 4.3 Zloty

100 Zloty = US $46.41
US $1 =2.26 Zloty

WARSAW

Introduction

Nestled in central northern Europe, Poland occupies a pivotal geographic position and is a stepping stone between the east and west of the continent. Thanks to its situation, it is rapidly becoming one of Europe's key business regions and continues to receive high levels of FDI. In 2006 FDI totalled €15,061m (Statistics from National Bank of Poland), an 81.9% increase from the previous 12 months, 87.9% of which was invested from European countries alone.

Alongside its prevalent commercial strengths, the country is also blessed with a rich culture. Home to both contemporary and medieval towns, the land maintains the essence of its ancient traditions whilst keeping abreast of modernity. Peppered with a mix of towering mountains, gushing streams, and the oldest primeval forest in Europe, Poland is home to the last of the European bison and the coveted amber gemstone.

Since joining the EU in 2004, Poland's economy has gone from strength to strength with a GDP that is equally distributed between the consumption, investment and export sectors. Year on year, the country has shown healthy growth, often outperforming predictions and achieved 6.5% GDP growth in 2007. Unemployment in Poland is still high compared with the EU average but continues to decrease gradually, currently standing at 11%, with the majority of unemployed people living in rural areas. Economic growth is expected to increase dramatically when Poland joins the Euro zone in 2009 and when it hosts the 2012 UEFA Football Championships.

> *'There is no doubt that Poland is taken very seriously by educated investors and with residential yields in popular cities such as Warsaw reaching 7%, it is easy to understand why'*

2007 saw supply match demand and almost beat it; however, there was an overall drop in demand levels compared to previous years due to interest rate hikes, banks tightening mortgage lending policies, higher prices and the suggestions of a global crisis in the property sector. This carried on into the first quarter of 2008 when Poland's largest homebuilder JW Construction revealed that sales for the first quarter of 2008 had dropped to a third of their usual output (OPP magazine June 2008). Investors then, seem to have become more cautious, meaning developments are beginning to fill the gap between supply and demand. In reality though, there is still a shortage of 1.5 million apartments in Poland, and substantial efforts are being made to meet demands. Indeed 220,000 building permits have been issued for 2008 alone, significantly more than in previous years. Experts have predicated that 2008 will become known as the year for stabilisation in terms of property prices, as the country steadies itself in light of recent high appreciation levels. As such, prices in some cities are expected to decrease slightly.

Considered to be one of the safest countries to buy in Central and Eastern Europe and just three hours from London, BMI, Easy Jet, Ryan Air, Wizz Air and British Airways now fly direct to Poland, at relatively low prices, making access quick and affordable. Capital appreciation for certain new developments is estimated to be as much as 28% over one year or 66% over the next five years. Further, with mortgage loans currently amounting to 8% of the GDP, Polish salaries are clearly increasing and with them, individuals' purchasing power and the ease of obtaining mortgages.

Is this a good place to buy?

There is no doubt that Poland is taken very seriously by educated investors and with residential yields in popular cities such as Warsaw reaching 7%, it is easy to understand why. Indeed, whether Poland can still be classed as 'emerging' is debatable; it is now deemed the fastest growing housing market within the EU. Some of the bigger cities are said to have already peaked, with buyers looking outside of city centres to more neglected areas to bag a bargain. For those seeking to break the tradition which has seen investors flock to popular cities such as Krakow, second-tier cities are recommended with their strong potential for price appreciation. Although popular cities still offer affordability in pockets and a guaranteed rental income, prices have generally matured and are now beginning to level out. The choice of investment destination within Poland then becomes crucial as far as returns are concerned. Generally speaking the rental market in Poland is a strong one, with yields ranging from 4%–9%.

Set to receive €67.2bn in EU funding between 2007 and 2013 for infrastructure, education and environmental improvements, Poland's infrastructure will soon mirror EU standards with the construction of 500km of freeways and more than 1,600km of expressways. The missing strips of the A1 freeway to Gdańsk and Katowice will also be built, and the E59 road linking Wrocław, Poznań and Szczecin will be repaired. Funds will also be used to modernise airports and the air control system, to repair railway lines and to construct a high-speed railway project.

Realkapital, a real estate investment funds management company, recently announced plans to raise €200m for the development of residential real estate in countries such as Poland, Russia, Slovakia and Romania which again will aid Poland's economic plight.

Which type of property should you go for?

When Poland joined the EU in 2004, interest from foreign investors was channelled towards the bigger cities, and new apartment blocks were the most popular choice for foreign buyers. Today there is a noticeable shift in the market, with foreign investors looking to lesser developed districts that have remained untouched by the property boom and are now in need of restoration. The rural market is subsequently receiving a facelift, with city suburbs such as Olsztyn, Bialystok, Bydgoszcz, Katowice and Lublin hot tipped for success and showing apartment price increases of between 20%–30% already. It is not only foreign interest pushing the rural areas of Polish property upwards: many expat Poles are returning home wanting more for their money and are therefore looking to the suburbs for lower-cost market entry.

Such properties are suitable for renting to Poland's growing local middle classes and expatriate communities and can return a reliable rental yield of 6%–7%. Older properties are also a good buy, especially turn of the century apartments with high ceilings which can command high prices. Developers are now turning their attention to renovating townhouses before sub-dividing them into apartments. With growing numbers of young Poles moving to the cities, the opportunity to purchase ex communist apartments has become available, and although aesthetically unattractive, they can be bought for as little as L60,000 and are good quality builds. Rental income is guaranteed as most of these blocks are perfect to rent to students within easy reach of education establishments.

There is still a market for new apartment developments in the cities, especially amongst Polish first-time buyers although this particular sector has become very specific and one-bedroom non-luxury properties are the most popular. Demand is coming from young Polish professionals wanting to buy first-time apartments with their growing salaries but unable to afford high-end prices. Between February 2007 and 2008, 33.7% more flats were completed to meet demand and as such, 2008/2009 is expected to see a rise in demand for one-bed apartments. Poles are expected to borrow €68bn in mortgage loans during 2008, showing how attractive Poland's market has become to both local and foreign buyers.

 INSIDER TIP **Land in Poland is difficult to buy; however, a permit from the Ministry of Internal Affairs is normally all that is needed to confirm a purchase. In order to maintain demand, a number of incentives are in place for buyers. These include VAT reductions, 5%–10% discount if paying in cash and 3%–5% discount for the last units on a development as well as legal, financial and architectural counselling and moving assistance.**

Hotspots

Warsaw

Warsaw is the cultural, entertainment and financial centre of Poland. The capital city has become the driving force for increased development of the country's economy and the focal point for foreign investment. With an attractive business environment unemployment in Warsaw is low and the city has been named as the 18th best business location. Warsaw is the most expensive of the cities and specialists say that over the last two years the residential market has changed entirely. There was a 32% rise in property prices in 2007 followed by a 5% fall, with more falls predicted to follow. Many foreigners have exited the market causing a slowdown, although yields of 4.8%–6% are still available. Less capital growth is expected in 2008 than previous years although Warsaw is continuing to construct thousands of apartments in the city centre and surrounding districts. Warsaw still claims to be short of 63,000 housing units so there are still good investment opportunities if buying to rent. Although limited capital appreciation is achievable, Warsaw still remains one of the most low-risk areas in the country showing good returns.

1. The Abu Tig Marina bordering Ancient Sands Golf Resort on the Red Sea Riviera (Egypt) where 5% guarenteed rental schemes are being offered, p.267

2. Booming Sao Paulo, Brazil's richest city where yields in the region of 9%–14% can be achieved, p.310

3. Stunning villa at Natal Ocean Club in the north east of Brazil where cheap land and construction prices are creating an environment of rapid capital appreciation, p.311

4. Montenegro has numerous vacant stone buildings which are perfect for renovation projects, p.145

5. Pearl Island in the Philippines is a private tropical island of 52 hectares. Luxury villas here will be coveted by the discerning traveller, p.245

6. Spectacular Shanghai, home of the powerful Shanghai Stock Exchange, one of the world's most important trade and finance centres and one of Asia's most exciting investment hotspots, p.206

7. Cattle grazing over the sprauling Mongolia terrain. Urban investments in the coutry's capital generate yields of up to 20%, p.236

8. Grenada is one of the Carribbean's most promising investment islands with low-cost entry and healthy yields, p.328

9. Luxury villa in 5-star Bacolet Bay Resort and Spa, Grenada with potential for net yields of between 6.5% and 15% per annum, p.328

10. The Tatras mountain range bordering Slovakia and Poland enjoys both summer and winter seasons creating a prime investment climate, p.41

11. Look to the emerging ski resorts of the Tatras mountains to secure great capital appreciation and alpine standard skiing to rival European counterparts, p.153

12. Olympic residence, bordering the embassy and shopping districts in Ulaan Baator, Mongolia. Luxury apartment will meet high demand from business professioanls, p.239

13. Tobago is a Carribbean hotspot. Its sister island Trinidad is the world's largest supplier of ammonia and methanol, providing 70% of the USA's liquified natural gas requiremnt, p.326

14. Interior of a penthouse at Zablocie Mill in Krakow, Poland, where 90% LTV mortgages are available, p.153

15. The spectacular sprawling landscape in Argentina's Cordoba province where capital appreciation and rental yields are high, p.232

16. The sought after town of El Gouna, Egypt, is popular with wealthy Egyptians and discerning international visitors. Demand here is high and guaranteed yields are offered on high-end resort properties, p.267

17. The Petronas Towers in Kuala Lumpur city centre where capital appreciation is just over double that of the rest of the country, p.299

18. Tranquil jungle retreats at the heart of the rainforest in Belize. Half acre land plots are available from £25,000, p.305

19. Village clusters characteristic of the Philippines, where well chosen properties can secure high returns, p241

20. Oil refinery on the Canadian oil sands – prime investemtn territory where house prices have risen 114% over the last five years, p.315

Krakow

Krakow attracts interest because of its place on the UNESCO world heritage list and status as a favourite weekend break and inter-rail destination. Tipped as a property hotspot for 2007, it did not disappoint. Whilst unsustainable capital gains of 100% were achieved in 2006, prices have now levelled out somewhat and 2008, although considerably less dramatic, should still see good growth.

Unlike the cold, lifeless ex-communist city that Krakow may conjure up in one's head it is in fact beautiful, with Europe's largest medieval square, 200 million works of art and modern Polish culture mixing with old traditional architecture. The city is split into two districts and Kazimierz, the old Jewish quarter, is predicted to become popular thanks to its bohemian feel. Prices for one-bedroom apartments start at £70,000. Although specialists are of the opinion that prices will now remain level, the city is likely to remain popular with technology companies and students, creating a young, qualified working population.

Gdansk

Prices in Gdansk are currently some of the lowest in Poland because the property market is in its infancy, meaning there is huge potential for growth. As a result, interest in the area from investors has been overwhelming. Centrally located apartments are available between €690–€875 per square metre. Alongside the low prices, the city also offers some of the highest rental yields. With large government and municipal expenditure developing the Tri-City rail and road networks, the Special Economic Zone of Sopot to attract business, and the very high level of education, Gdansk should continue to attract multinational companies and pose as a strong investment hub in the future. The large student population in Gdansk means rental demand is continuously high and investing in buy to let is a growing market.

Zakopane

Located in southern Poland against the Tatras Mountains, Zakopane is Poland's premier ski resort attracting two and a half million visitors a year. With good access to Poprad airport across the Slovakian border and the proposal for a new motorway intersection linking Zakopane and Krakow airport, transfer times should soon be reduced to only an hour. Budget flights now fly into both Poprad and Krakow Airports from the UK meaning flight costs are pleasingly low. Thanks to the area's varied leisure activities, Zakopane caters for both the summer and winter tourist seasons giving a rental window of around eight months each year. Holiday homes in Zakopane are currently most popular amongst the Polish, meaning the value of property has remained steady and affordable. One-bedroom apartments in the Zakopane resort are available from £45,000 + VAT (7% of property value) and two-bed apartments from £50,000. Outside the resort, new developments are being sold for £77,000 with estimated rental yields of 5%. Yields in the resort are between 7% and 9%.

Lodz

Lodz, set against the stunning Sulejowskie and Jeziorsko lakes is the fastest growing second-tier city in Poland, experiencing 4.1% growth per month. With good transport links and a growing economy, the city is a regenerating manufacturing base offering attractive property investments. Capital appreciation was expected to be between 25%–50% in 2007 whilst GDP growth reached 6.5%. During the first four months of 2007 property prices in Lodz rose by 16% but are still low by regional comparison. One-bedroom apartments are available at £10,000 to £15,000 less than Warsaw prices. Loft-style apartments in renovated warehouses have been particularly popular amongst foreign investors costing approximately £35,000 for a one-bed in a good area. Buy to let is not yet a largely profitable sector but has the potential to develop thanks to the growing number of people moving to Lodz to work as well as the large student community. As a result, rental yields of between 8%–9% are reportedly achievable. Lodz has also been ranked 7th out of the sixteen most attractive provinces in which to invest, with an absorbent market and low labour costs.

Katowice

Known as 'Poland's sleeping giant', Katowice, although a wealthy mining city, has property prices significantly lower than similar industrial cities such as Lodz. With three million permanent residents, Katowice is the most urban and industrial city in Poland. It has an impressive infrastructure and a large and dynamic workforce creating a thirst for quality residential property. The current quality of housing is poor and housing stock is ageing, meaning the demand for new modern apartments is high, not least because of the high purchasing power of young residents working for large companies in the area. Recent price rises may indicate the start of a trend.

Buyer's guide

Since joining the EU in 2004 foreigners have been able to purchase Polish property with minimal restrictions providing they have a permit from the Minister of Internal Affairs and Administration. (Source: http://www.mswia.gov.pl/index_a.html)

The most common property rights in Poland are the *Perpetual Usufructs*. Under this system, land is owned by the State Treasury or by local authorities. The rights over the land are similar to ownership although there is a limited duration (typically 99 years) and an obligation to pay an annual fee whilst the perpetual usufructuary automatically becomes the owner of any building constructed on the land. Easement, lease and tenancy property rights are also available in Poland.

(Source: Gide Loyrette Nouel, *The International Comparative Legal Guide to Real Estate 2008: Poland*, available at www.iclg.co.uk)

Mortgages

LTV %	TERM	CURRENCIES	RATES %	STATUS	SPECIAL CONDITIONS
100	40	EUR, PLN, CHF, USD, GBP	5	Employed or self-employed	

Key risks

Poland has experienced difficulties in the past with unscrupulous developers although this tends to be in areas where development is something new. Developers selling in mature markets such as Warsaw or Krakow should be able to recommend previous successful projects and contracts to safeguard against this risk. Sadly it is the less mature markets such as Szczecin, Bialystok, Bydgoszcz, Gliwice, Rzeszow or Lublin that offer the best returns but an equally higher risk. These areas will see considerably higher growth rates as their economies explode, although there will also be less support for the foreign investor and more uncertainty in the area. Those buying property for renovation need to bear in mind that the majority of skilled Polish labourers have relocated to countries offering higher wages, meaning support in this sector will be limited and consequently costly.

Rating: ⚠ ⚠ ⚠

Key opportunities

In general terms, Poland is still a good investment destination with relatively low-cost entry, the potential for medium-term growth in most cities and higher growth from suburbs and third-tier cities. Showing consistently healthy increases in property prices and economic structure over the last few years it is regarded as one of the EU's most successful entrants and has a strong economic future ahead.

Rating: $$$$

Portugal

Currency: Euro

Exchange rates:
100 Euro = £79
£1 = 1.3 Euro

100 Euro = US $157
US $1 = 0.64 Euro

LISBON

Introduction

Portugal's history is characterised by intrepid explorers, its culture is flamboyant and artistic and its geography is richly diverse with lush mountains and popular coastal outcrops. Seafaring habitants and natural explorers in the 15th and 16th centuries promoted Portugal to a world power with the discovery and seizure of a sizeable empire including colonies in South America, Africa and Asia. Modern day Portugal still contains reminders of times gone by, embracing a deep-rooted mix of vibrant origins and ancient civilisations. It is also the elite haunt of some of the world's most exclusive golf courses and attracts enthusiasts from around the world.

As one of the warmest European countries with beautiful countryside, quintessential coastlines, elegant cities, Oriental architecture and a Mediterranean ambience, Portugal has become one of the world's most popular tourist and second-home destinations. It is now classed as the third most popular second-home destination in the world with its most famous Algarve region rated as the number one destination for investment according to Channel 4's *A Place in the Sun*.

Indeed, the Algarve is one of Portugal's success stories and is one of the country's most affluent areas catering for the more elite visitor. It is especially favoured amongst golf enthusiasts and British investors who have already laid claim to 50,000 properties along the region's coast. Having said that, northern Portugal should not be overlooked. It has coastal regions of equal merit and an increasing number of high-quality golf developments under way to rival the existing array in the south. For wine lovers, the Duoro Valley and city of Porto are well worth a visit, famous for their exports of Port and Vinho Verde.

'As one of the earliest investors in golf tourism, Portugal now boasts some of the finest mature courses in the world and is recognised as a prime golfing region. Demand for properties close to golf courses then is understandably considerable'

Economically though, Portugal does not paint such a rosy picture. Since joining the EU in 1986, the country has struggled to meet the 3% average growth figures stipulated by the managing body, reporting only 1.3% GDP growth in 2007. Although 2008 growth is expected to reach 2.1%, this is still significantly below its neighbour Spain, who for the last decade has showed growth of over 3% per annum.

Tourism in this already popular destination is still increasing with 11% growth recorded in June 2007 and predictions that tourism will increase by 3% every year between now and 2017.

Indicative of the country's overall wealth is the progress and activity in its capital Lisbon. This city provides a snapshot of the general economy as a whole and is now showing signs of recovery after a long period of decline and neglect. Restoration work, new infrastructure, improved services and an expansion of its airport appear to signal that the city, and indeed on a larger scale the country, is on a positive upward trajectory.

Is this a good place to buy?

Following a spate of governments with minimal shelf lives, Portugal has recently gained a new-found stability and is functioning well as a democratic republic. The solid euro-based banking system, easy purchase process and EU-fuelled FDI increases make the prospect of investing in Portugal an appealing one. Add to this 10–15% price appreciation since the millennium and a high build quality and Portugal's investment potential speaks for itself.

According to *A Place in the Sun*, returns of up to 360% will be achievable from the Portuguese property market over the next 10 years. Whether this figure is likely or even achievable though remains to be seen, not least because property prices rose only 17% between 2001 and 2006. Of course, those willing to take a risk and invest in less developed areas can secure higher returns but at the same time risk significant losses.

Following political and economic upheaval over the past few years, Portugal is now seen very much as one of the more stable and established EU countries. Developers are taking care to ensure that the country's natural landscape is not spoilt by overdevelopment and strong buy-to-let markets in smaller less developed areas are defining themselves as investment hotspots. With reasonable entry level prices, it is no surprise that people continually look to Portugal to invest. An estimated 38,000 UK residents currently live in Portugal, with a further 11,000 owning holiday homes there.

As one of the earliest investors in golf tourism, Portugal now boasts some of the finest mature courses in the world and is recognised as a prime golfing region. Demand for properties close to golf courses then is understandably considerable.

Which type of property should you go for?

The obvious choice for the best short-term rentals and capital appreciation is golf property and the area between Lagos and Tavira on the Algarve is particularly suited to this kind of investment. Investors should know though, that due to their guaranteed desirability, golf properties can come with up to a 50% higher price tag.

Newly developed properties on the outskirts of cities are often better equipped with amenities such as gardens and swimming pools, than original apartments – a key concern for investors looking to meet tourist needs. Those thinking of purchasing a more authentic rural property meanwhile and wanting the chance to restore an older building, need to be prepared to finance it themselves. Most banks will not lend money for rural retreats, instead preferring to lend in the bigger cities where mortgages are easier to secure. Anyone considering buy-to-let purchases should be aware that net rental income is taxed at the 25% main corporate income tax rate plus a local surtax usually in the region of 1.5%. (Source: Price Waterhouse Coopers Going Global Report 2007.)

Hotspots

The Algarve remains popular with returning tourists and golf enthusiasts, and while long-term appreciation is guaranteed here, however, areas along the less-trodden path have been highlighted for investment potential, meaning investors must be willing to take the risk in these less developed areas to see better returns on their money.

Algarve

Mention investment in the Algarve, moreover Portugal, and one of the first things that springs to mind are sprawling white villas serviced by deep-blue pools and picture perfect views. Indeed, true to its renowned reputation, the Algarve is the country's most popular region and one which exerts timeless appeal over second-home buyers, particularly those with a penchant for golf. Almost 50% of Portugal's golf courses are in this region, meaning it generates a lot of inward investment. The Algarve is also blessed with international marinas, 150km of sandy coastline and 280 days of sunshine a year. Inevitably prices have always been on the up and are continuing to rise thanks to increased demand from golfing and sun-seeking tourists. It is also one of Portugal's most profitable regions as far as investors are concerned engendering price appreciation of 10% in recent years.

Happily there is also a good range of property available so buyers won't be disappointed. Whether they are looking for a small functional studio or a sizable beach villa, they will be presented with a broad choice. Average property prices in the Algarve vary dramatically depending on the resort and the proximity to golf courses or the beach. Entry prices for apartments start from €150,000 and can top €600,000 for high-end luxury finishes. Central areas of the Algarve around Albufeira, Vilamoura and Faro are those that have witnessed the heaviest development as far as tourism and property are concerned but have still managed to maintain their original charm and continue to attract high volumes of tourists year on year. Here prices will be higher but those looking for slightly lower-cost entry should look to the east where prices are 30% cheaper.

Demand is currently in line with supply throughout the region, making the Algarve a good bet as far as investors are concerned. What is more, a collection of svelte new golf resorts coming to the market over the next few months are expected to generate at least double figure yields. The beauty of purchasing here is that local authorities have enforced stringent regulations in order to protect the beauty of the landscape, particularly near the beach. Building within 500m of the beachfront is now prohibited, as are buildings of more than four stories. With intelligent protection methods in place, and prices still lower than France and Spain, the Algarve then has a lot to offer.

Vale Do Lobo

Situated at the heart of the Algarve and often dubbed Europe's finest golf and beach resort, Vale Do Lobo is highlighted as a prime area for property investment. Just 20 minutes from Faro International Airport, this resort is centred around leisure and luxury and, with direct flights from other major European cities less than three hours away, it is extremely accessible. There is an array of accommodation to suit all holiday makers, from sports enthusiasts and spa lovers to sun worshippers, with simple apartments at the lowest end of the range to luxury villas with private pool and garden.

Lisbon

Portugal's capital city, Lisbon is home to 20 centuries worth of history, a great climate, easy accessibility to the coast and is fast becoming a very popular tourist city break destination. With a number of low-budget airlines opening up the city's accessibility from across Europe, in particular the UK, and an improving infrastructure, the city is simultaneously becoming a property hotspot. EU funding has concentrated on strengthening the city as a tourist attraction over the last few years, with improvements to buildings and plans in the pipeline for a high speed rail link to Madrid. As a UN World Heritage Site, high-rise buildings cannot be built, meaning the medieval beauty of the city will be preserved.

Apartments are mostly old and in need of restoration, offering charming original features. Having said that, new-build stand-alone properties on the outskirts of the city are also becoming increasingly popular with buyers. Prices are more affordable here than other parts of Western Europe as appreciation has not risen much above inflation, meaning excellent value for money can be found. Investors can expect to pay £2,000– £2,400 per square metre in the best areas of the city and as little as £1,300 in some suburbs. Rental income is estimated at £50–£70 per night for character properties and prices are expected to grow in line with the ongoing improvements to the city. As such, long-term investment in Lisbon is a very good option.

The Lisbon Coast embargo

Within 30 minutes of Lisbon are the coastal magnets of Cascais and Estoril, popular with those who live in Lisbon as a weekend retreat and with those who choose to live there and commute into the city. In general, these resorts have a sophisticated reputation and property (and its prices) reflects this, with apartments hard to find for less than €150,000.

Silver Coast

This is an area that has been earmarked by experts as somewhere with great potential. Property here is considerably cheaper than the Algarve but no less desirable, surrounded by quaint fishing villages, lush countryside and interesting historical sites. The Silver Coast is viewed as the prime up-and-coming area of Portugal and one generating much interest and popularity with tourists and investors alike.

Development is on the increase and several large residential and golf complexes, such as Praia d'el Rey and Bom Successo have already opened.

A plot of land can be bought for €12,500 and a farm or country house in need of restoration can cost as little as €40,000. **Coimbra**, the ancient capital and home to one of the oldest universities, and **Nazare**, a popular fishing village, are two of the coast's most desirable locations.

Costa Verde

This is an area receiving increased interest from British buyers. Prices here are the cheapest in the country at £30,000 for a farmhouse in need of renovation. Apartments on the coast can be obtained for similar prices.

The Alentejo

Dubbed the 'new Tuscany', Alentejo has a rich cultural heritage, deliciously rustic food and beautiful scenery that splits between a dramatic coastline and rolling countryside dotted with vineyards and olive groves, Alentejo ticks all the Tuscan boxes while remaining appealingly undeveloped. Although covering a third of the whole of Portugal, it is only home to 5% of the country's population.

Investors should keep a shrewd eye on this area where prices have remained stagnant for the last 10 years. Again you can get a lot more for your money here than you can on the Algarve. Average apartments cost from £60,000 whilst houses are generally available from £100,000. The market though is becoming increasingly competitive as overseas buyers strive to buy before the price 'boom'. As two airports near Alentejo have recently gained international licenses and will operate daily flights from the UK the area will become extremely accessible which will push prices up and up.

The most northerly province untouched by the property boom, Minho is unspoilt by mass tourism. Good returns can be expected over the next few years with starting prices for rustic traditional properties at £40,000.

Buyer's guide

Non-residents, both individuals and corporations can purchase real estate in Portugal without restriction although in rural areas rights are somewhat more limited.

Mortgages

LTV %	TERM	CURRENCIES	RATES %	STATUS	SPECIAL CONDITIONS
80	30	EUR	5.56	Employed or self-employed	

Europe

PORTUGAL

Key risks

The one thing to be aware of in Portugal is subrogation. In short, property debts including mortgage payments, local taxes and community charges stay with a property when it is sold and are inherited by the buyer. Ensuring that a property is free of debts therefore (usually by obtaining a certificate from the local Land Registry) is an absolute must for anyone purchasing in the country.

Those specifically looking for investment gains will need to make sure that they choose their property carefully, ensuring that they purchase in a place supported by real fundamentals of demand. Otherwise they may like to look to more emerging countries.

Rating: ⚠

Key opportunities

Although not the most exotic of destinations, Portugal has a very appealing climate and a decidedly more exciting investment potential than its closest rivals, i.e. the likes of Spain and Italy. The strong buy-to-let market and international banks that are well established throughout the country make it easy for foreigners to buy property. Low crime levels, low terrorism risk alongside the country's natural charm, beauty, hospitable people, delicious cuisine, laid-back lifestyle and excellent quality of life confirm why increasing numbers are investing on its sunny shores.

Occupying an important position within Europe the country is generally well regarded, has a growing tourism industry and, despite occasional downward blips, offers relatively secure investment opportunities. Capital appreciation is not as spectacular as in other countries but if it continues to grow in line with the tourism and development sectors, investment here should be profitable.

Rating: $$$

Romania

Currency: Romania New Lei

Exchange rates:
100 New Lei = £22
£1 = 5 New Lei

100 New Lei = US $43
US $1 = 2.45 New Lei

BUCHAREST

Introduction

With fairytale castles, majestic mountains, seaside resorts, traditional villages and cities full of architecture, Romania has been said to be where the Czech Republic was around a decade ago in terms of its tourism status. Lying in south-eastern Europe, the country is bordered by Ukraine, Moldova, Bulgaria, Hungary, Serbia, Montenegro and the Black Sea and is therefore ideally placed for trading with its Eastern European neighbours.

Despite worries that Romania was not financially or socially ready to join the EU it became a member in January 2007 having met a number of stringent targets for improvement. It is generally acknowledged that the country still has a long way to go but it is hoped that improvements in infrastructure, increased commercial investment and growth of the tourism and property markets will help to bring greater stability to the country.

Romania's GDP increased 51% between 2002 and 2006 and was maintained at a healthy 6% in 2007. Meanwhile, the country's skilled and numerate young workforce has cornered the software industry, drawing in multinationals such as Microsoft, Alcatel and Hewlett-Packard, especially to the north of the country. Many more traditional manufacturers have also moved into Romania, including Wrigleys, Nestlé and Renault, with Nokia and Ford both planning to open operations in 2008. This influx of multinational companies is partly to take advantage of new markets and also to benefit from the large, well-educated and skilled workforce and their low wages.

> **'Romania is a country offering low-cost entry into a property market ripe with the potential for high rewards and good long-term capital growth'**

In the Ernst and Young Southeast Europe Attractiveness Survey 2008, Romania ranked the highest in terms of attracting investor interest whilst a recent survey of private and institutional investors in the region conducted by the Centre for European Economic Research (ZEW) again named Romania as the most 'attractive' investment destination. Of those polled 37% believed Romania to be the most important investment destination heading into 2009.

Is this a good place to buy?

With a growing economy, high levels of inward investment and receiving the highest levels of EU structural funds (€30bn by 2013), Romania should have a stable future ahead of it. According to the Romanian finance minister, GDP per capita increased 63% between 2004 and 2007 to €4,240, which is indicative of the increasing wealth and productivity of locals. As domestic wealth increases so does purchasing power, meaning the Romanian property market is experiencing increased demand from within the bounds of its own country.

Research conducted by PMR focuses on a national shortage of over one million properties. It claims that the residential construction output in 2007 increased 20% and neared 46,000 and expects it to continue to rise to 50,000 per year by 2010. Questions remain as to whether or not this will be enough to alleviate the current housing deficit – good news as far as investors are concerned. Further, with price appreciation expected to be between 20–25% for 2008 (according to Anglo-Romanian Development ARD), prospects within the Romanian investment market look very strong.

Infrastructure improvements are currently being prioritised, with the Romanian government hoping to implement 1,800km of new motorways as well as the construction of a second bridge over the Danube planned for completion 2010. This will vastly improve the Pan-European Transport Corridor and make the country considerably more accessible. Further aiding accessibility has been the recent announcement of new low-cost flights into the country. Both Easyjet and Ryanair now fly into Romania from as little as £29.99, boosting the country's tourism market.

As far as property investment is concerned, Romania is fast ascending the popularity polls. According to a survey conducted on www.movechannel.com, enquiries into Romanian real estate rose in April 2008 positioning the country as the 16th most searched in the world. Forecasts as to the market's potential in 2008 are very positive with the National Union of Notaries Public Romania (UNNPR) estimating that €23bn worth of residential property transactions will take place.

Property can still be found at prices significantly lower than in other European counterparts and with expected price gains in the region of 20%, the potential for capital appreciation in Romania is a strong one. According to Anglo-Romanian Development, the average property price increased 40% in 2007 thanks to increasing local wealth. If market analysts Mercer are accurate in their projections that wages will rise at 11.5% in 2008 (the highest rate in Europe and 4th highest in the world) then demand from the increasingly wealthy locals is likely to be maintained. Moreover, with the government expecting that average salaries will increase by 75% by 2013, this demand is likely to continue over the long term. (Source: www.homesoverseas.co.uk)

'Those looking for cheaper property outside of the city centre may want to investigate the suburbs and outskirts of Bucharest which offer low cost entry with the potential for substantial long-term returns as the city expands'

On average, prices for standard new-build properties start from around £45,000, for luxury city apartments £60,000 whilst more rural country properties are available from around £25,000. (Source: www.channel4homes.com)

Low rates of personal and corporate tax and favourable taxation on new-build property as well as a low cost of living are just some of the incentives enticing investors to buy in Romania although they should be aware of the astromonical inflation levels. The National Bank of Romania had to raise interest rates to 9% in February 2008 in a bid to combat the 6.6% inflation recorded in 2007.

Which type of property should you go for?

Romania has a strong ownership-centred culture, meaning that the property market is very well suited to capital growth. Having said that, the increase in multinational companies moving into major cities means that the expatriate community is developing and creating a need for rented accommodation. The country's rapidly developing tourism industry also means that demand for short- term holiday accommodation is likely to increase over the coming months, again creating opportunities for buy-to-let investments. Investors need to be aware though that the very short summer season means their property may lie vacant for as many as eight months a year. Opting for property close to other winter attractions will therefore be essential if occupancy and rental yields are to be maximised.

Foreign investment in Romania tends to centre around dwellings and business property as non-resident foreigners can only buy land by forming a Romanian registered company – a restriction that is due to be reviewed by 2013.

There is a range of property on offer throughout the country from swish capital city apartments, to rural *conac* cottages, to chalets in up-and-coming ski resorts as well as property along the Black Sea Coast. Apartments in Bucharest range from £56,000 to £336,000 depending on their location and finish whilst a large detached villa just 150m from the beach can be bought for £307,000. Ski apartments near up-and-coming resorts can be bought for as little as £44,500.

Hotspots

Bucharest

The capital of Romania holds the nickname 'Little Paris', thanks to its wide, tree-lined streets and imposing architecture. However, the Communist era has left its mark in many areas, especially the central district, much of which was razed and rebuilt by former dictator Ceaucescu. The city is an interesting mix of French-style Belle Epoque buildings, traditional Romanian architecture, Communist-era Neo-classicism and faceless Soviet-style blocks.

Prices in the city have risen between 20% and 30% over the last few years and experts are optimistic that growth should continue. As such, the city is becoming comparable in terms of price with other areas of Europe though it still remains one of the cheaper capital cities.

According to www.emergingrealestate.com there is a need for 200,000 extra homes within the city to cater, in particular, for the emerging middle classes, a statement confirmed by DTZ who comment on limited supply in the luxury market segment. As such, high-end projects aimed at the wealthier buyer can cost from £165,000 and top £236,000 for apartments in the most sought-after areas, whilst those in less desirable suburbs cost from £39,000. Net yields of 5% can be achieved for properties in well-located areas.

Iasi

Lasi is Romania's second largest city with around 800,000 citizens. Predominantly an industrial and student city it is also the fastest growing region to accede to the EU since 2004. Local GDP growth stands at around 8.5%. Home to the largest EU funding commitment in Romania, Iasi boasts a €250m mixed-use development project behind the city's palace, including residential, recreational (water-sports etc), office and cultural (exhibition, theatre etc) zones. With 130,000 households (mostly old communist buildings) and a rapidly growing wealth, supply is wholly out of line with demand, meaning the housing market is heavily under-supplied. There is, therefore, a huge squeeze on medium and high-grade real estate, meaning capital values are rocketing. Yields for top-grade accommodation are in the region of 8% whilst capital appreciation can be in the region of 20%.

Those looking for cheaper property outside of the city centre may want to investigate the suburbs and outskirts of Bucharest which offer low-cost entry with the potential for substantial long-term returns as the city expands and properties in these areas become more integrated.

Timisoara

Known as Little Venice, this is one of Romania's richest cities, on the western border with Serbia and surrounded by the lovely countryside of the Banat region. Positioned on the European North-South superhighway, it is an excellent logistical hub and attracts a lot of commercial investment including big names such as Procter & Gamble and Nestlé. The town council and mayor have been working together in a bid to replace all infrastructures within the town including drains, electricity, telephone, road, railways, buses and trams, making Timisoara's future prospects very good ones.

The property market here is thriving with many residents moving away from city-centre apartments and seeking new villas in the suburbs and surrounding countryside. Rental rates, according to www.romanian-cc.com are very high at between 10%–20%. Prices in the region start from around £52,110 for a simple apartment but can reach £440,935 for a six-bed villa with a pool. (Source: www.properazzi.com)

INSIDER TIP

Hotly tipped as the next big investment location, Arad benefits from a free trade-zone just west of the city where there are no import taxes and profit is only taxed at 5%. As a result the area is attracting heavy industry and businesses. Situated on the proposed new Bucharest-Budapest route it is well placed for trade links and prices start at around £54,800 for a one-bed apartment.

Transylvania

The central region of **Transylvania** is forever associated with the myth of Count Dracula and pulls in substantial tourism as a result. It is also a rural paradise of forests, fairytale castles and the Carpathian mountains. Cities worth considering for investment include, **Cluj-Napoca**, a populous and thriving hub for many corporations. There are also good transport connections including an airport scheduled for expansion and the new motorway connections with Bucharest and the Black Sea. A large student population may make it a good buy-to-let option whilst the potential for capital appreciation is also strong. Entry prices for a high-quality apartment in Western Cluj are £42,800 whilst off-plan apartments near to Bran with views over Dracula's castle can sell for as much as £205,700. **Brasov** in southern Transylvania has good commercial links and a large university. Property here consists of new apartments in the slightly sprawling industrialised areas and contemporary and older-style family homes. Apartments in an off-plan development close to the centre are available from £33,000.

Sibiu

Sibiu, a beautiful and historic town, was the 2007 European Capital of Culture and has enjoyed increased media and tourism interest as a result. Substantial investment has gone into infrastructure and commercial investment. Property here is in short supply and therefore prices are on the rise although new apartments can still be found for around £32,800.

Ski resorts

Poiana Brasov, Predeal and **Sinaia** are Romania's main ski resorts and as such offer investment as well as second-home opportunities. With the potential for year-round rentals unlike on the coast, prices start from around £38,000 for new-build apartments and from £360 per square metre for luxurious log ski cabins. (Source: www.romaniareport.com)

Black Sea Coast resorts

The country's Black Sea Coast resorts are not as well known or developed as those of neighbouring Bulgaria and the short summer rental season of only four months each year has curtailed investment. Nevertheless, the towns of **Constanta, Costinesti** and **Mamaia** are busy with Eastern European tourists all summer and prices have been rising. Property is available from around £23,000 for new-build apartments whilst a seven-bedroom house close to the Black Sea is available for £92,000.

Buyer's guide

Foreigners are able to gain ownership rights for buildings without restriction in Romania although constraints are in place on ownership of land. If private EU individuals who do not live in Romania want to own land, they will need to set up a Romanian company. In this way, the current legal restrictions can be avoided as the company is viewed as being of Romanian nationality. EU citizens/ nationals resident in Romania can own land without restraint.

(Source: Pachiu & Associates, Attorneys at Law *The International Comparative Legal Guide to Real Estate 2008: Romania*, available at www.iclg.co.uk Anghel Stabb Law office, Romania, www.stabblaw.com)

Mortgages

LTV %	TERM	CURRENCIES	RATES %	STATUS	SPECIAL CONDITIONS
75	20	RON, EUR, CHF	6.95	Employed	

Key risks

There is an element of risk when dealing with any country that is finding its feet, so Romania may be too unpredictable an opportunity for the more cautious investor. Rocketing inflation levels and high interest rates need to be borne in mind although measures are in place to combat these problems. Perhaps then, the most important thing to remember when investing in Romania is to proceed with vigilance and care as much can change, legally, politically and economically. That said though, investors should not overlook Romania's very real potential.

Rating: ⚠

Key opportunities

With healthy GDP of around $264bn, enjoying increasing levels of FDI and as the largest recipient of EU structural funding, Romania is considered an upper- middle income economy. Unemployment in Romania was encouragingly low at 3.9% in September 2007 – a figure well below other middle-sized or large European countries and recent cuts in income tax to 16% mean consumer confidence and spending power have both increased.

As a culture, Romania is much more orientated towards ownership than renting and so investors would probably be best advised to concentrate on capital growth rather than rental yields. That said, well-chosen properties in popular industrial and university towns do have the potential for strong rental returns. In short, Romania is a country offering low-cost entry into a property market ripe with the potential for high rewards and good long-term capital growth.

Rating: $$$$

Slovakia

Currency: Koruna
Exchange rates:
1,000 Koruna = £26.08
£1 = 38.33 Koruna

1,000 Koruna = US $51.65
US$1= 20 Koruna

BRATISLAVA

Introduction

Peppered with a mixture of fortresses and castles, Gothic churches and 15th-century town squares, evidence of Slovakia's vibrant history is prominent. A previously understated tourism destination, the country has managed to stave off much of the rampant commercialism which has overtaken some of Western Europe, perhaps because of its Communist past. Peasant traditions and quaint farm practices are still prevalent in many rural villages and townships giving the country an authentic, original feel. With nine national parks and acres of untouched countryside as well as several castles, spas and picturesque lakes, Slovakia has a lot to offer as a tourist destination and is enjoying growing popularity.

Nestled in the very centre of Europe the republic is bordered by Austria, the Czech Republic, Poland and Hungary. It links the prosperous western countries with the new emerging markets and manufacturing wealth of Eastern Europe. Furthermore, Slovakia has more natural beauty than most of the markets which provide direct competition, and as advertising budgets become more generous, travel and tourism figures are increasing. Slovakia saw a 38.6% increase in UK tourists between 2006 and 2007, and the availability of cheap flights to and from Western European cities such as London, Paris, Berlin and Dublin mean tourism is expected to rise 5.3% in each year between 2008 and 2017. Flights are available from Britain to Slovakia with budget airlines such as Sky Europe offering return flights from £60.

For those who prefer skiing or mountain walking to overcrowded beaches or concreted resorts, Slovakia is the ideal place for a second home whilst also offering promising investment opportunities. Many of the purchasers who come here combine Slovakia's dual market strengths and often have a second home for personal use before looking for an investment property.

Is this a good place to buy?

The Slovak Republic enjoys rising prosperity and an ideal central European location and as such has great investment potential. Whilst joining the EU in 2004 did not necessarily help Slovakia to stabilise or ensure any immediate returns on investment, it did guarantee EU legal rights to all investors. Since May 2004, foreign nationals have no longer needed to establish a company to purchase a property, meaning the purchase process is straightforward.

Slovakia has one of the fastest growing economies in Europe and has out-performed all of its neighbouring countries over the last two years. GDP growth in real terms reached 8.8% in 2007, and growth is expected to continue at the same rate. As a result of such strong economic progression, the European Commission has recommended that Slovakia adopt the euro from 1 January 2009. A final decision will be made in July but if successful, it is expected that property prices will simultaneously rise.

'Demand for property in all areas of Slovakia is now booming and exceeding existing supply, meaning the property market is enjoying a period of great growth'

In 2004 Slovakia introduced a flat tax system, which has since been adopted across Central Europe. The government created a foreign investment boom by luring foreign investors and high-earning Europeans into the country with the temptation of new, low rates, including a flat tax of 19%. In April 2007, the National Bank of Slovakia cut the interest rate to 4.25% making the cost of borrowing cheaper with the hope of enticing more people to invest. As a result, property prices should be bolstered.

Although Slovakia has the second highest rate of unemployment in Europe after Poland, things are changing. Unemployment rates were very high in 2003 and 2004, with 18% unemployed; however, this had dropped to a much healthier 8.6% by 2007 and the situation is expected to continue to improve throughout 2008. What is more, thanks to the introduction of the government scheme 'Tourism Development Strategy' which will run until 2013, increased tourist visitor arrivals should be fostered.

Which type of property should you go for?

The current shortage of properties and significant domestic demand will continue to push property prices up – especially new flats built in popular residential areas. Strategically placed new-build developments are therefore likely to offer the best investment opportunities and should avoid problems with title. The quality of build on new homes is also likely to be of a more reliable quality than older properties.

Within Bratislava, attractive older properties are likely to sell at a premium, but may also be subject to problems with property title and planning permission for those who want to renovate. Although an older home may exude greater aesthetic charm, renovation might not be worth the time and effort. Investors should also remember that winters in Slovakia can be severe, with temperatures dropping as low as –20°C meaning reliable heating systems in older properties, although costly, are essential.

Hotspots
Bratislava
Bratislava is one of the most popular places to invest in Slovakia and, as the country's capital, attracts a constant stream of tourists. Downtown Bratislava has been tipped as the best place to buy, thanks to local government efforts to install a beautification programme. When the new highway between Bratislava and Vienna is built, living in and around Bratislava will become even more desirable as commutes between each city will be reduced to 45 minutes. Yields in central Bratislava are currently at around 6% whilst a central three-bedroom apartment costs from around €293,984.

Tatras
Although it is a beautiful capital with extensive investment opportunities, Bratislava is not the only place to buy. The high Tatras are one of the most attractive high mountain ranges in Europe, offering the only truly alpine standard skiing in Eastern Europe. Enjoying both winter skiing and mountain summers, the Tatras provide year-round appeal. Investors, however, must be prepared to suffer slow transport links especially if their property is in the depths of the countryside.

INSIDER TIP With a significant portion of the Slovakian property market aimed at the younger generation, another place to consider which is more affordable is Trnava. Just 20 minutes' drive from Bratislava, this university town has cheap property prices where one-bed apartments can be bought for €42,000 and rental yields of 8% achieved.

Poprad

Another good place to consider is Poprad, Slovakia's luxury holiday resort overlooked by the Tatras Mountains. With an international airport, good quality amenities and surrounded by stunning countryside, Poprad's property prices should rise in the near future. A studio apartment in a fully furnished golf, ski and spa resort is available from €55,000.

Liptov

Liptov is a final area worthy of consideration. A resort between the High and Low Tatras, the area has a reputation for being both beautiful and affordable.

Buyer's guide

Aside from agricultural and forestry land, foreign investors can acquire ownership rights to real estate. For Slovak companies meanwhile, even if they are owned from abroad, there are no restrictions at all.

(Source: Konecna and Safar, *The International Comparative Legal Guide to Real Estate 2008: Argentina,* available at www.iclg.co.uk)

Mortgages

LTV %	TERM	CURRENCIES	RATES %	STATUS	SPECIAL CONDITIONS
80	30	SKK	4.94	Employed or self-employed	

Key risks

Despite Slovakia's record of high returns and its sustained period of growth, it is always worth taking fundamental precautions. The main risks in Slovakia relate to title and a lack of transparency in local property prices. Buyers should employ a good lawyer and ensure that they research the area well to make sure that they are paying a fair price. Buyers should ask to see ownership papers, and check that the property is registered under this name at the land registry. Your solicitor should also make a search to determine whether there are any unpaid taxes or other charges. Older properties may have problems with title and it is important to confirm that the house is correctly zoned and that any alterations have planning permission.

As Slovakia is getting richer, there is some confusion about the 'right price' for property. Sellers may quote prices widely divergent from those that a house or apartment would fetch on the local market. A good way to check whether you are being quoted an unreal price is to visit internet expatriate forums and ask people with local knowledge. There is a particularly good forum for Slovakia run by a local English language paper which can be found at www.slovakspectator.sk.

Rating: ⚠ ⚠ ⚠

Key opportunities

The Slovakian economy is renowned for providing high rewards at low risk and is the best emerging market in terms of its location in Europe. Demand for property in all areas of Slovakia is now booming and exceeding existing supply, meaning the property market is enjoying a period of great growth. New development, especially in the ski areas should continue to attract local and international investors as well as ski enthusiasts. Investors who purchase now, are buying into a market with a period of prolonged expansion ahead of it, and as such are more then likely to receive worthwhile rewards.

Rating: $$$

Slovenia

Currency: Euro
Exchange Rates:
100 Euro = £79.00
£1 = 1.3 Euro

100 Euro = US $157
US $1 = 0.64 Euro

LJUBLJANA

Introduction

An Alpine coastal country in southern central Europe, Slovenia is renowned for its unspoiled countryside, beautiful lakes and snow-capped mountains that cover 30% of the country. Contained in a space smaller than Wales, all these natural attractions are within easy reach of each other. Occupying an excellent location, bordered by the successful and established countries of Hungary, Italy, Austria and Croatia, Slovenia is in a position to flourish. For those who enjoy outdoor pursuits, Slovenia has a lot to offer: from hiking, skiing and snow board-ing, to riding, climbing, golfing or simply strolling in the midst of awe-inspiring scenery. It also boasts 46km of Adriatic coastline, bordering the popular Istrian peninsula that the country shares with Croatia.

Slovenia joined the EU in May 2004 and the Eurozone in January 2007 and is a popular investment location with British, Irish and other northern Europeans. The country's economic growth may have been slower than other emerging mar-kets but it has the highest GDP per capita in Central Europe and was the first of the 2004 entrants to adopt the euro. GDP growth was a steady 5.8% in 2007 up from 2006's 5.2% and in 2007, the interest rate was 5.6%. The workforce is gen-erally well-educated and unemployment is currently lower than it has been in the past, at 4.6% in 2007. An educated and expanding workforce combined with higher wages should therefore broaden Slovenia's property market in the future.

The country also has excellent infrastructure and improving international connections including a new motorway link between Llubljana and the Austrian border. Budget airlines such as Easy Jet and Whizz Air fly regularly from the UK into the capital Ljubljana and the flight time from London is just two hours.

Europe

SLOVENIA

Tourism is Slovenia's fastest growing industry welcoming 1.2 million foreign tourists a year and travel and tourism activity as a whole is expected to grow by 3.9% per annum between 2008 and 2017.

Is this a good place to buy?

Slovenia, in investment terms, is seen predominantly as a country offering good potential for further growth while still remaining unspoiled by mass tourism and development. With diverse scenery stretching from the snow-capped Julian Alps, to the beautiful Lake Bled and the sliver of Adriatic coastline, Slovenia enjoys an expanding property market, driven by foreign investors, rising local employment and wage increases.

Reforms in taxes and the business sector have paved the way for increased overseas investment into the country, particularly from Western European buyers; however, investment levels are still low in comparison to other leading European destinations. House prices have risen substantially since EU entry in 2004 and are expected to increase a further 280% by 2018.

INSIDER TIP

Most Slovenian property purchases from overseas buyers are for second or holiday homes rather than for pure buy-to-let investment. However, investors should be aware that there are growing opportunities in the buy-to-let sector as tourism expands. Average rents in the popular areas of Kranjska Gora and Lake Bled are between £400 and £700 per week depending on the quality and size of the property and season. An increase in tourist numbers offers opportunities for buy to let and entices visitors who may wish to own after holidaying there.

The buying process is uncomplicated, relatively fast, and since EU accession, legislation allowing foreign property ownership has been introduced. Having said this, though private purchase is legal, the government has created a loophole allowing it to restrict property sales to foreigners for up to seven years if deemed necessary.

'Slovenia offers strong opportunities for investment in an emerging market with the best GDP per capita and economic growth of all of the other transitioning economies of Central Europe'

Much of the industrial sector is still state-owned leaving a workforce that remains resistant to change and businesses that are uncompetitive in a global market place. The current government has pledged to work towards lower taxes and the privatisation of state-operated industries in order to get the economy moving faster, although this current situation may hinder to some extent the success of the property market.

Which type of property should you go for?

Available property consists of idyllic mountain lodges, rural farmhouses and cottages ripe for renovation. Many of these properties, although cheap, may well be isolated or in poor condition so investors will incur transportation and renovation costs on top of the original purchase price.

Holiday homes and buy-to-let purchases can also be found in ski resorts and major cities and with tourist numbers increasing, these are the types of property which will be worth investing in. Cities such as the capital, Ljubljana, offer the potential to rent to students and young professionals, with yields of around 6%. On a more negative note though it should be remembered that rental income tax is high and owners will be forced to pay 25% tax on 75% of their rental income.

Hotspots

The Julian Alps and ski resorts

The Julian Alps in the north-west of the country attract winter sports enthusiasts but also enjoy good summer trade from the likes of walkers, riders and cyclists. Popular tourist haunts also include the Triglav National Park, an area of outstanding beauty dominated by Mount Triglav. **Kranjska Gora** and **Bovec** are the two best-known ski resorts in the region designed mainly in an Alpine style offering a range of skiing at all levels. At over 1,700m, Bovec has a long season marred only by the fact that it is in an earthquake zone. Small houses here are available from around €89,000. Renovated Gorenjska style buildings in a mountain village 15 minutes from Kranjska Gora with access to ski slopes are available from €103,000.

Lake Bled and Lake Bohinj

Lake Bled and Lake Bohinj are also favourite spots with holidaymakers, golfers and second-home owners. Smaller apartments start at just £52,123. The island of Bled with its famous church is one of the country's most recognisable landmarks. As well as a location for waterside holidays, the resort offers direct access via chairlift to the ski area of Straza. Property in traditional, family-sized chalets is pricey and averages around £250,000. One and two-bedroom apartments cost around £139,000.

Maribor

Maribor is a key hotspot for investors. Slovenia's second city, it also offers a gateway to the Prekmurje, the wine-growing region and the Mariborsko Pohorje mountain range. Ryanair started a service to Maribor in June 2007 opening up the region to further investment and tourism. The area includes famous thermal spas and the Goricko Regional Park and is undergoing a programme of development. A new motorway will increase access from Ljubliana. Property here is still relatively affordable with rustic cottages and new-build apartments available from around £30,000 to £142,000.

Piran

Piran, on the beautiful and popular Istrian peninsula has Venetian roots, pretty beaches and an outdoor café culture. Nearby Koper and Potoroz are also of interest. Expect to pay around £40,600 to £54,100 for a traditional house inland, with larger and newer properties priced between £70,550 and £138,000.

Ljubljana

Ljubljana is Slovenia's historic capital city with many beautiful baroque, art nouveau and contemporary buildings. It also boasts a young population and cosmopolitan atmosphere. Approximately 15% of the country's population live here and the university brings in a large student population. Young professionals and students offer good opportunities for long-term rental prospects. The most sought-after properties are the attractive character apartments in the city centre and, as a result, they tend to be highly priced with current average costs of £1,700 per square metre. Prices over a million euros aren't unknown. More affordable new-build developments and small houses can be found in the outer suburbs, where one-bedroom apartments are available from £120,000.

Buyer's guide

Citizens of the EU member states can buy property in Slovenia under the same condition as nationals. Further, providing reciprocity is secured, nationals from EU candidate countries can also purchase real estate in the country .

(Source: Schoenherr Attorneys at Law, *The International Comparative Legal Guide to Real Estate 2008: Argentina,* available at www.iclg.co.uk)

Mortgages

LTV %	TERM	CURRENCIES	RATES %	STATUS	SPECIAL CONDITIONS
70	25	EUR	Variable 12 month Euribor + 2.75	Employed or self-employed	Minimum loan Euro 40,000

Key risks

Currently FDI in Slovenia is one of the lowest in Europe on a per capita basis, although there are hopes that this will improve in a spiral of investment as new opportunities emerge and new business and infrastructure projects are planned.

Disadvantages in investing in Slovenian property include the high tax on rental income and the potential risk of the government restricting foreign purchase; there is a loophole enabling them to restrict foreign purchase for up to seven years.

Rating: ⚠ ⚠

Key opportunities

Slovenia provides the great combination of a strong post-transitional economy and a new market with good potential. Entry prices are still quite low and tourist numbers and foreign investment are set to increase. As a result, a market has been created where investment in a holiday home or buy to let property is an attractive prospect especially as prices are rising so strongly at the moment.

Slovenia offers strong opportunities for investment in an emerging market with the best GDP per capita and economic growth of all of the other transitioning economies of central Europe. Entry prices are still very low by European standards and outside the centre of Ljubljana, good potential for investment in both second homes and buy-to-let purchases are available.

Rating: $$$

Europe

SLOVENIA

Spain

Currency: Euro

Exchange rates:
100 Euro = £79
£1 = 1.3 Euro

100 Euro = US $157
US $1 = 0.64 Euro

MADRID

Introduction

Spain, the land of matadors, flamenco dancing and Gaudi's modern architectural lines, occupies 85% of the Iberian Peninsula, and is Europe's third largest nation. As the second most mountainous country on the continent, flat land is limited and housing is mostly concentrated on the coastal strip alongside the Mediterranean. Without doubt, the attractions of this vast and varied country are obvious: beautiful beaches, 320 days of sunshine a year, delicious food and wine, the mountains of Andalucía, and the magnificence of cities such as Madrid and Barcelona. Spain also has one of the most fascinating cultures, with the bonus of an easy-going and laid-back lifestyle.

These are all good reasons to visit Spain and the fantastic infrastructure, range of activities and enthralling countryside mean it is eternally popular with tourists. In fact the country is currently the second most popular tourist destination in the world, welcoming 59.2 million tourists in 2007 (a 2.1% increase on 2006), and expecting 60.7 million tourists in 2008.

> *'Spain is still one of the most appealing overseas home destinations for Brits because of its excellent lifestyle and property prices to suit all budgets'*

Spain has continued to show healthy GDP growth with figures exceeding 3% every year for the last decade (excluding 2002), and reaching 3.7% in

2007 – this is significantly higher than the EU average of 2.9%. Government statistics would lead us to believe that property prices are rising too, with prices in Murcia allegedly growing 10.7% in 2007. However, specialists in the market counteract this claim suggesting that such declarations are quite simply untrue. Destinations once popular with Brits are decreasing in price at a more than rapid rate, causing property businesses to shut down and developers to halt construction. As a result, unemployment rates in the construction sector are escalating with an increase of 8.62% seen in just 12 months between January 2007 and January 2008. The future of this market then, is somewhat in limbo and if nothing else, has got industry experts worldwide speculating as to its sustainability.

Is this a good place to buy?

Anyone interested in property will have heard the recent rumblings of Spain's difficulties, especially in light of last year's credit crunch. According to the Spanish Instituto Nacional de Estadista (INE), property transfers across the country fell by 14.1% between February 2007 and 2008, whilst CB Richard Ellis recently announced that there is now oversupply equating to around one million residential units – 50,000 to 100,000 of which are in the Valencia region. A high percentage of apartments on the Costa del Sol also sit empty and new developments are taking up to four years to sell, so it's no wonder foreign investors are taking a step back. Or are they? A thoroughly established market, Spain is still one of the most appealing overseas home destinations for Brits because of its excellent lifestyle and property prices to suit all budgets. Indeed the AIPP (Association of International Property Professionals) rank it second favourite for Brits buying holiday homes overseas.

At the start of 2008 though, the Spanish property market was not the best place to be from an investor's point of view; buyer interest was down, especially on the coast, new developments sat unsold, estate agent closures swept the country, developers lost confidence and unemployment in the construction sector soared. And with 500,000 new homes due to be built in 2008, questions pondering whether there is adequate demand are rife.

The tightening credit crunch has only worked to aggravate the problem and completed house sales for January 2008 showed a drop of 27% year on year, according to the National Statistics Institute (INE). Banks are lending at unreasonable terms and a 28% drop was experienced in lending to home owners. The exchange rate has also moved against British buyers, with the GBP now weak against the euro. The time it takes to sell a property has also suffered, jumping from six months in 2006 to 24 months in 2008. All these statistics then, intimate a floundering property market but strangely people are still buying. International property media panders to audience interest and continues to talk consistently about purchasing in Spain and it is rare that you pick up an overseas investment magazine without it featuring property in Spain in one form or another.

'This market is operating at almost full capacity and is undoubtedly more suited to the lifestyle buyer than the serious investor. With prices expected to drop a further 6.5% by 2010, this is not the market for capital gains'

Further, Jose Luis Rodriguez Zapatero, leader of the Spanish Socialist Party, was re-elected recently, bringing promises of regulating the somewhat brittle property market. The drive to boost the buy-to-let market through mortgages and elimination of the wealth tax are two incentives aimed at convincing future investors of Spain's worth and reliability and offsetting the housing downturn. Similarly, retaining incentives are being provided for the mass of unskilled labourers now without jobs. What is more, large-scale infrastructure improvements are sweeping the country, adding to its appeal. The introduction of a 185 mile per hour bullet train has reduced travelling times between Madrid and Barcelona to just two and a half hours, whilst Madrid and Malaga are only two and a half hours' away and Madrid and Valladolid less than an hour. Plans are also being drawn up for a prolific rail network which would include links to London. It seems then, that Spain is aware of the precarious state of its market and is taking its fate into its own hands.

Having said that, investments can be made that give you a lot for your money providing the quality is high. This market then, is operating at almost full capacity and is undoubtedly more suited to the lifestyle buyer than the serious investor. With prices expected to drop a further 6.5% by 2010, this is not the market for capital gains.

Whether this is a gentle correction or a full-blown crisis remains to be seen, however, Spanish authorities are confident that this recession will be a bee sting in Spanish property history, sharp and short. The property sector has been fundamental to economic development over the past decade, accounting for 7.5% of the country's economic output.

Which type of property should you go for?

Since the 1960s, Spain has been offering package holidays to foreigners, meaning the existing infrastructure is years ahead of emerging markets, financing is easy and the country is one of the most accessible in Europe. It is also home to the most expensive property in the world with plush pads on the market for a whopping £48m. Spain also offers property for those with a more modest budget and the type of property a buyer chooses will usually depend on personal preference, what their aims are, or on the location in which they intend to buy.

Apartments offer the cheapest prices and the highest potential for returns, but bring with them privacy issues. Linked and terraced properties are comparatively cheap and easy to resell whilst townhouses give easy access to amenities, and have the additional benefits of modern surroundings. Corner properties are also cheap and are frequently used as holiday homes, while detached properties offer more privacy but at greater cost. Traditional homes are common and community properties with a shared area are always popular.

INSIDER TIP **Most new homes on the Costas are sold off-plan; however, since the price dip it is not recommended to buy off-plan developments as many developers are starting new builds and having to halt construction halfway through, sometimes never finishing because of extensive oversupply. Shrewd investors will also avoid big building projects with thousands of dwellings as well as property with unrealistic letting promises. Those hoping to exploit the buy-to-let market should also take care. Many foreigners are unaware that under Spanish law a licence must be acquired before a property can be used for rental purposes and if this difficult procedure is not honoured, owners could face fines of up to £20,000.**

Buyers should also be aware of a 'tradition' which sees purchasers 'help' the vendor in reducing his capital gains tax liability. Generally speaking the vendor will ask for a greatly reduced purchase price to be stipulated in the purchase contract and for the buyer to make up the difference between the contract price and the actual price in cash. This is illegal, and could have unfortunate repercussions when it comes to your turn to sell – you will either have to persuade a buyer to go through the same process, or pay substantially more gains tax than you should have to.

Hotspots

Murcia

Murcia is hot tipped as a prime emerging region located between Costa del Sol and Costa Blanca. The new Corvera airport, due to open in 2009, will make Murcia more accessible and hopes to attract increased tourist numbers cutting transfer times to resorts to 20 minutes. Fondly known as 'The Market Garden of Spain' the region enjoys unspoilt beaches along the Costa Calida coastline and extensive walking trails winding through pine tree lined parks. Nicknamed the 'Baroque Capital of Spain' due to its wealth of buildings, beautiful monasteries, gardens, parks and Cathedral de Santa Maria, there is much to explore. The area's natural beauty and conservation scheme appeals to those buying for longer-term potential or relocation. Large areas in Murcia have been set aside as National and Regional Parks and as such cannot be built on. This is an attempt to avoid the problems of overcrowding and oversupply associated with the Costas. There are currently six golf courses and most of the new resorts do focus on golf. Property prices in the area have increased 12.9% with the village Lorca showing an impressive 17.2% rise. Average prices in the Murcia region for an apartment are £100,000, £120,000 for a country house and £150,000 for a villa on the coast.

Andulucia

Andulucia is a region becoming extremely popular with overseas buyers and an 84% increase in visitor numbers was seen between 2006 and 2007. **Huelva** is located in the Andalucia region and is the fastest growing destination for golf tourism in Spain. With a new airport opening on the western fringes of Spain's Costa de la Luz, a surge of new tourists into the area is predicted. Another popular destination in south-west Spain is **Galera.** Both Huelva and Galera would suit people with a smaller budget wanting peace and quiet away from the coast and walking and cycling facilities. Renovated cave houses are common in these areas and are available from as little as €18,000 un-restored or between €55,000 to €70,000 fully restored. Jerez de la Frontera, in southern Spain, offers property 46% cheaper per square metre than the Spanish average and 77% less than property in Cadiz or Seville. A planned AVE high speed train connection will cut journey times between Seville and Jerez to 20 minutes, making the area much more accessible.

Islands

There has been a noticeable shift in focus from foreign buyers, moving their money away from the problems in mainland Spain to neighbouring islands. The **Canary Islands** have done particularly well with a 73% increase in property purchases since 2006. La Gomera is the second smallest Canary Island and has been nicknamed 'Tenerife's younger sister'. The Island is noticeably untouched by development and boasts Europe's only rainforest with banana and avocado plantations. Unlike Tenerife which has been subjected to numerous concrete, high-rise builds, La Gomera has maintained a quieter existence with hiking and cycling through the national park. The reason this island has been so unaffected by development is because it cannot be built upon and as a result, property prices are higher than on the Spanish mainland.

Northern areas

Searching for a more authentic Spanish getaway, northerly areas such as **Galicia** and **Asturias** are becoming popular with middle-class buyers. If escaping somewhere away from the overcrowded and overdeveloped 'Costa's' of Spain is what you want then these quiet unspoilt coastlines with secret coves and peaceful beaches are for you. Luscious green countryside, friendly locals and a great cuisine combine with low property prices. In Galicia original stone buildings can be obtained for as little as €70,000. Asturias is more expensive with original buildings costing around €200,000; however, property in need of restoration can be picked up in both locations for minimal costs.

Buyer's guide

Before foreigners can buy property in Spain they will need to apply for a 'Numero de Identificacion de Extanjero' (NIE), a process which can take up to six weeks. Whilst in the past it was possible to apply for an NIE post-purchase it is now obligatory to get one before. NIEs can be obtained from National Police Headquarters following an application. Other than this, foreigners face no restrictions.

(Source: According to a Halifax press release posted on www.hbosplc.com/media/pressreleases/articles/halifax)

Mortgages

LTV %	TERM	CURRENCIES	RATES %	STATUS	SPECIAL CONDITIONS
90	40	EUR	4.35	Employed or self-employed	

Key risks

The most prominent and ongoing threat to Spain's housing market has to be its fragility. The country is facing a challenging time and prices have been dropping, with many of the newer developments grinding to a halt. Having said that, it is a buyer's market and there are affordable properties available in a very few emerging pockets of the country. Vendors are more likely to accept lower offers at this trying time so negotiating is highly recommended.

Thankfully the controversial Valencia Land Grab Laws which allowed unscrupulous investors to expropriate land from private owners were overhauled in June 2008. Investors need to be aware though, that similar laws are still in existence in Andalucia and Murcia meaning investors may still be vulnerable to such acts.

To combat the huge problems Spain has experienced with overdevelopment, a stringent system is in place where PGOUSs regulate zones that can be built upon and those that cannot. In this way, remaining Spanish land will be protected from mass building although it is a shame these enforcements were not in place earlier.

For those planning to tackle the buy-to-let market the application for the compulsory licence (which must be acquired before a property can be used for rental purposes) can be arduous and time consuming and should be borne in mind.

Rather unfortunately Spain seems to have become the country that emerging markets compare themselves to in terms of 'what not to do'. The extreme growth seen over the last decade has resulted in high prices disabling strong appreciation whilst overdevelopment means demand has dwindled.

Rating: ⚠ ⚠ ⚠

Key opportunities

Whilst there is no denying that Spain makes a fantastic second home or retirement destination, high inflation is driving avid new investors to countries where property and life are still cheap and the terrain less developed.

Rating: $

Turkey

Currency: New Lira
Exchange rates:
100 New Lira = £41.35
£1 = 2.42 New Lira

100 New Lira = US $81.42
US $1 = 1.243 New Lira

Introduction

An ancient country steeped in history, Turkey comprises picturesque seaside resorts and cosmopolitan cities, supported by extensive public facilities. Balmy climes, exotic food, genuine local hospitality, and surprisingly low house prices compared to equivalent Mediterranean resorts make Turkey a popular choice with overseas investors. According to *A Place in the Sun*, Turkey has been named the third most popular country for overseas investment in 2008 behind recurrent favourites, France and Spain. With a longer summer, beautiful scenery, low living costs and the opportunity to still pick up a bargain along much of the coast, Turkey has been tipped to take over the property investor giants Spain and France as 2008 matures.

The country is actively involved in increasing tourism and infrastructure and hopes to achieve EU accession and euro currency before 2015. If this happens, Turkey will soon rival, if not beat, the most popular lifestyle investment destination, Spain, and will come to the fore as one of Europe's most popular countries. Of those buying property in 2008, one third are expected to buy specifically for investment returns, with a further 29% predicted to buy for both investment and lifestyle purposes.

Although the tourist industry suffered a heavy blow throughout 2006 with the outbreak of bird flu, proximity to the Iraq war and increase of widespread terrorism threats, recent political calm means tourism is steadily recovering. 2007 showed an increase in foreign visitors of 18% and there are high hopes of a further 15% increase in 2008. The World Travel and Tourism Council predict a 4.8% annual increase in real terms over the next 10 years.

Is this a good place to buy?

If this book was merely about choosing a nice place to build a second home, Turkey would be high on the list. The climate, Mediterranean lifestyle, wonderful food, beaches and hospitality combine to make Turkey very appealing to second-home buyers. However, this book is also about investment and choosing a property which might increase in value. Whether Turkey deserves a place on this list is therefore questionable.

At the start of 2007, foreign buyers looking to invest in Turkish property were few and far between, the non-existent mortgage market, ongoing altercation surrounding Turkey's entry to the EU and the political instability of the country did not make for a safe investment. However, the second half of the year showed changes aimed at transforming Turkey into an appealing destination for holiday makers and property investors alike. A new mortgage law introduced in April 2007 threw open Turkey's property market to foreign and local investors alike and with 100% LTV available (subject to status) there is little on the financial front to stand in investors' ways. It is not just the mortgage situation though which will have long-term effects on the market – Turkey is getting richer and as domestic wealth increases, house prices are expected to rise simultaneously. Further, experiencing historic levels of FDI, deemed a top five developing country, and enjoying predicted GDP growth of 6% in 2008, the country's economy is strong, as are its investment credentials.

INSIDER TIP

Recent suggestions that Turkey will not be made a member of the European Union until 2015 has dampened some of the wilder optimism of local property agents. Although the required legal and financial services reforms will help to place the market on a sounder footing, some feel that the market is now so dynamic that entry itself will not be the catalyst it might once have been. Regardless of undecided EU entry, 2008 is still expected to be the year that most investors will choose to buy in Turkey. Prices are expected to double over the next three years on the back of 40% increases since 2004, meaning those who invest now will benefit.

At the time of writing (June 2008), the issuing of title deeds to foreign buyers has been temporarily suspended to allow re-drafting of legislation detailing foreign corporations' rights to buy agricultural land. This is merely to ascertain not whether foreign nationals are allowed to own land, but whether restrictions as to the size of land foreigners can purchase should be relaxed assures John Howell from International Law Partnership. Expected to be resolved by July 2008, this amendment is only likely to have a temporary impact on investors.

'Whilst all the major Turkish cities offer interesting investment opportunities, it is the historic areas of Istanbul, in desperate need of reconstruction and renovation, which offer some of the best investments'

Which type of property should you go for?

Whilst all the major Turkish cities offer interesting investment opportunities, it is the historic areas of Istanbul, in desperate need of reconstruction and renovation, which offer some of the best investments. Istanbul has just been ranked as one of the top ten European development and investment cities for 2008. The reverse of these intercity properties are the more rural seaside locations that do not require renovation, and are becoming popular with the longer-term overseas investor interested in a dual purpose purchase. These properties can be bought with both retirement and buy-to-let options in mind. South-western areas such as Kalkan and smaller villages along 'The Lycian Coast' are establishing themselves as popular haunts of British long-term investors.

Hotspots

Aegean Resorts

The most developed areas in Turkey are centred in the Aegean resorts; **Bodrum, Kusadasi** and **Marmaris** – and continue to provide healthy price appreciation. Alanya, set against a backdrop of Taurus Mountains and golden beaches to the east and the west is an area expected to enjoy significant appreciation following recent airport expansion. With entry levels as low as €50,000, investors purchasing soon and joining the 17,000 overseas investors who have already bought here should enjoy healthy returns. The 300,000 population of the town offers a mix of old and new and year-round appeal. A working town, Alanya has numerous restaurants and bars along its so-called 'party strip' and harbour. The traditional Ottoman-style buildings have been turned into smart hotels and prices have risen 13%–15% over the last few years with entry prices around £40,000. An extra £10,000 will afford you the best area 'Oba' that has recently benefited from a new Tesco store. There is an overwhelming element of community in Alanya and a European Social Centre has been built to bring together locals and expats socially. The opening of the airport on 10 April 2008 will only serve to increase the area's potential with three additional flights per week from the UK. Investors should also be made aware of plans to build a ski resort to accommodate 3,600 skiers a day just 40km from Alanya.

Europe

TURKEY

Coastline towns

Areas such as **Bodrum, Dalaman, Didim**, and **Fethiye** will continue to be good holiday investment hotspots. These coastline towns are not necessarily any more attractive than others but offer a better infrastructure and are established tourist destinations with an existing expat community and regular international flights.

Kusadasi although not new to the knowledgeable Turkish property investor, has only recently come to the fore as a promising destination. The most northern Mediterranean resort, it admittedly does not offer the cheapest property prices but is loaded with potential. Three-bed properties can be bought for £80,000 to £150,000.

Along the south-west coast of Turkey, the small fishing village of **Kalkan**, often referred to as 'The Pirate Coast', is becoming a popular tourist hotspot for those in search of a more authentic Turkish Getaway. The charming village of Kalkan is located along the Lycian Coast that boasts miles of unspoilt beaches, 'The Lycian Way' Walk and historic Roman ruins. Only a 90-minute drive from Dalaman airport and 20 minutes' car drive from nearby city Patara, this resort has been kept a secret amongst locals and the scattering of tourists who happen upon the area. It is exactly this exclusivity that makes Kalkan so appealing to foreign visitors and investors as, unlike westernised Turkish towns such as Bodrum, a very 'Turkish' atmosphere is maintained with authentic fish restaurants situated near the harbour and tiny meandering streets with boutique shops spilling out onto the pavement. Investments in this area are often bought as holiday homes and apartments can achieve weekly rents of £495 for a hillside property and £595 for a sea-view property during peak seasons. Luxury apartments are increasingly being built in the area; however, much of what is already built is protected by a 'land belt law' meaning the current views will not be spoilt by new builds.

INSIDER TIP

Another alternative way in which to invest in Turkey and secure your perfect holiday home is to buy a plot of land and build the property yourself. Areas such as Uzumlu, **just outside Fethiye, offer plots from £113,000.**

Buyer's guide

Foreign nationals are entitled to purchase property in Turkey as long as it is to be used for residential purposes and is located within the boundaries of implementation zoning plans or regional development plans. 'Military Permission' must be sought from Turkish authorities in all cases, a process which can take in excess of six months. Investors are limited to 25,000 square metres per person and can't acquire property in strategic, military and agricultural zones.

As stated earlier, issuing of title deeds to foreign buyers of residential land in Turkey has been temporarily suspended, a problem expected to be resolved by July 2008.

(Source: Paksoy Attorneys at Law, *The International Comparative Legal Guide to Real Estate 2008: Turkey,* available at www.iclg.co.uk. Also www.lawoverseas.com)

Mortgages

LTV %	TERM	CURRENCIES	RATES %	STATUS	SPECIAL CONDITIONS
100	20	EUR, GBP	6.4	Employed or self-employed	

Key risks

At the start of 2007, foreign buyers looking to invest in Turkish property were few and far between. Deterred by the non-existent mortgage market and political instability of the country, investors did not view this as a safe investment. Although mortgages are now available, a measure that has thrown the doors of the property market right open, it will take a while before Turkey is considered one of the top investment markets.

This is due, in part to the country's floundering attempts to gain access to the EU. Rumours are rife that Turkey may not even be granted accession until 2015, a fact that is understandably dampening the optimism of local property agents.

Further to this, the re-adjusting of ownership laws for foreign investors by the Turkish government in the early months of 2008 put many investors in vulnerable positions.

Rating: ⚠ ⚠ ⚠

Key opportunities

Aside from its failed attempts to enter the EU, Turkey has many of the ingredients of an excellent investment location: prices are low and there are good fundamentals making the country popular as a tourism and holiday-home destination. Mass urbanisation will continue to create a strong market in the major cities with a forecast need for more than five million new houses by 2010. For pure investment potential, our recommendation would be to buy in Istanbul or emerging southern markets located near the newly built Alanya airport.

There is no longer a risk of over development in coastal regions as Turkey claims to have 'learnt from Spain's mistakes', putting planning restrictions in place so that affluent areas will not become over popularised or developed. Planning in up-and-coming areas such as Alanya is limited to five floors with the level decreasing the closer the property is to the mountains.

In March 2008 the law allowing sale of real estate to companies established by foreign firms was cancelled, although the annulment of this law is not expected to adversely affect the average UK buyer. As such, property in Turkey is still considered to offer relatively safe investment opportunities in well-chosen destinations with prices hoped to increase steadily between 5% and 10% per annum.

Although entry levels have risen in recent years, they are still low by Mediterranean standards meaning that Turkey, supported by strong market fundamentals, has a healthy investment future.

Rating: $$$$

Ukraine

Currency: Hryvnia (UAH)

Exchange Rates:
100 UAH = £11
£1 = 9.2 UAH

100 UAH = $21.50
$1 = 5 UAH

Introduction

A fascinating mixture of spectacular landscapes, unique architecture and a rich history, Ukraine is home to one of the most beautiful cities in Europe. Kyiv, the capital city and heart of the country is one of Eastern Europe's most picturesque capitals and attracts a consistent stream of visitors throughout the year. Of equal appeal are the country's miles of natural beauty, rich natural resources and deep-rooted history and culture making the country increasingly popular with tourists.

The Carpathian and Crimea mountain ranges attract keen skiers and hikers as well as those seeking solace in mountain spas or rich historical sites. The city of Lviv, home to an old medieval town, is the main cultural centre of the country and is renowned for its extravagant and distinctive architecture.

Realising its potential as a tourist destination, visitors are seeking coastal resorts in increasingly numbers. As one of the biggest centres for sugar production in the world, Ukraine's economy is supported by a strong export sector.

'Those willing to take a punt may well get their hands on a good deal, although those seeking stable investment opportunities may be better off looking elsewhere'

Is this a good place to buy?

Occupying a strategic location in Eastern Europe, Ukraine has enormous development potential. A refreshing alternative to the now over-saturated markets of central Europe, Ukraine's property investment market is in the early stages of development, offering the potential for strong and high yields.

Supported by significant FDI inflows, exchange rate stability, the expansion of domestic demand and improving external market conditions, GDP growth reached 7.1% in 2007.

At present there is a somewhat limited supply of investment grade buildings, meaning those properties of the relevant quality are in high demand. The growing purchasing power of individuals and the general expansion of the Ukrainian economy are creating an increasingly healthy investment environment and although issues with regulation, unwarranted prices and quality of product do exist, it is important to state that Ukraine does still possess potential.

As of 1 January 2007, capital gains levied on dwellings (houses, apartments, summer houses) measuring 100 square metres or less were abolished leaving investors free to realise their profits more fully. Those with properties exceeding 100 square metres are subject only to a 1% tax. Capital gains earned on the second and any additional sale of similar real estate property (any size) within the same tax year are subject to 5% tax. Capital gain acquired by a non-Ukrainian resident from the sale of property will be subjected to a 15% withholding tax (Source: Price Waterhouse Coopers Going Global Report 2007).

Flaws plaguing their economy a few years ago have now given way to strong economic growth particularly in the real estate sector, with price increases of 50% witnessed on property and as much as 100% on land. As a result, the country is experiencing high rental yields, especially in built-up cities such as Kiev. This, coupled with moderate rental income tax, a pro-landlord rental market and low transaction costs between the buyer and sellers, presents a strong opportunity to potential investors.

Although in the past there were problems with supply of skilled workers, Ukrainian nationals in recent years have shown an eagerness and willingness to learn new skills, take on employment and take full advantage of the education provided. In time then, the country's workforce will improve.

Ukraine has shown good economic growth over the last few years and many cities are now being re-developed. Improvements to public services as well as incentives to attract higher levels of tourism and FDI are being implemented. And it would appear that such methods are working. Thanks to increased government transparency and a relaxation of entry barriers into the financing sector, FDI in the first six months of 2007 increased by 50.3% compared to the same period of 2006 totalling USD $3,276.3m (according to State Statistics Committee).

Pressures from the international community and international financial institutions, pre-empting Ukraine's WTO accession and a closer EU relationship will continue to encourage consistent structural reform.

Something to be aware of however, is the country's limited finance options, its imperfect financial system and frequent and abrupt changes in legislation, all of which can inhibit the smooth passage of investments.

Which type of property should you go for?

Kyiv is currently earning the highest rental yields in Ukraine and many foreign investors are investing in apartments in the city centre on a buy-to-let basis. Alternatively, residential houses in prime locations have the best prospects for capital growth but need to be carefully selected to ensure they are close to necessary amenities.

Hotspots

Kyiv

Kyiv is the capital and largest city of Ukraine and one of the oldest cities in Eastern Europe. With many picturesque facades, an ancient cave monastery, cathedral, up-market boutiques as well as a business centre, Kyiv has a lot to offer and is popular with tourists.

Land prices are reported to have increased threefold in certain parts of the city over the last 18 months whilst rental rates are rocketing. In 2007, office, retail and hotel transactions worth over $300m were registered on the Kyiv property market with another $500m in the pipeline.

 INSIDER TIP

Such high demand and sluggish supply in one of the least developed hospitality markets in central and Eastern Europe therefore makes for a strong investment climate where room rates are rocketing. The virtual absence of renowned hotel chains then means there is something of a void in the market leaving excellent opportunities for development in this sector of the market. In addition, with a strong landlord's market and high demand for rental apartments, investment in Kyiv has healthy prospects for the shrewd investor. It must be considered however, whether these prices and growth are sustainable or whether, as some experts believe, the market is very overpriced. Considering the current lack of appropriate supply though, it is likely that prices will continue to rise over the short-term.

Lviv

Lviv is situated in the western part of the Ukraine and is easily accessible with an international airport close by. It is another beautiful city with a history dating back 750 years and is in close proximity to popular Ukrainian ski resorts. Already deemed a World Heritage Site it has a flourishing tourist industry and is expected to experience a surge in property prices as its popularity grows. With a thriving nightlife, relaxing café culture, inexpensive food and cheap accommodation, it is an ideal getaway.

Odessa

Situated next to the Black Sea, Odessa is a colourful city and important trade centre. Known as 'the pearl of the Black Sea', it is one of the largest Black Sea ports and has many beaches which are popular during summer months. Currently it is enjoying significant infrastructure and foreign direct investment and is becoming an increasingly renowned holiday spot for holidaymakers seeking an accessible destination. As its appeal blossoms more and more jobs are becoming available and increasing numbers are moving to the city. Short to medium-term gains here are likely to be attractive.

Yalta

Yalta is a resort town on the Crimea peninsula, a beautiful and unspoilt stretch in southern Ukraine and a popular destination with Ukrainian and Russian tourists alike. It is gradually making its way onto the international tourism map as the rest of the world becomes aware of its beauty. With dazzling beaches and intricate architecture, property prices here are on the up, but at present are still affordable.

Those wishing to take advantage of the buy-to-let tourism market, can make use of the many property management companies whereas those wishing to tap into the local market will be well placed to sell to the affluent Ukrainians and Russians seeking holiday homes in this quaint town.

Buyer's guide

Foreign investors are subject to certain restrictions when looking to purchase land plots in Ukraine although they can acquire non-land real estate without imposition. Providing they are not buying agricultural land, foreign individuals can gain ownership title to land within settlements as well as plots outside settlements if they already own the property standing on it.

(Source: Schoenherr Attorneys at Law, *The International Comparative Legal Guide to Real Estate 2008: Ukraine*, available at www.iclg.co.uk)

Mortgages

Finance is not yet available in Ukraine.

Key risks

Whether Ukraine's recent rapid growth, both in its economic and property sectors, can be maintained is hard to determine and investors should be very cautious for this reason.

Ukrainian inflation rates have soared in recent months, forcing many locals to invest in property in a bid to safeguard their wealth. It is this that has contributed to a property boom. Investors will find that some stock is now being sold at extortionate, unsustainable prices as a result. The stability of the current property market then, is somewhat questionable as recent price rises were not necessarily based on strong market fundamentals, but more on speculative decisions. It is likely then, that the supply and demand balance could become malevolent and returns will drop. The country still has debts which are higher than other, more successful economies and although structural reforms are taking place they are at a very slow pace which is restricting the country.

Ukraine then, has an unsure future.

Rating: ⚠ ⚠ ⚠

Key opportunities

Currently enjoying high rental yields (especially in Kyiv), moderate rental income tax and a pro-landlord rental market, investors may be attracted to this market. Continuous rises in foreign investment, particularly in key cities, are also encouraging and indicative of a strengthening economy.

Some experts claim that the property market has reached its peak and that housing prices will soon drop off whereas others are just starting to whisper about its potential. Those willing to take a punt may well get their hands on a good deal, although those seeking stable investment opportunities may be better off looking elsewhere.

Rating: $$$

Cambodia

Currency: Riel
Exchange Rates:
100,000 Riel = £12.62
£1 = 7,918 Riel

100,000 Riel = $24.96
$1 = $4,006

Introduction

Cambodia, hidden in a corner of South East Asia, is gradually making its debut onto the global stage. With over 400km of beautifully pristine beaches, huge areas of wild, tropical jungle alternating with luscious paddy fields, Cambodia is emerging from its dark history leaving the past firmly behind it.

Closed to the rest of the world for three decades at the end of the 20th century as a result of the despotic rule of the Khmer Rouge, Cambodia missed out on the development her neighbouring countries have benefited from. Thailand (to the north) and Vietnam (to the south) have become successful countries, despite ongoing poverty, with rapidly developing economies and export markets, and a strong tourism industry that brings year-round international interest. Cambodia is just beginning to start on the path that her neighbours have trodden.

Thanks to the imprisonment of the area, Cambodia has retained the beauty of an untouched country. The marks of the tourist industry are not yet imprinted on the land, and there are many areas of the country that are wild and undiscovered. The long, sandy beaches that escort the pure azure waters of the Gulf of Thailand are expansive and uncrowded, often empty entirely. The wondrous and incomprehensible temples of Angkor remain as they were when created thousands of years ago; squatting and huge, engulfed by the tendrils of the jungle. Remnants of Cambodia's French rule can be seen in the colonial architecture that characterises many of the buildings, especially in Phnom Penh, the country's capital. Even the horrific remains of the Khmer Rouge's genocide are preserved in the Killing Fields which afford a very real view into its murky past.

Cambodia offers so much to the international visitor that it is not hard to explain the rapidly enlarging tourism industry. The fascinating blend of heritage, culture and astounding natural beauty makes Cambodia one of the most exciting places to visit today.

Is this a good place to buy?

Due to severe communist restrictions, the development of Cambodia froze during the rule of the Khmer Rouge. Following their fall from power Cambodia was opened up to the world and found itself far behind other countries in many ways, crucially, in economic and political terms. Since then, it has raced to catch up with the developed world.

'Providing comprehensive legal advice is sought, and purchasers stick to developed areas of the country, this high-risk market could also be one characterised by high returns'

Cambodia's economy has traditionally been dominated by the textile and tourism industries, perhaps a somewhat narrow economic base if the country is to develop as it hopes. However, the imminent expansion of the mining industry following the discovery of various minerals on-land, coupled with potentially huge oil and gas deposits in fields offshore in the Gulf of Thailand, mean its economic future is one ripe with potential. Tourism continues to thrive and with visitor arrivals estimated to reach three million per annum by 2010 bringing in an estimated $780 a head, the value of this industry in economic terms is undeniable.

In the South East Asian arena, Cambodia is second only to China in terms of GDP growth over the last few years, sustaining an average growth rate of just over 10%. Further, its accession to the WTO in 2004 serves to confirm further the country's credibility as an international competitor.

Cambodia's rapid development owes a great deal to the huge amount of foreign investment poured into the country by neighbouring Asian countries, namely China. Foreign direct investment rose from $121m in 2004 to $475m in 2006, and looks set to multiply at an expeditious rate following the recent natural resources discoveries. The range of investment projects, from IT companies to shopping malls, golf and entertainment complexes, to roads and a new airport, all combine to present a burgeoning, modern and pro-foreign Cambodia that is working to secure its position within a developed world.

Asia

CAMBODIA

In the property market the collapse of the Khmer Rouge left Cambodians in an unusual position. Under communist rule relatively few had any physical possessions or material wealth, but after the Khmer Rouge's departure Cambodians found that, amongst other things, the land they had been living on for years suddenly had considerable value. This has enabled a large number of Cambodians to engage with the property market, many suddenly achieving middle-class status as a result of selling land. Cambodian property ownership is very high and as a consequence the property market has grown to become vibrant and competitive.

The legacy from the Khmer Rouge is a property market that has little developed history – there are no freely available statistics or trends with which one can analyse the potential and the security of the market. This obviously creates an element of risk, but it also presents the possibility of making some huge investment gains. The market's immature status means property is widely undervalued and there is only one way for prices to move.

INSIDER TIP **Foreign investors are taking advantage of this young and emerging market, the evidence of which is widespread. Many luxury apartment buildings and renovations are springing up across the country's main cities, and in remote corners of the luscious jungles, high-end villa complexes are being created for the ultimate experience in indulgent living. Many high-end investors are purchasing fully renovated colonial-era properties, thus eliminating the pitfalls that can arise when dealing with constructors and developers. Demand for high-end rental properties is so great that some developers are offering a guaranteed rental return of 10% net for the first two years of ownership whilst capital appreciation is estimated at a conservative 20%–25%.**

As in most Asian countries, there are limitations on complete foreign ownership. Current law offers two options to the foreign investor: long-term leaseholds of up to 99 years, or to form a company and take on Cambodian nationals as partners, with the foreign investor taking the 51% controlling share. There are pressures on the government to make it easier for foreigners to buy so this situation may improve in the near future. Investors should look out for fake property papers, corruption, unscrupulous developers and the lack of transparency in many sectors. As with any overseas purchase, the use of an experienced lawyer will prove invaluable.

Whilst Cambodia is progressing at such an expedient and encouraging rate and developing a much brighter future, it would be unwise to ignore the less salubrious side to Cambodia. The unstable foundations on which Cambodia is trying to rebuild itself have engendered crippling corruption, severe poverty, and a shocking trade industry in people and child-sex. The country's desperation to catch up with its counterparts has led to the poor being swept aside to make room for foreign developers' new creations, leaving them in a much worse condition out in the countryside lacking even proper sanitation. Cambodia *is* developing, but a prospective investor should keep a watchful eye on its complete development as a nation, not just as an economic field.

Which type of property should you go for?

The property investor looking to put money into Cambodian property is almost universally advised to stick to prime development areas of the big cities, especially Phnom Penh. Property in regional areas may be tempting with cheap prices but there is no guarantee that prices will rise. The short property market history has shown significant demand and development in the cities. Most of the properties in Phnom Penh take one of two forms: renovated colonial apartments, or brand new luxury developments in high-rise buildings. Along the coast luxury villa complexes are emerging to take advantage of fantastic ocean vistas from the peace of a secluded corner of the tropical jungle.

Hotspots

Property-wise, advice is unanimous in recommending that investors stick to purchasing property in the developed areas; anything outside is regarded as too much of a gamble, with no guarantees of market demand, trends or even potential return.

The majority of modern development is taking place in three main areas: the comparatively large cities of **Phnom Penh** and **Siem Reap**, and the smaller but popular beach resort of **Sihanoukville**. All three areas have international airports situated close by, with the airport at Sihanoukville undergoing major renovations which will make it the country's main airport in the future. The rest of Cambodia is rarely mentioned when talking of investment potential, although this could change as the number of tourists entering the country increases.

Phnom Penh

Once known as 'The Paris of the East', Phnom Penh retains the architectural evidence of its French colonial rule, with the old French Quarter being the most desirable part of the city to live. Developers in the area maintain the beauty of the historical architecture by merely renovating the interiors of buildings, thus creating a stunning juxtaposition of old and new. Situated on the river, the French Quarter hosts the Old Market, and boasts a café culture that would rival any Western European city. The nearby Royal Palace adds a dash of majestic splendour to the neighbourhood, as do the many palaces and *wats* (temples) that season the colonial city with relics from its ancient history.

The skyline of Phnom Penh is destined to change as Korean developers muscle in to gain a piece of the market with plans to create giant high-rise buildings and condominiums with up to 42 storeys.

Siem Reap

Siem Reap, the gateway to the world-famous Temples of Angkor, draws thousands of tourists every year. The proximity of the city to the UNESCO World Heritage Site makes it an ideal location for a few days' stopover on the great tourist trail, and consequently there is a high – and still growing – demand for accommodation for the many world travellers. The city itself is relatively small and easily accessible to the average pedestrian, with its fair share of restaurants and hotels – many under construction and renovation to cope with increasing demand.

Sihanoukville

230km south-west of Phnom Penh, lies Sihanoukville, a town in its adolescence, created in the 1960s and promptly stifled by the repressive regime in power. Now though, it is emerging as a hotspot destination thanks to its dream beaches with swathes of white sands and deep blue waters. Luxury villa complexes are springing up along the miles of beach front, selling the luxury lifestyle to those wanting to cash in entirely on the fantasy beach existence, offering, in turn, an enticing investment opportunity to both lifestyle and investment buyers.

Buyer's guide

Foreign ownership of Cambodian land is prohibited and Prime Minister Hun Sen recently stated that non-Khmer nationals will never be able to own land outright. Currently 99-year leases are available in Cambodia. In order to side-step current hurdles, foreign investors have coupled up with Khmer partners and gone about investing in Cambodian property this way. However, more often than not these business relationships are forged on trust alone, leaving the foreign investor in an extremely vulnerable and unregulated situation. It is hoped that the government will soon make changes, in line with the rest of Asia, regarding the right of foreigners to own property. When such changes might be implemented though remains to be seen.

(Source: *The Phnom Penh Post*, available at http://www.phnompenhpost.com/ index.php/20080403338/Real-Estate-2008/Freehold-still-a-dream-for-foreigners.html)

Mortgages

Finance is not yet available in Cambodia.

Key risks

No matter how positive Cambodia's recovery, there is no denying that this is still a country underscored by some very real elements of risk. The infancy of its property market coupled with a government that is still finding its feet in the modern world means the country is open to fluctuations that may hinder its progress. Infrastructure throughout requires upgrading and the banking sector still has a significantly long way to go before it can be described as confident. Furthermore, the buying process can be complicated, corruption is still rife in most parts of the country and issues with land title are common.

Rating: ⚠ ⚠ ⚠ ⚠

Key opportunities

Cambodia is a now thriving country, a phoenix rising from its terrible ashes, and fast becoming an established country in the international arena. High GDP growth rates indicate a booming economy that is developing at a phenomenal rate, and when coupled with the country's low inflation rate of 3%, the overall economic outlook is extremely bright. With the projected continued expansion in the tourism sector and its subsequent effect on the property market, and with the oil, gas and mineral discoveries, the country's economic future appears inimitable.

At present, property prices are significantly undervalued but are expected to rise dramatically over the coming months, creating strong opportunities for healthy capital growth. With the market far below saturation point, this growth should continue for the foreseeable future. As such, a healthy relationship between supply and demand should be maintained, supported by rising local wealth and the thriving tourist industry. Those willing to shoulder the risk then, could buy into one of the investment markets of the future. Providing comprehensive legal advice is sought, and purchasers stick to developed areas of the country, this high risk-market could also be one characterised by high returns.

Rating: $$$$

Asia

CAMBODIA

China

Currency: Chinese Yuan Renminbi (CNY)

Exchange rates:
1,000 CNY = £73.69
£1 = 14 CNY

1,000 CNY= $145.34
$1 = 7 CNY

Introduction

One the world's oldest civilizations, with cultures dating back more than six millennia, China is drenched in a fascinating history. The source of some of the world's greatest inventions and home to the world's longest written language system, the culture is unique and engaging. As the world's most populous and fastest growing country, and with the globe's second largest single economy, China is an economic powerhouse and one of the world's most important markets in almost all industry sectors. (Source: The World Factbook, 2007, CIA, Rank Order – GDP (purchasing power parity) [Online] Available at: https://www.cia.gov/library/publications/the-world-factbook/rankorder/2001rank.html Accessed 16 June 2008.)

Since the start of the Chinese Economic Reform in the late 1970s, China's extraordinary economic growth has been widely acknowledged by the international community and with GDP growth averaging between 8% and 9% for the past quarter of a century it is not hard to understand why. In 2007, China's estimated GDP was $6.99 trillion at the current exchange rate, an increase of 11.9% over the previous year. For five years in a row, China's economic growth has reached or slightly exceeded 10% without significant inflation. According to a 2007 Ernst and Young survey China was rated the most attractive country to foreign visitors.

According to the Global Competitiveness Report 2007–2008 published by the World Economic Forum, China was ranked 7th out of 131 countries in terms of its macroeconomic stability and 34th overall.

Is this a good place to buy?

China has showed openness to progress and development by its accession to the World Trade Organisation (WTO) in 2001 and, in a bid to encourage more FDI and non-FDI inflow, China also has dual taxation agreements with 78 countries, including the UK (further details of these agreements can be found at www.chinatax.gov.cn/ssxd.jsp).

'China has possibly the strongest underlying fundamental reasons for property price growth of any country in the world'

A key element of China's new-found economic freedom was the introduction of property rights in 2004 which guaranteed that legally obtained private property of citizens would not be violated. The constitution further cites that the state may, for the necessity of public interest, requisition or expropriate citizens' private property and pay compensation in accordance with law.

The most recent adoption of China's Property Rights Law (PRL, passed by China's National People's Congress in March 2007, and implemented from October 2007) is a milestone in China's legal system and goes further in defining and systematically regulating general property rights. The PRL emphasises that, for the first time in China's history, private, collective and public property are equally important and enjoy the same level of protection. Part IV of the law states that land use rights in residential property are for 70 years and will automatically be renewed at the end of their term.

The recent moves made by the Chinese government regarding real estate ownership have made property investment a far more secure prospect for the foreign potential investor.

Which type of property should you go for?

High-end luxury apartments in prime city-centre locations will be in the highest demand and are likely to generate the most reliable returns for investors.

All property in China is under a 'land use right' system, similar to the western leasehold concept. There are three types of lease on land: residential, which is run on a 70-year renewable lease, and commercial and industrial land which are on 40 to 50-year leases.

Although the Chinese economy has grown rapidly for the past quarter of a century, its per capita GDP in 2007 was approximately $2,200, still low by world standards. To ensure that the majority of the Chinese people will be able to afford homes in the future, the Chinese government has introduced new measures to restrict foreign purchases. Foreign individuals can acquire one home having been a resident in China for over a year (they will need to have obtained a residence visa for over a year). Alternatively, properties can be purchased by foreigners through a local vehicle, either by setting up a fully owned foreign enterprise (WOFE) or a joint venture company (JV). Registering such companies however, can be time-consuming as well as costly.

These measures are likely to be relaxed in the near future once the central government can see that the real estate sector has maintained a good period of sturdy growth.

Hotspots

There are a number of different regions attracting investment in China each with differing legal requirements and investment opportunities. The major cities, or first-tier cities, remain **Shanghai**, **Beijing**, **Guangzhou**, **Hong Kong**, **Shenzhen** and **Macau**. The secondary cities, or second tier cities, have increasingly become very good investment locations due to recent domestic economic growth and inflow of capital. These cities include **Chongqing**, **Chengdu**, **Tianjin**, **Wuhan**, **Qingdao**, **Hangzhou**, **Suzhou**, **Nanjing** and **Dalina**. Due to rapidly rising local wealth, domestic tourism is also taking off in China, meaning it may well be profitable to invest in either ski or beach resorts.

For the purposes of this book and due to shortage of space, Shanghai, Beijing, Chongqing and Macau will be considered in detail.

'The property markets in China's secondary cities and cities like Macau have not yet been targeted by too many foreign opportunity funds or speculative investors, making now an ideal time to invest'

Shanghai

Home to the powerful Shanghai Stock Exchange, Shanghai rubs proverbial shoulders with New York, Tokyo and London and is one of the world's most important trade and finance centres. Its GDP growth exceeded 1.2 trillion yuan in 2007, the 16th consecutive year of double-digit growth, with expectations that it will reach 2 trillion yuan by 2012.

Having won its bid to host the World Expo in 2010, the city is enjoying $2.3bn dedicated to new urban infrastructure. The resulting influx of people has caused demand for property to far outstrip supply and stands the market in very good stead.

Considering the city's current status, the price of property remains attractive – you can purchase here at a fraction of the cost of other world financial centres, and at half or even a third of the prices in Hong Kong or Taipei. This means that the potential for capital growth is substantial, and prices are likely to rise sturdily over coming years.

The real estate market in Shanghai is very healthy due to constant demand for luxury residential units. Transaction rates are high and construction is increasing to match demand. Fuelled by surges in the residential market and a rising consumer price index, average rental prices have increased to $22.5 per square metre per month. The luxury residential market is a stable one with an optimistic future as demand seems set to increase further. Meanwhile confidence in the market is compounded by the many new construction projects planned for the city.

Beijing

Beijing is the capital, main political and cultural centre of China and enjoyed a thriving GDP growth rate of 12.6% in 2007. The host of the 2008 Olympics, the city will without doubt become a property investment hotspot, augmented by the $41bn that has been budgeted for the city's transformation and development of infrastructure.

As the centre of China's tourism and therefore seeing a high level of transient population, serviced apartments and hotels in the city represent a good buy and are set to benefit greatly from the increased levels of Olympic tourism. In addition, excellent infrastructure should ensure that the city maintains it position as a key investment destination long after the Olympics have finished.

In the luxury residential property sector, prices are averaging U$3,000 per square metre, whilst rental prices have risen to $22.8 per square metre per month. Although rental yields for luxury properties (predicated at around 5.5% for 2008) are better than many of the world's other metropolises, the vacancy rate is alarmingly high, currently standing at 25.43%.

Chongqing

The yield compression in first-tier cities is diverting some institutional investors' attention to second-tier cities. Among the second-tier cities, Chongqing becomes the most obvious hotspot.

Chongqing is located in central China at the confluence of the Yangzte and Jiangling Rivers and, following Chinese government policies aimed to further develop western China, Chonngqing has become somewhat of a 'Gateway to the West'. Chinese central government has committed $2bn annually to improve Chongqing's infrastructure, support that is predicted to continue for at least a decade. According to the Chongqing Municipal Government, the growth rate of its economy ranks third across the country and increased 15.6% in 2007 compared to the same period in 2006. This was its fastest growth since 1997.

Central government's 'go west' plan is providing an enormous boost to the city and the Three Gorges Dam project (impacting tourism and the relocation of residents) and increasing FDI will result in increased demand for commercial space and accommodation.

The Chongqing real estate market is showing steady growth, with the number of residential housing transactions up 34.65% in May 2008 from the previous month. The market seems unaffected by the recent earthquake in the neighbouring Sichuan province. The Chongqing Municipality have also earmarked 10 billion yuan ($13bn) for the demolition and renovation of all old and dangerous buildings in its nine urban districts, planned to occur over the next five years. This bodes well for the up-and-coming city, providing a huge boost to the housing market as well as to the overall potential of this city.

As a secondary city, Chongqing is beginning to be recognised as an upcoming market with enormous potential for high rental yields and capital appreciation.

Macau

Dubbed the Las Vegas of the Far East, Macau is one of world's most famous off-shore banking centres and tax havens. Only 70km south-west of Hong Kong, property prices in this small territory (only 23 square km) are about a third of Hong Kong's.

The revenue from its gaming industry was greater than Las Vegas in 2007 (about $10.3bn), up 46% on the previous year's total. After the completion of Sands Macau, the world's biggest casino in 2004, Wynn Macau in 2006, and MGM and Venetian in 2007, 15 new casinos will become operational by the end of 2009, along with a number of new hotels and should draw higher levels of tourists. Macau already receives 27 million tourists annually so its future is very positive.

GDP growth has been averaging 10% per year since 2001, with 2007 seeing a growth rate of 27.3%. It is even rumoured that Macau's GDP may soon outstrip Hong Kong's. Meanwhile, unemployment stands at a low 2.9%.

With its robust economic performance, continual wealth enhancement, booming gaming and gaming-related tourism industries, Macau's property market is attracting more and more sophisticated property investors and property prices have already increased by over 100% between 2002 and 2005. The supply of new dwellings is very limited and the property vacancy rate is low, making Macau a prime market with great potential. Rental yields for residential properties are about 4% to 6% but are expected to grow quickly as large numbers of foreign expatriates and highly educated staff move to Macau to take advantage of the burgeoning gaming and tourism industries.

Asia

CHINA

Buyer's guide

To many, investment in China may seem like a difficult prospect. Apart from language and cultural differences, concerns range from opaque laws and regulations, to complicated bureaucracy.

Most importantly, investors first of all need to check whether they are even in a position to purchase a property in China – i.e. a foreign resident in China for over a year or one who has registered a WOFE or a JV.

Before purchasing a property, certain checks must be made on both the seller and the property. During the purchase process itself, a number of legal documents must be signed and require legalising by the Chinese Embassy or Consulate. Some of this documentation must be completed in China, but this can be done through an agent and a power of attorney arrangement.

Once you have decided to buy, it is necessary to open a local bank account and to register this with the appropriate authorities. This bank account will be the base for any transactions, such as rent payments, to be made with regard to the property. A bank with internet and telephone banking is recommended for this process, as buyers are thereby able to keep track of transactions and funds.

To reserve a property it is necessary to pay a small deposit. The buyer and seller will then enter into an *official sales contract*, which must be notarised if the purchaser is foreign. If property is off-plan, payments are often made in stages, which vary depending on the seller. Once the property is completed and the full payment is made, application will then be made to the government Deed and Title Office for the deed transfer from the seller to the buyer, on payment of the relevant taxes and fees (which will typically amount to around 5% of the purchase price). Before this transfer can be made, the seller must have paid off any existing mortgage on the property. This payment schedule also varies depending on the developer.

Mortgages

LTV %	TERM	CURRENCIES	RATES %	STATUS	SPECIAL CONDITIONS
70	30	CNY	6		Must be eligible to buy properties in China as a private individual

Key risks

Property prices and supply in certain districts in China's major cities are no longer sustainable, meaning investors have to be cautious when choosing the location of their investment. Furthermore, China's legal system, as well as its tax system, are still not very transparent, making it essential to procure reliable legal and tax advice before and whilst investing.

There are many perceived risks in China, predominantly related to politics and the protection of private property. However, private property rights are now protected in the Chinese constitution and the Property Rights Law and China's recent accession to the WTO should continue to ensure that the government maintains an investor-friendly approach. In some cities, prices have increased rapidly in recent years, creating fears of a bubble; however, while in the short term there may be some price deflation, these locations still present good medium to long-term opportunities.

The only thing that may hold foreigners back though is their eligibility to buy. Investors may be put off by the processes they have to go through before they are able to purchase property – namely setting up a fully owned foreign enterprise (WOFE) or a joint venture company (JV) or having been resident in China for at least a year.

Rating: ⚠ ⚠

Key opportunities

The implementation of the Property Rights Law should provide more security on private property rights and give domestic and foreign investors more comfort when investing in China's property market. The property markets in China's secondary cities and cities like Macau have not yet been targeted by too many foreign opportunity funds or speculative investors, making now an ideal time to invest.

With China set to become the world's biggest economy by 2020, demand for property is growing enormously both locally and internationally, and the country has possibly the strongest underlying fundamental reasons for property price growth of any country in the world.

According to China Intercontinental Communication Network Centre, the property supply will continue to be lower than demand over the next few decades. Meanwhile, China's government official website states that property price growth is unlikely to drop below 10% per year for the next 15 years.

Rating: $$$$

Guam

Currency: US dollar (USD)
Exchange Rates:
US$ 100 = £51
£1 = US$2

HAGÅTÑA

Introduction

The hub of the Western Pacific and one of Micronesia's most cosmopolitan destinations, Guam is infused with a rich, exotic culture and beautiful landscape. Its unforgettable coastline of striking sandy beaches and crystal clear water coupled with its absorbing history, fragrant cuisine and traditional music and dances make Guam an increasingly popular international holiday destination. Situated in the heart of the Mariana Islands, Guam is currently the biggest island in Micronesia and is bursting with natural beauty. It also features one of the best deep-draft harbours in the Western Pacific making it an important naval hub.

Aware of its potential as a strong tourist destination, Guam's government is committed to developing the island so that it offers visitors hotels and accommodation at international standards as well as a range of other island amenities. The beaches lacing the island offer many different water sports including spectacular scuba diving among the coral reefs and shipwrecks dating back to the world wars. Diving here is some of the least expensive in the world but no less spectacular. Guam waters are home to the world's tallest ocean mountain and the world's deepest known point: the Marianas Trench.

Although Guam isn't particularly well known for its night life, a New York style night club has recently opened and there are many elegant restaurants and hotels offering a variety of cuisine. If golf is more your thing, there are several courses to choose from. The late 80's boom in hotel and golf course developments forced Guam's hotel room inventory up by more than 300% between 1985 and 2000 and prompted the creation of three high-profile golf courses, making Guam a popular choice with avid golfers.

Is this a good place to buy?

As a territory of America, Guam's economy is structured under US laws and uses US currency – its purchase processes and legalities are therefore more transparent than some of the other Pacific countries. With a recent history of political stability, Guam's economic growth has seen a healthy period with the island's Gross Island Product (GIP) increasing by nearly 50% since 1996. Further, investments of between $8–$10bn have recently been injected into the country directed in particular towards infrastructure, housing and support facilities which should attract increasing levels of FDI and tourists.

The state of Guam's modern real estate was decided back in the Second World War when, following the United States' victory, the federal government acquired a substantial portion of the island for strategic military purposes. The federal government still retains control of approximately 30% of the island, with the local government owning another 30%, leaving the remaining 40% in the hands of private landowners.

'Guam's property market is recovering and opportunistic investors, armed with in-depth property information, face attractive investment opportunities'

Since the 1960s, prices and the health of the real estate market have fluctuated severely with several short-lived booms and busts meaning the market is now viewed with some caution. Many regard it as an extremely volatile property market.

However, with economic forces from tourism and military sectors providing the foundation for the local real estate market, it is likely that recent and proposed increases in military activity will further support the sector. Although characterised by severe peaks and troughs, Guam's property market does have some deliverance. Strong market fundamentals such as US laws and currency, close proximity to Japan and Asia, political stability, tropical climate and adequate tourist infrastructure should couple with military growth and foreign investment to support the long-term recovery of Guam's real estate market.

It is probable that Guam's next boom will occur between 2015 and 2020, as newly rich Chinese look for vacation properties, and Japanese, Korean, and Taiwanese investors return in earnest. Pre-empting this, it is hoped that authorities will put measures in place to preclude the severity of the busts which historically follow.

Guam is the sophisticated destination in Micronesia and following its recent strong tourism growth, the country is now experiencing a construction boom with property prices beginning to rise. Buying property in Guam is a relatively straightforward process for the foreign investor, with few restrictions on foreign ownership. Although property prices are steadily increasing, rental income tax is low and non-resident foreigners earning rental income are only taxed at corporate tax rates. This means that rental yields currently sit high, at around 14%; an attractive prospect for investors. Prices for residential property are currently around $1,100 to $1,450 per square metre.

 INSIDER TIP

Transaction costs for buying and selling property in Guam are also low, currently sitting between only 6.6%–12.6% of the property value. With the tenancy law in Guam pro-landlord and a year-round sunny climate, Guam does have some credentials which present positive investment opportunities for foreign investors, especially on a buy-to-let basis.

As an up-and-coming country undergoing continuous development supported by a blossoming tourist industry, house prices over the island are expected to rise and investors with the courage to invest in a risky market may well enjoy healthy gains.

Which type of property should you go for?

As a growing tourist destination, Guam has a good array of tourist accommodation including luxury resorts, business hotels, family-style accommodations and bed and breakfast inns. Renowned operators such as Hilton, Westin, Hyatt Regency, Outrigger, Nikko, Pacific Islands Club (PIC), Hotel Okura, Marriott, and other international and regional hotel chains now have developments throughout the island.

Although Guam doesn't have a huge population, most people reside in the north of the country. Tumon Bay is particularly popular, especially with tourists, thanks to its impressive beaches and spectacular seafront property. Property along the seafront though, can be expensive, meaning many people looking to buy property opt for the areas of Mong Mong, Toto, Maite or Mangilao which are only 10–15 minutes' drive from Tumon Bay but considerably cheaper. Apartments and condominiums bought on a buy-to-let basis are popular with foreign investors as are all properties with a sea view. It is these units that typically earn the highest rental income.

Asia

GUAM

Hotspots

As property prices rise throughout Guam's popular cities, certain areas are defining themselves as investment hubs.

Dededo

Situated in northern Guam this is the most populated town on the island offering a shopping mall of 130 stores, elegant restaurants, an amusement park and a mall theatre. It also has a pretty beachfront, a little way along which is the Guam golf resort, containing many sporting and leisure facilities as well as several good restaurants.

Tamuning

The country's economic and business centre, Tamuning also offers a wide variety of entertainment venues and is a popular tourist town. With various shopping amenities such as the Harmon flea market, the duty-free boutiques and premium outlets, there are also many places to eat both in and around the city. The city borders Agana Bay which has several good quality hotels such as Palace Hotel and the Onward Beach Resort. There are also many beach and water activities further along the coast, all within walking distance of the big hotels.

Hagatna (Agana)

The capital of Guam, may not have a large population but does contain some of the island's main tourist attractions such as the historic site of Dulce Nobre de Maria Cathedral-Basilica, Chamorro Village and Latte Stone Park; a man-made historical stone setting. To the south of Guam lie several inactive volcanoes providing an absolutely stunning backdrop to the island. Several travel companies on the island offer complete tours showing all the popular sites and attractions including waterfalls, viewpoints and various historic sites.

Buyer's guide

Although there are a few restrictions for foreign individuals wanting to buy property in Guam, these can be avoided by investing through a Guam registered company. If going down this route, properties can be purchased freely. Title insurance is available to protect buyers (www.investguam.com).

Mortgages

Finance is not yet available in Guam.

Key risks

Although Guam's property market does have many appealing attributes, the country is still military based and it is difficult to guarantee that it will continue to progress and develop at a rate necessary to make investments profitable. The near-term future of the real estate market then, remains largely unstable and susceptible to external forces in the region, particularly from Japan. Highly susceptible to volatility due to external pressures, the property sector is likely to suffer in line with regional economic downturns.

Rating: ⚠ ⚠ ⚠

Key opportunities

There are no restrictions on foreign ownership in Guam except that foreigners can only buy one occupied house in their name unless they are registering as a permanent resident. Those able to form a Guam corporation, with a minimum of three incorporators (at least one of which should be a Guam resident) are able to buy properties without restriction. Total buying costs are low at between only 6.6%–12.6% thanks to low transaction costs.

With rising tourism, a strong US economy, infrastructure improvements and high levels of construction, Guam's property market is recovering and opportunistic investors, armed with in-depth property information, face attractive investment opportunities so long as they are prepared to shoulder the many risks associated with buying here.

Rating: $$$

Asia

GUAM

India

Currency: Indian Rupee
Exchange rates:
1,000 Rupees = £11.81
£1 = 84.63 Rupees

1,000 Rupees = US $23.34
US $1 = 42.95 Rupees

Introduction

As diverse a country as India cannot be summarised in a few words. Home to the most populated city, most prolific film industry and one of the most favoured cuisines in the world, India has a lot to offer. From northern Mumbai, home to both the Indian Stock Exchange and Bollywood, characterised to the south by paddy fields and coconut plantations, India is a land of colourful diversity. With a plethora of languages, customs, religions and arts, the country has always been a popular tourist destination.

India is undoubtedly an emerging market and as such has very good potential for capital appreciation. On top of this it is a market where transactions take place in English, finance and banking is straightforward, and a growing middle class ensures a healthy rental market. The rocketing population creates a constant demand for property, meaning that India unarguably presents an interesting and very real prospect for investors.

There is, however, a catch. The opportunity to buy is largely restricted to people with strong personal links to India, defined as either non-resident Indians (NRI) or persons of Indian origin (PIO). This means either Indian citizens living abroad or people who have held an Indian passport at some time, have a parent or grandparent with Indian citizenship or are married to an Indian citizen. Technically foreign citizens of Indian origin also need agreement from the Reserve Bank, but a general permission to buy immoveable property has been granted.

If the buyer has status as an NRI or PIO the rule is as follows:

An Indian citizen residing outside India (NRI) can acquire by way of purchase, any immovable property in India other than agricultural, plantation or farm house. He is allowed to transfer such kind of immovable property to a person resident outside India who is a citizen of India, or to a person of Indian origin resident outside India, or a person resident in India. (Source: www.yesweb.org)

A useful website to consult may be the Reserve Bank of India (www.rbi.org.in) which has up-to-date information on the legal regulations for property purchase.

'India's stability, lack of a communist government, and the right to freehold property makes the real estate market here in many ways preferable to that in China'

It should be noted that foreigners are able to get around the strict rules by opening a properly registered business in India thereby entitling them to own property, but this in itself can be problematic as the business often has to be registered in more than one name and be able to show assets as well as a proportion of Indian ownership. Foreigners are also technically allowed to buy property having resided in the country for 182 days – but with the Indian tourist visa expiring at 181 days this is usually harder than it sounds. As a result of many foreigners ignoring these rules and buying illegally the Indian government is cracking down on foreigners buying property, and many are finding themselves in trouble having proceeded through the buying process believing that they were acting legally. Any foray into the Indian property market should be done cautiously with independent advice from proven-reputable agents and lawyers.

Is this a good place to buy?

If you are entitled to buy in India, then there are many options open to you in this emerging market. The economy has posted an average growth rate of more than 7% in the decade since 1996 and Merrill Lynch predicts a sevenfold increase in the property market by 2015. With a GDP growth rate of 8.5% in 2007, the Indian economy is among the fastest growing in the world and is still growing at a rate double that achieved by the West during the Industrial Revolution.

India's stability, lack of a communist government, and the right to freehold property makes the real estate market here in many ways preferable to that in China. Eligible emerging market investors then, who might otherwise turn to China may prefer the greater degree of stability and ease of investing that India offers. Encouragingly, it isn't just economic growth which is tempting people to buy, meaning there should be ample room for the real estate industry to develop.

Over half the current population is under the age of 25, so with increasing education creating a professional population and a growing modern attitude towards independence, the result is going to be a sudden surge of demand for housing over the next few decades. As it stands at the moment, official government figures show a shortfall of 20 million housing units according to a spokesman for www.Navyroof.com. At the same time, the middle class, developing in size and wealth now finds it has disposable income and can afford better housing, and so add further to demand. With the population growing by 15–20 million people every year half of the population will be categorised as middle class by 2025.

Net income in India has grown 100% over the last 10 years and population growth is expected to help India take China's place as the most populous country by 2030. 20 million houses will be needed in the next five years if supply is to keep up with demand meaning investors couldn't ask for a better set of market fundamentals.

There are over 25 million non-resident Indians and they retain close links to the country. Remittances by overseas Indians are higher than for any other country in the world and latest figures show that remittances from overseas totalled US \$24.6bn from 2005 to 2006: ahead of India's two closest followers, China and Mexico. Overseas and non-resident Indians often like to maintain a base in the country and their wealth provides a constant boost to a property market which has been one of the strongest internationally over the past few years.

Massive infrastructure improvements are being planned for new international airports at Bangalore, Hyderbad and Pune while 'The Golden Quadrilateral' project to provide an interstate road link between Delhi, Mumbai, Kolkata and Chennai is nearly complete. The current thirst for infrastructure improvements is likely to have a favourable stimulus on the Indian economy, real estate and tourism markets.

Which type of property should you go for?

Local property consultants tip high-quality apartments and villas in central locations as the best stock to invest in. Whilst property prices in the countryside or suburbs of different cities may remain static, prime property values in most major cities should continue on an upwards trajectory. In keeping with the rapid development of certain industries, the property market is also expanding and as a result much of the property available, especially for investment purposes, comes in the form of large, new off-plan apartment complexes.

Hotspots

Those looking for a pure investment buy will probably be tempted by cities such as **Mumbai**, **Delhi**, **Bangalore** and **Chennai** which have all undergone radical growth in the last few years. Indeed, the country is urbanising at a rapid rate of 2.5% a year. By 2015 India's 'Mega-Cities' of Mumbai and Delhi will be the world's second and third largest cities.

Mumbai

Generally regarded as expensive, especially south of the city. Identified as the commercial and financial capital of India and with a fantastic public transport network, no area is out of reach and property is in high demand. Apartment prices in South Mumbai are the equivalent of those in many of the world's leading cities. A leading Indian real estate site (www.Magicbricks.com) offers an idea of prices, with property in the western suburbs of Mumbai costing from as little as £24 ($46) per square foot, to £727 ($1,412) per square foot in southern Mumbai.

A degree of caution needs to be exercised when investing in Delhi or Mumbai as severe price drops in residential property prices occurred during 2007. That said, providing you choose your development and area carefully, a profit can still be made.

Buyers would do best to invest in other rapidly developing cities such as Bangalore in India's 'Silicon Valley' (Karnataka) or Jaipur (Rajastan).

Bangalore

Firmly established as a technology hub, its economy is rising rapidly. Here, total demand for apartments is estimated at 24,000 units each year, with an expected annual growth rate of 20% over the next several years. Average prices in Bangalore range from £217–£540 ($421–$1,048) per square metre.

Jaipur

Jaipur forms part of the 'Golden Triangle' of Delhi-Agra-Jaipur. Popular with tourists, it is universally famous as the 'Pink city' with stunning lakes, forts and palaces. It is also the site for substantial IT and industrial development. To keep pace with the business development there are a growing number of residential complexes being created, with prices starting from £9,400 ($18,257) on a complex of town houses and apartments, and from £23,194 ($45,048) on a complex of villas that can be built to personal specification.

INSIDER TIP Other fast-moving cities include Chennai (Tamil Nadu), Hyderabad (Andrhra Pradesh) and Pune (Maharastra) which are proving to be highly attractive business locations, thus attracting residential demand. IT and retail are key drivers of the real estate in Pune. Its transformation into a vibrant corporate city with close proximity to Mumbai has made Pune a hot destination for the real estate investor. Choice can vary across a plethora of new real estate builds, with luxury apartments starting from as little as £30,000 ($58,273) whilst top of the range property is around £150,000 ($291,367).

Rudrapur

Expected to see huge amounts of growth in the near future after the government designated it a Special Economic Zone and offered tax incentives to encourage companies into the area. With around 450 factories being built, the predicted work force is expected to reach 300,000, with at least 50,000 expected to be employed from outside the region. It is expected that those living locally will also choose to move out of family homes as their wages increase so demand could continue to grow for a number of years, creating a solvent and sustainable investment opportunity.

For buyers looking to pick up a second home for holiday use or for the holiday market, the best letting opportunities are in Goa and Kerala in southern India.

Goa

With 100km of stunning beaches, over 400,000 tourist arrivals a year and prices that have risen over 25% in the last three years, Goa is a hot destination for investors. The Goan government is cracking down on rogue agents and sales to non-Indians have to be reported to the government to ensure they are legally conducted. Often nicknamed 'India for Beginners' it is a delightful blend of East and West that has already attracted some 5,000 foreign investors, 3,000 of which are British. It is also rated as one of India's best states to live in and one of the safest Indian regions, becoming increasingly popular with retirees from the west. Rental yields on Goan property are estimated at around 6%–8%.

Kerala

Kerala, also known as the 'Queen of the Arabian sea', is a collection of islands and narrow peninsulas with a warm tropical climate. The area has become increasingly popular with tourists over the past few years and has a sustainable tourism industry, almost year-round.

In both Goa and Kerala, an apartment in a gated compound can be a good buy. Remember that a sub-tropical climate can have a harsh effect on buildings so buying into a serviced apartment block means less can go wrong in your absence. Prices in Goa range the whole spectrum, from cheap, individually sold apartments at £5,000–£20,000, ($9,712–$38,848), whilst more expensive villas in gated complexes start from £70,000 ($135,968) and up. Recent 2008 reports from developers based in Goa have reported a thriving resale market with increases of 40%–50% over a 12-month period on the sale price of an off-plan property.

Wherever you choose to buy, you will find India well supplied with research resources. www.Indiaproperties.com for example, has a regional market section which gives up-to-date information on costs in different areas of major cities.

Buyer's guide

There are very severe restrictions in place for any foreigners looking to buy property in India. To be eligible they need to be either a non-resident Indian or a person of Indian origin. Neither NRIs or PIOs are entitled to acquire agricultural land/plantation properties or farmhouses in India without approval from the Reserve Bank.

Foreign nationals of non-Indian origin cannot purchase any immovable property in the country but are permitted to take residential accommodation on a lease provided that the lease period does not exceed five years. (Source: www.rbi.org.in)

Foreigners can partake in real estate transactions by establishing a foreign company although this needs to have at least a 60% non-resident Indian (NRI) holding. Further, the immovable property they purchase should be necessary or incidental to carrying on their business activity. (Source: www.rbi.org.in)

Great care needs to be taken when buying any land or property as the title deed registration process is outdated and insecure. (Source: www. amberlamb.com)

Mortgages

Finance in India is only available to local and non-resident Indians.

Key risks

There have been concerns that rapid price rises in some urban areas could lead to a potential bubble in the market and in 2007 some prices in Delhi and Mumbai suburbs began to fall after their rapid rise. As yet, there have been no drastic changes in the Indian real estate market, although it would be prudent to check the state of a particular local market, easily found in the property sections of local English language newspapers.

The biggest concern regarding purchasing property in India is the eligibility-to-buy factor. All ventures into any real estate investment market should be made with caution but extra care must be taken with India. It is essential at every level to ensure that transactions are carried out transparently and legally, leaving no cause for the government to have issue with your purchase. Repatriation of funds can also be a problem. According to Price Waterhouse Coopers, NRIs/PIOs are permitted repatriation of sale proceeds up to $1m per financial year for a maximum of two houses. However, the property must have been paid for from a rupee account and repatriation of funds is only permitted up to the amount originally invested. Unless investment laws are further liberalised, this suggests that returns have to be made from rental income rather than capital appreciation. Non-resident Indians are allowed to rent out property and to repatriate the income earned through the banker/authorized dealer. For foreigners this is slightly harder but developers have methods to get around this legally so it is best to get up-to-date advice from them as well as independent legal advice at all stages. All use of offshore accounts is totally illegal, for both buyer and any local developer or agent.

Corruption is still a very relevant problem in the country and all caution should be taken to avoid this.

Rating: ⚠ ⚠ ⚠ ⚠

Key opportunities

The burgeoning Indian economy and a rapidly growing middle class make India an outstanding investment opportunity, albeit for a restricted market. Demand for accommodation is expected to increase greatly over the next few decades thanks to increasing wealth, a rapidly growing younger population, and comparatively cheap property prices. India is fast becoming a world player on the economic field: the internationalisation of the economy and the country's emergence as an economic force should equate to excellent long-term performance in the real estate market.

Rating: $$$$

Kazakhstan

Currency: Tenge
Exchange Rates:
£100 = 23.84 Tenge
£1 = 238.39 Tenge

$100 = 12.07 Tenge
$1 = 120.7 Tenge

Introduction

Kazakhstan is an unlikely jewel in the property market crown; with a growing economy, beautiful landscape and low property prices, it presents a very interesting opportunity to the foreign investor.

Subtle nuances left over from Russian travellers are apparent throughout the country and the Great Silk Route that ran through the south of the country has inspired varied architecture and some spectacular monuments. The Al Matinsky Nature Reserve, Kol-Say Lakes and the Aksu-Jabaghy Nature Reserve, the largest Natural Park and home to numerous rare species, are all testament to the beauty of the natural landscape. For the more adventurous, many outdoor activities, including horse riding, swimming, fishing, hiking and skiing are set amidst breathtaking surroundings and available throughout the year.

> *'Kazakhstan appears to have the credentials for a healthy real estate future and those investing sooner rather than later are likely to enjoy the greatest returns'*

In 2006 the release of *Borat: Cultural Learnings of America For Make Benefit Glorious Nation of Kazakhstan* starring Sacha Baron Cohen brought Kazakhstan to the cinema screen, however the country's portrayal was inaccurate and the film met with mixed reviews. Although the film caused controversy, tourist interest in Kazakhstan since its release has grown a staggering 300% and the government are embracing this surge of foreign interest.

Its economy is also on an upward trajectory. Kazakhstan was the first country to repay its debt to IMF in 2000, seven years ahead of schedule and was successfully upgraded to market economy status under US trade law as a result.

Is this a good place to buy?

Of the world's emerging markets, Kazakhstan is perhaps one with some of the greatest potential. With major deposits of oil, petroleum, natural gas, coal, iron ore, tin and gold, the country's export trade is a strong one and thanks to its wealth of natural resources Kazakhstan attracts high levels of FDI – over $40bn since 1993. With GDP growth of 9.7% in the first nine months of 2007, Kazakhstan's economy is considered to be among the fastest growing in the world. Home to the Caspian Sea region's largest recoverable crude reserves, oil is the backbone of Kazakhstan's economy, drawing a consistent stream of mining companies and executives. At the outset of its growth and reform cycle, the country should mature into a prime investment destination providing political stability is preserved.

On 19 September 2002, Kazakhstan became the first country in the Commonwealth of Independent States to reach an investment grade status with Moody's, a credit rating agency, upgrading the republic by two notches to 'Baa3 ' – the same rating as Saudi Arabia and Bahrain. Further, Kazakhstan by right, is considered the leading Commonwealth of Independent States (CIS) country in terms of investment opportunity, evidenced by Kazakhstan's investment ratings from both Moody's and Standard & Poor's and Fitch. The findings of surveys conducted by other international experts and international organisations have further confirmed its auspicious status.

The property market in Kazakhstan is currently the most open that it has ever been for both local and foreign investors. International investors are becoming increasingly interested in the Kazakh market and since 1999, the number of companies with foreign involvement has increased by a staggering 564%. Keen to secure higher levels of FDI, the country is striving to implement constructions that will attract more foreigners to the country and improve infrastructure. Public transport is one area that the government are especially keen to improve as buses and trains, at present, are not very reliable. Although trains are cheap, they are also slow and overcrowded whilst buses, although more frequent, have an increasing association with crime. Internal flights are recommended, but not always available: a problem that the authorities need to address.

Laws have also been put in place to make the purchase process more straightforward and with tourism on the rise, it is likely that this will become a very significant industry for Kazakhstan's growing economy.

Which type of property should you go for?

Apartment prices in the larger cities of Kazakhstan, such as Astana the capital, and Almaty have seen a continuous price growth over the last seven years. However, these increases are not expected to continue as most locals are now priced out of the market. A new scheme by the government aiming to lower credit interest rates and make mortgage loans more accessible for the poorer people of Kazakhstan, should allow more local home ownership. Authorities are convinced that implementing a lower credit rate will encourage locals and foreigners to invest in property, resulting in a more lively and competitive market.

INSIDER TIP **The next big project is Esentai Park in Almaty, a 342,000 square metre mixed-use development designed by Skidmore, Owings and Merrill in New York, at the heart of which is a 162m tower with breathtaking views of the Zaili Alatau Mountains. A JW Marriott and 450 upscale residences will be included in the complex which should kick-start Kazakhstan's property market.**

Hotspots

The north of Kazakhstan is the industrialised and highly populated area of the country but still boasts stunning surroundings. A testament to its appeal are the 15,000 tourists a year who visit the area for its sandy beaches and ancient pine forests.

Central Kazakhstan has one of the largest lakes in the world, one half made up of salt water, the other comprising fresh water. **Astana**, the capital city of Kazakhstan, is also located in this region.

The east of Kazakhstan is the more mountainous region, with plunging forested canyons and beautiful cedar forests. Russian travellers' homes from years ago are preserved here as museums and offer a quaint insight into times gone by.

West Kazakhstan is the meeting point of Europe and Asia and home to some of the country's most interesting architectural sites such as the Shakpak-Ata Mosque.

Atyrau

Atyrau is the regional capital with a population of 141,800 people. The city has well-developed fishing and oil industries, as well as machine-building facilities and extensive crop production. A number of air carriers are successfully operating here and the number of passenger flights into the city is steadily increasing. An extensive programme was recently drawn up for the development of the airport and is currently being realised.

Over 55 enterprises with foreign capital now work here and are mainly engaged in the business of oil extraction. Such companies are bringing workers, professionals and increasing wealth to the region.

As far as the oil industry is concerned, **Tengiz** plays a pivotal role. Home to a substantial oil deposit, development of the Tengiz supply started a few years ago and has started energy experts talking across the globe. It is likely that such supplies will continue to draw many large companies and workers to the region over the coming years especially as there are several prospective oil and gas deposits in the north-eastern part of the Caspian seabed which are still to be fully explored.

Almaty

Almaty was the official capital of Kazakhstan for more than 70 years and has a lot to offer visitors. Home to five stadiums, a hippodrome, and mountain sport complexes with unique skating rings and 60m ski jumps, sports enthusiasts flock here. Just fifteen minutes outside of the city is the famous international mountain-climber camp 'Khan-Tengri', popular with mountaineers from all over the world on their way to climb the highest peak in Kazakhstan – the Khan-Tengri.

Almaty's astounding ability to adapt to the changing times whilst remaining ecologically responsible earns it great acclaim.

Astana

Astana has been the capital of Kazakhstan since 1997 and is the most popular area for property investment. The capital is a thriving modern city developing at rapid speed and is the political and cultural centre for Kazakhstan. Centrally located in the republic of Kazakhstan, Astana is the crossroads between China and Europe and is a busy transport hub.

Boasting a five-star hotel and variety of further high-quality accommodation for visitors, Astana has apartment blocks that are built to European standards whilst government and office buildings are prolific in the city centre. The city also has the benefit of well-constructed modern roads and a picturesque river.

Since 1997 the population of Astana has nearly doubled in size with an estimated 500,000 people now living and working there. This rise is attributable to the increase in government and office jobs now available in the capital.

Determined to attract increased foreign investment, Astana is undergoing extensive construction which, it is hoped, will attract further businesses and tourist arrivals. To cater for rising visitor numbers, its airport is undergoing major renovation including the construction of a new runway.

Actau

The city of Aqtau is considerably cheaper than other cities in the country and therefore should be noted by investors. It is a relatively new city – built in 1961 to service the burgeoning oil industry and as such should experience high demand and growth over the coming years as more and more companies flock to extract the precious oil.

Buyer's guide

Following the country's release from communism, laws were privatised and liberalised whilst several changes were made to land registration laws, making the purchase process more straightforward. All foreign investments now have the advantage of being protected by the government which should encourage foreigners, although of course it is essential that all land titles are checked more than once to verify legality of ownership.
(Source: http://kazakhstan.offplanproperty.info/visas.html)

Mortgages

Finance is not yet available in Kazakhstan.

Asia

KAZAKHSTAN

Asia

KAZAKHSTAN

Key risks

Kazakhstan's climate is not especially accommodating: summers tend to be extremely hot and winters bitterly cold so visiting in spring or autumn, the more temperate months, is recommended. Flights are often grounded in the winter and eating out can be difficult out of season as most of the restaurants close.

Terrorism is obviously a risk that anyone considering purchasing property in Kazakhstan must be aware of. Recent terrorist attacks in neighbouring Uzbekistan have led to increased military presence on the border.

Rating: ⚠ ⚠

Key opportunities

Kazakhstan is a huge country that is still growing both economically and culturally. Generally considered safe, it has a stable political climate and a steadily rising economy. House prices are growing but are still relatively cheap when compared with house prices in Western Europe, the main attraction for foreign investors. Those investing in key oil regions are likely to secure high occupancy levels and strong rental yields.

The recent simplification of the purchase process means it is easier for foreigners to buy here and shows Kazakhstan's commitment to encouraging Foreign Direct Investment. All foreign sales are now protected by the government; however, it is still strongly advised that all property titles are verified in detail before exchanging. Kazakhstan then, appears to have the credentials for a healthy real estate future and those investing sooner rather than later are likely to enjoy the greatest returns.

Rating: $$$

Malaysia

Currency: Ringgit
Exchange rates:
100 Ringgit = £15.55
£1 = 6.43 Ringgit

100 Ringgit = US $30.71
US $1 = 3.36 Ringgit

KUALA LUMPUR

Introduction

Malaysia is spread across the South China Sea, occupying a peninsula bordering Thailand and a third of the Island of Borneo. The area is one of the most beautiful corners of the world, famous for palm-fringed white beaches, gentle seas and rainforest, and is a key point for shipping and trade in South East Asia.

Geographically it has beautiful coastal areas, including the popular resorts of Penang and Langkawi, and a tropical interior. Several mountain ranges run through the country, with forests of native sandalwood, teak and ebony. Malaysia also has abundant mineral resources, oil and gas reserves, and a large agricultural base.

Early introduction of rubber trees was highly successful and became a main export for over a century. A former British colony, the country's political structure is based on the UK's. Independent since 1963, the country is now one of the main dragon economies that saw huge growth in the mid-1990s but suffered economic downturn in 1997. Economic reforms instigated in the early part of this decade have proved fruitful and stability appears to have been achieved. Now highly developed economically and commercially, the government has implemented an ongoing programme encouraging inward investment from overseas corporations and individuals.

Malaysia takes the education of its workforce seriously, literacy rates are high at just under 90% and Malaysian workers tend to be highly motivated, especially in the services sector. Labour laws in the country are relatively well-formulated to offer employment security. These days, the country's main exports are electronic goods and electrical machinery, with much of the domestic production based on manufacturing and export of goods and services. The GDP grew at a rate of 6.1% in 2007, higher than predictions from the previous year and has positively withstood setbacks such as political unrest in areas along the Thai border and health scares such as SARS. The country is moving forward with a policy of creating a strong knowledge base in the fields of technology, research and development. Free Trade Zones and high-spec technology parks have also been set up across the country to aid businesses and research companies.

The country's infrastructure is well developed. Major new road schemes link all commercial hubs, including the seven international shipping ports (95% of Malaysia's trade is via the sea). In addition a well-run rail freight service has begun operations between Kuala Lumpur and Bangkok and will eventually form the Trans-Asia Rail Link connecting all the countries in the region. The country also has five international airports with the largest, Kuala Lumpur International, being highly regarded and capable of accommodating up to 25 million passengers per year.

'The best long-term opportunities of all lie in the buy-to-let market of Kuala Lumpur, particularly with high-end or serviced apartments'

Recent elections, however have shaken the government and the country. Although the Parliamentary election was won by BN, the prime minister's ruling party, the results were some of the worst in history, prompting criticism of the prime minister from many areas. For the first time the party did not win the two-thirds majority necessary to pass amendments to the Malaysian constitution and this has unleashed a national tirade against what some feel was a dirty election. This political uncertainty, coupled with concerns of the slowdown of the global market, has led to some doubt from foreign investors; however, the US statement that it is happy to co-operate with the Malaysian government should allay fears and instil confidence in the Malaysian market.

Many non-nationals are drawn to Malaysia by the quality of life, the sunny, tropical climate, safe environment, good healthcare and education services, and the low cost of living and property. Coastal areas tend to be most popular, with Penang drawing a large number of residents.

To this cultural and geographical vibrancy Malaysia adds flourishing financial and high-tech industries based in Kuala Lumpur. Popularly known as KL, Malaysia's capital has a modern cityscape dominated by the Petronas Twin Towers, at present the third tallest building in the world. With a rapidly expanding population and an urbanisation rate of 10% per annum, Kuala Lumpur is growing fast and the city has become more heavily developed as demand for property has intensified over the past few years.

Is this a good place to buy?

Overseas investment in the property market concentrates on Kuala Lumpur, whilst a secondary market exists in the resorts and islands.

The Malaysian government scrapped capital gains tax on property in early 2007 and relaxed its laws on foreign ownership. In addition it is promoting investment and relocation via the Malaysia My Second Home scheme (MM2H) (see www.malaysia-my-second-home.com), aimed at allowing individuals with a certain level of income to take up long-term residency. The policy has encouraged a mix of overseas buyers and it is hoped that the removal of capital gains tax will increase demand and capital appreciation over the medium term, which has remained at around 6% in recent years. At the start of 2007 a large number of cash-rich buyers from India began to invest heavily in Malaysia and it is likely that this trend will continue.

'Property is cheap, especially compared to Malaysia's Asian counterparts, and there are clear exit strategies available as supply has not yet caught up with demand'

Demand has also been fuelled by a flourishing tourist industry. Over 19.1 million tourists visited Malaysia in 2007, nearly 20% more than the figures recorded for 2006. A new budget airline, Airasia X, is proposing to expand its flight destinations to include London – projected to happen over the next few years. When this does happen the tourism market will be enhanced and demand is likely to increase in the key tourist areas of Kuala Lumpur and along the coast.

Which type of property should you go for?

Regarding the property market, there are two trends discernable: firstly, there is a concentration of affordable luxury properties with the numbers of gated housing projects and non-landed luxury units increasing. Secondly, there is growing demand for serviced apartments, particularly in central locations. This demand is attributable to the large number of professionals who relocate to the

Asia

MALAYSIA

city every year either on a permanent basis or more commonly, for between three and six months. As a result, serviced apartments are a relatively safe bet as far as investment is concerned.

The best long-term opportunities of all lie in the buy-to-let market of Kuala Lumpur, particularly with high-end or serviced apartments. The rise of Malaysia as a tourist destination has also awoken the resort markets in Langkawi and Penang. In these locations, luxury property can seem very cheap and the year- round climate means that annual rental yields from short-term holiday lets can be attractive.

Hotspots

Kuala Lumpur

Fast developing into a highly cosmopolitan, high-tech city, Kuala Lumpur is attracting increasing levels of investment from commercial sectors and is seeing larger numbers of immigrants. It is often the first location property buyers consider and as a result prices here are the highest in the country. New residents are drawn from both overseas and local markets and tend to be young professionals seeking better employment prospects in a growing city. Property is mainly in tower blocks, with many developers offering luxury, serviced apartments, often with guaranteed rentals of between 6%–8% for those wanting a buy-to-let investment.

Strong economic growth, low interest rates, the ease of mortgage borrowing and an element of volatility have all pushed prices in Kuala Lumpur up over the past few years. Capital appreciation is high here in comparison with the rest of the country, and prices on average vary from £700–£1,600 ($1,377–$3,150) per square metre, producing annual yields of up to 10%. A well-located, spacious two-bedroom apartment is unlikely to go for anything under £80,000 ($157,400).

 INSIDER TIP Suburban locations are also popular and many new developments are targeting high-income families with new communities offering on-site facilities such as golf courses, pools, shops and services. The Klang Valley and Monte Kiara in particular are attracting high levels of investors and developers. A new development in the Klang Valley is offering affordable units from £30,000 ($60,050) to £50,000 ($98,400), whilst more high-end properties are being sold for between £75,000 ($147,600) and £160,000 ($315,000).

Sepang Gold Coast

This 22-kilometre stretch of coastline on the western coast, around 25 minutes from Kuala Lumpur airport, is already the location for the Formula 1 Grand Prix circuit and is earmarked for further development. A great coastal project is planned featuring hotels, retail outlets, leisure parks and a whole new residential town. The first development is the vast Golden Palm, which will be built offshore. Prices for properties in the first phase start at £80,110 ($157,500). The resort is expected to attract a lot of interest from buy-to-let investors.

Port Dickson

Port Dickson is a popular coastal resort, around an hour's drive from Kuala Lumpur, and is attractive to the weekend and second-home market. There has been an increase in development in this area over the past three years with large numbers of condominiums and water chalets appearing. Prices start at around £40,000 ($78,700) for a standard one-bedroom apartment or chalet, whilst larger properties sell for between £70,000 ($137,800) and £150,000 ($295,350). Much buy-to-let property is in evidence here with lots of developers offering guaranteed rental returns of around 8%. Though the resort has attractive beaches to the south there are also petrochemical plants further north and this may deter some buyers.

Penang

Penang is a heavily developed tourist island with a growing resident population. Many believe it is now overdeveloped, with a large number of new complexes and condominium buildings. Most of the development is on the west coast with prices for average apartments starting at around £40,000 ($78,700). High-end condominiums have prices heading towards £150,000 ($295,350), whilst a luxury villa could see prices reaching £500,000 ($984,500).

Langkawi

Langkawi is actually a cluster of 99 islands on the Straits of Malacca, around an hour's flight from Kuala Lumpur. Most people holiday and buy on the main island of the same name. Measuring around 25km, the island is known for its long, white sand beaches, traditional stilted fishing villages and upmarket resort complexes. Much of the land here is jungle and designated as reserve land, which means it cannot be sold to non-nationals. The property market here is not as developed as in Penang and private sales are common, with a standard-size townhouse or apartment in a new development costing from £30,000 ($60,050) to £40,000 ($78,700). The whole of the island of Langkawi is a duty-free haven.

Sarawak and Sabah

Situated on the island of Borneo, Sarawak is the largest state in Malaysia and is a heavily forested region that the government is actively targeting for growth. Tax incentives and protection of foreign investment are two of the steps it has taken to encourage investment in the region. Tourism is a major activity, as is palm oil production. Property comes mainly in the form of new-build developments with prices starting from £125,000 ($246,000) per unit, rising to over £400,000 ($787,400) for luxury villas. High occupancy figures issued by the regional tourist board are estimated to be 70% and with a shortage of holiday beds, prospects for investors are strong. Further, with 4 million tourists expected in the region by 2010, there should be increased demand.

Buyer's guide

Leasehold as well as freehold title can be acquired even for condominiums throughout the country although in Sabah state, freehold titles are only granted to native lands which can only be acquired by natives and Malays. In general, foreigners can acquire immovable properties in Malaysia providing they are worth more than £40,000 without approval from the Foreign Investment Committee. State Authority consent though, is always required before foreigners acquire immovable properties.

As far as the fiscal system goes, Malaysia is subject to moderate tax rates and has a double taxation agreement with 60 countries.

Mortgages

LTV %	TERM	CURRENCIES	RATES %	STATUS	SPECIAL CONDITIONS
80	20	MYR	4.75	Employed or self-employed	

Key risks

There is little about Malaysia that should cause concern to the property investor. The economy has recovered from the Asian Financial Crisis of over a decade ago and continues to improve, although some commentators argue that it has yet to return to levels seen before the crash. The recent political developments have caused some disruption and may continue to cause unrest amongst some Malaysians but it is unlikely to have too severe an effect on the economy and the real estate market as a whole. Although the country is one of the most stable in Asia, racial and religious tensions do exist and have been a recurring theme in the recent election.

Rating: ⚠

Key opportunities

Malaysia is a modern, efficient country with a stable and high-performing economy. It has excellent infrastructure and is a recipient of large amounts of foreign investment supporting development within the country. The government is extremely pro-foreign investment, resulting in beneficial incentives for foreign property purchasers, including automatic residency for any property owner, tax breaks and relaxation of foreign property ownership laws. With a low-cost but high standard of living as well as some of the most beautiful beaches and fascinating jungle to explore, Malaysia has a thriving tourism industry that creates a high rental demand and offers good rental yields. Property is cheap, especially compared to Malaysia's Asian counterparts, and there are clear exit strategies available as supply has not yet caught up with demand, meaning there is always a buyer waiting in the wings. The process of buying and integrating with the country is facilitated by the fact that Malaysia is an ex-British colony and has modelled the legal system on that of Westminster's Parliament. With English a widely spoken language the purchase transactions are transparent and easier to comprehend.

Rating: $$$$$

Asia

MALAYSIA

Mongolia

Currency: Mongolia Tugriks (MNT)
Exchange Rates:
100,000 Tugriks = £43.70
£1 = 2,384 MNT

100 Tugriks = $86.51
$1 = 1,157.00 MNT

ULAANBAATAR

Introduction

Mention Mongolia and it evokes romantic visions of another era. Far removed from the 21st century, one imagines a sprawling empire where natives traverse the lands on horseback, clad in animal skins. Mongolia is, after all, probably best known for its great grandfather, the famous adventurer and warrior Gengis Khaan.

Located between two of the global economic superpowers of the future, Russia and China, Mongolia is the second largest landlocked and least densely populated independent country in the world. Home to a striking terrain of mountains, lakes, deserts and grasslands, the country also enjoys a vibrant capital city. It is a commodity-rich country abundant in natural resources, minerals and ores including coal, molybdenum, tin tungsten and gold as well as the largest underdeveloped copper mine in the world. Upon completion this mine alone is expected to double the GDP of Mongolia in a very short period of time. In recent years, Mongolia has seen many high-profile mining companies such as BHP, Ivanhoe Mines and Rio Tinto, relocate operations to its capital in order to take advantage of these untapped resources.

Today then, Mongolia is a country full of excitement, hope and energy with a buzzing economy and a tourism industry that is going from strength to strength. What is more, the country offers an astonishing opportunity to savvy real estate investors with an eye for the unusual.

Is this a good place to buy?

Over the past 15 years, the Mongolian economy has undergone major structural changes. The old centrally planned economic system has been abolished and measures have been taken towards privatisation, price and trade liberalisation, banking reform, and a general opening up of the economy. As a result, Mongolia is currently experiencing an economic boom and a rapidly developing tourism industry.

'Mongolia is a country whose fiscal future is set to flourish, displaying many of the positive signs of an economy with large expansion ahead of it'

The Mongolian economy has suffered a series of setbacks due to a combination of communist interference from both the People's Republic of China and the former USSR, natural disasters and the knock-on effects of international financial crises. However, Mongolia has weathered these storms and has a rapidly developing economy to show for it: GDP growth in 2007 stood at a healthy 9.9%, up on the 2003–2006 average of 8.7%. Having traditionally been an economy based on agriculture, the more recent discoveries of mineral deposits have led to a huge rush to extract them by some of the world's leading mining companies. As a result, mining is now a key industry accounting for two-thirds of the country's exports in 2007. Foreign Direct Investment into the country increased in 2007 by just over a third to $500m, two-thirds of that amount being invested into the mining industry.

Mongolia now enjoys a parliamentary democracy and won the award for the Best New Democracy in 2006. It joined The World Trade Organisation in 1997 and is also a full member of the Multilateral Investment Guarantee Agency of the World Bank Group. In July 2006 Mongolia was accepted as an EBRD (European Bank for Reconstruction and Development) country of operations, helping to foster market economies and democracies. This admission allowed the EBRD to start financing projects in the country by October of the same year. Mongolia has also prepared a complete set of measures for the stabilisation of the banking sector, which should result in an increase in public confidence.

Mongolia's tourism sector is also expanding rapidly with the dynamic moving away from back-packers towards a greater percentage of high net worth individuals. The recent emergence of well-known hotels such as the Hilton and Shangri-La in Ulaan Baatar confirm that the capital is developing into a more popular tourist destination. Mongolia now welcomes 500,000 visitors each summer, a figure that is expected to increase at a rate of between 15%–20% a year, contributing to increased demand for short-term accommodation.

The property market in Ulaan Baatar is therefore becoming extremely lucrative. Rapidly appreciating land values and increasing salaries have

Asia

MONGOLIA

pushed up rents meaning yields currently sit at around 20% whilst the emerging economy has engendered a real estate market that is seeing growth rates of up to 30%. Land and construction costs throughout the country are still low making purchase prices incredibly attractive.

There have been concerns voiced that Ulaan Baatar is in danger of becoming overdeveloped, that there is too much construction going on and soon there will be an oversupply of property. However, with 50% of the capital still living in traditional gers, this seems unlikely over the short term. Further, there is a proportion of development under way that is being conducted illegally by cowboy constructors which is unlikely to ever see completion. Lack of sufficient funding, distraction by other schemes and restrictive winters can also hinder progress and mean that some properties never get built. When buying then, it is essential that every effort is made to avoid unscrupulous constructors and ensure that ownership certificates can be produced. Such official documents act as the legal tender for the property, facilitating processes such as mortgage applications.

It is also necessary to take into consideration probable increases in demand. Pending the forthcoming election (at time of writing) in June 2008 and the signature of an investment agreement between Ivanhoe Mines and the government, the mining industry is set to trampoline, bringing with it an influx of business officials and executives who will expect high-end property to match their budgets.

As the country's economy expands and is supported by the burgeoning mineral extraction industry, Mongolia's workforce will industrialise further and in turn, create a wealthier community. Demand should also mushroom amongst locals who look to make the transition from the portable traditional *ger* or *yurt* (tent-like construction) accommodating half of the population, to more permanent property. This then, is a country ripe with potential.

Which type of property should you go for?

As mentioned above, the demand for medium-grade apartments to supplement traditional *ger* accommodation is rocketing. With around half of the capital's population still to house in immovable property, it can be assumed that low to medium-grade accommodation is likely to remain in high demand over the coming years and should not only benefit from substantial capital appreciation but regular and sustainable rent. There is also an annual surge at winter time as the Mongolians living outside of the big cities rush to get ensconced in more protective accommodation before the harsh winters take hold.

However, mid-range accommodation does not necessarily present the most promising investment opportunity. Many of the multinational corporation executives moving to the city to exploit the mining opportunities are issued with accommodation budgets of up to $6,000 per month, but the top-end prices for current rental property barely meet that figure. There is a notable absence then of good quality housing, leaving a huge gap of potential that needs to be filled.

With land prices and construction costs still relatively low, final purchase values can be very attractive for high-grade city centre apartments. Taking into account high-demand, high-end rentals can command anything from between $14 per square metre per month to $25 per square metre per month, delivering annual yields of approximately 10%.

Hotspots

Ulaan Baatar

With the recent influx of mining executives and the migration of locals from traditional *ger* settlements into medium-grade apartments, the capital Ulaan Baatar currently offers the best investment opportunities in Mongolia. Described by British press in 2007 as 'the new hot destination for foreign-property buyers', media reports also suggest that Mongolia offers the highest rental yields in Asia. Recent high-end developments sell luxury, one to three-bed apartments for prices between $175,00 to $670,000.

Buyer's guide

Foreigners can acquire immovable properties but although they can own the dwellings outright, they cannot own but rather have to lease the land. Once a property has been obtained, private property rights are fully protected and income and corporate tax rates are moderate. Double taxation agreements with various countries including the UK, Germany, China, France, India and Russia have been signed.

Mortgages

Finance is not yet available in Mongolia.

Asia

MONGOLIA

Key risks

Although the Mongolian economy looks to be going from strength to strength it is tainted by high inflation which forced the Bank of Mongolia to tighten its monetary policies, meaning interest rates rose twice in 2007. The future of the mining industry is also in question following the introduction of a new prime minister in November 2007. Whilst his predecessor actively supported the mining industry's maturation, a change of policies and reticence to sign an investment agreement with a leading extraction company means progress has been hindered. With regards to the real-estate industry, Mongolia's market is not yet firmly established meaning build quality is sometimes questionable and unscrupulous developers can be a problem. Although the tourist industry is developing, winters here are harsh with temperatures plummeting to as low as -40°C, meaning this is not a country to visit out of season. The cold snap also interferes with construction as it is often simply too cold to work, resulting in lengthy building progress.

Due to its geographical location, Mongolia is understandably very reliant on its two neighbours. China accounts for 72% of Mongolia's outward trade, and together Russia and China account for 64% of all Mongolia's imports. Any negative changes in these neighbouring economies then, will directly affect Mongolia's economic performance.

Rating: ⚠ ⚠ ⚠

Key opportunities

Mongolia is a country whose fiscal future is set to flourish. It is displaying many of the positive signs of an economy with large expansion ahead of it, such as good GDP growth, capital appreciation and interest rates that are beginning to fall. Funds entering the country from the EBRD, Asia Investment Bank and the IMF display a confidence in the economy that looks set to increase whilst the developing mineral extraction industry also encourages regular influxes of foreign investment. It also means that demand for high-end accommodation is maintained. As this sector is currently undersupplied, the gap between supply and demand is a very healthy one for investors. With low entry costs, dependable demand and high yields, confidence in the real estate market is flourishing. As and when Mongolian banks begin to offer mortgages to nationals, purchasing power amongst locals should increase along with demand, meaning the future here should be one loaded with potential.

Rating: $$$$

Philippines

Currency: Philippine Pesos

Exchange rates:
1,000 Php = £11.370
£1 = 87.953 Php

1,000 Php= $22.52
US $1 = 44.53 Php

MANILA

Introduction

The archipelagic nation of the Philippines comprises 7,107 islands clustered just north of Malaysia in the South China Sea. Bearing the brunt of a tirade of bad press, the Philippines is unfortunately associated with corruption, dictatorship, terrorism activity, economic weakness and natural disasters. Although the undertones of all these problems do ripple throughout the country, the merits of the Philippines should also be prevalent. With an array of eco-tourism sites, a treasure trove of underwater meccas and a captivating landscape dominated by the country's numerous volcanoes, Philippines is a stunning place to visit.

Its diverse natural environment, with a warm and humid tropical climate, boasts swathes of jungle and forest, beautiful beaches, fertile farmlands and a handful of active volcanoes. Mud-walled rice terraces, an ancient town teetering on the lip of a volcanic crater and the Chocolate Hills (which if legend would have it are the teardrops of a heartbroken giant), are just some of the Philippine's delights.

Tourist numbers in recent years have been growing steadily and reached a record three million through 2007. A key industry for the country, tourism contributed nearly $5m to the Philippine economy in the same year, most of which was re-invested into infrastructure improvements. As such, Joseph Durano from the Philippine Department of Tourism is confident that his country will see visitors in excess of five million by 2010 and has put several measures in place to encourage this. Of all the islands, Cebu remains the most popular and experienced an increase in visitor numbers of 24% in the first four months of 2007.

The country has a reputation for being warm and friendly and the cost of living is low. Whilst many believe the Philippines could mature to rival other South East Asian countries in terms of business and tourism there are several hurdles to be overcome before then. The country's well-documented battle with corruption and bribery mean many investors are put off buying in this unpredictable and unregulated climate. This coupled with terrorism threats, high transaction costs and a lack of security for tourists mean the property market is yet to realise its full potential.

Although domestic growth has been well managed in recent years and is expected to increase a further 5.6% in 2008, this is still an emerging economy where problems with poverty, reform of education, health and general welfare are rife.

Is this a good place to buy?

Despite the country's numerous shortfalls, it still managed to achieve GDP growth of 7.3% in 2007 (www.asiarisk.com), meaning seasonally adjusted GDP is now on its 27th quarter of positive growths according to www.nscb.gov.ph. This growth is expected to be maintained over 2008 and 2009 at a rate of around 5.8%. In addition, the Philippine Central Bank (BSP) expects foreign direct investment to increase by a substantial 100% over 2008 to $6.9bn (www.property-investor-news.com), a reflection of the confidence other countries have in the Philippines' future. And with interest rates at historic lows and over €61m of EU aid (even though the Philippines are theoretically a little outside the EU catchment area) to be dedicated to ameliorating basic social services including health and the protection of human rights, it is easy to see why this country is beginning to make waves across the developed world. Indeed, the president is engaged in plans to upgrade up to 20 airports as well as many railway, road, bridge, port and irrigation improvements (www.businessmonitor.com/infra/philippines.html).

It is clear then that the Philippines is engaged in an economic recovery of sorts and is striving to become a main player in the global economy. Surprising news for some may be that analysts believe this goal to be wholly achievable providing the economy continues on its current fortuitous course. The government is more stable than it has been for many years and was recently re-elected, and higher levels of inward investment and tourism are an additional and very significant boost for the economy. Authorities are treating the development of the tourism industry as a priority and aim to create 20,000 new hotel rooms, predominantly in luxury resorts.

As far as the property market is concerned, hopes are high here as well. Credit Suisse rate the Philippine property sector as 'overweight', an idiom referring to the raw strength of the market supported by low interest rates and strong demand which they believe will sustain the robust growth of real estate companies. With one of the lowest mortgages to GDP ratios in the world at just 2%, Credit Suisse suggest that the property sector is boosted by the reliable US dollar remittances of overseas Filipino workers who buy residential properties in their home country (www.property-investor-news.com). On top of this, David Stanley Redfern's head of international research explains that, as far as potential growth is concerned, Philippines' property is some of the best poised in the world. Rental yields are currently between 8% and 10%, should be around 12% by the end of the year and could continue to generate even higher returns in years to come.

'It is clear that the Philippines is engaged in an economic recovery of sorts and is striving to become a main player in the global economy'

Overseas investors though will need to consider the restrictions on ownership if they wish to buy here. By law, foreigners are not permitted to privately own land but can acquire up to 40% of the equity in a domestic company that owns land in the country. The most usual route foreigners wishing to buy property follow is to invest through a corporation in a joint venture with Filipino individuals or Filipino-owned corporations. (Source: Going Global 2008 Report, Price Waterhouse Coopers.) Further to The Condominium Act of the Philippines, foreigners can obtain condominium units providing they do not account for more than 40% of the total and outstanding capital stock of a Filipino owned or controlled condominium corporation (www.real-estate-guide.philsite.net). Under the Investors' Lease Act of 1993, foreign investors are allowed to lease land for a straight period of 50 years if it is to be used for certain industrial and agricultural projects. (Source: Going Global 2008 Report, Price Waterhouse Coopers.)

Despite the waves of optimism staring global uncertainty in the face, there are several rather troubling issues that investors in the Philippines have to contend with. High unemployment, acute poverty, poor human rights, slave labour, unequal distribution of wealth, inflation rates of 8.3% (in April 2008, according to www.census.gov.ph), regular terrorism, astronomical food prices and predominant corruption deter all but the gutsiest foreign investors.

In a survey of some 1,400 expatriates, the Philippines topped a poll of the most corrupt Asian nations scoring a shocking nine out of a possible 10 points under a grading system used by PERC, whereby 10 is the worst. This perception was backed up by internal Filipino surveys with around seven out of 10 Filipinos distrusting the president Mrs. Arroyo and her spouse. It seems then that the country needs to address the very bonds holding the country together before it can present itself as a true global player.

INSIDER TIP For those who do decide to shoulder the risk and invest, prices are extremely low by European standards and it is here that the opportunities lie. Although the distance from Europe may make it too far for a holiday-home destination, the country undoubtedly offers excellent potential for buy-to-let investments with a focus on long-term capital growth. Having said that, the costs of owning and renting here can be lofty, with all income, including rental returns, earned by non-residents charged at 35%. A further 12% of VAT is levied on the gross selling price of the real property, meaning profits can be severely undercut. (Source: Going Global Report 2008. Price Waterhouse Coopers.)

Which type of property should you go for?

Because of the restrictions on foreign ownership it is easier for overseas investors to buy into apartment blocks than houses with land. This makes commercial sense as well, seeing as the most substantial gains are to be made from small city-centre apartments. In recent years the most sought-after property in the Metro Manila area has been apartments, bringing in average annual returns of around 8% to 15%. Historically, the smaller the apartment the larger return it generates – a reflection perhaps of the increasing wealth of the young professional workforce who have little need for space.

Beachfront property is also an attractive option for those seeking a holiday home in an exotic location. However, non-nationals will have to buy through a company or own on a leasehold basis, which may not suit all investors.

Hotspots

Though the Philippines has a large number of coastal locations and rural areas, the most weighty investment gains will be made in a very small proportion of the country – namely around Manila and the larger Metro Manila region and at the nearby coastal area of Batangas.

Metro Manila

The country's capital, Manila, is a city of high rises and high expectations. It is also home to a fascinating historic area, founded by Spanish settlers in the

16th century. **Istramuros** is one of the oldest walled cities in the Far East and a delight for history-hungry visitors. Aside from this are a large number of open squares, parks and public gardens as well as the river which bisects the city in two. On completion of the expansion of the light railway system Manila will also benefit from efficient and swift transport links.

Manila lies on Manila Bay and is part of a wider area called Metro Manila situated on the island of Luzon. Metro Manila is divided into 17 cities and municipalities, including former capital Quezon City and bustling Makati. Unfurnished studios in a Manila high rise are typically available from £28,000, whilst luxury fully furnished, fully fitted and fully serviced residences start from £36,900. With 1,660,714 people living within its bounds, Manila has the highest population density of any major city in the world including Paris and Shanghai.

Although a popular spot for visitors, foreigners do need to be aware of crime levels especially considering that threats of kidnapping and religious tension are fairly high.

Palawan

Palawan is an archipelago of 1,700 islands gaining prominence as the eco-tourism destination of the future. Located in the South China Seas, this is a natural safe haven protected from extreme weather in a region free of earthquakes and away from the typhoon belt. It is home to 2000km of coastline, two World Heritage Sites and four marine reserves. Within striking distance of local financial centres Singapore, Hong Kong and Manila, and with an airport upgrade due in 2008, direct international flights to the capital Puerto Princesa will soon be available.

Batangas

Around two hours' drive from central Manila is the popular coastal area of Batangas. Offering attractive beaches, decent diving, historical colonial architecture and increasing amounts of tourist resorts, this region has been identified as one of the Philippines' key growth areas. Batanga City has seen a programme of development over the past 10 years along with the local port, which is one of the most important trading hubs in the country. A hectare farm here costs from £30,600 whilst a four-bedroom modern house close to amenities will start from around £52,000. Land plots within 525 metres of the beach with views of the South China Sea are available from Php 6400–8000/square metres.

Cebu

An island in the middle of the main Philippine archipelago, Cebu is arguably the country's most sought-after destination attracting divers, tourists and anyone doing business in busy Cebu City. In line with its popularity especially among expats, property here isn't cheap especially in the more mountainous locations which are often more sought after than the beachside locations. Properties tend to be in gated communities though a proliferation of apartment buildings being sold off-plan are beginning to arise. A 25 square metre condo is available from £30,900, a two-bedroom house from Php 500,000 and a luxurious five-bed house in Cebu City from Php 15,000,000. Rental yields on some developments are expected to be in the region of 8%.

Boracay

Boracay Island in the Western Visayan group is another popular coastal destination, although a particularly concentrated development comprising a number of bars and restaurants has reportedly begun to damage the famous 14km powder-white sand beach and clean seas. Despite this, the area continues to attract large numbers of visitors. Prices for an apartment bordering the renowned Fairways and Bluewater Golf Course on the world-famous Borocay Island start from around £45,000, whilst flats in the prestigious Pearl development can cost from £70,000.

Investors and tourists alike are strongly discouraged from visiting Mindanao because of ongoing terrorist activity, the most recent of which was a bomb on 22 November 2007. This is not a safe or secure place to visit or invest in.

Buyer's guide

Unless buying a property site before the 1935 enactment which limited land ownership strictly to Filipinos, foreigners cannot purchase land. They can, however, purchase condominium units providing that less than 40% of the project is owned by foreigners and enter into a long-term land lease. (Source: www.realestate.cebunetwork.com) Land can be acquired through a corporation providing 60% of the shares are owned by Filipinos. Foreigners can own buildings in the Philippines. (Source: www.kittelsoncarpo.com/philippines-property-onweship.htm)

Mortgages

Finance is not yet available in the Philippines.

Key risks

What is likely to inhibit the Philippines' success as far as investors are concerned are the weighty problems it faces with corruption, lack of belief in its government, tangled bureaucracy, poverty and the threat of terrorism and crime. If the country does not work significantly harder to improve aspects of government, social and welfare reform it may be left behind by its more dynamic and secure neighbours.

In general terms, overseas investors need better incentives to move into a country that has a poor reputation for efficiency, safety and fair trading. With high transaction costs and rental income taxes, plus the hurdles foreigners need to overcome to buy land, investing here may be more trouble than it's worth.

Prone to repeated typhoons, earthquakes and volcanic eruptions, these are threats visitors need to be aware of.

Rating: ⚠ ⚠ ⚠

Key opportunities

Having said that, there is no doubt that the Philippines is engaged in economic recovery which should bring with it increased stability. The country does then have the potential to increase its commercial and tourism sectors over the next five to 10 years. Businesses seeking low-cost environments from which to run operations and tourists looking for more exotic and off-the-beaten track locations will find that the Philippines can meet their needs in more ways than one.

A fundamental change that would mobilise the property market would be the relaxation of ownership laws and creation of a more transparent purchase process although when such changes might come into effect remains to be seen.

The Philippines does have several of the credentials necessary for a successful emerging market. Economic growth is slow but steady, annual nominal house price changes were 10% in 2007 (www.property-magazine.eu), entry costs are low and the potential for good returns high.

If investors are willing to shoulder the risk that comes hand in hand with investing here, there is a good chance that their investments will pay off.

Rating: $$

Vietnam

Currency: Vietnamese Dong (VND)

Exchange Rates:
£1 = 32.802 VND
100,000 VND = £3.06

$1 = 16.607 VND
100,000 VND = $6.06

Introduction

Curving along the eastern coast of the Indochinese Peninsula nestles Vietnam, a long snaking country that stretches from China, down to the Gulf of Thailand. Just under 3,500km of coastline provide stunning beaches whilst the interior contains densely forested mountains; flat, emerald paddy fields; tropical jungles full of diverse wildlife; plunging lakes and towering; mineral escarpments. Vietnam's turbulent history has made for an interesting cultural heritage, with influences varying from the French colonial to extreme Soviet visible across the countryside and in the cities.

Under Chinese rule for a thousand years, Vietnam was colonised by the French in the mid-19th century, only for them to be finally expelled in the middle of the 20th century after a long period of resistance and struggle. The country was left politically divided and fighting between the north and the south led to intervention from the French, the Americans, communist allies of the north and various other nations. The Vietnam War ensued, lasting for just under two decades. Emerging to power after this destructive period, the Communist government tried to implement government policies designed to reinvigorate the economy but to little success.

Ravaged and divided by decades of violent war and restrained by communist intervention, Vietnam suffered dreadfully, both economically and culturally. However, following the institution of significant economic and political reforms implemented in the mid-1980s, the country has recovered to such a vast extent that it is now the second fastest growing economy in Asia and is rapidly becoming a favourite with international investors looking to buy in South East Asia.

> **'The growth in middle-class wealth has enabled more of the population to consider owning property, meaning domestic demand is now much higher, although supply remains low'**

Vietnam is also gaining popularity with the tourists. Over four million international visitors were welcomed to the country in 2007 (up from 3.6 million in 2006) whilst the World Travel and Tourism Council predict that Vietnam will be amongst the top 10 tourist destinations in the world within the next 10 years. The main cities are seeing low vacancy levels and beach resorts are growing both in popularity and size as more developers move in to profit from the lack of supply.

Is this a good place to buy?

Vietnam has seen immense growth in its economy over a relatively short period of time. A sustained growth rate of around 8% for over 15 years shows great progression and is one of many reasons for the increasing number of foreign investors. Vietnam received over $20bn of foreign direct investment in 2007, a record amount with an increase of 70% on 2006 figures, and saw almost 1,500 new projects licensed in the same year. Although the economy is developing at a rapid rate, entry costs for investors are still low, and cheap labour costs coupled with a young, literate workforce make business investment a very attractive and lucrative prospect.

The strong growth of the economy has been supported by thriving manufacturing, information technology and high-tech industries and a rapidly expanding oil exporting industry – Vietnam is now the third largest oil producer in Asia. Retail is also becoming an influential sector and it is estimated that it will continue to grow with double digits throughout 2008. Accession to the World Trade Organisation in 2006 furthered Vietnam's popularity in the international arena as well as ensuring the continuation of reforms and creating trade expansion opportunities.

Vietnam's real estate market has also witnessed rapid growth. From the point of view of a foreign investor the real estate industry is focussed predominantly in the two main cities of Hanoi and Ho Chi Minh City, with opportunities to be found in tourist resorts emerging in the coastal areas. Hand in hand with the growth in the commercial and retail market comes demand for property development. Over half of the 85 million strong population are under 30 years old and many of these are middle class with an increasing disposable income at hand. This has increased the demand for retail and leisure opportunities, and as a result luxury apartment and multi-use leisure complexes are springing up across the main cities. Of the US5.44bn received in foreign direct investment in the first quarter of 2008, 90% has been spent in the service sector.

The growth in middle-class wealth has enabled more of the population to consider owning property, meaning domestic demand is now much higher, although supply remains low. It has not been uncommon to witness queues of Vietnamese waiting to purchase real estate as it comes onto the market. In recent years it has become increasingly fashionable for middle class Vietnamese to live in luxury city-centre apartments and in 2007 prices for luxury city apartments in Ho Chi Minh City tripled due to high demand.

Demand also originates from a thriving tourist industry. There is currently a lack of quality hotel rooms to accommodate the millions of tourists each year (4.2 million in 2007), whilst the growing expatriate communities are demanding well-located, serviced apartments, which are also in short supply. Rents are therefore growing rapidly for villas in popular districts, and rents for serviced apartments are expected to increase by 15%–20% in 2008. Yields vary from location to location and depend on the type of property, but a serviced apartment in Hanoi can produce rental yields of 13%–14%, whilst the same in Ho Chi Minh City produces yields of 10%–13%.

However, owning property as a foreigner in Vietnam is not straightforward. Current law does not permit foreign ownership of real estate. The common procedure is for property to be leased on a 70-year basis with the option to renew or, if the law changes, to convert to freehold. Buying is effectively a transfer of leasing rights. Recent legislation changes to allow perpetual leasing mean that Vietnam now has one of the most open property markets in Asia, as neighbouring countries offer only limited leases. This also means that foreigners are effectively in the same position as Vietnamese in regards to real estate ownership. Changes to legislation regarding foreigners' ability to buy property will come into effect in 2009 when certain categories of foreigners will become eligible to purchase apartments as part of a government-run pilot programme.

Although recent statistics show Vietnam in a favourable investment light, it is critical to take note of the country's current economic situation. As with any nation witnessing rapid development there has to come a point where the current growth rate is unsustainable, and it seems that Vietnam has reached this juncture. Goldman Sachs predict that the economic growth rate will slow from 8.5% in 2007 to 7.3% in 2008. Most crucially though, is the high inflation rate that the country is currently trying to contain. The annual figure rose to 21.4% in April 2008, one of the highest rates since 1991. Global factors are partly to blame for rising inflation but the fast price rises specific to Vietnam and not its neighbours suggest that domestic factors are also culpable. The government is making strong efforts to curb the growth of inflation through a combination of methods, including stricter lending rules, raising interest rates and increasing compulsory bank reserves.

A slowdown in growth is not reason for concern in itself though as this is typical cyclical economic behaviour, and the inflation could be curbed if the government exercises tighter monetary control. The real estate market continues to see an influx of foreign investment and there is no immediate reason why this should decrease.

Which type of property should you go for?

INSIDER TIP Vietnam offers a wide range of property to the potential investor. The best types of property from an investor's perspective are high-end, serviced apartments and office spaces in the prime locations of Hanoi and Ho Chi Minh City. These satisfy demand from middle-class Vietnamese, expatriate business workers and, to a degree, tourists. Quality is of the essence here, as demand is especially high at the upper end of the spectrum. Villa resorts in coastal areas will also provide excellent tourist rental opportunities.

Hotspots

The largest and most well-renowned cities of Vietnam, Ho Chi Minh City and Hanoi offer the widest range of investment opportunity and are generally considered to be reliable in terms of risk.

Hanoi

Hanoi is the political capital of the country. Located in north Vietnam it is situated on the banks of the Red River and is a cultural wonder to the foreign tourist, embodying a fascinating mix of influences from East and West, the presence of the French and the Chinese evident in the architecture. Its growing population of over 3.4 million and the continuing influx of foreigners make for an evolving property market. Rental prices for apartments vary from £500 to £2,000 ($1,000 to $4,000) a month, whilst villas tend to have monthly rental prices from £760 to £3,200 ($1,500 to $6,500).

Ho Chi Minh City

This is the larger of the two cities, with a population of over 6.2 million. It is the economic and financial hub of the country and has a very busy and bustling atmosphere. It is often known as the 'Pearl of the Far East' or the 'Paris in the Orient' due to the strong French colonial influences still evident in the city. The average rent in the city is $15 per square metre and it is not uncommon to see rental yields of 10%–14%. Serviced apartments in downtown Ho Chi Minh City have a monthly rental price bracket of £1,700 to £2,000 ($3,500 to $4,000), whilst downtown villas can have a price tag of anything up to £2,530 ($5,000) per month. Both cities are witnessing great amounts of development and construction in many sectors of the economy.

Nha Trang

Aside from the main cities, coastal areas are responsible for attracting a large number of tourists, creating more opportunities for the potential investor. Nha Trang, a resort on the south-east coast of Vietnam, is growing in popularity with backpackers as well as more affluent travellers. It is said to be one of the most beautiful bays in the world, and is host to summer festivals that draw tourists in every year. Its selection as the site of the Miss Universe pageant 2008 shows the growing international popularity of the resort and will put it on the international map. Additions of golf courses, a marina and a yacht club will increase its tourist appeal. Currently with over 300,000 inhabitants, the population is expected to reach 600,000 by 2020.

Halong Bay

A world-famous UNESCO heritage site, Halong Bay is reported to attract 90% of visitors to Vietnam and it is said that until you have visited the bay you haven't visited Vietnam. The iconic bay, full of monolithic limestone towers and islands, attracts thousands of tourists and as a result has seen much development in the form of hotels, restaurants and shopping opportunities.

Buyer's guide

Land in Vietnam is administered by the state and all land users will be issued a Land Use Rights Certificate (LURC) from the state. The rights of the land user will depend on what the land will be used for and the status of the user. Foreigners are not permitted to own land in Vietnam and can only own properties via leasehold. The length of the leasehold is determined by the Investment Certificate although according to Decree 84 issued by the Government dated 25 May 2007, a 70-year lease may be acquired by foreign investors and may be extended without additional land rental.

(Source: Communist Party of Vietnam Online Newspaper http://www.cpv.org. vn/english/news/details.asp?topic=12&subtopic=105&leader_topic= 175&id=BT1240850700.

Allens Arthur Robinson, 2008, *Vietnam Legal Update August 2007* [Online] Available at: http://www.vietnamlaws.com/vlu/aug_2007.pdf. Accessed 4 June 2008.)

Mortgages

Finance is not yet available in Vietnam.

Key risks

Although it offers much opportunity, investors must bear in mind that the Vietnam property market is still young and its immaturity can work against its favour: there is little history to work from, transparency is low and the administrative process can be somewhat frustrating. There is no land ownership in Vietnam, either for national citizens or foreigners, which restricts the options open to investors. The forecast slowdown in economic growth has started but this shouldn't be a huge cause for concern, especially as growth is still progressing at a healthy rate and readjustment was necessary following such a prolonged period of high growth. Inflation *is* a cause for concern and the government's progress in trying to limit this should be carefully monitored, although at present the real estate market is still benefiting from large amounts of foreign investment. If locals start being priced out of the market, problems will arise for investors.

Rating: ⚠ ⚠ ⚠

Key opportunities

Despite experiencing a tough economic period many spectators are not too worried about Vietnam's future, seeing the current problems as short-term correction. In the long-term, growth is expected to continue as it has done supported by the large amounts of foreign investment that are still being poured into the country. The real estate market is still showing very promising growth rates. Tourism is another strong market in Vietnam, with excellent growth prospects for the future, ensuring ongoing demand in the rental market and competitive high yields. Current undersupply in the real estate market means that demand continues to be high, and with restrictions to foreigners entering the Vietnamese property market relaxing, the opportunities to profit are getting easier. Investment here is more geared towards the medium to long-term.

Rating: $$$$

Angola

Currency: kwanza (AOA)
Exchange Rates:
100 kwanza = $1.34
£1 = 147.808 kwanza

100 Kwanza = £0.69
$1 = 74.85 kwanza

LUANDA

Introduction

Situated on the west coast of Africa, Angola borders the Atlantic Ocean, Namibia, Zambia and the Congo. Unfortunately associated with war and destruction, few are aware of the country's 1,650km white sand coastline, untouched wildlife parks and raw natural beauty. Dogged by many physical reminders of its civil war of independence, Angola is still recovering both socially and economically. Formally brought to an end in 2002, the 27-year conflict left Angola one of the poorest countries in the world.

The country's economy is driven almost entirely by the burgeoning oil industry, supported by gas resources, hydroelectric production and diamond mines. Such resources have helped redeem Angola's fortunes, turning it into the second fastest growing economy in Africa and one of the fastest in the world.

'Due to the infancy of the property market, entry level prices are very low and so offer excellent opportunities for capital appreciation'

Although still a developing country Angola has a lot to offer prospective tourists including a wide variety of leisure activities along the Mussolo peninsula, sailing along the coast, fishing in Santiago and the second largest waterfall in Africa, the Kalanduo Falls. Luanda, the capital, is the country's largest city, is home to its largest seaport and offers fascinating day trips to nearby destinations Bimbe and Tundavala. Further, its quaint old town is a popular attraction for tourists.

Is this a good place to buy?

Thanks to its prominent oil industry, Angola's future is promising. Accounting for over 90% of the country's exports, this sector is what will remedy the country's ailing wealth. Known as the 'Kuwait of Africa', it is now Africa's second largest oil producer with an output of one million barrels per day. By next year it is expected that Angola will overtake Nigeria and become Africa's number one supplier. As well as oil, the country has several other profitable exports including diamonds, gold and iron ores. Angola also has a promising agricultural sector thanks to its appropriate climate, soil, and topography which allow for the large-scale agricultural production of a wide range of crops. Furthermore, with significant hydropower, forest, and fishery potential, Angola could soon regain its pre-war stance as the most productive agriculture industry on the continent. The country then does have the potential to generate economic stability and with a government dedicated to achieving this end, improvements should soon become evident.

Both domestic and foreign investment is being encouraged by the government who ensure that equal treatment, fiscal and custom incentives, a simplified investment application process and affordable levels of required investment capital make the investment process as straightforward as possible. Although a lot more needs to be done to achieve satisfactory govern-ance and satisfactory rule of law and to lower corruption risks, steps to make national practices more transparent have been enforced. Under pressure from the international community, the government now publishes financial reports, prevents extra-budgetary expenditures and is a signatory to the UN Conven-tion Against Corruption in a bid to lower investment risks and provide greater assurance to investors. As a result FDI is gradually increasing and according to recent findings, Angola received $800m in FDI during the first half of 2006 and was the largest overall recipient in Sub-Saharan Africa between 1999 and 2004.

As far as the property market is concerned, Angola is a country is desperate need of restoration. Decades of war and a lack of appropriate economic and legal reforms have posed a widespread housing problem. Throughout the war for independence, Portuguese residents were forced to abandon their homes which were then confiscated by the government. Refugees returning to dwell-ings were either met with repossessed homes or nothing but empty fields. As a result, recent UN findings state that about 90% of urban residents live in set-tlements without a clearly defined legal status. Of these, most live in multi-family dwellings constructed in the 1960s which have now deteriorated so that basic utilities are limited or unavailable. The demand for local housing then is very high and a main priority in the redevelopment process.

Africa & Middle East

ANGOLA

In theory, all urban land in Angola is considered state property although the management and administration of houses are under the directive of provincial governments, meaning the intricacies of exact property regulations are still hazy. Indeed, land can be leased to private entities. Angolan parliament has passed a new Law on Land and Urban Planning which came into effect in September 2004 affirming that all land ultimately belongs to the state, although most urban and some non-urban land will effectively become privately owned through long-term renewable leases. Owners must, however, wait five years after purchase before selling land.

Angola then, due to its developing political and economic situation, still has a long way to go before it can be classed as a stable country. That is not to say though that opportunities don't exist, they do, but are merely shrouded by an element of severe risk.

Which type of property should you go for?

With Angola striving to attract foreign investors, the real estate market is slowly beginning to take off and property is being sold. Many foreign investors are buying houses and apartments for vacational rents where rental income can be good depending on the location.

INSIDER TIP — **Good quality properties to house urban residents are in short supply and are therefore likely to equate to some of the more profitable investment opportunities for investors.**

Hotspots

Angola has several towns and cities as well as clusters of smaller villages.

Benguela

Founded by the Portuguese, Benguela is the second biggest city in the country. Situated along the western coast, the city escaped the worst of the destruction caused by the civil war meaning its architecture remains intact. The city is full of life with many fine beaches and a vibrant culture.

Lobito

Also along the western coast, is Lobito, one of Africa's best natural harbours protected by a three-mile sand pit. Beach huts are available to rent along the coast and there are beach bars to eat and drink at as well as restaurants and hotels in the city centre. An interesting place to visit is a town on the outskirts of the city, made of only mud and corrugated iron.

Mussulo and Luanda

A few kilometres from the capital Luanda lies the unspoilt island of **Mussulo**, a favourite with many tourists and commonly described as paradise. Luanda itself has several restaurants offering a variety of different cuisine as well as a lively nightlife, with many bars and restaurants open to early hours in the morning.

Buyer's guide

In theory, Angola is open to foreign investment although its regulatory and legal infrastructure do not necessarily allow ease of purchase and hazy laws that are yet to be clarified mean all foreign investors need to conduct thorough research before considering buying here. Before purchasing, an updated ownership certificate needs to be sought from the Registry as well as an updated tax certificate from the relevant tax office.

Mortgages

Finance is not yet available in Angola.

Key risks

Although the government of Angola is encouraging foreign investment, the country is still recovering from years of war and is considered to be one of the poorest countries in the world. The country's economic and political state therefore is far from stable, which may deter many investors. The land titling process is also complicated and lengthy with procedures taking up to 334 days. Property registries themselves in Angola are poorly organised so provide little security of ownership. There are also still problems with security and crime in certain areas so investors would be well advised to conduct comprehensive and in-depth research before buying property here.

Rating: ⚠ ⚠ ⚠ ⚠

Key opportunities

The Angolan government appear serious about attracting FDI, and have set up the National Private Investment Agency (ANIP) in order to streamline foreign investment and ensure that investors are tempted by a range of incentives. Due to the infancy of the property market, entry level prices are very low and so offer excellent opportunities for capital appreciation should the real estate market mature as some experts would hope.

Further, in line with Angola's developing tourist industry, the economy is becoming increasingly strong.

Rating: $$$

Cape Verde

Currency: Cape Verde Escudo
Exchange rates:
10,000 Escudo = £71.40
£1 = 140.551 Escudo

10,000 Escudo = US $141.60
US $1 = 71.3 Escudo

PRAIA

Introduction

Lying just off the coast of Africa, 16 degrees north and 24 degrees west, a thread of tropical islands pepper the deep blue waters of the North Atlantic Ocean. The Cape Verde Islands lie in a delicate cluster and are graced with some of the most unspoilt beaches and beautiful scenery in the world today. Already dubbed the African Caribbean and expected to rival, if not supersede the success of the Canary Islands, these treasured islands are beginning to enjoy a surge in popularity and prosperity.

In 1975, the islands separated from Portugal, and have since been an independent republic. Their interiors are wild and volcanic offering a captivating backdrop to the array of beautiful beaches and all enjoy a consistently temperate climate never varying much from an average 25°C.

With leading travel companies and holiday programmes predicting Cape Verde to be one of the top holiday destinations of the future, the number of visitors to the islands has increased. Expedia touted the area as one of the top 10 destinations for 2008 and as a result, Cape Verde is now the most popular location for British holiday home buyers after Europe.

Statistical data goes yet further in confirming the Island's promise and growing popularity. Real economic growth in the country has averaged 6% over the past few years with GDP growth reaching 7% in 2007. Tourism figures have also rapidly increased along with growing amounts of foreign investment. Significantly, the largest quota of FDI has been injected into the tourism industry representing a 54% share. The services-orientated economy contributes 73.9% of the country's overall GDP.

Africa & Middle East

CAPE VERDE

> *'Paralleling the climes, beauty and low crime rates of the Caribbean yet resting safely outside the hurricane belt and only a five and a half hour flight from Europe, these charming islands could mature into a lucrative property market'*

That more development is needed on the islands is certain: the lack of schools and roads mean that this is not yet the place to look for a second home. The country still suffers from water shortages and the economy has a poor natural resources base. However, Cape Verde has been rated as having excellent standards of health, with most facilities reaching Western standards. These islands are not renowned for their practicality; however, their antiquity is, to a certain extent, part of their charm. Cape Verde has retained a sense of peace and tranquillity that more developed islands and Eastern Europe have now lost.

Encouragingly, the government sees tourism and the second home-market as the best way in which to guarantee prosperity for Cape Verde so infrastructure and amenities are likely to see continual improvement over the coming years.

Is this a good place to buy?

Cape Verde's accessibility has improved dramatically in the last few years with direct flights from the UK now available with a number of airlines, flying predominantly from London Gatwick, Manchester and Birmingham. There are also flights from Belfast, Dublin, Edinburgh, Glasgow and the Channel Islands, as well as direct flights from Italy, Portugal, Germany, Denmark, Holland, Senegal and Brazil. Currently there are international airports on three of the islands, Sal, Santiago and Boa Vista, with smaller local airports on some of the other islands. The local airport on Sao Vicente is currently under conversion to accept long-haul aircraft, with completion anticipated by the end of 2008. Cape Verde is one of just three sub-Saharan countries with category one status under the US Open Sky policy, meaning that aircraft leaving the island are authorised to land directly in the US.

Inconvenient and time-consuming travel connections are therefore no longer a deterrent and, with increasingly positive media coverage, Cape Verde is expected to attract growing numbers of tourists over the next few years. Property experts fully expect that the now emerging real estate industry will grow simultaneously with the tourism market and believe it has the potential to provide profitable returns. Buying into an off-plan development that is due to complete in the next two years should put investors in a good position to reap the benefits of the burgeoning tourist industry. In a couple of years they will be able to sell on their property to tourists looking for finished second homes.

On average, tourist arrivals to Cape Verde are said to be growing at a rate of 22% per annum, meaning annual visitor numbers are expected to exceed one million by 2015. Tourism now contributes 27.5% to Cape Verde's GDP. Aiming to do all they can to facilitate the growth of the tourist and investment markets, Cape Verde authorities approved of investment projects totalling $300m in 2006 alone, with more than a few other million dollar projects announced since.

Investors should also be encouraged by the stability of the country's political and economic positioning. The American CIA sees Cape Verde as a country that 'continues to exhibit one of Africa's most stable democratic governments' whilst the British Foreign and Commonwealth Office believes Cape Verde to have 'an efficient and generally un-corrupt bureaucracy'. What is more, investors need not worry about severe exchange rate risks as the Cape Verde Escudo has been pegged to the euro since January 1999, maintaining low inflation.

In a bid to foster all the foreign investment that it can, the Cape Verde government has constructed several incentives for foreign investors. For the initial five years, buyers enjoy a tax holiday as well as an exemption on import duties for building materials. Private investors who invest more than £23,673 or employ in excess of 13 nationals are entitled to residency. The government also gives foreign investors important guarantees such as privately managed foreign currency accounts that can be credited only in foreign currency from abroad or from other foreign accounts in Cape Verde. It also allows unrestricted repatriation of dividends, profits and capital from foreign investment operations.

In short then, Cape Verde appears to offer a very promising investment market. Paralleling the climes, beauty and low crime rates of the Caribbean yet resting safely outside the hurricane belt and only a five and a half hour flight from Europe, these charming islands could mature into a lucrative property market. Low purchase costs of 7% make property investment an attractive concept. Importantly, authorities are keen to avoid Spain's problems with over-development so environment-sensitive developments are favoured and very much encouraged. Due to the islands' relative underdevelopment, the build quality of off-plan developments is hard to measure and is something that potential investors should look into thoroughly.

Which type of property should you go for?

The lack of infrastructure means that it can be difficult to refurbish and furnish an older property to your satisfaction. A furnished off-plan apartment or villa will therefore be the easiest and most popular option for investors. It is also likely to be easier to access a new-build unit as infrastructure around newer developments is likely to be more advanced. If opting for an older property, be aware of its build quality. Standards have greatly improved over the last six years so anything constructed prior to 2002 may be of questionable quality. A surveyor will therefore be an essential authority as far as this is concerned. Inflated prices are also a factor to be aware of as some developers try to maximise their gain from tourists. Shop around and don't be limited to one island.

Hotspots

Development so far has been mainly concentrated on the islands of Sal and Santiago as these two islands offer the most developed infrastructure, including international airports. However, San Vicente and Boa Vista are also starting to take off within the Cape Verde property market.

Sal

The first stop for almost every international visitor, Sal offers a more developed infrastructure to cope with increased visitor numbers. With a mix of different nationalities and some of the best beaches and diving opportunities just off their golden sands, Sal is hugely popular. A large tourist resort, developed in the south of the island in the town of Santa Maria, Sal is where the concentration of international tourists can be found, with property development to match the increasing demand. However, Santa Maria Sal is in the throes of development, and whilst this bodes well for a few years' time, it doesn't make for the most relaxing atmosphere. A two-bedroom apartment can be bought for £60,000 ($118,470) to £110,000 ($217,200), and a three-bedroom villa for £200,000 ($394,910) and above. A new tourist complex worth over $130m is being developed outside Santa Maria due for completion in 2009.

Santiago

This is an island that investors should take a close look at. The largest of the Cape Verde Islands, it combines bustling nightlife in the capital **Praia** with calm landscapes offering tranquil escapism. It is touted as being the island for people who have an interest in local culture and wildlife. It is also described as the most African of the islands, with a more varied terrain than most of Cape Verde, even boasting mountain ranges. Sambala Developments are developing a huge resort situated within 20 square kilometres of lush, mountain valleys that will contain tourism villages, villa complexes, five-star hotels, golf courses, marinas and more. Plots have already sold out on the first stage of the development.

San Vicente

This island also offers interesting investment opportunities. It has long been the island of culture and history with strong Portuguese influences, but is now undergoing plans that should transform it into an elite holiday destination and thriving business centre. The west side will become the island's business hub whilst the completion of the grand marina will mean the island has the capacity to welcome a host of flotilla and light craft.

INSIDER TIP As of May 2007 Cape Verde Developments (one of the most prestigious property developers of the islands) and Nikki Beach (one of the world's leading lifestyle brands) joined forces to create an ultimate luxury experience in the shape of a five-star renovation of the fort situated in the island's capital, Mindelo. Prices start at £228,000 ($450,197) for apartments and £677,000 ($1,336,797) for luxury villas. For those with simpler tastes, smaller apartments begin at £75,000 ($148,094) and villas from £145,000 ($286,315). Development of a new golf resort should also augment the island's tourist appeal whilst an extension to the airport's main runway near San Pedro will allow smaller international charter flights to access San Vicente and should help encourage and cater for the growing visitor arrivals. The island has also signed an agreement with Spain's Canary Islands and the Portuguese archipelago of Madeira to promote and operate cruises in the mid-Atlantic which should again deliver an increased number of tourists to San Vicente's shores. Units in a new development on the west coast will be available from £80,000 ($157,967).

Buyer's guide

There are no restrictions on foreigners owning property in Cape Verde and foreign investors are treated the same as nationals. Foreign investors have the right to private ownership and establishment whilst property rights are recognised and guaranteed in several Cape Verde laws. Acquisition and disposition of property rights are protected by legal systems. (Source: U.S Department of State www.state.gov.com)

Mortgages

LTV %	TERM	CURRENCIES	RATES %	STATUS	SPECIAL CONDITIONS
85	35	EUR, CVE	8.5	Employed or self-employed	

Key risks

The Cape Verde market is still in its infancy, both in terms of property and as a tourist destination, meaning it is likely to take some years for the country to become fully established. That is not to say that it should be avoided however, but merely that a touch of realism is required so as to avoid frustration at the lack of infrastructure etc.

Rating: ⚠ ⚠ ⚠

Key opportunities

Cape Verde should offer good long-term opportunities as the islands develop into a mainstream tourist destination. There is a great amount of optimism invested in the country, with realtors offering achievable gains of 15%–20% over the long term. With so much high-end foreign investment being poured into the country – most notably as luxury developments – it is not hard to foresee the huge increase in popularity this small group of islands will soon experience.

Rating: $$$

Africa & Middle East

CAPE VERDE

Egypt

Currency: Egyptian Pound (EGP)

Exchange Rate:
100 EGP = £9.41
£1 = 10.61 EGP

100 EGP = $18.69
$1 = 5.35 EGP

CAIRO

Introduction

Record numbers of foreigners are attracted to Egypt year-on-year to visit the myriad ancient monuments of the Pharaohs amongst the arid plains of the Sahara Desert. Over a million square kilometres in area, with almost two and a half thousand kilometres of coastline, Egypt is a large country with a lot to offer the foreign visitor. The vast Sahara desert claims over 90% of Egypt's land, forcing its 80 million people to inhabit the luscious, life-giving Nile Valley and Delta, and the coastlines, thus creating close-knit communities that have a long-established history.

Whilst the pyramids, sphinxes, tombs and ancient hieroglyphs have drawn an endless stream of tourists for hundreds of years, a new tourist market has developed, capitalising on the astounding natural attributes of the country. The Red Sea is fast becoming one of the top diving destinations of the world as divers come to experience the amazingly clear waters that are home to multitudes of dazzling tropical fish, whilst others take advantage of the many water sports schools that pepper the coastlines. Diving enthusiasts are spoilt for choice with the diving haven of the Red Sea Riviera and warm, sophisticated waters of the Mediterranean coast. A strong golfing community is also taking root in the sands of Egypt, with many significant and upmarket golfing resorts under development.

> *'The Red Sea is fast becoming one of the top diving destinations of the world as divers come to experience the amazingly clear waters that are home to multitudes of dazzling tropical fish'*

Whilst these attractions are all very appealing, there is something else responsible for attracting the record number of tourists and investors alike. A year-round sunny climate and minimal rainfall mean Egypt is the ideal holiday destination every month of the year.

Is this a good place to buy?

With a forward-thinking, pro-foreign prime minister, Egypt's economic climate has developed to become rather appealing to the foreign investor. The IMF has rated Egypt as one of the world's top countries in terms of economic reform, a statement that is supported by 25% annual capital growth, 7%–8% annual GDP growth and a total annual FDI input of over $11bn. As the GDP growth rate and the country's official reserves increase and national debt falls, the country only looks to be getting richer. Recent economic success is attributable to the privatisation of certain sector industries, and reforms introduced by the government to customs, income and taxation.

Increasing domestic wealth has engendered a burgeoning middle class with both the means and intent to invest in their local property market. This has had a direct effect on demand for housing. Cairo was initially built with a population of three to five million in mind, but currently has a population somewhere between 15 and 20 million. With an annual population growth rate of 1.7% per annum it is estimated that an extra 400,000 properties are needed each year to accommodate this growth and the ongoing demand for property from outside investors. To satisfy this demand and to readdress the outdated infrastructure, brand new satellite cities are being developed on the outskirts of main cities, designed to offer those living in polluted centres a better standard of living. These cities are created as an entire city structure, with houses, offices, flagship malls and designer shopping boulevards, parks, gardens and a cosmopolitan centre that reflects the national heritage in traditional architecture.

To date, the Egyptian government has sold around 35 million square metres of land for private real-estate developments, and demand is still growing. Competition from foreign investors is creating healthy land prices, as one might expect, but Egypt still has a long way to go before it starts matching the property prices of some of its neighbours. In a list of 46 countries produced by the

Global Property Guide, Egypt has the lowest price per square metre, starting at only $569.

'With an annual population growth rate of 1.7% per annum it is estimated that an extra 400,000 properties are needed each year to accommodate this growth'

Happily for the foreign investor, rental returns on Egyptian property are amongst the highest in the world and can top 17% in well-chosen districts, whilst capital growth is a very healthy 25%. Thanks to recent tax reforms, investment into Egypt is now far more attractive to the foreign buyer as there is 0% purchase and capital gains tax, whilst stamp duty and income tax are low. Having said that, roundtrip transaction costs are a high 11%.

Unlike in many Middle East countries, foreigners may now own, sell and let Egyptian property freely. Unfortunately, the property registry is out of date, with only an estimated 10% of Egyptian properties actually registered, meaning issues with title often ensue. For the foreign buyer wishing to purchase undeveloped land or an older, established resale property it is highly recommended that an independent lawyer familiar with Egyptian real-estate law is employed to ensure that the transaction is completed legally. Language barriers and intricate land registering processes can then be more easily negotiated. For buyers purchasing off-plan or property under construction on large multi-site developments, contracts are usually written and arranged privately, so that properties can be rented or sold immediately.

Investors need also bear in mind the building standards of any potential purchase. Standards across the board are likely to vary considerably as the Egyptian community is well known for different interpretations of quality. More crucially, Egypt sits on many fault lines and has suffered direct earthquakes, earth tremors and aftershocks. Buildings therefore need to be built to a standard able to withstand such threats, especially if they are more than a few storeys high. If the property in question is low-rise, buyers should also be aware of what is built nearby.

The country appears to be on track to achieving tourism ministers' aims to welcome 14 million tourists by 2011. In 2007, tourist numbers rocketed 20% to reach 10 million according to the United Nations World Tourism Organisation UNWTO. Such robust increases will undoubtedly bolster the real estate market, feeding it with higher levels of demand which will put prices up and increase the need for supply.

Which type of property should you go for?

The majority of investment properties in Egypt are large-scale, tourist-orientated developments, usually situated on the coast, offering the expected range from large villas to one-bedroom apartments. Historically, developers have favoured apartments meaning these are slightly easier to come by. Searches for property are usually contained within the areas of Sharm El Sheikh on the Sinai Peninsula, Hurghada on the Red Sea coast, Cairo, Luxor/Aswan, and the Mediterranean coast. Investors will find that there is little property available that is not on a development, but this isn't actually a big deal as it avoids problems caused by land registry processes and structural history. The average house price in Egypt currently sits at around £72,000 , with the average apartment costing in the region of £47,000, and the average villa £114,000.

Hotspots

Sharm El Sheikh

Renowned for world-famous diving, Sharm El Sheikh is the most popular tourist holiday spot in Egypt, drawing in the younger end of the tourist scale with its reputation as a fun resort with a lively nightlife. The extraordinary waters of the Red Sea offer some of the best diving in the world and are revered amid the diving community. With its own international airport, Sharm El Sheikh is easily accessible from major European capitals. With so many developments situated in and around Sharm El Sheikh, there is a wealth of property to choose from. Three-bedroom apartments are available from £120,000, and it is not unusual for the use of central resort amenities to be included in the purchase price.

Hurghada

South-west of Sharm El Sheikh on the Red Sea Riviera is Hurghada, once a small fishing village but now an up-market tourist destination that attracts a stream of Europeans and Americans, and also visitors from other Arab states. Property ranges from cheaper town-centre apartments, popular with divers on shoestring budgets, to wealthier, luxurious 'tourist villages', such as **El Gouna**. El Gouna is a purpose built, self-contained and self-sustainable complex built on 10km of coastline, with 14 hotels, a large marina, a mature golf course and a population of around 10,000. Villa prices on the new developments can range between £170,000 and £600,000.

Cairo

The property market in Cairo is developing rapidly with a focus on the luxury end of the market to cater for the increasingly wealthy Egyptian classes and generate inward revenue. Despite recent construction booms there is still a lack of high-end tourist accommodation meaning the supply and demand relationship is a healthy one. Satellite cities outside Cairo offer a cleaner, healthier and often updated lifestyle, with land prices starting from around £200 per square metre.

The Mediterranean coast

Tipped as the Côte d'Azur of the future, the Mediterranean coast of Egypt is said to have an atmosphere that is more Mediterranean than Middle Eastern, and offers the still, turquoise waters that can be found gracing its European counterparts at a fraction of the cost. Founded by Alexander the Great, Alexandria is bursting with cultural history from its position as a centre point between African, Middle Eastern, Greek and Roman empires.

INSIDER TIP The Mediterranean Coast is an area yet to be developed by foreigners but expected to experience similar levels of development to more popular areas of the country as more people discover the charm of the Mediterranean Sea from the Egyptian view. Now then is a shrewd time to invest and take advantage of lower prices before demand forces them up.

Buyer's guide

Foreigners in Egypt are entitled to the same rights as nationals and can own property and land in the country.

(Source: Http://www.lincomrealestate.com/investment-guide/legal-consulting/)

Mortgages

LTV %	TERM	CURRENCIES	RATES %	STATUS	SPECIAL CONDITIONS
60	10	EGP	8	Employed or Self-Employed	

Key risks

Investors need to bear in mind the build quality of potential purchases. Standards across the board are likely to vary considerably as the Egyptian community is well known for different interpretations of 'quality'. As such, purchasers need to ensure they will not be supplied with a dissatisfactory end-product.

More crucially, Egypt sits on many fault lines and has suffered direct earthquakes, earth tremors and aftershocks. Buildings therefore need to be built to a standard able to withstand such threats, especially if they are more than a few storeys high.

Rating: ⚠ ⚠

Key opportunities

Egypt, then, is a country with the potential to offer significant financial return on well-chosen investments and backed by a stable economy, flourishing tourism market and government that is pro-actively focussed on 21st century development and foreign interest, this sector looks to have a stable future.

Although the best investment opportunities are limited to plots on large-scale developments, this shouldn't deter the serious investor who should not be swayed by the aesthetic appeal of his property, or its fiscal promise.

Opportunities to pick up a bargain do still exist throughout the country but may not be around for too much longer as demand is set to increase in line with the blooming tourist industry. In turn, prices are likely to shoot up. The earlier investors commit to this market, the greater appreciation they are likely to experience.

Rating: $$$$

Africa & Middle East

EGYPT

Morocco

Currency: Dirham
Exchange rates:
1,000 Dirham = £69.08
£1 = 14.5 Dirham

1,000 Dirham = US $136.283
US $1 = 7.34 Dirham

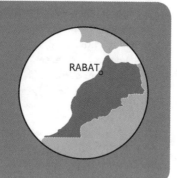

RABAT

Introduction

Morocco, on the edge of north-west Africa, is a country brimming with the enticing allure of a foreign land. Oozing colour, charm and a deep-rooted culture, the country boasts an enthralling history and a varied and beautiful landscape. Sun-drenched terracotta buildings, a sultry, fragrant air and deep blue skies are home to a rich and fascinating culture. The buzzing *souks* and an aromatic cuisine, considered one of the best in the world, together with year-round high temperatures tempt visitors to return time and again.

With snow-capped mountain peaks, miles of white beaches, undulating hills and old towns bustling with life, Morocco has an enduring appeal which has attracted people from all walks of life. Since the Beckhams' visit to Morocco in 2006, Morocco's reputation for becoming the next trendy footballer haven has rocketed with Rio Ferdinand, Gary Neville and John Terry all buying into 'Plan Azur' Projects in the up-and-coming Tangier resorts. Winston Churchill, Jean Paul Gaultier and the Rolling Stones as well as Kate Moss and P Diddy, have also succumbed to Morocco's charm and fallen for the country's timeless appeal.

Recent figures confirm the country's growing popularity. In 2006 mainstream tourism was up by 18% and foreign property investment was rife. In 2007 7.45 million holidaymakers visited Morocco, a 13% increase from the previous 12 months, and Morocco was named the fastest growing tourist market for the second year in a row. Revenue created from tourism showed a 30% increase resulting in 53 billion dirham - an all-time high. There is a strong belief that 'Vision 2010' will achieve its goal of attracting 10 million tourists to Morocco annually, thanks to a massive €2.5m which has been given to refresh current advertising campaigns, a 20% increase in the advertising budget set out for 2007. New print, poster and television advertisements will work to encourage more British tourists to visit Morocco. Even now, the tourist industry is contributing a significant amount to Morocco's GDP and is considered to be a key sector in the national economy, with growth predicted to be 6.8% in 2008.

'Morocco has all the high expectations that an emerging market should have and has successfully shrugged off its dangerous image'

As Europe's 'Gateway to Africa', Morocco enjoys long-established trade links with the UK, and commerce between the two countries has increased three-fold in the last decade alone, with the UK now one of Morocco's top six investors. At the end of November 2007, FDI into Morocco exceeded $4bn for the first time ever – an 18.8% increase, indicative of the increasing global interest in the country's tourism and investment markets.

Morocco is a deeply traditional country led by a young ruler who is spearheading changes. The expansion and promotion of Moroccan property to rival Spain's higher prices aims to show investors a sophisticated market, no longer in its infancy. Plan Azur is the driving force behind the country's healthy figures and now in 2008, the project is well under way, with the first and biggest resort, Mediterranean Saidia, to be completed at the end of 2009. Plan Azur's main aims are to attract five times the number of tourists in 2010 than in 2002, 10 million in total, and to create 600,000 jobs in the tourist industry. A further six coastal resorts are already under construction, all offering high-quality properties and facilities. With £2.2bn being injected into infrastructure, the EU plans to invest €650m before 2010 to help support economic and social reforms. These plans aim to increase tourism contribution to GDP by 8.5% annually so as to reach 20% by 2010. Importantly, the largest property development company in the world, Emaar Properties, has committed billions of dollars to the further expansion of the Moroccan property market, suggesting a boom in international investment is imminent.

Following the introduction of an open skies agreement last year, Morocco has now become increasingly accessible and should plans for a proposed twin track tunnel under the Gibralter Strait go ahead, Morocco could be within an hour and a half's train ride from European shores. Morocco then, is the most exotic short haul destination, currently nine miles and an hour's ferry ride from southern Europe, with prices similar to those in Spain 10 years ago. Britons are starting to realise the close proximity and affordability and are favouring it as a holiday and investment destination.

Is this a good place to buy?

The last five years have seen a considerable rise not only in the number of visiting foreigners but foreigners buying houses in Morocco, partly attributable to the fact that King Mohammed VI is actively encouraging foreign investment and, in 2001, changed the law to allow foreign investors to take proceeds of property sales out of the country; 100% repatriation of funds is therefore achievable and a very appealing factor for non-resident foreign investors. The government has also created the Investment Promotion Unit in order to attract further foreign investment and does not legally differentiate between foreign and domestic investors.

2007 saw an unexpected drop in the economy due to a severe drought, and the 8.1% GDP real growth achieved in 2006 slumped to 2.1%, emphasising the high dependency that Morocco still has on agricultural output. Since the 'Plan Azur' reforms, the economic climate has been more appealing but never stable. The Moroccan currency is tied very closely to the euro to minimise volatility, meaning GBP/EUR and GBP/MAD have similar patterns. A foreign exchange rate anchor, a well-managed monetary policy and inflation rates have all been held to the levels of industrialised countries for the last decade and according to World Bank and IMF reports, the dirham has appreciated by 18% in real terms since 1990.

House prices are a third lower than those in the UK and living costs are between 6 and 10 times lower. Moroccan property therefore represents extremely good value for money – other European markets are around 50% more expensive. On top of this, the country enjoys 300 days of sunshine per year, allowing for a year-round tourist market with excellent rental opportunities.

Which type of property should you go for?

In determining which type of property to purchase, there are several things to consider, including location, age, size, architectural value, condition, title and ownership, and the cost of purchase and restoration. Morocco really has everything to offer in terms of variety with Spanish, Arab and French influences.

In Morocco there are three main types of investment: either a renovation project in the form of a *riad* or *dars*, buying existing property such as a villa with its own swimming pool and land, or buying off-plan. Riads or dars are traditional houses that can be found inside the *medina* (the old town enclosed in ramparts accessed through imposing gates, with maze-like streets), and offer the investor a creative output through renovation. These types of project can be costly and buyers looking to restore an older more traditional building should set aside 50%–100% of the purchase price for building costs. Title deeds are also more difficult to obtain due to the 'Melkia Law' which involves gaining permission from all family members before a sale can be completed.

The second investment option is a villa. Villas are more expensive to buy than apartments; however, rental income will be higher than an apartment and you get the privacy that apartment blocks cannot offer. Nonetheless, research the area and make sure there is access to local amenities – if the property does not already have electricity or internet and phone connections look into prices to have these fitted.

The third investment option is an off-plan apartment, currently very trendy for buyers who won't be spending a lot of time in the country and are buying as an investment only. Most off-plan properties show an increase of capital appreciation before they are even built and gaining title deeds is a lot simpler than with older properties. Since 2003 a VEFA contract has been put in place for off-plan purchases, ensuring that the seller builds the property within an agreed time limit and that the purchaser makes scheduled payments throughout the construction process.

Land in Morocco is less easy to purchase than property. In fact foreigners cannot buy land outside the urban perimeter. However, in a bid to attract investors, the Moroccan State can authorise the change of the legal nature of the land from agricultural to residential. Investors then need to apply for a VNA, Vocation Non Agricole, a procedure which is quite complex. For this, government permission is required, which can take months, and an architect and surveyor are usually appointed. To avoid the sometimes arduous process of obtaining permission, you can buy direct from a developer who has already bought the land and therefore completed the process. Many developers in the main coastal resorts are willing to sell portions of land for sub-developments, so this is an option for people with the money and expertise. Land has reportedly increased in value four-fold in the last two years so it is definitely worth thinking about for those wanting fast returns.

INSIDER TIP
If you intend to buy a number of properties it may be worth setting up a Moroccan Private Limited Company (set-up time is about three weeks), the minimum equity capital for which is 100,000 dirhams (around £6,000). This is a good mechanism for unifying your Moroccan property investment activities and will make managing your various profit streams for repatriation considerably easier.

Hotspots

The most popular places for property sales in Morocco are Marrakech, Fez and Essaouira, although the new resort developments along the coast also offer some opportunities. Sidi ifni, Agadir, Essaouira, El Jadida, Tangier and Casablanca are all areas along the Atlantic coast and Ceuta, Tetouan and Nadir can be found along the Mediterranean coast. Marrakech is located inland.

Plan Azur

Although there is no rental market as yet, the interest surrounding these developments combined with the country's increasing number of tourists means occupancy will be high. A lot of the 'Plan Azur' resorts are centred on golf, the sport is a big passion of the kings, therefore some of the world's greatest golf courses are to be built here and when buying a property it is worth checking if golf membership is included in the price. Samanah Country Club is one of the new developments due for completion in 2010, with 600 villas across a 700-acre site. A three-bedroom property with a pool can be bought €237,000, although it does not include membership to the resort's golf course. Tagazout is another new 'Plan Azur' resort 25 miles south of Agadir compromising a 4.5km beach, two hotels, a golf course, a golf academy and a spa and fitness centre. With so many resorts to choose from, be sure to see what extras are included in the property price. Investors at 'The Salama Valley Resort' receive a €900 card to spend in the resort, free return flights for the first three years, free healthcare and free house keeping. The £101,000 price tag also comes with a nine-year buyback guarantee and 7% annual rental income guaranteed.

INSIDER TIP There is neither a better nor worse coast for investment: it is merely a matter of personal preference. Choose the Mediterranean coast if you prefer a warmer climate and the Atlantic coast if you want to catch the 'Alizee', the local name given to the strong winds that offer perfect conditions for wind sports.

Essaouira

Located along the Atlantic coast, Essaouira has been nicknamed the 'surfing capital' of Morocco, alongside other attractions such as sailing, horse riding, yoga and kite surfing. Essaouira attracts thrill-seeking holiday makers all year round and June is its busiest month. It is not only adrenalin junkies that travel here though, the walled old town hides spice and fish souks and labyrinth streets affording a rare glimpse of times gone by.

Two and a half hours from Marrakech on the Atlantic coast, Essaouira is the second most popular destination for homebuyers after Marrakech. Although there is no official price index, property prices here are said to have increased 200% over the last four years. The city was once the port for Timbuctoo, and as a result has a wide mix of cultures. Essaouira has the only medina with a grid system, as it was one of the first towns to have an urban planning policy. The area has also proved popular with film-makers, and was the location for Oliver Stone's *Alexander* and Ridley Scott's *Kingdom of Heaven*. The new mayor however, has placed restrictions on the construction of guest houses after a surge in the numbers being built provided too much competition for the larger hotels. The market here is particularly suited to second-home buyers with property cheaper than in both Marrakech and Fez.

Marrakech

Known as the 'entertainment capital' of the country, Marrakech has long been the most popular tourist destination due to its year-round desert heat, its rose-red medina, its boutiques and now Marrakech's answer to the famous nightclub chain Pacha, hosting events with world-renowned DJs and attracting a famous crowd. It also has the most developed property market with 85% occupancy rates achievable during the high season, making it great for rental income. A fabulous mix of traditional and modern, the city is within easy reach of ski slopes and also boasts three golf courses, with seven more planned in the coming years. It has attracted stars such as Jean-Paul Gaultier and Yves Saint-Laurent, and until recently was the most accessible Moroccan destination from the UK. This made it the most sought-after place to buy property, and prices reflect this. The current trend for property developers is to buy old houses in the commercial district of Gueliz, knock them down and build modern apartment blocks in their place, creating a pied à terre market for long weekenders from Europe. Whilst Marrakech still presents good opportunities for investment and is an exciting destination, prices here may be prohibitive; a villa currently costs upwards of £237,000.

Countryside

An alternative option is to buy land in the countryside around Marrakech and to build on it: the **Route d'Ourika**, the **Route d'Ouarzazate** and the **Route de Fez** are three areas which are gaining in popularity, the first due to the stunning views and the second two due to their proximity to facilities such as the American School, large supermarkets and Club Amelkis, a new 18-hole golf course.

Rabat

As the country's capital Rabat is more cosmopolitan than some of Morocco's other cities and boasts some of the region's best golf courses which are a popular allure amongst tourists. Economic reforms have had a substantial impact on the property market meaning that in the last few years it has experienced exceptional growth.

Tangier

A less popular destination but one set to dominate the Moroccan property market in coming years, is **Tangier**. Located on the northern tip of Morocco this bustling port enjoys lively markets, a superb bay and delectable beaches. Seaside homes can be bought for less than £200,000 and Mayor Mohammed Hassud has been head hunted by the young king to change this area from an industrial hub into a tourist one. The city's landmarks are to be cleaned up and 5km of coast has been set aside for property and hotels. What is more, if the proposed tunnel link with Europe goes ahead it will welcome a constant stream of pleasure-seeking tourists each year. Prospects for short-term letting options are encouraging and with the UK just a two and a half hour flight away, Tangier's accessibility is one of the easiest in the country. Experts are finding that there is also growing demand for long-term rental property, making it ideal for an investor seeking stable investment options.

Fez

A Moroccan Florence, Fez prides itself on having the most elegant and highly-decorated houses in the country. It is also considered to be the best preserved medieval medina in the world and has been described as 'the most beautiful city'. Although it is somewhat quieter than other Moroccan hotspots, it is the ideal place to go to get your hands on a traditional home at a bargain price. Indeed, property can be 50% cheaper than Marrakech with the potential for between 20%–30% capital, appreciation every six months. The city, once the nation's capital, has a significant number of run-down properties left vacant or poorly maintained when inhabitants fled to the new capital Rabat and new commercial hub Casablanca in 1912. All these properties are apparently for sale and offer great opportunities for developers wanting to build stylish hotels, or individuals lured by the challenge of a restoration project. It must be remembered, however, that this is a time-consuming and expensive process. It is also important to obtain a building permit or *roska* from the government office. It costs 100 dirhams and is generally obtainable in a couple of days.

Buying an apartment in one of the old palaces, once inhabited by ruling oligarchy, could also prove to be a shrewd move. Traditional un-renovated dars here are available from anything between £6,800 to £40,580 whilst riads generally cost between £24,870 and £74,609. The fact that riads are so sought after is reflected in their elevated prices, meaning it is often better to opt for a dar which is more easily obtainable and therefore cheaper. It is unlikely that Fez's property market will mirror the success story that is now Marrakech within the short term; however, for those willing to invest in a long-term market, Fez may well be the ideal location. Those interested in taking advantage of the growing tourist industry should be cheered by the fact that the Moroccan Tourist Ministry have made it easy for foreigners to obtain licences to operate bed and breakfasts. Whilst other cities have restrictions on such permits, the government's aims to encourage foreign direct investment, bolster the tourism industry and renovate the medina in Fez mean that this type of enterprise is encouraged.

Saidia

An example of an area benefiting from Plan Azur investment and emerging as a promising investment hub, is **Saidia**. This large master planned resort development is three hours by air from the UK, has a perfect Mediterranean climate and is being built by one of the largest developers in Spain. It is also the only Plan Azur area situated on the Mediterranean coast and has a variety of villas, apartments and penthouses for sale. The €1.6bn 7,000,000 square metre development of Mediterrania Saidia is due to complete in 2009 and is poised to create a region blessed with world-class amenities which will create a series of resorts that have already been billed as 'Europe's new holiday centre'. The increase in tourism is likely to create a situation where demand significantly outstrips supply, and at least over the next five years, capital appreciation should be very good. One-bedroom apartments at Mediterrania Saidia are available from £52,600 and appreciation on these properties is expected to be strong.

Buyer's guide

In a bid to encourage increased levels of international investment the Moroccan government has recently made it easier and more attractive for foreign investors to own and profit from real estate in the country. Now overseas investors looking to invest in the county are subject only to the restrictions faced by Moroccan persons and are entitled to 100% repatriation of profits.

Mortgages

LTV %	TERM	CURRENCIES	RATES %	STATUS	SPECIAL CONDITIONS
70	25	Dirams	4.08	Employed or self-employed	

Key risks

Morocco is so dedicated to its programme of diversification and vast expansion of its tourist industry that it is in danger of forgetting the smaller things. The employment rate which stands at 15% throughout the country nears 20% in urbanised areas, and has failed to improve. Further, the economic drop experienced in 2007 highlighted the strong dependency that Morocco still has on its agricultural industry, and will continue to have until all intended tourism aims are met. Although Morocco is keen to become one of the top tourist destinations and is encouraging large-scale projects throughout the country, it has not yet managed to stabilise the smaller business sector providing income for many local businesses.

One of the main problems with buying property in Morocco is issues which arise with regard to title. Some properties do not have title deeds, and if anything, have a scroll written by an *adoul*, an official scribe, documenting ownership which sometimes goes back hundreds of years. As inheritance laws state that everybody with a claim to the property must agree to a sale (this can be a sizeable group of people), it is a good idea to employ a lawyer well-versed in the intricacies of Moroccan property law to trace the title holders and to arrange the purchase. If possible, it is better to buy from one or two owners who have owned the property for a long time. Official title can also be gained by paying 1% of the purchase price during the buying process. Evidently houses with secure title are more likely to sell at a higher price in the future.

Rating: ⚠ ⚠

Key opportunities

Morocco has all the high expectations that an emerging market should have and has successfully shrugged off its dangerous image, now offering a variety of holidays in exciting crime-free destinations.

It is currently possible to buy an existing property for a very good price in the country although it is important to bear in mind that renovated properties may mask a multitude of building flaws, so check everything thoroughly before making a purchase.

Morocco's accessible geographic location, burgeoning tourist industry, stable economy and emerging market status are all strong credentials for a healthy investment. Providing proper legal proceedings are adhered to and destinations are hand picked in terms of amenities and accessibility, Morocco is likely to provide strong investment opportunities.

Rating: $$$$

South Africa

Currency: Rand
Exchange rates:
1000 Rand = £63.38
£1 = 15.75 Rand

1000 Rand = US $125.34
US $1 = 7.99 Rand

Introduction

South Africa is a country with a breathtaking natural landscape and vast opportunities for adventure, either through safari, mountain walking, city or beach
life. The natural terrain varies from savannah to snow-covered mountains, forests to swamps, endless beaches and peaceful rivers to bustling towns and cities. Unsurprisingly, there is plenty to explore: vibrant Cape Town, Robben
Island where Nelson Mandela was imprisoned, the Cradle of Humankind near
Johannesburg, the Kruger National Park, Table Mountain and the Garden Route
which comprises 600km of coastline between Cape Town and the Tsitsikamma
Forest. The country has gone through impressive changes over the last 15 years
and its tourism market has opened up significantly. Indeed, visitor numbers
increased by 9% in 2007 and were estimated to be worth around €31.2bn, a
figure that is expected to soar to €60bn by 2017.

Economically, South Africa is considered to be an emerging market with
an abundant supply of natural resources. The financial, legal, communications, energy and transport sectors are well-developed, and the country
has a modern infrastructure. However, growth has not been strong enough
to substantially lower South Africa's high unemployment rate (which was at
24.2% in 2007), and the economic problems from the apartheid era remain
serious, especially regarding poverty and a lack of economic empowerment
among disadvantaged groups. Economic policy is currently focusing on targeting inflation and liberalising trade, hoping to increase job growth and
household income. GDP growth in 2006 and 2007 was 5%, up from 3.7%

in 2004 and 4.5% in 2005, while inflation in 2007 stood at 6.5%. This improvement has been steady and the country is showing good potential for the future. The Economist Intelligence Unit anticipates that real GDP will accelerate again and the 2008 budget promises infrastructure investment towards railways, harbours and ports whilst $7.7bn dollars will be directed at improving the generation capacity of Eskom, South Africa's state-run electricity company.

> *'Because South Africa has a stable economy, relative security, plus possibilities for good rental potential and capital growth, it will continue to attract more serious investors looking for returns on their investment'*

On the back of this growth and new-found prosperity, the demand for property has also increased, particularly among a new black middle class and overseas buyers lured by the warmer climate.

Is this a good place to buy?

South Africa is a country of great variety, offering something for everyone. There are beautiful beaches, unspoiled countryside with an abundance of wild-life, mountains, bustling cities with a vibrant night scene (including Cape Town, one of the most popular cities in the world), impressive relics from the dawn of humanity, fine wines and a range of cuisines. South Africa is especially popular with Brits seeking winter sunshine, and has the advantage of being only two hours ahead of Greenwich Mean Time, whilst boasting a considerably cheaper cost of living.

House prices here are much lower than in the UK or USA, and in some areas prices are less than a tenth of prices in the south of England. Standard family homes are available from around £65,000 ($132,000) and two-bed-room apartments start from about £42,000 ($85,300) – though prices vary depending on location, style of property and local amenities. Over the last seven years, prices have reportedly risen 16.7% annually (according to *Homes Overseas* Magazine, July edition) and although such high growth lev-els may not be sustainable, prices are still expected to appreciate over the next few years especially as the country is to host the Football World Cup in 2010.

As a second-home, holiday or retirement destination, therefore, the country is an attractive proposition. This is compounded by the fact that, as long as they are in the country legally at all times, owners of property in South Africa are permitted to reside there for as long as they wish. From a legal point of view, South Africa is one of the safer countries in which to buy a home. Non-residents who own in the country have all the normal rights of ownership, including the right to recover rental income.

South Africa is reputed to have the best deeds registration system in the world, with an exceptional degree of accuracy and tenure guaranteed as long as the proper precautions are taken regarding contracts, deposits and obtaining proper title. Property can be owned individually, jointly in undivided shares or by an entity such as a company, a close corporation or trust or a similar entity registered outside the country. There are, however, procedures and requirements which must be complied with in certain circumstances. In the case where a foreign entity purchases property in South Africa, it needs to be registered locally. In the case where the shares of a local company are owned by a non-resident, a South African resident public officer will need to be appointed for accounting purposes. In the event of a non-resident purchasing property in the country with the intention of residing for longer periods, permanent residency will have to be applied for in accordance with the given requirements and procedures of South African law.

South Africa has proven especially popular with those looking for holiday or retirement homes and thanks to its stable economy, relative security, plus possibilities for good rental potential and capital growth, it will continue to attract more serious investors looking for returns on their investment. These factors mean that demand is likely to stay high, and that investing here offers relatively safe prospects. Having said that, the announcement that 30,000 South African estate agents have failed to renew their licence for 2008 (according to South Africa's Estate Agency Affairs Board) intimates that even this market is likely to face a slowdown of sorts.

Which type of property should you go for?

There is no shortage of properties in South Africa, so whatever type you are looking for, there is likely to be plenty to choose from. Most properties for sale tend to be apartments, villas and duplexes in new-build developments, or older properties such as farmhouses and cottages, though it is also possible to buy a plot of land and build on it. Provided the title deeds have been endorsed 'non-resident', any funds put into a property and any income received, including profit from sales, can be repatriated easily.

INSIDER TIP

Cluster homes, which are part of security complexes, are convenient and popular with overseas buyers as 'lock up and leave' properties. Although new properties may lack the charm and character of older buildings, they have advantages in that there are no costs associated with modernisation or renovation, while heating and maintenance are generally cheaper. The standard of modern development in the country is strictly regulated and is producing higher quality properties than were constructed previously (check that the developer is reputable, though, and have all aspects of the building checked before signing). Delayed payment options add to this appeal.

More modern properties also have good resale potential and are considered a good investment by South African buyers, although they are usually smaller than older properties and rarely come with a large amount of land.

Despite these factors, there are advantages to buying a resale property. Such properties are likely to be in a more developed area with good local facilities and services. They are also more likely to have an individual design and style and avoid the usual teething problems associated with a new property. There will also be no need to install water, communications or electricity meters and buyers are likely to get more for their money, in the form of a larger plot of land, an established garden, and extras such as furniture included in the price.

The previously strong buy-to-let sector has recently diminished in line with falling rental yields although for those who can afford to buy with cash, the buy-to-let sector still represents a good investment. Potential first-time buyers are renting, finding it more cost-effective than buying on finance and although yields are dropping, demand for rental accommodation is still high. Oversupply is unlikely to become an issue, because building costs are rising. In addition, the boom in commercial property developments and infrastructure projects is likely to take capacity away from the residential sector.

'South Africa's ever-present security risks have not seemed to have discouraged foreign interest in the country either although they need to be borne in mind'

Yields remain highest in the luxury segments whilst inner-city rentals can also be a good investment. Johannesburg's luxury segment offers yields of between 8% and 10%, because of its slower house price growth rate. The luxury market of Cape Town has lower yields at 3.4% to 5.3%, while middle segment properties yield around 4.7% to 6.6%. Properties in Durban have lower yields again. For those who are looking for rental returns and can pay up front, then apartments generally offer the best value, and will have year-round rental potential in good locations. Despite the recent slowdown, rental rates in 2007 were still predicted to rise by 12%–15%, according to South African property experts.

Hotspots

Cape Peninsula

The most popular area for overseas buyers is the Cape Peninsula, one of the most desirable places in the world. White sandy beaches, proximity to the Garden Route and Cape Town's cosmopolitan urban centre have all combined to raise the profile of the property market. On the Cape Peninsula, the average house price is £97,000 ($188,000) whist prices on the Eastern Cape are cheaper at an average of £76,000 ($148,000). (ABSA data for the last quarter of 2007).

Cape Town

Cape Town has been heralded as the 'Saint Tropez of Africa', and the dynamic city is home to a wealth of cafes, bars, museums, shops and restaurants. With a highly desirable location and easy access from the UK, it receives 1.6 million foreign tourists a year. More than £1.07bn has been invested in the city since 2000 and the fact that it is due to host the 2010 FIFA World Cup is bolstering the city's investment popularity. Indeed, studies conducted following the World Cup 1998 in France reported that property prices rose by 60% in the year prior to the competition and it is predicted that the tournament will have a similarly beneficial effect on house prices in Cape Town and the surrounding area.

Properties are still available in central Cape Town for under £80,000 ($140,000), but demand is strong, so this will not be the case for long. Cape Town's southern suburbs perhaps represent one of the most desirable areas of the city: it is safe and family friendly, and close to amenities. A two-bedroom apartment on a secure complex in the popular Hout Bay area costs from £59,000 ($115,300).

Western Cape

Most properties bought by Brits are in the Western Cape, which stretches from St Helena Bay in the west to Durban in the east. The Garden Route, the

Africa & Middle East

SOUTH AFRICA

coastline of the Western Cape, has long been a popular holiday spot for South Africans from inland areas as well as foreign investors. Although prices are still low, this is not the price haven that it used to be with an average house costing £81,000 ($157,000).(ABSA data for the last quarter of 2007).

Plettenburg Bay and Knysna
Over the Christmas holidays, Plettenburg Bay is transformed from a sleepy coastal town to a bustling holiday resort. There is much that appeals here, and Knysna's arty lagoon community and Plettenburg Bay's beaches have begun to attract outside interest, pushing prices up and creating good rental potential.

Durban
Durban is a recent addition to South Africa's investment scene. The south coast around Durban has long been popular with locals who have been visiting the area's seaside resort towns for years. There are stunning beaches and a number of golf resorts, another factor which makes the area a popular one. Moreover, Durban will be one of the hubs for the football World Cup in 2010. It is upgrading its airport and direct flights from the UK will follow. As a result many recent developments are starting to focus on this area. For example, the Blythedale Development built along an untouched stretch of coast north-east of Durban has prices from £54,000 ($109,800) for a three-bedroom townhouse overlooking the golf course. The development includes three resorts centred around forest, beach and golf and will contain 4,500 homes.

Gauteng and Pretoria
Gauteng, formerly Johannesburg's environs, is the main commercial hub of the country. Demand for property from the local market is therefore strong, and as prices here are lower than in Cape Town, this is tipped as a good investment area. Pretoria is also reputed to represent a good investment opportunity where owners are seeing the best increases in rental returns. Over the past 10 years, rents for flats grew by an average of 12% per annum in Pretoria, compared with 9% in Cape Town and Port Elizabeth.

When it comes to favoured locations, the above areas are the ones attracting most overseas investors. However, increasing interest is also being seen in Kwa-Zulu Natal, **where prices since 2004 have risen by as much as 36% in areas such as Balito and Umhlanga. In Kwa-Zulu Natal, on the South Coast, the average house price is £72,000 ($140,000).**

Buyer's guide

There are currently no restrictions for foreigners wanting to own property in South Africa although there are certain procedures and requirements that need to be adhered to in certain circumstances. Generally foreigners are granted the same rights as locals. In the case where a foreign entity purchases property in South Africa, it needs to be registered locally. In the case where the shares of a local company are owned by a non-resident, a South African resident public officer will need to be appointed for accounting purposes. In the event of a non-resident purchasing property in the country with the intention of residing for longer periods, permanent residency will have to be applied for in accordance with the given requirements and procedures of South African law.
(Source: www.sunshineestates.net)

Mortgages

LTV %	TERM	CURRENCIES	RATES %	STATUS	SPECIAL CONDITIONS
50	20	ZAR	15.5	Employed or self-employed	

Key risks

There are risks associated with buying properties in South Africa, so it is advisable to employ a solicitor before signing any contracts or paying any money. Buyers must be aware that there is a chance that some properties will be seized and redistributed to original African owners who can prove a claim to the land if clear title is not carefully researched. All municipalities have lists of claimed lands, and they are free to view so either request that your solicitor checks them, or do so yourself.

In recent years, the possibility of a moratorium on the buying and selling of property by foreign investors has been considered by the South African government, but this has not yet been implemented. The aim of such legislation would be to control escalating property prices and would consist of a governmental 'land audit' to ascertain the extent of foreign ownership. This could be followed by laws banning foreigners from buying freehold properties, and restricting the length of their leaseholds. However, property prices are now rising at a steadier, more sustainable rate and the idea of the moratorium has fallen out of favour for now. South Africa's ever-present security risks have not seemed to have discouraged foreign interest in the country either although they need to be borne in mind.

Rating: ⚠ ⚠ ⚠

Key opportunities

Despite significant price rises over the last few years, entry prices are still reasonable in many parts of the country, meaning there is the potential to achieve good capital appreciation. Good rental opportunities are available for those in a position to make cash purchases or to raise finance in other countries where interest rates are lower.

Rating: $$

United Arab Emirates

ABU DHABI

Introduction

Over the last 40 years the United Arab Emirates (UAE) have gathered momentum as an economic force and top tourist retreat and have now stormed onto the global scene. A unique amalgamation of mountains, beaches, deserts, oases and thriving city centres, the seven-state United Arab Emirates sit along the Arabian Peninsular. Abu Dhabi, Ajman, Dubai, Fujairah, Ras al-Khaimah, Sharjah and Umm al-Quwain comprise the UAE, each bringing their own individual influence. As the biggest state, Abu Dhabi is the capital of the federation whilst Dubai is undoubtedly the most well-known, commercialised and developed state. It is also the country with the fastest growing population in the world, with new figures suggesting that up to 857 people move to Dubai each day, therefore totalling 5,000 a week. A flurry of media hype surrounding this particular emirate has propelled it to astounding heights as far as investment is concerned, painting a very merry picture of high returns and yields. As a result investors in their masses have paid their Dirhams and now own their little slice of this super city. In fact, latest figures from the Dubai Land Department show that British companies now account for over 1,900,000 square feet of prime real estate land and as a country we are now the number one overseas investors in land in Dubai.

Attracted by low rental taxes and low transaction costs, the UAE is also a highly industrialised nation and one of the most stable countries in the whole of the Middle East. As such it offers prosperous investment opportunities.

> **'For prospective real estate investors, the UAE has a lot to offer, not least thanks to its low rental tax and transaction costs'**

Whilst the bigger states of Dubai and Abu Dhabi offer city slickers all that they could wish for, from tempting tax-free shopping to an array of international eateries, as well as some spectacular scenery, the smaller emirates such as Fujairah and Al Ain have a much more laid-back atmosphere with several sights and attractions. The country is served with several international airports making all emirates easily accessible for both business and tourism.

Is this a good place to buy?

There is no questioning that the UAE has recently flourished as far as business and tourism are concerned, but whether this country still offers healthy property investment opportunities is a subject widely debated in the media. With Dubai's population growth being the fastest in the world, demand, in theory, should keep up with supply. However, this population growth has been abnormally high and is unlikely to remain at such astronomical levels. As a result, there are increasing concerns that the market will be hit with a glut of supply that even the rapidly expanding population will not be able to fill. In recent years, Dubai has experienced mass development, much of it off-plan, but with a lot of this building now reaching completion, the market has become swamped with new housing. And this problem does not look set to abate any time soon. Between mid-2009 and 2010, around 277,000 further residential units will be delivered. The question remains then, for how long will property be first of all, in demand and second of all, profitable? Leading investment analysts questioned in the latest www.ArabianBusiness.com survey echo the media's scepticism about the state of this market, believing the market is a 'bubble waiting to burst'. A further 25% of those questioned believe Dubai offers no real long-term value. Dubai's fragility in investment terms is exacerbated by the fact that many purchasers have made buying decisions based on speculation rather than key market fundamentals, meaning effective exit strategies, especially amid the tides of new developments, are hard to come by.

Attempts to stabilise the market are to be implemented at some point in 2008 by the Real Estate Regulatory Agency (RERA) in the form of rental caps. These currently sit at 7% and are expected to be lowered imminently. Such measures should make the market in Dubai more resistant to erratic price increases and are expected, overall, to soothe the market's current volatility.

In Dubai's favour though, is its burgeoning tourist market which welcomed almost 750,000 UK visitors in 2007 alone. Add to this premium air traffic which is growing 20% year-on-year, and the emirate's tourist appeal becomes evident. In line with this increased demand, EOS recently announced that a daily flight from London Stansted to Dubai International will commence on 6 July 2008. British Airways has also recently added six extra flights per week from London Heathrow to Dubai to support the growing demand.

Aside from Dubai, excellent opportunities for investment exist in its less illustrious neighbours. Considered the 'richest city in the world' (Source:CNN), the UAE's capital Abu Dhabi is slowly but surely catching up. As the UAE's centre of government, business and commerce and comfortably producing 90% of the UAE's oil, property rentals are high whilst property prices are on the up. With supply falling short of demand, now is a very good time to invest. Abu Dhabi still offers the excitement and modern lifestyle of Dubai although it isn't as developed or discovered. There are several developments currently under construction which should offer some good opportunities to investors, especially as the authorities here are determined to draw on Dubai's successes whilst sidestepping its failures; that is, its 'brashness and crassness' (Source: Homes Overseas – April 2008). With its population expected to double over the decade commencing 2008, demand should remain healthy.

Ras al Khaimah (RAK) is another emirate the shrewd investor should sit up and take note of. Named the 'Rising Star of the Middle East' by Gulf News, with no personal and business taxes, a large university and some spectacular scenery, RAK's property market has the potential to afford hefty rewards on well chosen units.

In order to accommodate increasing visitor numbers throughout the UAE as a whole, it has been brought to the authorities' attention that there is a severe need for improved infrastructure to stave off problems with congestion and overcrowding. As a result, the president of the UAE, Sheikh Khalifa bin Zayad al-Nahayan, has announced that he will spend $4.4bn on infrastructure improvements across the seven emirates. Plans for the 350km Emirates Railway network have been conceived as well as intercity highways to improve connectivity.

Something to be aware of though, is the increased threat the UAE faces from terrorists. In June 2008, the Foreign and Commonwealth Office claimed that terrorists were planning to carry out attacks in the country and Britain consequently raised its terror warning for the UAE to the highest level.

Which type of property should you go for?

Whilst apartments remain very popular investments throughout the United Arab Emirates thanks to the high expatriate and young professional population,

Africa & Middle East

UNITED ARAB EMIRATES

it is also these properties which have been built in proliferation and now swamp the market place, particularly in Dubai. Having said that, rental yields on apartments can be very high and rental income tax is very low, especially in Dubai, so providing occupancy can be assured, they do make good investments.

Residential rather than commercial property in the UAE tends to be especially popular with investors as it caters for the vast number of executives that flock to the emirates on a weekly basis. It, therefore, provides the most reliable returns.

INSIDER TIP — **Investors should also keep an eye out for investment opportunities along the planned Arabian Canal which will be one of the world's most extravagant and impressive engineering projects predicted to cost around $61bn. Plans detail the creation of a 75km canal stretching from Palm Jebel Ali to the Palm Jumeirah as well as a $50bn city spanning 20,000 hectares along the canal's southern flank. This increased waterside development space will mean the creation of many 'waterside apartments' which are expected to be in high demand.**

Whilst smaller, functional urban apartments are popular in Dubai, emirates such as Ras al Khaimah (RAK) which are blessed with beautiful natural surroundings may find more scope for holiday/lifestyle orientated property. RAK, with the longest stretch of coastline in the emirates, is a thriving tourist destination and entices holiday makers seeking a five-star lifestyle.

Hotspots

Dubai

It goes without saying that Dubai is the most popular tourist destination in the UAE and attracts millions of visitors each year. It is an expensive, flamboyant city which has been subject to consistent development over the years. Known as 'the city of gold', Dubai offers a very high standard of living, a full range of five-star services and some of the best shopping in the world. It also has a range of man-made beaches, the most popular being Jumeirah Beach offering everything from jet skiing to volleyball.

As the mass of developments which have been cropping up all over the city over the last few years near completion, concerns are being raised as to whether demand will be unable to keep up with supply. This coupled with astronomical house prices rises in recent years, may contribute to a distinct 'cooling off' in this market.

INSIDER TIP Keep an eye out for the spectacular Dubai Waterfront, an 81 million square metre waterfront development bigger than Manhattan, comprising 250 master planned communities which is guaranteed to impress. Of even greater prowess promises to be Versace's personalised residential resort overlooking Dubai Creek. Here you will find £178 dinner plates, £1,700 bath robes and a special under-beach cooling so that guest don't burn their feet en-route to the sea!

Abu Dhabi

Named as the best Arab city to live in by *Saneou Al Hadath* magazine, the 'golden city of the Gulf' and emirate capital Abu Dhabi is a modern and exciting city which combines the culture and traditions of the Arabian people with diverse up-to-date real estate. Previously hidden in the shadow of its neighbouring city Dubai, Abu Dhabi, although not as lively, has recently proved its true potential as both a luxury and glamorous holiday destination and interesting investment choice. Around every corner, visitors will come across stylish hotels and eateries (including the Emirates Palace Hotel which is one of the most expensive hotels in the world), interspersed with amazing architectural sights including towering skyscrapers. The fortunes of this emirate will always be linked, to a certain extent, to the successes of Dubai but being slightly earlier on its development path, investors are not faced with quite the oversupply risks plaguing, or at least being talked about, in Dubai. Plans for an inter-city train and metro network complement the 'Plan Abu Dhabi 2030' which is striving to implement an expansion of the transport network in order to cater for increased visitor and resident numbers.

Ras Al Khaimah (RAK)

As the northernmost of all the emirates, Ras al Khaimah is politically safe, free from corporate and income taxes, has competitive labour, office and warehouse rates, a low cost of living, a progressive and fast-growing Free Zone, easy road, sea and air access and a beautiful 64km coastline. As such it is widely expected to become the premier tourist destination of the UAE and, with the government keen to preserve its country's natural beauty, will be protected from overdevelopment. High-density tower-blocks, over-crowding and congestion should all be kept to a minimum.

Development has focused on life-style and industrial sectors meaning RAK has attracted a high percentage of real estate, leisure, educational and hospitality investments. What is more, the increasing numbers of new and expanding industries mean RAK will soon own over 50% of UAE Total Production capacity. Indicative of its economic strength, was the 18% GDP growth achieved in 2007 (Source: Eman Al Baik). On the back of this growth, RAK's share of the entire region's wealth is predicted to grow 'exponentially' over the next few years according to a cross section of industry leaders at the RAK conference last year. Inward investment is expected to rocket to as much as AED50bn in the coming years and should maintain RAK's position as the emirate with the third-highest level of project investment relative to GDP in the UAE.

Appealingly, property prices in RAK sit at around one third of those in Dubai, with freehold ownership granted for every property. Frontline properties here are available from £50,000 and luxury 3-bedroom apartments sell for around £200,000.

Fujairah

Fujairah has a lot to offer the history-hungry visitor, with a high concentration of archeological sites, some of which date back as far as the Iron Age. It also boasts many beautiful waterfalls and beaches and a rich natural beauty. A law which would allow foreign property ownership (similar to Dubai's) is currently being considered, although at present the only opportunity for freehold investment for foreigners is the 270-apartment Al Jabar Tower. Otherwise, only leasehold investment opportunities have been open to expatriates for the last few years. As in other emirates, The Fujairah Free Zone offers the opportunity for 100% foreign-owned businesses. With confident plans to triple current tourist bedroom supply from 1,500 to 4,500 by 2012, tourist arrivals are expected to increase over the coming years and a proposed Dubai-Fujairah road due to complete in 2008 should boost numbers further by opening up accessibility.

Ajman

The smallest emirate, Ajman, has recently experienced an influx of foreign investment following the announcement that a new international airport will be in operation by 2011. Its popularity is therefore likely to proliferate over the next few years especially in line with a new £30bn coastal self-contained city to be co-developed by the government of Ajman and Solidere International. Aside from Dubai, Ajman is the only other emirate where foreigners can buy and own freehold villas and townhouses. It also has a growing Free Zone industrial area and a strategically located port. Reports from www.myglobalinvestments.com suggest that rental yields in the region of 8%–10% and capital appreciation in the region of 30% can be achieved. Villas in Ajman Green City are available from around £148,648.

Buyer's guide

Since 2006, buying property in Dubai has been straightforward for non-UAE nationals. Foreigners are entitled to freehold ownership of villas, apartments and land and can enjoy profits generated by renting it out for a period of up to 99 years. (Source: www.buying-property-in-dubai.com)

Foreign investors in the emirate capital Abu Dhabi are only entitled to buy property within three 'investment zones', although proposals are in place that, if approved by state government, would allow outright land ownership in certain areas of the capital. As the law stands at the moment, foreign investors are entitled to ownership, development, leasing and mortgaging of land and property for non-UAE nationals within these investment zones. They may also opt into various lease agreements lasting up to 99 years. (Source: www.thenational.ae)

Freehold properties in Ajman are available to foreigners in designated areas, although there are still some severe risks associated with title deeds.

Foreigners are awarded full ownership rights providing they are in the Ras al Khaimah Properties portfolio. (Source: www.bsa.ae)

In Fujairah freehold ownership for foreigners has not yet been granted so those wanting to invest have to lease hold properties for 99 years.

(Source: *An Overview of recent Legal Developments in the GCC Real Estate Sector and the Impact on Foreign Investors by Jimmy Haoula, Partner at the Bin Shabib and Associates (BSA)* available through http://www.bsa.ae/pdf/BSA%20Article%20-%20An%20Overview%20of%20recent%20Legal%20Developments%20in%20th.pdf)

Mortgages

DUBAI	LTV %	TERM	CURRENCIES	RATES %	STATUS	SPECIAL CONDITIONS
	70	25	EUR, PLN, CHF, USD, GBP	From 5+	Employed or self-employed	Certain developers only

RAK	LTV %	TERM	CURRENCIES	RATES %	STATUS	SPECIAL CONDITIONS
	70	10	AED	8.25	Employed or self-employed	

ABU DHABI	LTV %	TERM	CURRENCIES	RATES %	STATUS	SPECIAL CONDITIONS
	70	10	AED	8.25	Employed or self-employed	

Africa & Middle East

UNITED ARAB EMIRATES

Key risks

Although investing in real estate has become a lot easier in recent years, and many of the restrictions preventing foreigners buying have been lifted, buying property in some emirates still doesn't enable foreigners to freely work or live in the country without obtaining citizenship. Also in some emirates it is only possible to purchase property via leasehold schemes.

There is a high demand for property in the UAE, especially in major cities such as Dubai and Abu Dhabi but with not enough property to go around property prices can be high. Traffic is also a big problem for the country which faces a lot of congestion on its roads. Although plans have been made to introduce more public transport it is unsure how long these plans will take to implement.

What remains to be seen is whether the more popular emirate markets such as Dubai will be able to maintain demand for the vast numbers of residential properties nearing completion. Media speculation fears that demand simply won't be able to keep up with supply and if this happens, exit strategies will become strained and prices will start to fall.

Terror threats are also something the UAE is becoming increasingly plagued with and are something that the potential investor needs to be aware of.

Rating: ⚠ ⚠ ⚠

Key opportunities

One of the fastest growing tourist destinations in the world and with a modern healthcare, education and transport system, it is no wonder that the UAE is turning into one of the destinations of the century. For prospective real estate investors, it also has a lot to offer, not least thanks to its low rental tax and transaction costs. Shrewd investors will choose emirates where prices are still rising and demand is still untainted by oversupply.

Rating: $$

Argentina

Currency: Peso ($)
Exchange Rates:
100 Peso = £16.77
£1 = 6 peso

100 Peso = $32.96
$1 = 3.03peso

Introduction

From the subtropical flats in the north, across the rolling Pampas plains, down to the semi-arid steppes of Patagonia in the south, and bordered by the majestic Andes, Argentina has been said to contain almost every geographical feature imaginable.

With a total area of just under three million square kilometres (not counting the Antarctic land the Argentines lay claim to) Argentina is the 8th largest country in the world and offers an incredible range of diverse climates, landscapes and experiences. A deep-rooted and complex past gives Argentina its cosmopolitan and somewhat European air that bewitches visitors year after year.

The elegant, cultural capital of Buenos Aires is an enchanting mix of its European heritage and the South American passion that is embodied in the national dance, the tango. Large, leafy boulevards are host to cart sellers and street dancers who mingle with tourists and wealthy shoppers alike. Buenos Aires also draws avid theatre goers thanks to its multitude of opera-houses, theatres and dance exhibitions.

Argentina has a very successful tourist market, augmented by its wealth of variety and year-round season. Stretching from the Tropic of Capricorn down towards the chill of Antarctica, Argentina's differing climates allow for a range of sports from jungle exploration to high altitude skiing, with a plethora of outdoor activities in between: the possibilities for tourists are endless.

The high standard of living makes the country an attractive place to live or visit, but with the added bonus of a comparatively low cost of living it is easy to see why the country is so popular with international visitors. *The Economist* also suggests that it is one of the few South American countries to remain relatively unaffected by the weak state of the US dollar, meaning Argentina is unlikely to feel the pinch of the credit crunch currently affecting so many other countries.

Is this a good place to buy?

In 2001, following severe debt and national depression, Argentina suffered a real blow as a recession floored the economy. At this point, a peso equalled a dollar, devaluing the currency so much that the only people profiting were tourists taking advantage of the fantastic exchange rate. At this time GDP was 18% less than in 1998 and 60% of the population were below the poverty line. A determined government guided Argentina through the crisis though, declaring a default on the country's foreign debt and slowly rebuilding the economy to a state where it was able to pay off its debt to the IMF, totalling over $100bn. From its rock-bottom position in 2001 then, Argentina's GDP has grown at an average annual rate of 8%–9%, developing a much healthier economy that is set to stabilise further over the coming years.

'With recent figures displaying encouraging levels of GDP growth and capital appreciation, the future could be very positive for Argentina and investors choosing to buy property here may well enjoy excellent gains'

Unsurprisingly, the economic crisis had a severe effect on housing, with the property market devaluing by as much as 70%. International faith was lost in Latin American currency, meaning that most housing transactions now take place in US dollars. Further, because of an insubstantial lending market the majority of purchases are paid in full upfront. This state of affairs has had a number of ramifications on the real estate market. Firstly, the market is based on a much more solid and reliable base as any boom or bust movements within the market are real, transparent and not based on foreign speculation. Secondly, with 100% upfront payments necessary a large proportion of the middle and lower Argentines' classes are priced out of the purchase market. Having substantial disposable income available (although not quite enough with which to buy a house) many of these, especially the wealthy middle-class Argentines, turn to the rental market, and create a consistently strong demand.

Argentina's exports are predominantly agriculture based although the economy is supported by a number of other sectors. As the economy recovered from the economic crash, industries such as construction, textiles, food production and the robust natural resources industry, flourished and now contribute highly to annual GDP figures. Tourism is also a major earner, expected to bring in \$24.4bn in 2008, a figure that the World Travel and Tourism Council expects to grow to \$42.9bn by 2018. Confidence in the market is demonstrated by the recent move taken by British Airways to increase its London to Buenos Aires flights to a daily service. The tourism industry though, is not only thriving at an international level but is also proving very popular internally as Argentines become increasingly enthusiastic about travelling around their own country.

Aside from the booming tourist industry, the property market looks to be going from strength to strength. Since the economic downturn in 2002, property prices have risen by as much as 50% (most definitely in the capital, Buenos Aires) and are predicted to continue to rise over the next few years. A recent report by Credit Suisse suggests that property could still be undervalued by up to 20% or 30%, and as prices have yet to return to the peaks of the 1990s there is great potential for some strong capital appreciation. Yields are conservatively estimated at 10%, with some areas and developments seeing higher return. The purchase process is fast and relatively straightforward with few restrictions for foreign buyers; however, the market is less regulated than the European markets and unlicensed realtors do exist.

Politically, the country is looking at an uncertain few months ahead. The hardline economic procedures that the previous and current government have taken to pull the country out of financial crisis are starting to cause problems. The robust financial policies have led to high inflation which is unofficially estimated to be above 20%; officially inflation is stated as being 8% or 9% but suspected government intervention in the national statistics office renders these figures obsolete. Furthermore, high taxes are starting to affect certain industries and leading to strikes but President Fernández is refusing to back down. The recent resignation of Argentina's economy minister has only served to deepen the sense of economic instability, and the president is rapidly losing popularity. If her policies do not alter there are predictions that the country could slide into more troublesome economic conditions, but these forecasts vary from spectator to spectator and are still just speculations. This does not necessarily bode negatively for the potential investor, but the political situation should be carefully observed.

Which type of property should you go for?

Argentina offers a range of property to suit varying needs and requirements. The greatest demand for real estate comes from the local population so

The Americas

ARGENTINA

buy-to-let investors may want to look at the type of property that would appeal to native Argentines: this could be city-centre apartments suitable for businessmen, or family suburban homes within a community and close to the necessary amenities. There is also a strong internal and international tourism market prevailing, so property in popular hotspots would also prove viable options. This could be in the form of ski chalets, lakeside retreats or wilderness ranches on the doorstep of the great outdoors. Argentina is less likely to be chosen as a destination for a holiday home by British nationals or citizens living further east due to the lengthy travel time to Argentina (around 16 hours from London), but if it does take a visitor's fancy there are a plethora of styles and locations from which to choose.

INSIDER TIP Cheap land is available on a grand scale, whilst building costs are low, meaning investors have the chance to build bespoke properties in the best of surroundings. There are also a number of off-plan developments emerging in the bigger cities, with good yields offered and viable exit strategies through selling to locals.

Hotspots

Buenos Aires

The capital, Buenos Aires, is the obvious first choice for those looking to buy property in Argentina. It is the political hub of the country and has much to offer in terms of culture and history, making it a top tourist spot. It is also one of the cheapest developed cities in the world. The buy-to-let market is two-fold: there is a demand for property from locals, be they business employees needing an apartment in the Docklands-equivalent Puerto Madero district, or large families wanting a good-sized house in the popular northern suburbs; and then there is the short-term demand created by the steady stream of tourists who favour central city pads, conveniently placed for visiting the key attractions. Occupancy levels tend to be reliably high throughout the year.

Prices vary from neighbourhood to neighbourhood. Recoleta is likened to Knightsbridge, with typical prices per square metre being between £1,500 and £1,770 ($2,900–$3,500). Pueto Madero, the most coveted address recently, consists of high-rise office and tower blocks where a small one-bedroom apartment can cost from £100,000 ($197,700) and anything larger with views can sell from £350,000 ($692,000). This area has better long-term investment prospects than short-term due to the amount of property available. The areas recommended to give the best return are Recoleta, Plaza San Martin and the

Palermo areas where the 'clever money' is said to be going. Palermo Viejo is known as 'the new Hollywood', welcoming foreign investment as big-screen companies flock to use the facilities. A small, contemporary apartment can go for £35,000 ($69,200) to £60,000 ($118,600).

Córdoba

Outside of Buenos Aires, Córdoba is the next largest city. It is cosmopolitan with a wealth of history embedded in its streets. Córdoba is known as the cultural centre of Argentina as well as being an important industrial location and housing the first Argentine university. It is popular with tourists for the variety of activities within such a close proximity: the historical and cultural sightseeing juxtaposed with robust outdoor adventures and a thriving and energetic nightlife. A five-bedroom villa downtown can be found for just over £100,000 ($197,700), whilst further out a five-bedroom ranch with over 2000 acres of land is on the market for just under £180,000 ($355,900).

Mendoza

To the south of Córdoba lies Mendoza, nestling in the foothills of the Andes. It is the 5th largest wine producing region in the world and as such draws crowds of wine enthusiasts keen to experience part of the process. It is also a beautiful city, perfect as a base for outdoor enthusiasts to enjoy the plethora of mountain experiences such as hiking, mountaineering and skiing. Prices can vary from as little as £32,000 ($63,300) for a small three-bedroom country house, to around £60,000 ($118,600) for a small townhouse, to over £200,000 ($395,400) for a large townhouse with a pool.

San Carlos de Bariloche

Further south along the Andean foothills lies the town of San Carlos de Bariloche on the shores of the Nahuel Huapi Lake. Resembling a Swiss village, Bariloche is often called the St Moritz of the Andes due to the phenomenal skiing available in the nearby **Cerro Catedrale** ski resort. This resort is South America's first and largest, and enjoyed high levels of investment and expansion during 2006. Bariloche is a prime investment location due to its high popularity and the fact that it is popular all year round. Being in the southern hemisphere, Argentina offers fantastic skiing when the northern resorts are in the height of summer, and when the snow has receded up the Andean mountains, Bariloche makes for a charming summer mountain and lakeside holiday destination. Occupancy is high for the majority of the year thanks to the two high seasons. A four-bedroom house within close proximity to the resort can be found for just over £70,000 ($140,000).

INSIDER TIP There are many other areas that are worth a second glance, especially considering the rising popularity of range-style holidays. Various Argentines and expats alike have established resorts that offer tailored trips for fishing, hiking and horse trekking, to name but a few. Some development companies are selling plots of land in the more remote areas such as **Patagonia** to investors in order to cash in on the **Argentine's** predilection for adventure holidays away from the big cities.

Buyer's guide

There are no restrictions placed on foreigners owning either land or immovable property in Argentina except in frontier zones when consent from a Federal Agency needs to be granted. A full range of property rights are available including freeholds, leaseholds, easement rights, usufruct and so on. There is no title insurance system in place in Argentina and all title searches are carried out by a public notary. As far as taxes go Argentina has very high rates with top income and corporate tax levied at 35%. All lands not under the public domain must be registered with a real estate registry in the area where the land is situated. Argentina has a double taxation agreement with a number of countries.

(Source: Marvel, O'Farrell and Mairal in *The International Comparative Legal Guide to Real Estate 2008: Argentina* available at www.iclg.co.uk)

Mortgages

Finance is not yet available in Argentina.

Key risks

The main risk that could hamper the decision to invest in Argentina is its uncertain political future. It seems as if the current government is at a point where decisions that are made could tip the country in either direction: if the president fails to ameliorate current financial policies the short-term future for the country could be bleak and this may end up causing repercussions for investors. However, the situation could be carefully controlled and may not create any cause for concern. Regarding the purchase of property, having to produce the entire cost of the property upfront will mean that Argentina is not a plausible investment location for some people, whilst for others it may seem an unnecessary inconvenience. The currency transaction process is also more convoluted than in other countries and adds around 2% to the purchase costs.

It was only a relatively short time ago that Argentina faced a debilitating economic crisis, thus it is still an immature market. The levels of growth seen recently, whilst encouraging, will not last for ever and it is important to acknowledge that appreciation is likely to slow over the next few years, potentially placing a medium-term cap on investment plans.

Rating: ⚠ ⚠

Key opportunities

Over the last 12 months property investors have been getting very excited about the prospects in Argentina and, current political situations aside, it is not at all hard to see why. It is a beautiful, long-established and relatively secure country with excellent infrastructure and a booming tourist industry that enjoys a thriving mix of history, culture, food, sport and the great outdoors. Argentina really does offer something for everyone, and with cheap property and living costs it is an ideal location in which to capitalise on such a healthy industry. With prices still low, there is much profit to be gained, and yields of around 10% coupled with high, year-round demand will make for high returns on investment.

With recent figures displaying encouraging levels of GDP growth and capital appreciation, the future could be very positive for Argentina and investors choosing to buy property here may well enjoy excellent gains.

Rating: $$$$

The Americas

ARGENTINA

Belize

Currency: Belize Dollar (BZD)

Exchange Rates:
100 BZD = £25.78
£1 = 3.87 BZD

100 BZD = $50.63
$1 = 1.97 BZD

Introduction

Nestled between Mexico and Guatemala in Central America, Belize is part of the Caribbean community yet offers a real taste of the exotic. Vast swathes of rainforest and intriguing swamp lands complement 386km of Caribbean coastline which gives way to a number of fantastic beaches and the second largest barrier reef in the world. Scuba diving, snorkelling and fishing (deep sea, fly, trolling and bone) are world class and draw large numbers of enthusiasts, a few of whom may be lucky enough to brush fins with the renowned whale shark. Those who prefer to keep their feet on dry land meanwhile can spend days exploring ancient Mayan ruins, trekking through exciting Jaguar preserves, scaling Victoria Peak and spotting howler monkeys and toucans in and around the famous Monkey River.

'With no capital gains tax and a currency directly linked to the US dollar, Belize is a thriving offshore banking centre and offers excellent tax-free retirement packages'

Formerly known as British Honduras, Belize was granted independence from the British in 1981, meaning its legal and parliamentary systems are largely based on British practices. This also means that it is the only Central American country adopting English as its first language.

Although rich in natural beauty, the country is still classed as a poor nation where poverty issues are still rife. As the economy grows it can be hoped that these problems will diminish but investors at this stage should be aware that impoverished communities are prevalent, particularly in less built-up areas.

Is this a good place to buy?

Although small, the Belizean economy has experienced steady upward growth of about 4% per annum for the last nine years. It experienced particular fervour between 2006 and 2007 in line with the discovery of oil, a find that is likely to bolster the country for many years to come. Growth in Foreign Direct Investment (FDI) within Belize has also been good and in the four-year interim between 2002 and 2006, increased a staggering 134%. Belize's primary industry is currently tourism, followed by exports of marine products, citrus, sugarcane, bananas and garments.

Belize has recently enjoyed sustained demand from both North American and European investors and the real estate market over the past 18 to 24 months has shown annual capital appreciation levels of around 24%.

With no capital gains tax and a currency directly linked to the US dollar, Belize is a thriving offshore banking centre and offers excellent tax-free retirement packages. As such it is very popular with Americans looking to buy retirement homes. Indeed, Belize arguably offers the most attractive incentive programme for foreign retirees anywhere in the world: the Qualified Retired Persons Incentive Act. This program is designed to attract increasing numbers of retirees to the country and is available to anyone over 45 years old and of any nationality, providing they earn $2,000 a month. Successful applicants can include his or her dependents in the programme which, among other things, allows you to import your car, light aircraft, boat and personal belongings duty-free. Subsequently, another duty-free car is granted every five years. Furthermore, members don't pay tax on any income sourced outside or inside Belize, and can direct foreign business activities from within the country. There is a similar incentive program in place for businesses.

As far as British investors are concerned, the purchase process is relatively straightforward thanks to the country's grounding in UK legal practices.

Tourism in Belize has been steadily increasing since 2002 with visitor numbers growing a total of 24% in the four years leading up to 2006. Hotel employment increased 7.5% in 2006 whilst hotel revenues increased 9.2% over the same period. The country's aim to further develop its tourism industry whilst maintaining a strong 'eco-ethic' approach means it should rally well in years to come. Although currently most popular with North American visitors, direct services from Europe due to be in place in 2008 should mean that the market is opened up to a wealth of new tourists. In line with tourism growth, property and land prices are simultaneously expected to climb.

Although pockets of popularity are emerging within the property market, these areas are yet to command any significant returns. The rental market is currently pro-landlord which means rents can be freely agreed with the tenant. The rent restriction act however states that the rent may not exceed increases of more than 10% annually.

Which type of property should you go for?

Most investors in Belize are currently buying small properties or land to build on to cater for the expanding tourist industry. Although this is a very cost-effective way of acquiring property the process of buying land can cause problems. Investors should therefore check that they employ the help of a good lawyer to guide them through the various stages.

Coastal properties, either apartments or condominiums, are proving to be the most popular investment and although entry prices for these types of property can be higher, the rental returns are considerably better, especially during the tourist season.

Hotspots
Ambergris Caye

Ambergris Caye is the largest and most populated island situated just off the coast of Belize. The island's coastline is protected by the barrier reef making it a great place to go scuba diving, snorkelling or fishing. Once a fishing village, **San Pedro** is now one of the most popular tourist destinations in Belize, and the only inhabited town on the island San Pedro. As such it offers a quaint taste of traditional Belizean culture and lifestyle. Mexican and Caribbean style buildings mix with colonial English architecture along the streets of the town. Adapting to its status as a tourist destination, there are several bars, restaurants, cafes, shops and hotels on offer. Considered a high-end area, Ambergris Caye is very popular with investors and those shrewd enough to have entered the market 20 years ago have watched prices triple.

Punta Gorda

The southern-most town in Belize, situated within the Toledo district. In the midst of verdant jungle, the village has a very rural feel to it. Although not fully equipped to satisfy tourists' many whims, Punta Gorda is the perfect base for those eager to explore nearby rainforests, villages and historic sites and gives a real taste of Belizean life.

San Ignacio

Situated in a valley of seven hills, San Ignacio is the hub of the Cayo district and emerging as a popular tourist spot. Culturally diverse with a laid-back atmosphere, several outdoor activities and a good nightlife, this city should continue to mature into a favourite with visitors.

Belize City

The biggest urban area in the country, Belize City remains relatively untrodden by tourists. Here the true culture of the Belizean people is preserved along with historic cathedrals, handicraft centres and a commercial centre. Grans farm is very popular with tourists and locals alike. It is situated just outside the city and offers several activities such as canoeing, hiking, swimming and tours of the tropical botanical gardens. This has not yet become a property hotspot but with the rise in tourism, increased demand for real estate is expected.

Cayo

The lush and verdant Cayo district offers the very best of Belize's natural bounty. As well as breathtaking Mayan ruins to rival Machu Pichu in Peru, there are the stunning thousand-foot waterfalls, magical secret falls, hiking and horse riding in jungle-sheathed mountains and exhilarating river rafting. The Caribbean Sea's palm-fringed beaches, heavenly islands and world-class diving, fishing and snorkelling facilities are also within an hour's drive making this the ideal place to invest.

Buyer's guide

Both freehold and leasehold properties are available to foreign non-residents in Belize via a legal system which echoes that of the UK. The Belize Alien Landholding Act does impose certain restrictions though and those considered aliens – any citizen not of Belizean or Commonwealth descent, any person not living in Belize for over three years or a company under alien control – are only able to acquire land and title 'if the same is situated within the boundaries of a city or town and the total area does not exceed one and a half acres. If situated outside a city or town, the total area must not exceed 10 acres.'
(Source: www.belizelaw.org)

The Americas

BELIZE

Mortgages

LTV %	TERM	CURRENCIES	RATES %	STATUS	SPECIAL CONDITIONS
70	20	USD	5.25	Employed or self-employed	Minimum loan $250,000

Key risks

Transaction costs in Belize are relatively high and amount to between 23% and 29% of the overall value, adding a significant chunk to the overall costs.

Further, Belize's territorial dispute with its neighbour Guatemala (who claims that half of Belize is her own) may also be of concern to some investors. Prospective buyers are therefore urged to research this issue thoroughly prior to purchasing. The general cost of living is also something to be aware of. Higher than what might be imagined for such a young country it often takes visitors and investors by surprise.

Rating: ⚠ ⚠

Key opportunities

Belize is gradually edging its way onto the property investor's map and shrewd investors are already taking advantage of its potential. With only minor restrictions on foreign ownership, acquisition of property is relatively straightforward, especially for the British buyer. What is more, the absence of capital gains or inheritance tax is an appealing factor.

The pro-landlord marketplace and exceptional retirement schemes also act as key incentives to the foreign investor. It should be remembered though that properties even in the highest-end regions are still only achieving yields of 4.5%; however, as demand for property grows alongside the expanding tourist industry, it is expected that these figures will rise.

Rating: $$$

Brazil

Currency: Real (R$)

Exchange Rates:
100 Reais = £31.68
£1 = 3.15 R$

100 Reais = $62.28
$1 = 1.60 R$

BRASILIA

Introduction

The fifth largest country in the world, Brazil borders every country in South America except for Ecuador and Chile and straddles four time zones. It is 35 times the size of the United Kingdom, and boasts a huge variety of landscapes, from the dense jungle of the Amazon rainforest, to the beautiful white beaches of the 7,250km coastline, to the mountains, valleys and waterfalls of its interior. Such diversity, along with the climate, the rich cultural life and the hospitality and passion of the Brazilian people, has made Brazil one of the biggest tourist destinations in the world.

Historically, Brazil's economic fortunes have been mixed. However, it is now keen to assure the world that it is a country on the way up. In 2002, whilst America was focussing on security and a potential war against Iraq, Brazil became part of the BRIC alliance, signing a trade and cooperation agreement with Russia, India and China and securing an agreement to supply these countries with raw materials and natural resources. Since then, its annual GDP growth has enjoyed healthy increases particularly in 2007 when it increased by 5.4%, the fastest rate since 2004.

Since 2003, President Lula's administration has steadied exchange rates and aided social stability and confidence, meaning Brazil now ranks as the eighth largest economy on the planet – jumping a huge five places from 2007's ranking. What is more, Goldman Sachs has predicted that it will become the fifth largest economy by 2050, making it one of the most compelling equity investment cases among the world's large countries.

Is this a good place to buy?

With GDP growth expected to continue to grow by a healthy 4.8% in 2008 (Source: IMF staff estimates) and following a 100% increase in 2007's FDI, Brazil's economy is clearly going from strength to strength. As the largest exporter of iron ore and soya, the second largest exporter of frozen meat and grain, self-sufficient in oil and the world's second largest bio-fuel producer, Brazil does not rely on any one economy (particularly the US) and is thus protected from any global fluctuations. Moreover it doesn't face the stark energy crises many of the world's other countries are battling as 80% of its power is currently supplied by hydroelectric dams. Furthermore, the discovery of what is claimed to be the world's largest offshore oil field off the coast of Rio de Janeiro is expected to have a total value of $25bn– $60bn and to generate healthy industrial interest in the country.

'Low entry costs are resulting in very high gains and extremely palatable investment opportunities'

Since Standard and Poor raised the country's long-term foreign currency debt rating from BB minus to BBB minus and awarded it an investment grade rating for the first time, the country's benchmark stock market index has shot to a record high, further confirming Brazil's convincing economic maturation. This confidence was echoed by the Wall St Round Up who ranked Brazil at the number two spot on NuWire Investor's list of the Top five Latin American Real Estate Markets in 2007, whilst Morgan and Stanley's Capital International Global Emerging Markets pole named Brazil the world's biggest emerging market in 2007 (Source: www.knightfrank.com).

This coupled with the country's soaring tourism industry which is predicted to continue to rise by 5.3% per year until 2017, means Brazil is likely to develop not only into one of the world's hottest holiday destinations but also one of the globe's more lucrative investment hubs. Property and land prices, though rising, are still undervalued, meaning entry costs are lower than in much of Europe and leave a lot of room for growth. In some areas, capital growth has been as high as 20% in recent years and rental returns of between 9% and 14% per annum are achievable on well-placed units. Furthermore with the announcement that the 2014 Football World Cup will be held in Brazil it can be expected that demand across the breadth of the country will be bolstered.

Aside from the tropical climate, spectacular and varied scenery, the culture of enjoyment and the year-round sunshine (giving an annual potential occupancy rate of around 30 weeks), there are a number of practical reasons to buy property here. Brazil is considered low risk in terms of war, terrorism and natural disasters, and the economy, as figures show, is stable. Infrastructure improvements are being put in place throughout the country, thanks to the government scheme PRODETUR which is dedicated to implementing tourist infrastructure with funds of more than $670m. Following the success of PRODETUR I, a second phase is now in place which will channel an additional $400m into the country's infrastructure. Accessibility is therefore being increased and in line with these developments, British Airways recently announced that it is upping its London/Buenos Aires flight quota to a daily service. It has also announced that it will now fly direct to Rio, instead of via Sao Paulo, meaning almost two hours will be cut off this flight time (Source: www.propertyinvestornews.com).

Property can be purchased on a 100% freehold basis, and both property rights and title are secure. Taxes remain low and the purchase and selling processes are relatively straightforward for urban investments with simple transfer of title. The cost of living in Brazil is some 20% lower than in the UK and the currency exchange rate is also favourable. All of this means that demand for property in Brazil is on the increase

INSIDER TIP

The most attractive areas for property ownership are currently in the coastal north-east of the country, notably Natal, Ceara, and throughout Bahia. Here prices are still very affordable, but in areas where infrastructure improvements are under way they are rising extremely quickly. Rio de Janeiro is still an attractive area although the market here is much more developed, meaning entry prices are higher and percentage returns lower.

Aside from increased interest from foreign buyers it should also be noted that the lower end of the market is set to experience significant increases in demand over the next few months. As the Brazilian economy expands, domestic wealth is also likely to increase, meaning local inhabitants will be able to enter the market seeking medium-grade accommodation. Foreign investors opting for these kinds of purchase then have a secure exit strategy which should result in high returns. Wherever you buy in Brazil, it is important to ensure that your property is relatively close to key amenities – there is always higher demand for properties within easy reach of an international airport and the beach.

The Americas

BRAZIL

> *'Wherever you buy in Brazil, it is important to ensure that your property is relatively close to key amenities – there is always higher demand for properties within easy reach of an international airport and the beach'*

Something to be aware of is that due to Brazil's somewhat emergent status in property investment terms, buyers may face problems with inexperienced or unscrupulous developers. Where possible it is advisable to purchase from a developer with some kind of proven track record so that satisfactory completion of your property can be relied upon.

Which type of property should you go for?

In urban areas, the best option is probably to invest in a serviced apartment in a reputable and secure suburb. In major cities such as Sao Paulo, the highest returns can generally be made on smaller apartments which are in constant demand from the young professional population. Those wanting to invest inland might like to consider building a pousada, or guest house, in a small village in one of the chapadas (valleys) which can also be profitable.

The vast majority of Brazilians live within 300km of the coast and it is here that an increasing number of luxury resort developments are appearing. Properties with good access to the beach, nearby cities and an international airport, as well as a range of on-site facilities will always be popular with tourists and, thanks to the country's tropical climate, should secure relatively high occupancy figures for most of the year.

As in any market, ensure that the chosen property stands out from others in terms of quality and amenities.

Hotspots
Rio de Janeiro and São Paolo
As the largest and most famous cities in Brazil, Rio de Janeiro and São Paolo are the safest opportunities for investment, although prices are likely to be high in the desirable areas and percentage returns will diminish proportionately.

The two cities have a relationship similar to New York and Los Angeles – Sao Paolo is the centre of government and finance in the country, and is therefore likely to be popular with those looking for commercial and office properties or accommodation to serve the prolific professional population, whilst Rio, the 'cidade maravilhosa' (beautiful city), has a reputation for carnival and the arts.

Sandwiched between mountains and the sea, Rio has 45 miles of white sand seafront, including the famous Copacabana and Ipanema beaches, and is therefore likely to be popular with those wanting to take advantage of high tourist numbers and the city's reputation as one of the great romantic destinations.

Sao Paulo is the largest and richest city in Brazil with a modern infrastructure, educated workforce and one of the highest qualities of life in the country. Its real estate market is unique in that it is fuelled solely by local demand. Brazilian buyers in this booming city are generating high growth and even higher yields in the region of 9%–14% gross for functional serviced properties. Occupancy levels are extraordinarily high with minimal void periods, making this an excellent investment choice. Luxury one-bed apartments in desirable Campo Belo are available from £78,500 whilst one-bed apartments close to the city centre are available from £37,500.

Rio Grande do Norte and Ceara

Further north, investors will find more opportunities in the less developed and beautiful regions of Rio Grande do Norte and Ceara. With rainforest sweeping down to some of the finest beaches in the world, the north combines a fresh, unexplored feel with properties designed to a luxury standard. Confidence in this area is sufficiently high for some agents to offer guaranteed returns of up to 5%. According to www.uvl0.com at least 80,000 houses and apartments will have to be built in the north-east if existing demand is to be met. Supportive infrastructure is under development especially in Rio Grande do Norte where investment of around R$400m in hotel construction is scheduled over the next four years.

Aside from Rio Grande do Norte, other states which are proving popular in the north include Ceará which is just six hours from Europe, functions as a major tourist hub and has already reported significant returns on property. Ocean fronting plots can be bought for £12,000 whilst apartments with sea views sell for £23,096.

Natal

The city of **Natal** offers exceptional food, scenery and entertainment at a fraction of the cost of its more southerly competitors. Boasting the lowest crime rate and one of the highest quality of life rankings in the country, it is becoming a firm favourite amongst tourists, especially Europeans, who only have to fly seven hours to reach its sandy shores. With an average temperature of 30°C and 360 days of sunshine a year and some 400km of truly spectacular beaches it is not hard to understand Natal's popularity. Currently devoid of sophisticated luxury resort developments, investment in high-end property

The Americas

BRAZIL

is likely to be lucrative. The opening of a David Beckham soccer academy in nearby Cabo Sao Roque should also increase Natal's global profile.

Other areas worthy of consideration are Pernambuco, Alagoas, Sergipe, Paraíba, and Piauí whose interlinking infrastructure has recently undergone improvements.

Bahia

Bahia is also tipped for increased growth, although the tourist industry is already somewhat more developed here than in the above-mentioned areas. Supported by the national government, this town's economy is thriving and has one of Brazil's largest economic growth indexes with a cost of living that is 20%–40% less than in Europe. Infrastructure is modern and efficient and average annual temperatures of 25°C along with an absorbing landscape make Bahia a pleasure to visit. Coastal land plots here cost from £19,700, studio apartments with ocean views from £20,000, whilst more luxurious beachside apartments are available from £67,500.

Buyer's guide

Non-residents are given the same rights as foreign nationals when buying property in Brazil although special conditions apply for those wanting to buy near the coast, frontiers and certain areas designated as national security areas. Rural areas can be acquired by non-residents according to specific law denominations. Under Brazilian law, right of possession and right of ownership are both sanctioned.

Mortgages

Finance is not yet available in Brazil.

Key risks

There are a few risk factors associated with buying in Brazil, as there are with pretty much every country. Because of its emerging market status, dubious 'due diligence' and heavily-inflated prices there have been one or two horror stories in the past. Although comparing properties agent by agent is laborious, it does reveal discrepancies in pricing, which can differ by up to 25%. Rigorous analysis also uncovers the small print behind lofty promises of 15% guaranteed rentals etc. As the locals say, Brazilians 'sabe jogar' (know how to play) and any investor must make sure that he has his wits about him. Verification of all rental agreements as well as employing reputable agents will avoid the shortfalls which can beset the more naïve investor.

Trading practices also differ considerably from those in the UK and occasionally unusual pricing structures will be enforced. Prior research into all aspects of the contract should safeguard against nasty surprises.

Brazil's somewhat turbulent price history may discourage some investors as well as its lack of available finance; however, those able to see past these risks will realise that this country's strong potential does help to allay such fears.

Rating: ⚠

Key opportunities

On a more positive tack, rising tourism, encouraging economic growth and vast infrastructure improvements throughout the country all point towards Brazil's very bright future. Low entry costs are resulting in very high gains and extremely palatable investment opportunities. As the country powers towards its predicted economic prowess in the years to come, investors shrewd enough to have invested today will be able to sit back and enjoy their spiralling returns.

Rating: $$$$

The Americas

BRAZIL

Canada

Currency: Canadian Dollar (CAD)
Exchange rates:
100 CAD = £49.95
£1 = 2 CAD

100 CAD = US $98.20
US $1 = 1.01 CAD

Introduction

Canada is the second largest country in the world and the 11th richest. Generally it is well regarded for being easy-going, tolerant and stable with one of the fastest growing populations among industrialised nations, currently standing at 33.2 million. A recent national census revealed that increasing immigration and movement of the population from rural to urban areas was significantly altering the country's demographic profile. Much of the economic and political power base showed a westward trend, towards cities such as cosmopolitan Vancouver and Calgary in the oil-rich province of Alberta. Almost half the citizens of Canada live in or around big conurbations such as Montreal, Vancouver and Toronto.

Canada's economic fortunes are strongly linked to its US neighbour and account for 80% of its export income. GDP growth in the country was predicted by the Economist Intelligence Unit to be at only around 2.1% in 2007, due to effects generated by the slowing of the US economy and housing market. Final statistics showed that it was 2.7% for the year.

Politically, Canada is very stable. Part of the British Commonwealth, Canada, has two official languages: English and French. The country is regarded as a clean, safe and green place to live and work, and its main cities regularly rank highly in terms of quality of life. In the 2007 Mercer Human Resource Consulting survey of worldwide cities and their quality of life, all of Canada's major cities were in the top 25.

> **'Both the tourist regions, which are developing in step with demand, and the industrial hot spots particularly in oil regions, offer potential for investment returns'**

In addition to Canada's main industries of oil, gas, logging and agriculture, the service and tourism sector play an important role in the economy. With the latest figures available, the Canadian Tourism Commission claims there were approximately 18 million overnight international visitors in 2006, which were worth approximately $67bn in spending power. Following a survey of communities, 80% agreed that tourism plays a very important role in terms of their economic health, particularly for those in central and eastern Canada.

Is this a good place to buy?

Canada is somewhere that non-nationals have only recently started to buy for investment. Until around four years ago, the majority of people would only consider buying there if they holidayed there a lot, had family in the country or planned to relocate. However, Canada is well placed to take advantage of visitors from all areas of the world and the advent of reliable, cheap air transport, low property prices and a growing investment in tourism has altered the perception of the country. Now buyers from both Europe and the Pacific Rim are targeting Canadian cities and holiday areas in increasing numbers. At the beginning of June, David Stanley Redfern Ltd announced that Canada was their most searched for country and 4th most popular with browsers, indicating how prolific an investment destination this country is becoming.

As the world's largest source of oil, the Canadian Oil Sands play a pivotal role in Canada's economy and are named as the US's preferred energy solution. It is estimated that the country has a total reserve of 1.7 trillion barrels, only 311 billion of which are accessible with today's technology. It is the state of Alberta that contains almost all of Canada's reserves and as such, small towns at the epicentre of the oil rush are experiencing phenomenal levels of demand. Fort McMurray for instance has recently welcomed a huge influx of workers and its population climbed 6.8% per year between 2001 and 2004, with estimates stating that by 2011, 30,000 more inhabitants will descend on the small town creating a need for more than 14,000 houses. Fort McMurray is therefore experiencing an extreme housing deficit with current supply levels unable to keep up with demand; 100% occupancy and very high yields are therefore achievable.

'Politically stable and with an affiliation to both Britain and France, Canada is a country in which many European buyers feel safe and welcome'

In recent years it has been Canada's ski resorts that have seen some of the biggest levels of overseas investment and buy-to-let purchases. These areas are receiving a large amount of investment into their infrastructure and services. Resorts such as Banff, Whistler and Mont Tremblant rival many American and European areas in terms of numbers of visitors and popularity. By European standards, prices in Canadian resorts and cities remain low or, at least, offer better value than in many other developed countries. Canada has one of the longest ski seasons, lasting from November until early June and with warmer winters predicted to affect snow reliability in Europe and in lower lying regions, the higher areas of Canada's mountain ranges, areas of the Rockies in particular, are expected to offer one of the few reliable ski seasons in years to come. Canada's mountains and forests also lend themselves well to outdoor tourism, such as boating, white water rafting, climbing and hiking, all of which are becoming increasingly popular. Golf is another industry that Canadian developers are beginning to focus on so as to increase the year-round appeal and viability of tourist resorts.

Politically stable and with an affiliation to both Britain and France, Canada is a country in which many European buyers feel safe and welcome. In addition, crime is generally low and services, transport systems and amenities in cities are first class. Rising levels of immigration are likely to generate buy-to-let opportunities in urban locations. For the lower level investor, an apartment or chalet in a developing holiday location, which can be used by the owner as well as rented out, may prove an enjoyable option.

Canada is one of the main countries that appeals to those looking to relocate from Europe and the UK. The fact that it is both English and French-speaking plays an obvious part. The legal and parliamentary systems are based on Britain's and the quality of education, healthcare and social services are considered high in most areas. Furthermore, Canada is currently experiencing its lowest unemployment rate for over three decades.

Which type of property should you go for?

In terms of aiming at the local rental market, one or two-bedroom apartments in the main cities and areas with industrial growth are always likely to show good, steady appreciation. Avoid markets where prices are already high if you want good returns. In Vancouver, for example, yields are only just above 3% on average, while in Toronto, Ottawa and Montreal average yields pan out between 5.5 and 6.5%.

Property aimed at the tourist market can be a good long-term investment as far as capital appreciation is concerned whilst short-term rental potential can also be strong. Tourism in Canada is growing markedly, and mountain and waterfront property in particular are becoming more sought-after in terms of holiday lets and for long-term or retirement homes. The 2010 Winter Olympics to be held in Vancouver will increase demand in the short-term rental market, although some argue that financial gain from such events is often over-hyped. Potential rental and resale markets exist in both the local and overseas sectors, giving a wide pool of opportunity. Holiday apartments in a complex designed for year-round living or individual homes in resort areas, especially those offering summer as well as winter activities and within easy access of amenities are worth investigating for investment.

Hotspots

Alberta

The province of Alberta has large oil reserves and is the strongest economy in Canada. As a result, it has been pulling in vast numbers of migrant workers. **Calgary** saw the number of sales rise by 18% per month at the end of 2006; however, as predicted, 2007 saw a slowdown in the market due to a rise in the number of properties becoming available, increasing interest rates and a lack of affordability. House prices have started to decline and affordability has improved. **Edmonton** is also witnessing a decelerating market as the number of new housing units under construction (known as 'housing starts') are slowing dramatically. The average prices in both cities start at around £132,696 (US$ 260,974) for a standard apartment with family homes costing from around £198,416 (US$390,319). Interest from buy-to-let investors hoping to cash in on the increasing numbers of workers moving to the region may well be fuelling such rises. The slowdown is not necessarily heralding a 'boom or bust' scenario but rather bringing prices back down to create a buyers' market.

The Americas

CANADA

Fort McMurray

Buy-to-let investors may also care to look northwards for newly discovered investment potential. The town of Fort McMurray is at the epicentre of the globe's largest oil frontier and is estimated to have 311 billion barrels at its disposal. As such, it has become America's preferred oil solution with several oil companies and their workers flocking to the town forcing an acute squeeze on existing accommodation resulting in a severe housing deficit. With a population that has doubled over the last 10 years, the number of inhabitants are expected to continue increasing close to the 6.8% rate seen in recent years, meaning over 14,000 new houses will be needed by 2013. With 54 of the world's top 65 oil producing countries now in decline, and the discovery of new oil supplies decreasing, Fort McMurray's potential is overt. Further, the Canadian invention of an underground mining refinery which will cut greenhouse gas emissions by 50%, double current production and minimise production costs means McMurray's zenith is yet to come. Housing prices here are the most expensive in Alberta, having risen 114% in the last five years, showing huge capital appreciation, and with predicted rental yields of 9%–13%, the town offers more investment potential than most other areas in Canada put together.

Toronto

The revitalisation over the past five years of what was already an important industrial and commercial hub has increased interest in Toronto. Property sales figures in the city reached record levels in 2005 with prices rising by 6%–10% across the centre and suburbs. However, by 2006 this dropped to around 5.4% and early 2007 saw lower gains of 4%–6%. Early 2008 statistics show an 11% drop in sales figures from 12 months ago. Nevertheless, with increasing migration from rural to urban centres across the country, the city is still somewhere investors should consider. The average price of Toronto property is £177,125 (US$381963), with standard apartments starting at around $150,000 and rising to over $1m for property in the revitalised waterfront district. Houses prices also range widely, depending on location, starting from around $250,000 in less sought-after suburbs and maxing $2.5m for executive homes in Midtown Toronto. Those keen to invest in this city are now looking to its many suburbs as questions of affordability arise. Something for investors to be aware of is a new land transfer tax which looks set to add up to 2% to residential and commercial real estate transactions.

Quebec province

Certain areas of Quebec have become hot spots over recent years. Though not experiencing the gains of other major cities, at the start of 2007 **Montreal** and its suburbs saw rises in almost all areas with wide fluctuations in prices, depending on location. The average price of a standard Quebec apartment is £90,471 (US$177,939), with standard town houses costing from around £98,283 (US$193,061) and large family homes costing from around $450,000 to well over $1m in sought-after areas.

The Laurentian Mountains are around an hour and a half from Montreal and are becoming popular for weekend homes. **Mont Tremblant** is a ski resort that has drawn a huge amount of investment recently with celebrity purchases increasing its cachet. Prices for studios or one-bedroom apartments start at around £60,985 (US$120,000), condos and chalet prices start from £150,000 (US$295,150), while larger apartments in popular developments sell for between £115,000 (US$230,000) and £203,000 (US$400,000) on average. Property in more rural, waterside or non-resort locations sells for a wide variety of prices depending on size, location and outlook. Wood and shingle cabins, sometimes with lake frontage, can still be found for less than £100,000 (US$200,000), with more upscale properties retailing from upwards of around £150,000 (US$300,000). There is a big population of wealthy investors moving to the area, which is sending prices for large properties on several acres of land into the £2.5m (US$5m bracket).

Whistler and Vancouver

The city of Vancouver has long been popular for having a vibrant culture, fast-paced business environment and beautiful surroundings. As a result it also has some of the costliest real estate in Canada. Prices range from £224,000 (US$441,000) for a standard townhouse and from £153,900 (US$302,945) for standard apartments. The apartment market saw rises of more than 10% in early 2007, while housing saw gains of 8%–19%. Vancouver was voted the joint third best city in the world to live in, according to the 2007 Quality of Living Survey by Mercer Consultings.

Though some agents have reported flat sales for the past few years in Whistler, the resort is reputedly becoming more sought after again, thanks to the 2010 Winter Olympics. Appreciation may have slowed but there is little available for under £100,000 (US$200,000). Houses cost from around £150,000 (US$300,000) for something small in a less desirable area, going up to several million dollars for larger properties in sought after mountain or lakefront locations. Vancouver has just seen a 1% increase in property tax, which will effectively become a 3% increase due to tax redistribution. There are warnings that 2009 will see an increase of up to 11% on property taxes.

Buyer's guide

Foreign investors will be subject to varying restrictions depending on the state in which they are investing. In the Province of Ontario, foreign investors won't

The Americas

CANADA

face any direct restraints although certain tax, reporting and registration provisions may apply. The Extra Provincial Corporations Act (R.S.O 1990) stipulates that foreign registered or foreign controlled entities obtain licenses before any business can be carried out in the province. Quebec and British Columbia levy comparable registration restrictions. In the state of Alberta the Agricultural and Recreational Land Ownership Act means foreign purchasers face some restrictions and need to seek government approval for specific transactions. Finally the province of Prince Edward Island restricts land holdings by non-residents. Both freehold and leasehold title is available.

(Source: Blake, Cassels and Graydon LLP, *The International Comparative Legal Guide to Real Estate 2008: Canada* available at www.iclg.co.uk)

Mortgages

LTV %	TERM	CURRENCIES	RATES %	STATUS	SPECIAL CONDITIONS
80	25	EUR, PLN, CHF, USD, GBP	from 5%	Employed or self-employed	Selected areas only

Key risks

On a practical level there are no major risks associated with buying in Canada. The only issue for overseas nationals therefore, are the restrictions on residency that prohibit visits of more than six months per year without full residency status being granted by the government. In terms of investment risks, there are also worries that certain areas currently enjoying property booms, for example, Vancouver in British Columbia and Calgary and Edmonton in Alberta, will become overheated and suffer downturns. Here, price rises have leapt up rapidly over the last couple of years meaning issues of affordability have arisen and forced prices downwards.

In light of the recent credit crunch, fears have also arisen as to the security of Canada's economic future. Closely affiliated in economic terms to the United States, investors wait to see what effect the recent economic downturn will have on the market.

Rating: ⚠

Key opportunities

Of particular interest to investors should be Canada's booming oil industry which is creating exceptional opportunities in key mining towns. Acute undersupply means new-build developments are in extremely high demand and able to command lofty yields and capital appreciation.

Tourism meanwhile offers good buy-to-let opportunities in popular towns and cities as well as Canada's many ski resorts. Thanks to the long ski season, occupancy here will be consistent for many months of the year. Buying into a ski area that also has good access to golf facilities (one of the fastest growing sports in North America) is likely to prove a very shrewd decision.

An aging population is also boosting demand for leisure/retirement property such as waterfront cottages. Properties of this type saw gains of around 13% on average between 2006 and 2007.

There are currently a lot of opportunities for shrewd investors looking to buy in Canada. Both the tourist regions, which are developing in step with demand, and the industrial hot spots particularly in oil regions, offer potential for investment returns with regard to long-term capital appreciation and short-term rental gains.

Rating: $$$

The Americas

CANADA

Caribbean

ANTIGUA, DOMINICA, ST. VINCENT, GRENADINES, ST. LUCIA, GRENADA, ST. KITTS AND NEVIS –
Currency: East Caribbean Dollar (XCD)
Exchange Rates:
£1 = 5.25 XCD $1 = 2.65

BARBADOS –
Currency: Barbadian Dollar (BBD)
Exchange Rates:
£1 = 3.95 BBD $1 = 2 BBD

TRINIDAD AND TOBAGO –
Currency: Trinidad and Tobago Dollar (TTD)
Exchange Rates:
£1 = 12.04 TTD $1 = 6.08 TTD

THE CARIBBEAN

Introduction

Mention the Caribbean and it evokes idyllic visions of soft white beaches, brilliant turquoise seas and a luxurious pampered lifestyle. One of the most popular regions for romantic rendezvous and sun-kissed weddings, the dazzling Caribbean also appears regularly as the backdrop for various films including *James Bond* and *The Pirates of the Caribbean*. The living is laid back and easy, the locals are some of the most friendly on the planet and the climate is coveted by tourists the world over. It is no wonder then that the Caribbean is the destination of choice for wealthy holidaymakers, celebrities and affluent investors, with islands such as Barbados and the Bahamas constantly in the headlines. Now, however, less developed islands are getting talked about not only for their unspoilt beauty and lifestyle but for the exceptional investment opportunities they offer.

Recent developments in infrastructure, plus a diversification in the kind of property on offer means that the Caribbean has blossomed into a thriving investment market with high rental returns based on the region's year-round season. English is widely spoken and accessibility to the most frequented islands is relatively straightforward. Mortgages of up to 70% loan to value are available and there are low property and capital gains taxes on most of the islands. As a result Caribbean property prices are rising at up to 10% a year.

Is this a good place to buy?

There are plenty of investment opportunities to be found in the Caribbean with more than 100 islands or regions to choose from and a selection of reasonable properties for sale on many. Buyers will be able to take advantage of the massive tourist economy with good holiday rental options, while those looking to relocate or to buy a holiday home will gain access to year-round, crystal-clear seas, balmy temperatures, an extremely rich cultural heritage, incredible cuisine and a lifestyle that is second to none. Property taxes are low on most islands, as is the cost of living, and properties can cost as little as £24,000 in some areas. With the US dollar currently weak against the pound and the euro it is expected that the second-home real estate market should continue to be strong for potential European buyers.

Which type of property should you go for?

Property types range from plots of land, to studio apartments, to eight-bedroom villas each with their own benefits and selling points. The cost of building is low in most parts of the Caribbean, although it is a good idea to check what local regulations and requirements are in place. Apartments, houses and villas in tourist areas have good rental and capital growth potential whilst those looking for second-home or retirement properties will also be inundated with choice. What type of property you chose, in essence, comes down to personal choice. Some islands have more favourable residency allowances and regulations, others offer swathes of untouched countryside whilst others have buzzing local towns, so personal research is always worthwhile.

Due to the fact that the Caribbean is such a thriving tourist destination, the highest demand for property focuses largely on the holiday rentals sector. High-quality villa and hotel accommodation are most likely to offer the best returns in the coming years, not least because there is a distinct shortage of these properties on some of the less developed islands. Hotels and resorts are able to attain much higher incomes than standard holiday lets due to their ability to let accommodation on a nightly basis and offer comprehensive facilities and services. Equally, resort properties have a much higher occupancy level than private rentals ensuring consistent yields are secured.

The Caribbean has something for all those wishing to invest or to own property in a sun-lover's paradise. Accommodation is available to suit all budgets, although more serious investors would be advised to stick to the popular tourist destinations on the islands. Whilst this will often mean that investors wanting to own a piece of the Caribbean will require a fairly high sum of money to enter the market, exceptions do exist on those less developed islands where prices can be up to 27% lower. Those wanting to live or to have a second home in the Caribbean will be able to find something cheaper as their purchase choice will not be affected to such a high extent by the availability of amenities, potential rentability and infrastructure.

Travel costs for any buyer are likely to be their biggest outlay so it is a good idea to check how accessible an area is before settling there.

'Although traditionally associated with the rich and famous, the Caribbean does also offer fantastic opportunities for anyone wishing to own a holiday or retirement home or to invest in a tropical paradise'

Hotspots

With the sheer number of islands in the Caribbean, it is difficult to select 'hot' areas without having to include a huge number of destinations. The following, then, is a summary of some of the most profitable investment islands.

Antigua

Antigua has experienced a recent property boom thanks to improved flights and extensive investment around Jolly Harbour. The outstanding golf and yachting facilities on the west coast add to the allure of the island as does the legend that there is a beach for every day of the year. A low crime rate, laid-back lifestyle and rural feel combine to make the island very popular. Buying here is also financially advantageous, as it is one of the few countries in the world that does not levy personal income tax, capital gains tax, inheritance or wealth tax on its residents. Antigua's laws are based on English legislation, a fact which also makes it accessible for UK buyers. A plot of land here costs between £30,000 and £70,000 ($120,000), depending on location and views. In other locations, such as Jolly Harbour on the west coast, 2-bedroom properties can be bought from £112,000 ($220,500). A luxury resort on a nearby private island, Jumby Bay has seen property prices rise by between 60%– 100% over the last two years. Detached houses on the mainland have also doubled in price in the same period. Two luxury estates, developed by La Perla International are selling villas from £101,500 ($200,000) and have seen property on both estates sell out soon after coming to market. Prices here then are rather inflated and although property will always be in high demand, you will have to pay for the privilege of owning.

Barbados

Barbados too, is a popular choice for real estate as its infamous Gold Coast offers the delights of some of the region's most famous beaches. Indeed it is one of the most popular Caribbean islands amongst British investors thanks to its reputation as a 'traditional' holiday location. A vibrant party scene dominates the island and mixes calypso rhythms with reggae in a setting of stunning natural beauty. Barbados was one of the first Caribbean islands to employ tourism as a major economic tool and is, therefore, one of the most well-established and economically prosperous. However, as a result of its popularity, Barbados has become somewhat over-developed in recent years and property prices have risen to extortionate levels with villas on the west coast often selling for millions of dollars. Rental income is estimated at around 15% and the lack of capital gains tax and inheritance tax are appealing. Having said that, residents can be taxed on their world wide income – something to be aware of.

> **'Property taxes are low on most islands, as is the cost of living, and properties can cost as little as £24,000 in some areas'**

Guadeloupe

The volcanic island of Guadeloupe is characterised by rolling hills, tropical forests and banana plantations. The island is a '*département*' of France, uses the euro and is governed by French law, with 80% of its tourists coming from France. As such Guadeloupe has a real and very appealing air of France about it, a rare thing in the midst of the Tropics. Property here is comparable in price to buying in the south-west of France, and while there are expensive properties here, it is possible to find studio apartments in Guadeloupe's premier resort for as little as £24,000 ($47,181). The average price of a 120 square metre apartment is £114,980 ($226,000) with yields of 6%–7.3% expected. If purchasing, non-EU residents have to undergo more intricate processes to gain permission and clearance to reside on the island.

St Vincent and the Grenadines

This collection of 32 islands and cays were recently made famous by the success of the Pirates of the Caribbean movies, and give a feel of the real essence of the region. Several are privately owned, including **Mustique**, where villa prices start at around £3m. The best deals are likely to be found on other islands such as Bequia, an increasingly popular tourist destination in the area. Property prices here are rising, but it is still possible to find a bargain. With a wide range of property available and a thriving tourism industry that has created a rental pool that should maintain a property on a year-round basis, the island offers great investment opportunities. The average price for property on the island is

The Americas

CARIBBEAN

£1,170 ($2,300) per square metre. Potential purchasers will need an Alien Land Holding License before buying.

St. Lucia

Voted the world's most beautiful island, with 19 acres of rainforest and an array of outstanding beaches, St. Lucia rivals the more established Caribbean destinations. Thanks to the 2007 Cricket World Cup, it has received £11m investment in infrastructure making it one of the most modern and efficient islands. Stable government and exchange rates, excellent health facilities and direct flights from the UK, means St Lucia has a lot to offer both tourists and investors alike. More importantly, its property prices are around 27% below those on neighbouring Barbados, meaning properties have excellent potential for capital appreciation. Three-bedroom villas are available from £160,000 ($314,500). Average house prices are around £1,980 ($3,900) per square metre, whilst condos cost an average £1,170 ($2,300) per square metre. Foreigners will need to acquire a Land Holding License to buy property.

Trinidad & Tobago

Trinidad and Tobago is a tiny twin island republic of 1.3 million ethnically diverse people. It has an ecological and geographical diversity that is truly unmatched in the Caribbean. Located just off the tip of Venezuela, Trinidad, the larger and livelier of the two islands, is the energetic heart of the republic, a thriving and highly developed island boasting exciting nightlife and a robust industrial sector. Tobago, in contrast, is the islands' serene escape with its palm-lined white beaches, lush rainforest and some of the richest coral reefs in the Caribbean, home to over 600 species of fish. Being at the most southerly point in the Caribbean, Trinidad and Tobago are the only islands where yacht insurance against hurricanes is obtainable.

Trinidad and Tobago offer exciting investment opportunities. Trinidad is often described as a 'Tiger economy', due to its wealth of natural resources. It is the world's largest supplier of ammonia and methanol and it supplies 70% of the USA's Liquified Natural Gas requirement. As a result, this predominantly industrial island has sustained a GDP growth rate of 10% per annum over the last five years and is one of the wealthiest countries in the Caribbean.

The government is committed to a restricted and sustainable programme to control and enhance the tourism industry, making this a popular eco-destination for the discerning traveller. Looking to be granted developed country status in the near future, the government has granted a $380m budget to take its country further towards maturity. Declining inflation, unemployment and expansion of Tobago's airport all indicate the island's healthy economic status.

With Barbados now pricing itself out of the reach of many Brits, Tobago is one of the islands to step into the breach. Although prices are rising, the average price for coastal properties is £1,323 ($2,600) per square metre – which is still cheaper than most other islands. As such, the potential for strong capital appreciation is good. Prices in Tobago range from £132,800 ($260,950) for a three-bedroom bungalow with private swimming pool near to the beach, to villas costing upwards of £2.2m. In Trinidad a three-bedroom house with a shared pool in a gated community costs around £132,760 ($260,895). Rental yields are moderate at around 7.7%.

There is no capital gains tax on the island and outsiders can buy up to one acre of land for residential purposes without a licence. However, there are some disadvantages, namely high rental income taxes and relatively high buying costs, though not as high as on many of the nearby islands.

St Kitts & Nevis

Located in the northern part of the Leeward Islands in the east of the Caribbean, St Kitts and its smaller partner, Nevis, have long been disregarded by the tourist industry, thanks to a flourishing sugar cane industry that negated the need for any other form of income. Since the industry's close in 2005, however, St Kitts has been making concerted efforts to court the tourists. World renowned for its excellent preservation of eco systems, St Kitts is a natural wonder, with lava formations, tropical forests and seaside lagoons.

INSIDER TIP

The government is committed to the development of tourism and has welcomed some multi-million dollar developments that have increased the appeal of the island. As one of the host venues for the 2007 Cricket World Cup, the islands' infrastructure and services are of a high quality. The islands are also a tax haven with 0% income tax, capital gains tax (on property owned for 12 months or longer), wealth or inheritance tax – a very appealing prospect for the foreign investor. Also, when investing in an approved development and spending over $350,000 investors can gain economic citizenship on the island.

Relatively under-developed compared to other Caribbean islands, St Kitts has a property market in the throes of its youth. Sellers have been waiting for prices to increase and so market development has been slow. However, the pace of development has been increased by the arrival of certain big names in the hotel and property development worlds to create luxury resorts, with a deep water port also recently created for the cruise tourists in mind. A resort just outside of Basseterre, the island's capital, has luxury apartments and villas available from £160,678 ($316,656) to £384,961 ($758,889), and a rental pool with predicted yields of 8 to 13%.

Grenada

Arguably the most exciting investment market is Grenada. Renowned for its picturesque interior of rainforests and waterfalls and its coastline of protected bays and secluded beaches, Grenada is the last undiscovered jewel of the Caribbean but one whose popularity is rising rapidly. Visitor numbers in the first quarter of 2008 increased by 24% compared to the same period the previous year, reaching 191,276. Stay-over arrivals for the same quarter in 2008 increased by 8% compared to 2007 as did cruise ship arrivals, growing by 29%. Of the total number of stay-over arrivals, 37% stayed in hotels. Bolstering the tourist industry is a stable economy with GDP growth increasing by 3.1% in 2007 and FDI inflows reaching EC$255,463,153 for the same year.

Occupying an early stage in the development cycle, the island offers excellent value by regional standards. The over-saturation of development land on more established neighbouring islands has caused shrewd local investors to focus on islands such as Grenada and take advantage of their lower property prices.

Concerted government efforts to increase the number of high quality hotel rooms by 1,000, to keep up with current demand, means that the island is very investment friendly. High demand also means that prices and yields on resort properties are constantly being pushed up at a rapid rate.

Benefits such as tax exemptions and customs concessions for tourism market investors are being implemented and substantial infrastructure improvements are taking place. Accessibility is also improving with direct flights from the UK, USA and Continental Europe as well as two cruise ship terminals.

There are already a handful of new high-class developments under construction, including Prickly Bay Waterside development at Lance aux Epines, the proposed Four Seasons project on Mount Hartman Bay and Hog Island, five-star Bacolet Bay Resort and Spa in St. David's, whilst in the capital Port Louis, Trading Company is to develop a 400-berth international yacht club and marina in association with the Ritz Carlton. In line with the emergence of these high-end resorts, it is expected that there will be annual price rises of 10% or more over the medium term. As such land prices have started to reflect the growth in property development, with the average coastal property price being around £1,776 ($3,500) per square metre. Non-nationals must pay the Alien Land Holding Tax at 10% of the property's value to buy an Alien Land Holding License.

The Rest of the Caribbean

Other locations offer different benefits: in the prosperous Cayman Islands, a two-bed condominium can be bought for £130,000 ($450,000) with no taxes other than stamp duty at rates of up to 9% on transfers of real estate. Cayman also has no sales tax, no income tax, no capital gains tax, no property tax and no inheritance tax and the purchasing process is relatively easy. Local laws simply stipulate that the prospective buyers present personal documents, including certificates of identification and confirmation of the source of funds, to their real estate agent.

In the Bahamas, prior government approval is not required for non-Bahamians to purchase residential properties of less than five acres. Such acquisitions are, however, required to be registered with the Investments Board and the Central Bank. There are no taxes levied on capital gains, corporate earnings, personal income, sales, inheritance or dividends. Residents are also free from succession, inheritance, gift, or estate taxes. The only indirect taxation is a real property tax, ranging from 0.75% to 1% for owner-occupied property, 1% for unimproved property and 1%–2% on all other property.

It is not all good news however. In Cuba there are no private property rights to speak of, making the investment potential poor and risky. Similarly, Haiti's political problems should ward off any sensible investor. It is therefore a good idea to look into the different areas, backgrounds and benefits of each area carefully before deciding where to purchase in the Caribbean.

Buyer's guide

With the various island governments striving to encourage foreign investment, buying property in the Caribbean has now become a lot easier than in recent years. The legal restrictions surrounding foreign acquisition of property vary from country to country so it is impossible to give a comprehensive overview. What we advise is that you check with a lawyer familiar with the legalities of your chosen island. In general though, foreigners will not face debilitating restrictions.

Mortgages

GRENADA	LTV %	TERM	CURRENCIES	RATES %	STATUS	SPECIAL CONDITIONS
	70	20	USD, XCD	From 6.75	Employed or self-employed	

ST.KITTS	LTV %	TERM	CURRENCIES	RATES %	STATUS	SPECIAL CONDITIONS
	70	25	USD	From 7.25	Employed or self-employed	

TRINIDAD & TOBAGO	LTV %	TERM	CURRENCIES	RATES %	STATUS	SPECIAL CONDITIONS
	80	20–60	USD	From 9.25	Employed or self-employed	

Key risks

It can be expensive and difficult to enter the Caribbean property market, particularly if you do not conduct sufficient research. This research is a vital part of the purchase process as no two parts of the Caribbean will have the same policy regarding non-nationals buying property. Each region will also have its own tax and transfer costs, and rules vary according to whether you plan to build or plan to buy a completed property. Each area will also have a different degree of accessibility, something which will affect anyone with business or family interests elsewhere. These are all things to check before taking any action, and the local tourist board or a local real estate agent should be able to advise you of all the different costs and laws. Once the financial and legal details are established, those planning on relocation might like to try living in their chosen location for a while before purchasing, just to confirm that it is the right one for them.

For much of the Caribbean, a major risk is from hurricanes. This risk is relatively easily mitigated though with insurance, and buyers should also take comfort in the fact that even the worst-affected areas tend to recover relatively quickly. Remember the further south you go the less likely the island is to be hit by bad weather.

Rating: ⚠ ⚠

Key opportunities

Although traditionally associated with the rich and famous, the Caribbean does also offer fantastic opportunities for anyone wishing to own a holiday or retirement home or to invest in a tropical paradise. There is such variety here that there should be something for everyone, as long as the necessary research is conducted and precautions are taken. Capital appreciation in the region of 10% is achievable and several developments have guaranteed rental schemes in place. This is the ideal destination for those seeking to marry an investment and holiday purchase.

Rating: $$$$$

Panama

Currency: Balboa/US Dollar

Exchange Rates:
1,000 Balboa = £508.758
£1 = 1.97 Balboa

1,000 Balboa = US $1,000
US $1 = 1 Balboa

PANAMA

Introduction

Panama is the entire isthmus connecting Central and South America. It is bordered by Columbia and Costa Rica and has two long coastlines, on the Pacific and Caribbean. Enjoying a mountainous interior, it has a large number of protected national parks mostly comprising dense, tropical rainforest with a rich variety of flora and fauna. In addition there are long stretches of fine, sand beaches on both coasts with upmarket tourist resorts that are now starting to develop more fully. The Pacific coast offers good conditions for sports such as surfing and as a result tends to attract a younger, sporty set. Meanwhile the Caribbean coast offers coral reefs, island archipelagos still inhabited by the local Cuna Indian population, and quieter waters that are good for bathers and divers.

The Panama Canal was handed over from American control in 1999 and resulted in a surge of inward investment welcoming 5% of all seagoing trade per annum. It has recently been given the green light for a massive $5bn expansion project that will run over the next six years and should significantly boost FDI inflows. The country has benefited from increased press coverage and is already popular with Venezuelans, Columbians, North Americans, Canadians and Europeans for relocation, retirement and investment.

Unlike many other Central and South American countries, Panama does not tend to base its income around export of goods but in providing trade and service industries. The construction industry is the backbone of the country, and among Latin American countries, Panama is expected to show the highest GDP growth in 2008, between 7.5% and 9%.

Unemployment in Panama is decreasing and the expansion to the Canal means this will diminish further, as thousands of new jobs are created. Poverty though is still rife, especially in more rural, lesser-populated corners of the country. A $39.4m loan has been agreed by 'the World Bank to help productivity in the more rural areas targeting especially small-scale farmers and it is expected that the World Bank will provide sustained funding in this area until 2010.

> *'Currently there is a definite sense of forward momentum in the market and Panama has benefited from five years' worth of strong growth which is expected to continue for the next decade'*

'Health Tourism' remains a strong market in Panama with patients visiting for either cosmetic or health-related treatments, and often choosing to stay on for a holiday afterwards. Panama offers first-class US trained doctors at 50% less than in the US so it is no surprise that this market is expanding rapidly and helping to boost the tourist industry at the same time.

Is this a good place to buy?

Property development and investor speculation is on the rise and 2007 was the year tipped to see increased property purchases. As far as 2008 is concerned, price patterns continue to emulate those seen in the preceding year, with a 24% increase in the number of properties sold in the first quarter of 2007. Thirty-five high-rise buildings are currently under construction with a further 300 projects in the planning stage whilst 2010 should see the release of over 40,000 units into the market to meet growing demands. During the last 12 months, foreign investment into Panama has risen by 20% and the country has now defined itself as a multifaceted market away from a purely US focus.

Panama also has an added string to its bow thanks to its 'limited taxation regime': 20 years' tax exemption is applicable to new builds whose building permits were issued before 31 December 2009 whilst free taxes on property purchases from foreign investors are available until 2030. The extension to these tax leniencies has full government backing and should work to significantly increase purchases from international buyers. Such tax incentives are a reminder of the government's 100% encouragement towards foreign investment, and the reinstatement of the 90-day tourist visa is further proof of this. With equal buying rights for both locals and foreigners, the market is made up of investors from many different countries and offers properties to cater for a full variety of price tags.

Currently there is a definite sense of forward momentum in the market and Panama has benefited from five years' worth of strong growth which is expected to continue for the next decade. Prices are not as low as one would imagine for an emerging market; however, incentives (such as significant tax reduction) have been introduced to encourage property purchases. Furthermore, set to join CAFTA, the Central American Free Trade Agreement along with Columbia and South Korea, Panama has high hopes that its real estate and economic markets will flourish in the near future.

Foreign investors are subject to exactly the same laws on property owner-ship as Panamanians and are protected by an extremely advanced administrative system which means the real estate market is secure and being driven steadily upwards.

Whilst prices are currently slightly higher for foreign buyers they remain moderate for locals, resulting in two separate markets. Locals are offered gov-ernment assisted loans with low interest rates and as little as 5% down payment whilst international buyers are tempted by tax breaks. As a result, both the international and local markets are currently thriving. The purchase process in Panama is extremely simple and highly advanced and application for residency is also straightforward. One year after obtaining a resident's visa, foreign citi-zens may apply for permanent residency and after five years it is possible to apply for Panamanian nationality provided you have bought a property valued at a minimum of $200,000 and can prove solvency.

Alongside the tax benefits it offers to foreign investors, the Panamanian Government has devised one of the top retiree benefit programmes in the world and recently topped the list (alongside Cyprus) of countries with the most financial and lifestyle incentives for retirees. Laws to ensure that all purchasers are protected are also prevalent, which should encourage the more cautious investor. Large discounts are also available on medicines, treat-ment and public transport in Panama's 'Pensionado programme' package and these, alongside a warm climate and relatively affordable homes means Panama now rivals Florida as the top destination for senior buyers. Further incentives include the shipping of household goods tax-free and a law allow-ing new cars into the country tax-free every 24 months for personal use. There is also no tax on foreign earned income for those that retire in Panama and inheritance tax has been abolished. Unusually you do not have to be of retirement age to qualify for these benefits, which makes the country yet more appealing.

The recent credit crunch has had an effect on the amount of investment and tourism directed into the country from the USA, but with direct flights from London, Paris and Milan, Europeans have been making the most of this opening in the market.

Which type of property should you go for?

Any new, build property offers tax breaks and is therefore one of the most popular purchases. Developers though, are working to supply different types of living accommodation as demand for property in Panama increases.

A lot of the more recent construction projects are based in or around Panama City. The wealthier city dwellers are relocating to the outskirts of the city although demand for one-bedroom apartments in the city centre remains high, with a steady inflow of working professionals generating strong rental returns for buyers. Capital appreciation on residential units has topped 15%–20% and rental yields in Panama City and second city David are achieving upwards of 11% on 190 square metre properties.

In rural areas buyers may face difficulties with possession rights as there is a lot of territory that has not yet been officially inscribed, meaning people living or working on land for more than five years can claim ownership. Properties in these areas can still be bought, although the process may take longer to sort out and the areas may not be as safe as the more developed towns and cities. On average, property purchases in Panama take six weeks although this can vary depending on the circumstances.

Hotspots

There are nine provinces in Panama, eight of which have property developments under way. Home to the protected territory of the Kuna Indian Tribes, the self-governed **Kuna Yala** is the only region to remain untouched by developers. Whilst real estate originally prospered on the coffee-growing highlands of Boquete and the islands of the Bocas Del Toro, interest today has spread to towns such as **Penonome**, **Santa Fe** and **Boca Chica**. Holiday isles **Gorgona** and **Contadora** have also experienced increased growth with **Panama City** remaining a tourist highlight for visitors passing through on cruise ships. There is growing Japanese interest on the Pacific coast which is also favoured by wealthy Panamean second-home owners and China is expected to be the next country to invest in property here thanks to the countries' good relationship.

Panama City, Boquete and Bocas Del Toro are areas which have recently experienced a construction boom but are fast beginning to run out of space. Developers therefore are now looking inland where property still offers good value for money and areas have room to grow.

Penonome

Penonome is located two hours' drive from Panama City and is expected to have a strong 2008 in investment terms. Until recently it has avoided much of the construction boom seen in areas such as Panama City and Bocas Del Toro, and is only now becoming one of the more popular interior areas in which to invest. The area boasts some of the country's better scenery with mountain views, meandering rivers and pretty Spanish colonial towns that are enticing investors looking for renovation projects. Satisfactory infrastructure, proximity to Panama City, affordable homes and only a short distance from the beach mean that the area appeals to second homers, business professionals and investors looking for good capital appreciation opportunities.

Boca Chica

Boca Chica is a coastal region that until now has been overlooked in terms of development. A new airport in nearby David is soon to be built which will support the already adequate infrastructure and boost the area's appeal. With its immaculate white sandy coast and charming islands this area works to sell itself and is perfect for fishing and diving. Investors should watch this space for investments of the future.

Amador

Amador is another of Panama's more scenic spots offering spectacular views across Panama Canal and the ever growing Panama City skyline. Home of the Amador Causeway connecting islands Perico, Naos and Flamengo it already has a well-established tourist market generating a healthy amount of inward investment.

Panama City

Once an important trading point between colonial powers, Panama City is still a bustling, commercial hub situated on the Pacific coast and Panama Canal. The skyline is dominated by towering skyscrapers, in particular Donald Trump's $250m dollar creation. The '69 Trump Ocean Club' is expected to be complete in 2010 and has boosted the country's buying profile. Encouragingly, the city's population continues to grow and an estimated 3,242,173 people currently live here. Over the last two years, property prices have risen by 25%: encouraging news for investors. Many international and financial industries operate from within the city, creating good employment conditions and providing consistent rental demand. An apartment here costs on average $3,000 per square metre within the city and yields of 11% are achievable. Plans to extend the airport expanding the terminal building should further help to augment these returns as the city is made a more desirable and accessible destination.

The city is split into two areas, the modern district with its proliferation of high-rise condominiums, retail malls and office blocks, and the old town

(**Casco Viejo**), a colonial gem. The government has offered financial incentives for those investors willing to renovate properties in the Casco Viejo district and some trendy bars and hotels are evidence that things are starting to change here. For investors who like a challenge, property in this area represents opportunity to earn in the long term, with prices from under $100,000 for pretty, crumbling houses to over $350,000 for anything restored.

The area of **Balboa,** directly on the canal is already a large and important shipping port but is soon to be the centre of further economic growth. The port has been privatised and will be part of a $1bn project aimed at quadrupling capacity. Apartments in Balboa vary depending on size and area. A one-bedroom can be picked up for less than £100,000 while a luxury two-bedroom apartment can fetch over £300,000.

INSIDER TIP

Pacific coast resorts, such as Conorado, Gorgona and Punta Barco are around an hour from Panama City and have long been popular with both overseas visitors and Panamanians. Prices here though can be high – $160,000 will get you a standard one-bed apartment in a new-build, high-rise with beachfront access, whilst $190,000 will buy two-bedrooms or a small house in an inland location. Large villas with gardens or apartments in ritzier developments cost from $250,000 to over $600,000. Rental returns average between 7% and 15% depending on whether the property is a villa or apartment and its proximity to the beach.

Buyer's guide

Foreigners are granted the same rights as Panamanian nationals and there are over 12 laws in the country that have been enacted with a view to protecting foreign investors

(Source: www.centralamericasecondhomes.com).

Mortgages

LTV %	TERM	CURRENCIES	RATES %	STATUS	SPECIAL CONDITIONS
80	20	USD	6.75	Employed or self-employed	

Key risks

Knock on negative effects from the recent credit crunch may be felt as the US economy struggles to regain its momentum, but this will only become apparent over time.

Another area for possible concern is the threat of overdevelopment and industrialisation, which may adversely affect the country's best assets – the natural beauty and diversity of its rainforests, mountain habitats and coastal areas. However, with 30% of the country's land set aside for conservation and several ecological projects in progress, the country's government appears to be managing this threat quite successfully.

Rating: ⚠ ⚠

Key opportunities

Economically Panama remains strong and growth has outperformed expectations in recent years, averaging at 7.3%. Rumours that Panama is seeing an unsustainable economic bubble have therefore been quashed and specialists are sure that the property and construction sectors are strong. Tourism has grown considerably over the last few years; however, it is important to note that a lot of this growth is due to the increase of cruise ship passengers, many of whom don't venture further than the bounds of Panama City.

The country's very appealing retirement programme, lenient taxation system and straightforward purchase process will make investment here appealing to the foreign investor.

Rating: $$$

The Americas

PANAMA

Uruguay

Currency: Uruguay Pesos
Exchange Rates:
1,000 UYU = £26.04
£1 = 38.41 UYU

1,000 USU = £51.59
$1 = 19.38 UYU

Introduction

The second smallest country in South America, Uruguay is situated south of Brazil and to the east of Argentina. It offers 120 miles of Atlantic shoreline and a mild climate all year round.

Fast becoming the playground for the young and wealthy, Uruguay's metropolitan towns and cities sprinkled along the coastline offer attractive real estate prices and strong potential for investors. Although most are drawn to the sandy white beaches, the colonial towns and cities such as Uruguay's capital city Montevideo also exert charming appeal. Their assortment of architecture and European-style café culture attract tourists from around the world.

'Properties in Uruguay range from the most expensive in resorts along the Gold Coast to the ridiculously cheap, rural areas and satisfy a range of tastes and needs'

As well as affluent locals and travelling tourists, supermodel Naomi Campbell and literary brain Martin Amis, were some of the first celebrities to invest in property in Uruguay and scenes from the 2006 remake of Miami Vice starring Collin Farrell were also filmed in the old town area of Montevideo.

Set to become a successful competitor in 2008's top places to invest and unaffected by the problems its neighbouring countries suffer (unemployment, inequality, poverty and slums) Uruguay has a first-world feel and a high level of security.

Is this a good place to buy?

Uruguay as a whole has seen strong and stable economic growth which currently sits at 7%. Inflation has dropped consistently over the last five years and in 2008 the country will receive its highest levels of FDI ever – over $1.7bn towards two paper pulp mills. Uruguay is also considered one of the safest places in the world, the second least corrupt nation in South America and one where political and working conditions are among the freest on the continent. Taxes are also appealingly low, with rental income and capital gains both at 12% and inheritance and gift taxes at 0%. With the rental market strongly pro-landlord, and with relatively low transaction costs, the potential for healthy yields and price growth should be maintained by enormous tourist demand. Of further appeal is that, unusually, up to 70% LTV mortgages are in place allowing relatively low-cost investment.

The buying process in Uruguay has been made very simple to encourage investment from overseas and a foreigner now has the same rights as a Uruguayan national when it comes to purchasing property. Appealingly, all-round transaction costs only amount to around 14%.

Which type of property should you go for?

Properties in Uruguay range from the most expensive in resorts along the Gold Coast to the ridiculously cheap, rural areas and satisfy a range of tastes and needs. Whilst rural property may seem a bargain at first glance, electricity, internet and phone lines may be difficult and expensive to fit which will add significant costs to the initial purchase price. Alternatively, beach houses make for fantastic holiday homes in the summer months but will lie vacant out of season as temperatures plummet. Voids in occupancy and rental returns are therefore probable.

Property prices in Uruguay have now regained their previous heights prior to the 2002 economic crisis meaning a three-bedroom house with superb coastal views can be bought for around $180,000, still cheap by European standards. The limited supply of rental units means high yields of between 7.5% and 11.4% are achievable although with such a small rental market, (only 4%) investment in this sector is neither reliable or advised.

Hotspots
Punta Del Este
The St. Tropez of South America, Punta Del Este is the place to see and be seen in. A vibrant city in a stunning position, it offers reams of pristine beaches and an elite clientele. Anyone who's anyone in South America frequents this

coveted spot. Unsurprisingly, tourism is escalating and, with recent runway and terminal renovation at the city airport, visitors are due to increase by a staggering 60% this year. Growing demand for high-end property is provoking increased construction and laying the foundations for a very successful investment future, although this is already one of the most developed areas in the country and fears over its sustainability are arising. Located 130km to the east of the capital Montevideo, Punta del Este attracts 700,000 visitors every year with its white sandy beaches and buzzing nightlife. January and February are the busiest months when a handful of celebrities and wealthy yacht owners take over the 20 miles of picturesque beaches to enjoy the scorching summer temperatures. Out of season however, the city quietens and occupancy levels drop off.

Montevideo

Uruguay's capital is also the largest city offering cultural diversity and liveliness in a country that is otherwise calm and quiet. Spanish and art deco styles will appeal to architectural junkies, with the most captivating feature and public space, the Ciudad Vieja, a colonial core which is a must see for all visitors. Sadly Montevideo has been overshadowed in both tourist and investment terms by cities such as **Buenos Aires** meaning property prices have remained low. Entry prices for apartments are currently less than $100,000. Sensible investment property purchases here will either be in a well-equipped coastal development or in restorations of existing historical buildings, both of which should remain in demand and therefore provide a reliable exit strategy. The capital's year-round appeal is another lure for investors looking to obtain consistent rental returns.

INSIDER TIP The most westernised area of Uruguay is the east coast area, the Uruguayan Riviera. **This offers white sandy beaches ideal for water sports, golf courses and expensive beach resorts. Located on the Gold Coast, it mirrors the ever popular Punta del Este but has the benefit of being significantly less developed.**

Buyer's guide

Foreign individuals face no restrictions when buying in Uruguay and are granted the same rights and incentives as Uruguayan nationals. They are therefore free to transfer capital in and out of the country whilst enjoying 0% income and capital gains tax.

(Source: www.t5estates.com)

Mortgages

Finance is not yet available in Uruguay.

Key risks

In 2002 Uruguay suffered an economic crisis and although recovering, is still fragile. With an economy reliant on livestock and related exports from neighbouring countries Brazil and Argentina, there is the possibility of another crash in the future. Its economic stability then is somewhat volatile.

Rating: ⚠ ⚠ ⚠ ⚠

Key opportunities

Having said that, recent growth intimates definite recuperation and low taxes and entry levels are undeniably appealing to the international investor. With FDI steadily increasing and a purchase process favourable to the foreign investor, Uruguay does offer potential. Carefully chosen investments by those willing to take a risk are likely to perform well over the medium term.

Rating: $$$

The Americas

URUGUAY

United States of America

Currency: Dollar US$
Exchange rates:
100 USD = £50.856
£1 = 1.966 USD

100 USD = €64.414
€1 = 1.55 USD

Introduction

Arguably the most powerful nation in the world, the United States performs on a grand scale. The fourth largest country in terms of land mass and population and the largest economy in the world, the States is the embodiment of Western, developed-world culture.

Stretching from the Pacific coast to the Atlantic Coast, the land in between contains almost every geographical and geological feature imaginable, with weather conditions to match; from the frozen, open space of Alaska to the tropical wetlands of Florida; the arid deserts of Nevada and Utah to the verdant Great Lakes, the US is full of extremes. It also boasts some of the largest, wealthiest and most renowned cities – the iconic skyline of New York to the sun-kissed opulence of Los Angeles – from which herald a wealth of famous characters, be they from the silver screen or the White House.

Regarded by some as the only remaining superpower in the current era, the United States has vast political, economic and military influence on a global scale, and as such, comes under close scrutiny as the ramifications of its actions can have such a huge repercussive influence on many other countries. This is exemplified by the weakening dollar and the impact of the American sub-prime crisis and its subsequent ramifications worldwide. Its strong economy produces over a quarter of the gross world product at market exchange rates with a GDP of over $13 trillion and is the largest importer of goods worldwide.

Everything in America is large, whether it's the economy, the distances, the size of its cities or the milkshake from McDonalds (and this chapter for that matter!), and the same is true of the property market. An in-depth and cohesive chapter on the whole of the United States real estate market would probably end up being longer than this entire book so the focus of this chapter will predominantly be on the state of Florida where the majority of British interest lies, along with what are considered to be the best of the rest of the country's investment opportunities. For more information please see Buying a House in Florida, Crimson Publishing (September 2008).

Is this a good place to buy?

The current state of the US market has been hard to avoid given the number of column inches that broadsheets and tabloids alike have dedicated to the subject. It barely needs to be said therefore that the United States is experiencing a major crisis within the economy and the housing market. What is more important is how the investment potential within the country has been affected and to what extent. Is there any potential for investment amongst the doom and gloom of the crisis?

In 2006 rising house prices could no longer be supported and the housing bubble burst. This triggered a sub-prime mortgage crisis. The high-risk end of the lending market began to stumble as people defaulted on their payments or were forced into foreclosure on their property. As property prices began to fall through 2006–2007 the situation worsened. According to www.Realtytrac. com the total number of properties involved in foreclosure activity in 2007 amounted to just under 1.3 million. Banks and lenders became much more cautious and reduced lending, leading to a severe drop in investment activity as a growing number of corporations became unable to procure sufficient funds. The economy began to suffer as its drivers, consumer and business spending, dropped.

Advance GDP growth figures for the first quarter of 2008, published in the May forecast from the University of Central Florida Institute for Economic Competitiveness, show a growth rate of just 0.6%, with expectations of the rate slowing further in the second quarter of the year. In an effort to try and prevent recession, the US government cut interest rates to 2% (at the time of writing) whilst injecting disposable income into consumers' pockets in the form of tax breaks in the hope that it will encourage reluctant spenders to start buying again.

However, opinions vary as to the state of the US regarding recession. A recession is generally accepted to be occurring when two or more consecutive quarters of negative growth exist, and as such the economy is still showing positive – small as they are – growth figures. At the time of writing, retail sales figures showed an encouraging growth rate of 1% for the month of May, double

The Americas

UNITED STATES OF AMERICA

the forecast growth, which offers optimism that the economy is not as unhealthy as some predict, allowing the Federal Reserve to concentrate on limiting the extent of inflation.

'Population growth, coupled with the economic downturn, are creating a burgeoning rental market.'

Put together, the financial factors do not paint a particularly welcoming picture to the potential investor.

According to the Standard & Poor's/Case-Schiller national index, house prices fell by 14.1% in the 12 months leading to the first quarter of 2008, which is a greater rate than seen at any point during the Great Depression. If the difference between the deflation of the 1930s and the inflation of the current period is taken into account then the falling rate extends to an 18% difference in real terms over the last 12 months, and some commentators are of the opinion that there is further for prices to fall. Manhattan is one of the few, if only, exceptions to the current state of the market. Defying national trends, the area has seen an incredible 41% rise in property prices over the last 12 months due to low supply and constant demand from individuals who are less affected by the tightening financial situation. Areas hardest hit by declining prices have been the 'bubble states' of California, Nevada, parts of the Midwest and Florida.

In Florida, the declining prices and rising inflation are forcing many houses to fall into negative equity with foreclosure being an increasingly common option, whilst others race to sell before they get caught in financial mire. This has created a huge number of very cheap houses on the market and with the strength of the pound and euro against the dollar, British and European investors find themselves looking at some unexpected bargains. Construction designed to meet the demand during the housing boom is now surplus – at the beginning of 2008 more than 25,000 homes were on the market in the Orlando area; in March 2005 the figure was nearer 2,500 – and realtors were going to great lengths to sell property, often by heavily reducing the price, contributing to upgrades and closing costs or even by throwing in items such as a car into the deal. Some properties were even going to auction with no reserve prices. However, by June 2008 the Orlando Regional Realtors Association (ORRA) announced that its members sold 1,276 properties in May 2008 – 3.66% higher than in April 2008. Perhaps the market is beginning to show signs of recovery, although it should be pointed out that this figure is 26.88% down year on year on 2007 sales figures.

In the midst of the frenzy of bargain basement prices it is important to be aware of the practicalities of the situation. Anyone buying into the market must be prepared to be involved for the long term to wait for the economy to recover, which could take anything from a few months to a year or 10. Unlike many emerging markets, however, there is the element of security knowing that the American economy *will* recover: it has a solid economic base, a strong position in global economics, low unemployment and a very substantial and consistent tourism market.

Florida receives millions of visitors a year, with a thriving international market – the state saw 4.7 million foreign visitors throughout 2007 - whilst also benefiting from strong internal tourism as Americans from the colder, northern states travel down to take advantage of the 300 plus days of sunshine a year. Florida also enjoys a booming population as foreigners and Americans move to benefit from the sunshine and its robust job market. In the last four years Florida has welcomed over 1.3 million new residents and the population is expected to grow from over 17 million in 2008 to over 19 million by 2010. The bulk of the population gain is due to inward migration, making up 87% of the annual population increase.

Such population growth, coupled with the economic downturn, are creating a burgeoning rental market. As more and more people are unable to uphold the cost of owning their property, a greater percentage of the population is either choosing or being forced to rent property instead. Similarly, migrating jobseekers from other states, also suffering from the crisis, will be unable to afford to purchase a property, and will again contribute to the growing demand for rental property.

Which type of property should you go for?

A key factor when deciding what type of property to choose is its purpose. In the buy-to-let market, rental patterns show that the British tend to prefer villa properties with extras such as a pool, whilst American tourists favour condominium style properties. If aiming for a longer-term let then condominiums present the better investment. The target demographic of an investment rental plan is also important. The Gulf coast of Florida is favoured by wealthier Americans and retirees, whilst central Florida, around the Orlando area is hugely popular with tourists, especially those with families. Meanwhile the Atlantic side of the Florida peninsula includes some of America's most desirable and expensive locations popular with the young and wealthy.

INSIDER TIP Social groups will favour different styles of property with varying amenities so to reap the greatest gains it is usually more profitable to target one group specifically and tailor a property to their needs. Gated communities that include amenities such as a club house, pool and restaurant are very popular, especially with the British, whilst developments centred around golf courses are also in high demand.

Hotspots

Orlando

Over 50 million people visit Orlando and central Florida every year, attracted to the many tourist attractions such as Disney World, Sea World and Universal Studios, and the warmer, drier weather that tends to be found in the coastal regions. It is the area most popular with British tourists and is touted as being one of the most visited destinations in the world. It has a very healthy rental market driven by the tourism industry and is the area most likely to present the best returns. Property within a few miles radius of the tourist attractions tends to command the highest rental prices. Advice from www.holidayrental.co.uk suggests that a three-bedroom villa in the region could command £450 per week in high season, dropping to around £350 a week in low season, whilst a five-bedroom villa could command weekly rental rates of up to £700 in high season and £500 a week in low season. Reports for May 2008 from the Orlando Regional Realtor Association show the median price of a home is now $214,000 (£109,200), a 1.42% increase on the previous month's median price.

The Atlantic coast

The Atlantic coast of Florida boasts such famous locations as **Daytona Beach, Miami** and the **Florida Keys**, all of which are unlikely to ever go out of fashion, at least for the foreseeable future. Miami is a world-class city, with prices to match, and as the economy reignites these will rocket up. Miami has a reputation as a party city and the key demographic is the 25–35 year old age range. Daytona Beach and Palm Beach are ideal locations for retired couples who wish to use their property for a couple of months a year and rent it out for the remainder.

To the north of the coast is St Augustine, the USA's oldest city (founded 1565). It is a quieter, more refined version of Orlando, whilst still being a resort city, offering the added interest of a long history on top of the beaches, shopping and golfing attractions. A three-bedroom townhouse here can be found for under $300,000 (£153,875).

The Florida Keys are a string of small, interlinked islands that emerge from the southern tip of Florida and stretch down into the Gulf of Mexico. The opulent surroundings contain some of the most expensive and desirable properties, with prices on average 25% higher than the rest of the state. Due to its constant popularity a stable rental market is guaranteed.

The Gulf Coast

The Gulf Coast has a slightly wetter climate, especially in the months of July and August so tends to be less popular with families holidaying during the summer school vacations. However, it is still very popular with retirees, especially with those who originate from the colder northern states, earning themselves the nickname 'snowbirds'. Around two-thirds of the US's wealthiest citizens spend their winter at Naples, the most popular town resort on the coast, which boasts exquisite white beaches, luxury golf resorts and a bustling restaurant atmosphere. Subsequently, prices are much higher, with waterfront properties commanding prices that are around double the amount for a similar sized house in the Orlando area.

INSIDER TIP

Aside from the state of Florida, investors may be interested in making more of a lifestyle-motivated investment and head for the hills on the western side of the country. The spine of the Rocky Mountains **that runs from Alaska, through Canada and down the western side of the United States offers many excellent skiing investment opportunities, some rated the best in the world. The state of** Colorado **offers the majority of the well-known names, such as Aspen, Breckenridge and Vail, with other resorts, such as Winter Park, set to expand on a similar scale. The appeal of properties here is that they have a year-round market (either for renting out or personal use) as the mountains have both winter and summer seasons. Aspen is by far the most expensive, with properties easily reaching into the millions of dollars, whilst resorts like Breckenridge and Winter Park offer smaller properties that range between $200,000 (£101,800) and $300,000 (£152,800). A luxury, ski-in ski-out, three-bedroom condo in an excellent location in Breckenridge is on the market for $1.5m (£764,000).**

The Americas

UNITED STATES OF AMERICA

Buyer's guide

In general, foreigners are allowed to buy homes without restriction in the USA unless this affects national security. Investors may find that their rights are limited by various federal and state statutes which prohibit foreigners' ability to acquire or dispose of real estate or to make testamentary dispositions to foreigners from countries that forbid similar dispositions to US nationals. (Source: www.lawoverseas.com).

Overseas buyers will also need to take other factors into consideration such as additional tax withholdings when their property is sold, high finance down payments and strict visa allowances where non-residents are prohibited from staying in the country for more than six months unless they have a student or work visa. (Source: www.sfgate.com)

Mortgages

LTV %	TERM	CURRENCIES	RATES %	STATUS	SPECIAL CONDITIONS
80	30	EUR, PLN, CHF, USDM, GBP	4.5	Employed or self-employed	No early repayment charges

Key risks

The economic state of the USA understandably starts alarm bells ringing in investors' heads. The credit crisis means that banks and lenders are more wary and whilst mortgages are available, foreigners will find that the process is likely to take longer. It is highly recommended that a mortgage offer is confirmed before any commitment to buy is made.

The crash of the housing market has created many bargains as property prices tumble, but some are of the opinion that the Florida property market is being over-hyped. It is important to keep a cool head and look carefully at properties that have slashed prices or include huge purchase incentives. Although bargains can be found, beware of the pitfalls. Foreclosure properties can be a disaster as some can still have money owing and the new owner may end up being responsible for this. Be wary if buying off-plan as construction companies can find themselves going bankrupt, although the US system ensures buyers money is protected through the Escrow system.

At its peak, the Florida property market was a prime place to flip properties. In the current climate though, investors should be prepared to be involved for at least two to three years minimum. According to some commentators, certain areas of Florida could see still further price falls. The question is one of timing and judging the bottom of the market. Whilst buying today may mean that you buy before the market reaches rock bottom, over the medium to long term it is very likely that you will see good profits as prices regain ground.

Rating: ⚠ ⚠ ⚠ ⚠

Key opportunities

Despite the fact that the United States is experiencing an economic crisis, it can be safely assumed that within a matter of years the economy will be back to full strength, with recovery, predicted by some, starting within six months. The US is a key world player in economic, political and cultural spheres and as such will have the input necessary to help the economy to recover. The weak dollar is already proving a bonus in the tourism industry as foreigners with a stronger currency arrive to take advantage of the great exchange rate. This booming industry is helping support the economy as other industries flounder. Being one of the world's most visited locations, Florida is benefiting hugely from this increase in foreign visitors, and investors in the state can profit from the increase in demand for temporary property. Its popularity is consistently high, creating a reliable rental market. The two-fold nature of the tourism market, with demand from international tourists and internal migration, broadens the potential of the market and offers investors a wider choice of renter to target.

Rating: $$$$ (over the long term)

Australia

Currency: Australian Dollar (A$)

Exchange Rates:
100 A$= 48.41
£1 = 2.06 A$

100 A$= $95.94
$1 = 1.05 A$

CANBERRA

Introduction

The sixth largest country in the world and 30 times the size of Britain, it is hard to comprehend the size of Australia and summarise the diversity within it. It crosses three time zones and is made up of eight states and territories, each with its unique character, economy and legislature. The geographical variety is astounding, created and characterised by the climates that are encapsulated across the country's vast land mass: lush, tropical jungle; unending, arid plains; cultivated, rolling vineyards, and of course, the mile after mile of wonderful golden beaches that draw millions of visitors every year.

Australia is a multiculturally rich country with diverse ethnic persuasions that combine to offer captivating experiences, be they culinary, artistic or sporting, embodied in such national icons as the Sydney Opera House and the Great Barrier Reef. Australia's diversity is its wonderful selling point, being a favourite destination amongst dedicated surfers, refined wine enthusiasts and intrepid explorers alike.

Australia is also a primary destination for international residents looking to relocate abroad. Ask a handful of Brits where they would choose to live if they had the chance and without doubt, one will say Australia. It is not surprising then that around 20,000 British people make the move every year, attracted by a comparable culture and lifestyle but much improved climate and laid-back atmosphere topped off with a favourable exchange rate.

Is this a good place to buy?

The housing market in Australia is by no means straightforward. Aside from various complications in the national market related to the economy, population increases and affordability, each state has, more or less, its own market with different price fluctuations and situation to its neighbour. To analyse the potential of the Australian market therefore, individual states need to be assessed in isolation.

> *'There is absolutely no reason for Australia to see a drop in popularity, thus it can be depended on to have a steady population growth (both permanent and temporary) from which investors can profit'*

It barely needs to be mentioned that overall, the country's market is well established and mature, meaning it is not the place to look to for low entry costs and an easy exit strategy. Such opportunities simply do not exist in Australia. Further, there are serious affordability concerns following the rapid price rises and growing inflation rates of recent years, meaning domestic investors are struggling to afford to buy. However, Australia does offer other more positive factors which explain why so many thousands of Brits, and other foreign investors, are buying property in the country.

Historically, Sydney has always been a favourite place to buy partly due to its status as a prime tourism destination but, following a prolonged rise in prices, property values are expected to cool off throughout 2008. With the worst affordability rating in the whole of Australia, citizens are expected to pay a whopping eight and a half times their average annual salary for a house whilst the national average sits at 6.6 times (one of the highest rates in the world). As a result investors and potential citizens are turning their attention towards cities that have more favourable and crucially more affordable prospects. In Melbourne for example, it is predicted that prices could still rise by up to 20% over the next 12 to 18 months, although affordability is still an issue here as locals would have to pay on average 7.2 times their annual income. Meanwhile, Adelaide in Southern Australia has the best affordability of the country and is named as one of the prime places to invest over the next few years thanks to low entry prices. Similarly Brisbane saw prices rise 21.6% between 2006 and 2007, an impressive rate considering the average increases across the country rose only 12.3% over the same period.

Australasia

AUSTRALIA

Australian tourism is undoubtedly a robust and flourishing industry, and is, as ever, a key influence in regards to the property market. The most popular locations with tourists tend to be Sydney and Brisbane and the coast in between, especially the Gold Coast, and also the Sunshine Coast just north of Brisbane. These areas then, provide viable exit strategies especially if a property is located close to attractions, amenities and transport links. At present, Australia is experiencing minimal rental vacancies country-wide meaning a healthy demand and supply imbalance is in place – good news for those thinking of purchasing buy-to-let properties.

Aside from catering for tourists, there are other demographics fuelling demand for property. Mature couples looking to downsize and migrate towards Queensland as well as first-time buyers seeking small, reasonably priced properties mean demand in both these sectors remains high whilst supply is low. The sector, though, currently generating the highest demand is the mineral mining industry. A mining boom, with sites scattered predominantly over South Australia, northern Queensland and Western Australia, has boosted the Australian economy whilst creating a massive migrating population consisting of internationals and Australians alike who move to take advantage of the well-paid jobs. Australia can only just dig the mineral out fast enough to meet the growing demand, namely from China. This high demand is expected to equate to the industrial world's total current annual demand by the year 2020. The upshot of this from an investment perspective is that there is simply not enough current supply to satisfy the hungry medium-term market of industry workers and professionals. As a result occupancy levels, house prices and rental rates are all very high and expected to escalate over the coming months.

Which type of property should you go for?

As mentioned previously, the demand for medium-grade accommodation to cater for mining executives in prime locations is very high and is likely to result in some of Australia's highest opportunities for capital appreciation and rental yields.

There is also a great shortage of, and thus high demand for, good quality houses and apartments in top locations, especially houses of the fashionable period style. Location-wise, there is a need created by citizens moving out of the cities into the suburbs where good amenities and infrastructure can be found. This migration is pushing prices up so investors may want to look at the suburbs adjacent to popular areas where prices will be slightly cheaper, but likely to increase as popularity spills over.

INSIDER TIP Water-front properties will always command premium prices but can be guaranteed to generate constant demand. Conversely, properties further away from water locations and city centres will be cheaper and may offer more suitable price tags. The Australians, being avid lovers of the outdoors, greatly value properties with large outside areas so houses that can incorporate this usually sell for more. House and land packages are also popular with investors with the intention of renting out, but foreigners must be aware that any bare land bought with the intention of building must have the construction work begun within 12 months of purchase.

Hotspots

The cosmopolitan cities of Australia lie along its east coast and are obvious places for investment. However, demand for coastal property is high, and prices will reflect this so ocean-fronting units will not offer low-cost entry.

Sydney

Prices in Sydney are now the highest in Australia, with the average property costing over £230,000 (US$450,000). However, it is not the most expensive place to rent and due to a shortage of rental opportunities, yields can be high. It is recommended that longer-term rentals to locals will be more profitable than to the short-term tourist market.

Adelaide

Adelaide, Australia's capital, was reportedly the strongest performing Australian city as far as capital gains went in 2007, enjoying 26% price appreciation which equated to an average gain of $82,000 for Adelaide property owners. Despite this phenomenal growth the city is still one of the cheapest capital cities in which buy property with median prices now at $406,270. (Source: www.rpdata.net.au)

Melbourne

Voted the second most liveable city in the world in a survey by the Economist Intelligence Unit, Melbourne is considered the cultural, culinary and sporting capital of the country. It is a key location for commerce and industry, although statistics released claiming that average property prices dropped nearly 10% in the first quarter of 2008 compared to the preceding quarter contradict expectations and suggest its housing market may not be as robust as the city's popularity. That said, Melbourne's most popular districts, Kensington, Toorak, Prahran and Port Melbourne, still managed to record positive growth over the same period. The average house price in the city is now over £210,000 (US$411,000).

Brisbane

Brisbane is highly popular with foreign immigrants for its relative proximity to the stunning Gold and Sunshine Coasts, but it is also attractive due to the efforts of the local government striving to address the problems of affordability. The median house price recently hit the £200,000 (US$391,450) mark. As well as being able to apply for a grant, first-time buyers are exempt from stamp duty from September 2008, and from July 2008 mortgage duty will be abolished.

Perth

In Western Australia Perth can be a good bet-especially as it is well placed to enjoy the fruits of the natural resources boom. Prices have seen spectacular growth over the last few years and one suburb, Palmyra, achieved 38.3% growth in 2007, putting it in the Top 50 National Suburbs for Capital Growth in 2007. There are reports though that house prices waned by 3.34% over the December quarter of 2007 and with rents also quite low between 3% and 4%, investors should be slightly cautious about investments here. For the best investment potential it is advised that investors look towards the wealthier sub-urbs of the city where the median house price stands at around £225,000 (US$440,300). Something else to be aware of is that the length of time it takes to sell properties here is reportedly going up, which may not bode so well for the future.

Buyer's guide

Buying in Australia as a foreigner is carefully mitigated and each case is reviewed on an individual basis by the Foreign Investment Review Board which can take up to 130 days (usually 45). All freehold land in the Australian Capital Territory (ACT) is owned by the Commonwealth, meaning no one can own land in the ACT although 99-year crown leases will be granted. Aside from this, foreigners looking to buy property in Australia are subject to the Foreign Acquisitions Takeover Act 1975 which gives the Treasurer the authority to block real estate transactions if they are considered to be 'against national interest'. All residential real estate operations must be brought to the Treasurer's attention as a matter of course. Both freehold and leasehold estate rights are available in Australia.

Stamp duty is a complicated process as each state has its own convoluted method of calculating the amount, which can vary hugely depending on the area. Careful homework is required as this can add a considerable amount to the cost of a property.

Mortgages

LTV %	TERM	CURRENCIES	RATES %	STATUS	SPECIAL CONDITIONS
80	30	EUR, PLN CHF, USD, GBP	4.5	Employed or self-employed	No early repayment charges

Key risks

Australia has seen a considerable price boom over recent years and is now witnessing market correction as prices drop slightly to accommodate the influx, varying from state to state due to differing positions in the price cycle. Slower growth in the economy and real estate market is predicted for the future, thus reducing the chances of excellent profit. High property prices coupled with not so high yields (the maximum being around 6%) combine to suggest that Australia generally isn't a prime choice for pure investment, although there are certainly exceptions. The purchase process for foreigners is somewhat onerous and can hinder a speedy purchase. Australia is not a country that offers a quick return on investment, especially as it is currently a buyer's market, thus lacking in reliable exit strategies. Medium-term rental is more advisory.

Rating: ⚠ ⚠

Key opportunities

Australia is an internationally strong and thriving economy. It offers an excellent standard of living, augmented by good weather and a healthy outdoors lifestyle, that is responsible for attracting thousands of immigrants and tourists every year. There is absolutely no reason for Australia to see a drop in popularity, thus it can be depended on to have a steady population growth (both permanent and temporary) from which investors can profit. Although high property costs can be off-putting they have encouraged a very healthy rental market which offers much potential. The economy has seen an extra boost from the expansion of the natural resources mining industry and this looks set to continue for the near future, continuing to create demand for property.

Rating: $

Australasia

AUSTRALIA

New Zealand

Currency: NZ Dollar (NZD)

Exchange Rates:
100 NZD = £38.18
£1 = 2.62 NZD

100 NZD = $75.71
$1 = 1.32 NZD

WELLINGTON

Introduction

From the snow-capped peaks of the South Island's Alps, to the sub-tropical waters of the extensive marine reserves, New Zealand has a multitude of interests to entice the intrepid investor.

The country is made up of two main land masses: the North Island and South Island, separated by the Cook Strait, plus a wealth of smaller islands that surround the mainland, giving a total area of 268,680 square kilometres. The country boasts 15,134km of coastline from which an array of aquatic adventures can be launched, and with the protective haven of the marine reserves there is a multitude of flora and fauna waiting to be explored.

New Zealand is renowned for its healthy, outdoors lifestyle, and for good reason. The geography of the country, coupled with the temperate climate, creates an environment where there is no excuse to stay inside, and whether the choice is skiing or scuba-diving, the size of the country (it is not much larger than the UK) means that everything is within easy reach.

The relaxed way of life is one of New Zealand's great selling points and something that is, without doubt, partly due to the reduced crime levels, the lack of common discourtesy and the immigration issues that all seem to plague the UK today. Successful British migrants are swift to emphasise the friendly welcoming nature of the native residents, and the ease with which they settled into the communities.

Is this a good place to buy?

A member of the British Empire since 1840, New Zealand's economy has traditionally been controlled and influenced by the British market. In the last

20 years the New Zealand government has broken away from dependency on British market access to become an independent global competitor capable of dealing with some of the world market's leading players. This is reflected in the latest AT Kearney Global Top 20 ratings where New Zealand was placed 11th. The change in size of its economic arena fuelled a boost to incomes and New Zealand's wealth has developed as a result, with healthy GDP figures to show for it.

'New Zealand is not best suited for avid investors seeking high returns but its straightforward purchase process and appealing culture make it ideal for lifestyle buyers'

New Zealand has a reasonably stable economy but as the country relies heavily on trade, it can be vulnerable to international market fluctuations. Its principal exports are agriculture-based. Tourism plays a considerable role in New Zealand's economy, constituting around 9% of the country's GDP and providing jobs for a tenth of the native workforce. Unemployment is at a stable low of 3.4%, having successfully recovered from a recession in the early 1990s where unemployment hit 10%.

The cost of living in New Zealand compares favourably with that of the UK, and house prices are no exception. The New Zealand national median price is currently just under £135,500. To contextualise this, the current national median for the UK is £230,000. Although the property market witnessed considerable rises in house prices over the last few years, with a particular peak at the end of 2007, a change is now occurring and price growth is on the verge of negative appreciation. Rises in mortgage rates leading to a drop in mortgage applications are partly culpable for this slump, as are rising interest rates. For New Zealanders then, it is not a good time to sell, and for the investor, the lack of reliable exit strategy is likely to prove a deterrent.

New Zealand is definitely a desirable location for those searching for a complete change in lifestyle. The sunny climes (although it does rain too), the relaxed, outdoor lifestyle, and proximity to nature, are all key selling points and many people are emigrating to take advantage of a better way of life. The country is also financially desirable, with 0% stamp duty, 0% capital gains tax (unless the land being sold was acquired with the intention of resale, source: Price Waterhouse Coopers Going Global 2007 Report) and 0% land taxes, although interest rates are some of the highest in the developed world meaning mortgage repayments are steep.

Australasia

NEW ZEALAND

New Zealand as a destination then, is not best suited for avid investors seeking high returns but its straightforward purchase process and appealing culture make it ideal for lifestyle buyers.

Which type of property should you go for?

There is quite an array of different property types on the market, depending on what you're looking for. For personal investment – moving out to become a permanent resident or buy a second home – there is everything one might expect, from cosy cottages on the shores of a stunning lake, to trendy down-town apartments, to large suburban family houses. For the property investor, there are developments to be found offering guarantees on yields and rental terms. Many of these take the form of apartment developments, some off-plan, built within the close proximity of some of New Zealand's livelier locations where high occupancy can be relied upon.

Hotspots

The beauty of New Zealand lies in its stunning diversity. The South Island is the larger of the two islands, with the Southern Alps forging a stunning rift from the Pacific Ocean in the north, to the Antarctic gateway at the southern tip. Touted as being as far away as one can get from the UK, British citizens still feel at home in this terrain.

Canterbury

The Canterbury region is said to have it all: the vertiginous mountains which you can hurtle down on skis, the unending Canterbury Plains, the soothing Pacific Ocean, and of course, the city of **Christchurch**. Described as the most English city outside the UK, the cultural city boasts a multitude of parks and tree-lined avenues, havens of green in the bustling and vibrant atmosphere. This lively city offers all one might expect from a cosmopolitan area, including a huge variety of property. Property on offer reflects all elements of taste, but of especial interest may be the luxury apartment developments that are spring-ing up across the city, with the overseas investor in mind. Many come with rental guarantees, and with no capital gains tax or stamp duty, investment here is made attractive. As the tourist influx to New Zealand looks set to rise for the future, it can be safely assumed that demand for tourist accommodation can be relied upon.

Auckland

The northern part of the North Island has been partly fragmented into new islands as the ocean gradually reclaims the land that emerged from it so long ago. The Auckland region includes an array of enchanting sub-tropical islands, many that are used solely for holiday retreats. **Auckland City** itself sprawls across two harbours, spreading out over the two land masses on both sides and guarded all around by luscious rainforests. The Polynesian and Maori heritage pervades all aspects of this city, creating a multicultural atmosphere with unique experiences on offer to both the tourist and the resident.

Housing in Auckland tends to be more expensive than the national average, reflecting the desirable qualities of the location that are also reiterated through the consistent high rankings of the city in international lifestyle surveys. Forecasting that the city's population is to double by 2050 confirms the future need for accommodation, ensuring the fluidity of the market in years to come. In investment terms this translates to one of New Zealand's most promising opportunities for growth.

Central Otago

The soaring mountain peaks and the deep, cavernous gorges of the Otago region, forever immortalised in the visually indulgent The *Lord of the Rings* trilogy, constitute the backdrop for one of the country's fastest growing regions. Once the scene of a mighty gold rush, the valleys of the region are now covered with Pinot Noir vines as the New Zealand 'wine rush' takes root, with visitors coming from all over the world to visit the wineries. **Queenstown** is heralded as the adventure capital of New Zealand, with everything from snowmobiling, to luge-riding, to off-roading. The region's strong economic base, due to a year-round industry, fuels consistent demand for accommodation and creates a lucrative real estate market.

Dunedin

New Zealand's oldest city, Dunedin, is competitively priced, reflecting the quality of housing available. The architecture, culture and history of the city, with its proximity to the powerful landscapes nearby, make Dunedin a highly desirable second-home location.

Buyer's guide

Foreigners are free to buy land and property in New Zealand with minimal restriction although those wanting to buy land or property bordering rivers, lakes, streams or the ocean will need to seek additional approval (www. escapearticst.com). Investors acquiring 25% plus of a business or property

Australasia

NEW ZEALAND

valued at over $50m, land over five hectares or worth more than $10m and any land on off-shore islands will also need to obtain ministerial consent (Source: www.converge.org.nz).

Mortgages

LTV %	TERM	CURRENCIES	RATES %	STATUS	SPECIAL CONDITIONS
80	30	EUR, PLN, CHF, USD, GBP	4.5	Employed or self-employed	No early repayment charges

Key risks

Following a rise in mortgage rates, mortgage applications have dwindled and this, coupled with rising interest rates mean house prices are dropping quite dramatically. As far as the investor is concerned, there is now a definite lack of reliable exit strategy throughout the country, which is likely to act as a strong deterrent for anyone considering purchasing.

In line with this, capital appreciation is likely to perish in the near future.

Although New Zealand has a reasonably stable economy its heavy reliance on trade means it can be vulnerable to international market fluctuations.

Rating: ⚠ ⚠ ⚠

Key opportunities

New Zealand is undeniably attractive to the lifestyle buyer. The tax-friendly environment – 0% stamp duty, mortgage stamp duty, land tax, property purchase tax and capital gains tax – makes the prospect of buying property very palatable, especially when the rental guarantees that come with many investment properties are taken into consideration.

The strength of the tourist industry means occupancy in well-chosen developments close to amenities and attractions is likely to be high and as such, stable rental yields of between 5% and 7% are attainable.

Investors that are able to make cash investments and are willing to wait for their returns could consider New Zealand, but this is not the destination for first-time investment purchasers wanting fast returns.

Rating: $$

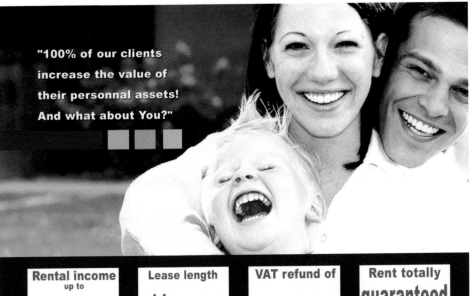

Groupe Menguy Investissements

Business Tourism residences in the heart of French towns.

GMI has been conceiving, developing, commercialising and managing business tourism residences in the heart of French towns and its neighbouring countries, under the brand Appart'City Cap Affaires®, for almost 20 years. With the expertise of its subsidiaries, this concept has known success and continued growth. The Group has now imposed itself as one of the majors in this market, with 40 residences in 2008 and close to 60 residences will be open to the public by 2009.

GROUPE FRANCE EPARGNE:

Commercialises under the brand GFE Epargne Retraite® the serviced apartments of the residences Appart'City Cap Affaires®. The rigorous selection of the locations is motivated by a long term strategy, and shows the want to satisfy the large demand for private investors who want a guaranteed complimentary income will building a portfolio of high quality property to prepare their retirement. With a secured rental income based on a long term renewable commercial lease with returns, one of the strongest of the market with an attractive fiscal status, the GFE Epargne Retraite® investment formula has already profited thousands of

investors across Europe.

The know-how and notoriety of the group, with its ability to respect its engagements, has given confidence to the biggest of promoters, like Vinci Immobilier, Kaufman & Broad, Bouygues, Capri, Sogeprom, Eiffage and many more. That's why in the next 3 years more than 10 000 apartments will be commercialised in quality locations.

DOM'VILLE'SERVICES:

Is the property management company, managing all the Appart'City Cap Affaires® residences. She offers complete piece of mind in the stability of the investment. The chain of serviced apartments in the heart of towns and cities, offers the opportunity to rent a fully furnished apartment with semi-hotel services attached, at the best ratio between comfort and price. They are tastefully decorated in a nautical theme, ready to live in from a few days to several months.

The sites are implanted in strategic locations close to shops, business centres and public transport only after a complete study of the local and national economical situation, with a strict adherence to the Appart'City Cap Affaires® quality chart. It answers a growing demand of quality accommodation for companies with travelling personnel, and mobile individuals.

With close to 75 residences in 2010, Appart'City Cap Affaires® will affirm its position as leader in this market.

The International Law Partnership LLP

(formerly John Howell & Co)

THE specialists in International Law

The International Law Partnership used to be known as John Howell & Co and it is often still referred to by that name.

We are a highly specialist and respected law firm, based in the UK but comprising lawyers qualified in many countries that deals with 'International' legal work – that is to say legal work for people who live in one country but who have legal problems in another. That is what we do. It is all we do. A large part of our work involves the buying, selling and development of real estate but we also deal with disputes and court cases, wills and inheritances, family matters, business issues and most other international legal and tax problems.

We also advise property investors about where and what is most likely to meet their investment requirements and we are also specialists in the use of SIPPs and investment clubs for the ownership of property overseas.

Over the last 25 years we have dealt with over 20,000 'international' transactions.

We offer legal services relating to 34 countries around the world and the number is growing all the time. We currently (January 2008) cover Algeria, Australia, Brazil, Canada, Cape Verde, Caribbean, Croatia, Cyprus, Czech Republic, Dominican Republic, Dubai, Egypt, England*, France, Germany, Hungary, Ireland*, Italy, Malta, Mexico, Montenegro, Morocco, New Zealand, Poland, Portugal, Romania, Russia, Scotland*, Slovakia, South Africa, Spain, Turkey, USA, Wales*.

(*=International work only)

This work requires knowledge of the legal and tax systems in both of the countries involved, necessary language skills and a familiarity with the culture of (and the cultural differences between) the two countries involved. But most of all it requires an 'International' approach that allows us to apply knowledge and skill gained in the law and legal system of one place to provide innovative and effective solutions to legal problems in another.

From our offices in London & Leeds our team of over 30 English and overseas qualified lawyers, paralegals and supporting staff, pride themselves on finding **cost effective** solutions to our clients' problems.

We are a truly international law firm that happens to be based in the UK, rather than a firm of English lawyers that happens to do some international work. Yet we are still regulated in

England and subject to all the same rules as your 'ordinary' English solicitor.

We are authors of the *Sunday Times*™ series of books on Buying a Property in Spain, France, Portugal, Italy, Turkey, Eastern Europe and Florida; the Cadogan Guides to setting up a small business in France and Spain and many other publications. We also appear as expert speakers at many conferences and seminars, on the radio and on television. We present regular (daily) programmes about overseas property issues on both Overseas Property TV (Sky channel 287) and Real Estate TV (Sky channel 273 & 274 and Virgin.)

John Howell & Co was voted Best International Property Lawyers by the Bentley Awards. It was a founder member of AIPP (The Association of International Property Professionals) and is a member of FOPDAC (The Federation of Overseas Property Developers Agents and Consultants.)

The International Law Partnership LLP

A limited liability partnership regulated by the Solicitors Regulation Authority
Registered in England under number OC321301
Registered Office: The Vaults, The Old Town Hall, 193-197 High Holborn, London WC1V 7BD

PRACTICING ADDRESSES & CONTACT DETAILS

London:
The Vaults, The Old Town Hall, 193-197 High Holborn, London WC1V 7BD, England
Tel: +44 20 7061 6700   Fax: +44 20 7061 6701   Email: London@LawOverseas.com

Leeds:
The Coach House, 75 Allerton Hill, Chapel Allerton, Leeds LS7 3QB, England
Tel: +44 11 3237 1118   Fax: +44 11 3237 1141   Email: Leeds@LawOverseas.com

Internet: www.LawOverseas.com

Buying a property abroad?

We guarantee you a great currency deal!

Save money on your currency transfer and make your new property more affordable with;

- Bank beating exchange rates
- Absolutely no commission
- Professional guidance and support
- Secure, fast and efficient service

Over the last 12 years our dedicated team of foreign currency specialists have helped thousands of people purchase property overseas and save thousands of pounds in the process.

Speak to a specialist on **0800 840 3304**

One Lawyer, One Estate Agent and a Foreign Currency Specialist

The road to buying property abroad can be a tricky one to navigate. There are many factors to take into consideration before final agreements can be made.

Getting it right requires a lot of research into location, property, budgets and payments, as well as an understanding of local rules, regulations and taxes.

Seeking advice from qualified professionals is crucial and will protect your long-term interests. In essence getting it right requires a good lawyer, an estate agent and a foreign currency specialist.

Use a good Lawyer:
Legal procedures involved with overseas purchases will vary, for example in Spain previous debt on a property can end up being inherited by the new buyer. So, it's essential that your lawyer is impartial and has a good grasp of English as well as the native language, to deal with the endless stream of rules and regulations.

Use an Estate Agent:
Prior research is vital and estate agents are also a good source of advice and will have sound knowledge of the property market in which you hope to invest. It's important you make sure that all information you receive is accurate and that your estate agent is officially registered and holds a license.

Use a Foreign Currency Specialist:
When transferring money overseas, using a currency specialist will not only save money but can protect your future mortgage repayments from currency fluctuations.

High street banks can charge up to 4% or more on exchange rates than a currency specialist. That works out as an extra £4000 on a £100,000 transaction. Banks often add further charges including commission fees and transfer fees.

A foreign currency specialist, like No.1 Currency promises bank beating exchange rates, transferring your money securely and providing expert guidance completely free of charge.

advertisement feature

Invest your soul in a lifestyle in *South Africa*

Why South Africa?

South Africa is considered to be an emerging market with abundant supply of natural resources. The financial, legal, communications, energy and transport sectors are well-developed, and the country has a modern infrastructure.

Is this a good place to buy?

South Africa is a country of great variety, offering something for everyone. There are beautiful and unspoilt beaches, countryside with abundance of wildlife, mountains, bustling cities with a vibrant night scene(including cape town, one of the most popular cities in the world), impressive relics from the dawn of humanity, fine wines and a range of cuisines. House prices here are much lower than in the UK or USA and in some areas, prices are less than a tenth of prices in the South of England. Non residents who own in the country have all the normal rights of ownership, including the right to recover rental income.

"Because South Africa has a stable economy, a good amount of security, possibilities for good rental potential and capital growth, demand is likely to stay high, and investing here offers relatively safe prospects."

South Africa is reputed to have the best deeds registration system in the world, with an exceptional degree of accuracy and tenure. Property can be owned individually, jointly in undivided shares or by an entity such as a company, a close corporation or trust or a similar entity registered outside the country.

Hotspots

The most popular area for overseas buyers is the Cape Peninsula, one of most desirable places in the world. White sandy beaches, proximity to the Garden Route and Cape Town's cosmopolitan urban center have all combined to raise the profile of the property market. Cape Town has been heralded as the 'Saint Tropez of Africa', and the dynamic city is home to a wealth of cafes, bars, museums, shops and restaurant. With a highly desirable location and easy access from UK, it recieves 1.6 million foreign tourists a year. Studies conducted following the World Cup '98 in France reported that property price rose by 60% in the year prior to the competition and it is predicted that the tournament will have a similarly beneficial effect on house prices in Cape Town and surrounding areas.

Economic Factors

- Substantial taxation breaks of up to 20% are on offer for real estate developers.
- The 2010 world cup in South africa is fuelling demand for rental properties.
- A 20% tax break on rental for 5 years is available on renovation projects.
- Housing property market is showing growth of about 13.9% in the Western Cape.
- The low rate of excange between the Rand and major world currencies, enables property purchasers to buy more for their money.

South Africa waits for you!

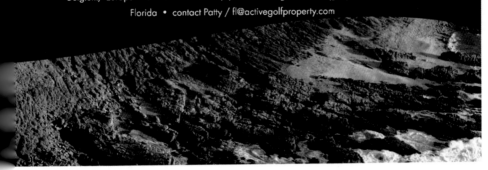

Allan Ballard Consultants Ltd

Tel +34 645 997 639   Email info@ab-consultants..com
www.ab-consultants..com

European Property
Consultants

Below Market Value
Properties

In Southern Spain

Allan Ballard Consultants Ltd

Due to the current market situation, we strongly believe that southern Spain is still one of the prime investment areas for U.K. based investors. Whether you are seeking a primary home, a rental income or a pure investment scenario, the Southern Costas represent a secure and increasingly mature market. The recent leveling of this dynamic area makes buying now an ideal time to acquire high quality properties at considerably below normal and soon to be re-attained prices.

We at Allan Ballard Consultants will only offer you properties that we have checked extensively for registry, mortgage and other issues. We also only offer properties that we feel offer exceptional value for money.

We are delighted to bring you a fabulous opportunity to buy genuine bargain distressed sale properties and developer repossessions at 10-45% under current property market values, thereby giving the possibility of 80-100% finance (subject to status and valuation).

Distressed sale doesn't mean there's a problem with the property – simply that the current buyer is struggling to raise finance to complete or sustain the purchase – usually due to a change in their personal circumstances. These buyers are therefore forced to either sell their properties quickly at bargain prices far less than the market value or have the property repossessed by the bank or developer and lose their credit status or deposit.

Remember in Spain, mortgages are loaned as a percentage of property value (not sales price), so astute investors can finance a high proportion of their purchase by borrowing (therefore minimal cash outlay) because of the discounts inherent in these bargain properties. We have a wide selection of mortgage brokers now working in Spain who can help with all your finance and reference requirements.

We are thoroughly committed to providing our customers with all the necessary help in locating the best priced and value for money properties and businesses available on the Costa del Sol, Costa Blanca and other areas. Whether interested in making a permanent move to Spain, finding a holiday or retirement home to suit your needs or sourcing the right Spanish property investment in today's buyer's market, we bring all our experience and resources to bear to make your goals a reality.

Allan Ballard Consulting uses an extensive network of agents and Spanish property finders enabling us to offer our clients numerous resale properties along the coasts as well as inland areas.

www.ab-consultants.com

Exclusive LOFTS in Berlin's trendiest area

- Reduced energy costs based on solar thermal systems and floor heating systems and top insulation
- Video entry phone
- Generously dimensioned terraces
- Parquet floors in the living areas
- Wood-burning stoves can be installed
- Designer bathroom fixtures
- Flat shower trays with glass cabins
- Beautiful common areas
- Underground parking with elevator

From 35 to 500m² for owner occupation or for investors with rentalrate guarantee

An impressive domicile in the centre of Berlin: The Kopernikusstrasse in Friedrichshain is one of the best residential addresses in the hippest, hottest and most creative district in Berlin

For more information: www.kopernikushoefe.com

Tel: 0049 30 346 757 50 Email: info@kopernikushoefe.com

Why Invest in Berlin Property market

Ten reasons to choose Berlin:

- Leading Economy
- Global Player
- High Productivity
- Excellent Workforce
- Innovative Power
- First-Class Infrastructure
- Inviting Incentives
- Competitive Tax Conditions
- Secure Investment Framework
- Quality of Life

Berlin real estate offers overseas property investors a great opportunity to benefit from low prices with great potential for capital gains. Although only 12% of Berliners own their property compared with 43% overall in Germany, the ownership trend is steadily rising with Berlin currently representing the most competitively priced property in Europe. Multi national companies are also fast taking advantage, swiftly moving in and snapping up large buildings while the low prices last.

Berlin is clearly a city in the upper echelon of Europe's business centres, this year ranking third in Fdi magazine's poll of desirable European investment locations at MIPIM, alongside London and Paris. The Financial Times Group publication selected 75 indicators to assess the locational attractiveness of more than 1000 European cities and regions, including factors such as gross domestic product, state-sponsored business promotion activity, major investment in 2007, marketing strategy, large-scale infrastructure and urban planning projects. Responses were compared to objective data on the areas overall economic potential, business friendliness, foreign direct investment, infrastructure, and the quality of the workforce. Berlin finished third in the overall evaluation, and fourth in the ranking for both infrastructure quality and workforce.

Berlin Urban Planning Senator Ingeborg Junge-Reyer said: "Berlin is one of the up-and-coming cities in Europe, a fact that is increasingly being realised internationally too. Berlin has space for economic growth and creative development."

More information for investors and the complete study can be found at: **www.berlin-partner.de**

The Portugal Realty Group's aim is to deliver a comprehensive service that will enable a prospective buyer to have a complete understanding of what they are investing in and the location they are buying in.

The products, developers and construction companies we have chosen to work with give you a wide selection of properties to match all budgets and reasons to purchase a property in Portugal from investors, retirees, people looking to buy a holiday home in the sun or planning to relocate to a warmer climate.

Ideally we like to present our products through a tailor-made viewing trip as we believe that this is the only way to get enough clear information to properly evaluate all the elements involved in the buying process; such as finance and tax questions, buying costs, the local property market, local facilities and local amenities.

Portugal is an excellent country for investment, retiring or re-locating to because of the stable government, steady capital growth, growing economy, good rental return, low cost of living, fantastic weather and it is **generally a safe place to buy property** with well developed property laws and strict planning regulations.

Property rights are secure in Portugal. The right to private property and the transfer of real estate during life and on death is enshrined in Article 62 of the Portuguese constitution. Property law and the various types of property are almost exclusively governed by the Portuguese Civil Code.

Property in Portugal is bought on a freehold basis as leasehold does not exist in Portuguese property law. However if property forms part of a shared building, the shared areas will be sold under the law of "propriedade" which specifies that a condominium association must be created to take care of cleaning and upkeep.

An important developing international tourist region of Portugal is the Silver Coast. The **Silver Coast** stretches between Lisbon and Porto along the Atlantic coastline.

Its strategic location with **easy access** to other large centers has contributed to its development. This region boasts outstanding unspoilt natural beauty, **beautiful beaches,** fishing towns and typical villages plus unique hospitality. This area is **one of the largest wine-growing areas in Portugal.** Full-bodied red wines with excellent alcohol content.

New regular low cost airlines fly in to Lisbon from the all over the UK and Ireland making the journey to your holiday home in the sun only a 3-4 hour hop from door to door. The Silver Coast is an excellent location to escape to for a weekend and with plenty of **Golf courses** in the area it is conveniently placed for the golfing enthusiast.

PORTUGAL = Excellent building quality – Good prospects for rental – Ideal investment value.

Come and visit us soon!

Costa Rica – A land of stunning scenery, sunshine, smiles and profitable property investments

Where we live in the Central Valley area of Costa Rica we enjoy spring-like weather all year round, no income taxes, no capital gains taxes, low property taxes, affordable property prices, low cost of living and an excellent quality of life.

I am British and moved to Costa Rica in 1999 and love living here so much I even wrote a book called 'How To Buy Costa Rica Real Estate Without Losing Your Camisa' and started WeLoveCostaRica.com

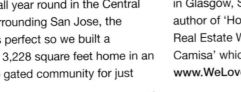

Costa Rica is a politically stable country, with no army located in Central America sandwiched between Nicaragua to the north and Panama and its citizens – the 'Ticos' – are an amiable and attractive people.

At an average temperature of 72 degrees all year round in the Central Valley surrounding San Jose, the climate is perfect so we built a luxurious 3,228 square feet home in an exclusive gated community for just £155,512 and you can find hundreds of new luxury flats for £100,000-£200,000.

We also recently sold an investment home for a 50% gain and paid zero capital gains taxes, and property taxes are only 0.25% which means we paid only £387 per year on that £155K home.

If you are living here and receive income from outside the country you will pay zero income taxes in Costa Rica and there's zero VAT charged on the purchase of a home.

The cost of living is a fraction of what it is in the UK and if you eat a diet full of fresh fruit, fresh vegetables, you will feel younger and fitter than you have in years...

Written by Scott Oliver who was born in Glasgow, Scotland. Scott is the author of 'How To Buy Costa Rica Real Estate Without Losing Your Camisa' which you can see at **www.WeLoveCostaRica.com**

WeLoveCostaRica.com
Expert Costa Rica Real Estate, Living & Retirement Information To Help You Live The Good Life

THE RISKS AND OPPORTUNITIES

COUNTRY	RISK RATING	OPPORTUNITY RATING	EASE OF PURCHASE
Angola	▲▲▲▲	$$$	Complicated
Argentina	▲▲	$$$$	Straight Forward
Australia	▲▲	$	Moderate
Baltics	▲▲▲▲	$$	Moderate
Belize	▲▲	$$$	Straight Forward
Brazil	▲	$$$$	Moderate
Bulgaria	▲▲▲▲▲	$	Complicated
Cambodia	▲▲▲▲	$$$$	Difficult
Canada	▲	$$$	Moderate
Cape Verde	▲▲▲	$$$	Moderate
Caribbean	▲▲	$$$$$	Moderate
China	▲▲	$$$$	Difficult
Croatia	▲▲	$$	Moderate
Cyprus North	▲▲▲▲▲	$$$	Difficult
Cyprus South	▲▲▲	$	Straight Forward
Denmark	▲▲▲	$$$	Moderate
Egypt	▲▲	$$$$	Straight Forward
France	▲▲	$$$	Moderate
Greece	▲▲	$$$	Moderate
Guam	▲▲▲	$$$	Moderate
India	▲▲▲▲	$$$$	Moderate
Italy	▲	$	Moderate
Kazakhstan	▲▲	$$$	Moderate
Malaysia	▲	$$$$$	Straight Forward
Mongolia	▲▲▲	$$$$	Moderate
Montenegro	▲▲▲	$$$$	Moderate
Morocco	▲▲	$$$$	Moderate
New Zealand	▲▲▲	$$	Straight Forward
Panama	▲▲	$$$	Moderate
Philippines	▲▲▲	$$	Moderate
Poland	▲▲▲	$$$$	Moderate
Portugal	▲	$$$	Moderate
Romania	▲	$$$$	Moderate
Slovakia	▲▲▲	$$$	Straight Forward
Slovenia	▲▲	$$$	Moderate
South Africa	▲▲▲	$$	Moderate
Spain	▲▲▲	$	Moderate
Turkey	▲▲▲	$$$$	Complicated
UAE	▲▲▲	$$	Moderate depending on emirate
Ukraine	▲▲▲	$$$	Moderate
Uruguay	▲▲▲▲	$$$	Straight Forward
USA	▲▲▲	$$$$	Moderate
Vietnam	▲▲▲	$$$$	Moderate